GHOSTS OF SPAIN

Giles Tremlett is the *Guardian*'s Madrid correspondent. He has lived in, and written extensively about, Spain almost continuously since graduating from Oxford University twenty years ago.

WITHDRAWN

Of related interest from Faber and Faber

THE DARK HEART OF ITALY
By Tobias Jones

Ghosts of Spain

Travels through a country's hidden past

GILES TREMLETT

LIS LIBRARY
Date 17/7/15
Fund f-Che
Order No 2604413
University of Chester

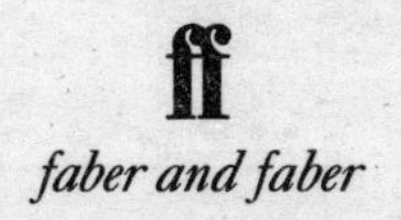

faber and faber

First published in 2006
by Faber and Faber Limited
3 Queen Square London WC1N 3AU

Typeset by Faber and Faber Limited
Printed in England by Mackays of Chatham Ltd, Kent

All rights reserved
© Giles Tremlett, 2006

The right of Giles Tremlett to be identified as author of this work has been asserted in accordance with Section 77 of the Copyright, Designs and Patents Act 1988

This book is sold subject to the condition that it shall not, by way of trade or otherwise, be lent, resold, hired out or otherwise circulated without the publisher's prior consent in any form of binding or cover other than that in which it is published and without a similar condition including this condition being imposed on the subsequent purchaser

A CIP record for this book
is available from the British Library

ISBN 978–0–571–22169–1

4 6 8 10 9 7 5 3

Contents

For Katharine Blanca Scott and our children,
Lucas Tremlett and Samuel Tremlett

INTRODUCTION

The Edge of a Barber's Razor

In Spain the dead are more alive than the dead of any other place in the world: their profile wounds like the edge of a barber's razor.
Federico García Lorca

It is shortly before 7.00 a.m. on a cool Madrid spring morning. The traffic is still just a purr, though it will soon be a rumble and, some time after that, the usual riot of horns, ambulance sirens and roaring motorbike exhausts. This should be a small moment of peace in what must be one of Europe's noisiest cities. A helicopter, however, has spent the past fifteen minutes poised noisily at roof-top level just a block down our street. The wide-open well of our six-storey apartment block is acting as a sound box that amplifies the relentless chugging and clattering. Sleep in our top-floor apartment seems, under these circumstances, impossible. I lie in bed worrying about whether the helicopter – which does this every few weeks – will wake the children. It is not as though they went to bed early, even though they have school today. One of them, a seven-year-old, got out of bed to take a phone call at 10 p.m. last night. It was another seven-year-old, excitedly inviting him to a birthday party at the weekend. Madrid boasts that it is a party town, a city that never sleeps. But does this really have to apply to the under eights?

I go out onto the balcony to wave a fist at the sleek white helicopter – wondering why on earth it is hovering there, so low, so loud and so early. I expect all the other balconies to be filled up with angry people roused from their beds. I am, however, alone. I stand, solitary, deranged and dishevelled, amongst the wilting geraniums. Even at this stage of the year, they are gasping for water. It is one of those moments when I am reminded that, although I now consider this to be my city, I am really an *extranjero*, a foreigner. Noise, in Madrid, in Spain as a whole, is just background. It is part of the atmosphere, like air or daylight. I realise that I have been caught with my guard down. During the day, after I have showered and slipped my daily coat of Madridness on, I would not care about the mere roar of a helicopter. Noise and bustle are normally part of what I like about this city. At night, when I sleep, though, I am returned to my natural condition as what Spaniards like to call an *anglosajón*, an Anglo-Saxon. This description for native English speakers – be they British, American, or from anywhere else – has always amused me. It makes me think of runes and lyres, of Beowulf and the Venerable Bede.

This country is famous for noise. Newspapers occasionally report on how the noise levels of Madrid or Barcelona pose a danger to health and sanity. One in four Madrid streets subjects its residents to noise beyond World Health Organisation limits, one report tells me. Half of fourteen to twenty-seven-year-olds in Barcelona suffer irreversible hearing damage, another one warns. Little wonder, then, that even noise-numbed Spaniards are occasionally driven berserk. I recall a scene from a Barcelona square, late on a summer's night, years ago. The square was packed with busy café tables. Teenagers with noisy mopeds were driving around it in circles, their high-pitched exhausts screaming out over the hubbub of conversation and laughter. An angry, elderly woman appeared on a roof top and started shouting and waving her arms. Everyone ignored her. Then she began hurling empty Coke bottles down at us. The glass bottles exploded on the ground, shattering into tiny, flying fragments. We ran.

Yet Spaniards seem to need noise. Televisions can stay on in people's homes all day long. 'It's like having a friend in the house,' someone once explained to me. Bars, where much of life takes place, have musical fruit machines, talking cigarette machines, coffee machines, microwaves and television sets (sometimes more than one, and set to different channels) all pinging, chattering, steaming, shouting and clattering at once. Raised voices, competing to be heard above the machines, add an extra layer to the noise.

Perhaps this need to be heard above the din is why Spanish – or more accurately, in this country of many languages, *castellano* – can be so hard and direct. 'It is a language in which one hears each word . . . and each word is as distinct as a pebble,' wrote V. S. Pritchett in his *The Spanish Temper*. 'It is a dry, harsh, stone-cracking tongue, a sort of desert Latin chipped off at the edges by its lisped consonants and dry-throated gutturals, its energetic "r's", but opened by its strong emphatic vowels.'

Verbal noise reaches its loudest in the *tertulias* – the hugely popular television and radio debate programmes whose daily audiences are counted in millions. At their best, *tertulias* are a serious business, a learned and informed exchange of ideas amongst knowledgeable people. Many, however, are little more than angry slanging matches. Spaniards are talented, if sometimes incontinent, talkers. *Tertulianos,* the people hired to take part in *tertulias,* are often angry people. That is their job. What they are angry about depends on what subject the show's anchor presents to them. The more inconsequential the topic, the louder everyone gets. The absolute peaks are reached in the programmes that specialise in gossip about singers, models, bullfighters and the legion of people who are famous simply for being famous.

Catch a taxi anywhere in Spain and you may find yourself sharing it with a handful of *tertulianos* vociferating on the radio. Your taxi driver – if he is not one of those immaculate, austere, proud *taxistas* who are too dignified and serious to sink to this level – may join in. Like them, he has strong opinions. If you have had a bad day, or feel strongly about the issue at hand, you are free to let rip yourself. Spanish offers you an earthy and sexually explicit vocabulary in which to unburden yourself. '*¡Joder, que no nos toquen los cojones¡*', 'Fuck, why don't they leave our balls alone?' one Madrid *taxista* threw at me recently. We were listening to a right-wing, Roman Catholic church-owned radio station as we sat in a morning jam on the M-30 ring road. The presenter began ranting about 'anti-Spaniards' in Catalonia and the Basque Country.

This provoked my *taxista* to unleash another tirade. '*Me cago en su puta madre . . .*', 'I shit on his whore-mother . . .' he began. This is not shocking language. I could, without seeming crude, have replied with a phrase in which pride of place was given to the female sexual organ, '*Coño . . .*'

A generous use of swear words is something we *anglosajones* share with Spaniards. Nobel laureate Camilo José Cela compiled a two-tome *Diccionario Secreto* of them. The author of *The Family of Pascual Duarte* included more than 800 terms for penis. They ranged from *arcabuz*, harquebus, to *zanahoria*, carrot.

'A Spaniard, if he does not let loose some Iberian expletives, has too much pressure in the cooker,' the writer, diplomat and Oxford don Salvador de Madariaga once explained. It can, indeed, be a most liberating experience. Step out of the taxi cab and the whole episode – the anger and indignation – is gone. For anger is worn lightly, and easily disposed of. Perhaps that is why Spaniards do not share that *anglosajón* weakness for fisticuffs. Road rage is considered fine, even healthy. You may sit in your car, blast your horn and insult anyone who takes your fancy. Nobody, however, steps out with hatred in their eyes and a car-jack in their hand.

Spain is my adopted home. I have lived here for well over a decade now, mostly in Madrid but also in its great rival – the charming, sophisticated Mediterranean port city of Barcelona. I first came here, living in Barcelona for two years, almost twenty years ago. Returning to London, I found it impossible to settle and so, eventually, came back. It is ironic that my Catalan friends, some of whom claim they are not really Spaniards, sparked my own long-term interest in Spain.

I make my living from writing, as a journalist, though I do not consider myself a typical foreign correspondent. I am not here on my way through to that dreamed-of posting in Paris or New York. I will go (almost) anywhere in the world to cover a story. This, however, is my home. If I ever leave again, it will be with the intention of coming back. That was not my original plan. Once here, however, I have found it impossible to leave. When I was younger and single, life was too much fun. The city *juerga* – the partying – was too inviting. With a family, though, it got even better. I had struck a sort of El Dorado for rearing children. Now I have a stake in this country. My own children are developing before my eyes as young Spaniards, or half-Spaniards. I have experienced the strange sensations – and concerns – of first-generation immigrants anywhere as they watch their children grow up, with enviable ease, in another culture. Spain's future matters to me. It may be theirs.

I have criss-crossed Spain many times pursuing stories to write, from north to south, from east to west and hopping from island to island. A colleague once complained that writing on Spain meant *toros*, *terroristas* and *tonterías* – bulls, terrorists and silliness. It is true that Spain, in newspaper jargon, provides 'good colour'. But then I have always liked that. Spain has a wealth of stories to tell. The open road beckons continuously – and there are few places in Europe as open, as generous with empty spaces and distant horizons, as Spain. Often, as I am driving through those vast spaces with some easy-listening *flamenquillo* music on the CD, I imagine this is more like America than Europe.

The story does not go stale either, for Spain changes at breakneck speed. Again, there is something American about this. Spaniards not only embrace change. They expect it.

No one is more aware of this capacity for mutation than a writer trying to capture the country in a moment of time. Grasp Spain firmly in your fist and almost immediately the grains of sand start to run out from between your fingers. 'How the commentators of Spain have aged!' observed the Catalan writer Josep Pla on 14 April 1931, after watching monarchy give way to republicanism in a single, eventful day. 'In one day they have all gone unbearably gaga.'

I experienced something similar over four ghastly, dramatic days in March 2004. These began with the killing of 191 people by Islamist radicals who planted bombs on early morning Madrid commuter trains. They ended with a general election in which Spaniards threw out a Conservative People's Party whose hold on power had seemed set in concrete. Spain shifted again, suddenly and swiftly. So, inevitably, did this book.

All this dizzying change did not start, however, in 2004. Spaniards have, in fact, spent almost a whole century playing catch-up – in a stop-start fashion – with the rest of Europe. 'You could say that in the *pueblo* where I was born (on 22 February 1900) the Middle Ages lasted until the First World War,' the avant-garde film-maker Luis Buñuel said of his home town in Aragón, Calanda.

Spaniards make my job simple. They are always ready to talk, to give an opinion, to tell you things about themselves. This is partly because, wherever you go, they believe theirs is the most fascinating corner of the world. It has, they will tell you, the best food and, often, the best wine. It is also because, generally, they are convinced that their opinion is as good as, if not better than, the next man's. Most of all, however, it is because they are naturally open and welcoming. Spain's position as a world superpower in tourism is not just down to sun, sand and *sangría*.

Spanish noise is fun, but it is also distraction. '*Mucho ruido y pocas nueces*' – a lot of noise but few walnuts – is what Spaniards say when something is all show and no substance. Few outsiders would place silence on this nation's list of attributes. I certainly would not have done so in my first years here. Nor, I suspect, would, Pope John Paul II. 'The Pope would also like to talk,' he found himself telling a chattering crowd at an open-air Mass in Madrid. Recently, however, things have happened that have forced me to think again – not just about silence, but about Spain itself.

If I had to blame one person for making me rethink Spain's relationship with silence, it would have to be Emilio. He was the first one to, quite literally, go digging in history. Emilio Silva is a journalist who went back to his grandfather's village, Priaranza del Bierzo, in the northern province of León in 2000. He wanted to tell the story of what had happened there six decades earlier, in 1936. That was the time when a military rising led by General Franco and others started the three-year round of fratricidal bloodletting known as the Spanish Civil War. Emilio ended up doing more than just story-telling, however. For he found the roadside mass grave where his grandfather, a civilian shot by a death squad of Franco supporters, was buried. Then he had him dug up, along with the other twelve corpses of those shot alongside him. DNA tests, carried out by Spanish forensic scientists with experience in digging up much more recent mass graves in Chile or Kosovo, finally enabled him to identify his grandfather. The bones are now in the local cemetery, alongside those of Emilio's grandmother. It was the first time a Civil War grave had been dug up like this, and the first time DNA tests had been used to identify the victims. When the 'Priaranza Thirteen' were found, however, it seemed like a one-off. I wrote about it, as a curiosity, and then forgot about it again.

Then, a couple of years later, I found myself standing by another Civil War mass grave. This one was also near the mountains of León, at a place called Piedrafita de Babia. It, too, had been dug up by volunteers. The elderly sister of one of the victims, Isabel, helped direct the mechanical diggers to the spot where they had been buried. For years she had been going, secretly, to lay flowers at the site once a year. Isabel still hated the men who had done it.

'Everybody knew the bodies were here. Back then, even after they were killed and secretly buried, people from the village came across the bones after they were exposed by rain,' she told me. 'The priest told them the *rojos*, the reds, were so vile that even the earth did not want them. Even now people remember the fear. They don't like to talk about it.'

Soon afterwards another grave was dug up, and then another and another. Suddenly, it turned out, there were graves all over the place. Spain was sitting on what campaigners claimed were tens of thousands of such corpses. They lay in mass graves, some in cemeteries, but many others beside roadside ditches, in forests or out in the open country. These were the victims of Franco's purges of *rojos*, reds or left-wingers, during and after the Civil War. That war had ended more than sixty years before, however, and Franco himself had died, peacefully and in his bed, in 1975. Nobody had done anything about them in the quarter-century since then. Now there were demands that the government should find them all, dig them up and rebury them.

In retrospect another catalyst for what was going on was probably José María Aznar. It was not so much a question of who he was, as what he symbolised. A few years earlier he had become Spain's first democratically elected right-wing prime minister since the 1930s. In a country where the right – in some people's minds – still meant Franco, that was always going to require a certain amount of readjustment. I never imagined, however, that it would raise the dead from their graves. They had been left to lie, after all, while the Socialists were in power for fourteen years. Somehow, however, the fact that the right was in power started people clamouring. Nobody was asking for justice – even though there still were, and still are, killers out there – but they did want dignity for the dead. The polemic continues today.

As history erupted from under the ground, I decided to turn my back on Spain's glittering, entertaining and enticing surface. I wanted to undertake what one Italian writer called 'that difficult voyage, to travel through time and space across the country'. It would, of course, be the voyage of an *anglosajón* – a Spain seen through foreign eyes, looking at some peculiarities which Spaniards themselves feel hardly warrant attention.

This would mean, in some respects, following a well-trodden road for foreign writers on Spain. Gypsies and flamenco music, for example, have long fascinated visitors here. But what, also, about some modern Spanish phenomena? The tireless pursuit of pleasure, the tourist ghettos flourishing on the coasts and, even, those gaudily lit brothels on Spanish motorways all have something to say about the priorities and attitudes of modern Spaniards. I had questions, too, about how women had fared in a country that had rocketed its way out of state-imposed, fundamentalist Catholicism into non-judgemental, 'live and let live' liberalism. Most of all, however, in a country where history weighed so heavily, my journey would be able to look at the past through the present, and the present through the past.

Informing Spanish friends about this project produced conflicting reactions. Spaniards are acutely, sensitively aware of what others say about them. They do not always like their intimate selves to be exposed. That is why they meet in bars, in the plaza or on the street. Their home is an intimate space – a family refuge. It may take years before a friend invites you into their house. Some of mine never have. The street – *la calle* – is far more than just a stretch of tarmac and paving stones. It is neutral ground, a space to meet and, why not, to show off.

'*¡Sí, sí,* Spain is different!' Mercedes exclaims. It is about time, she suggests, that someone pointed out that the country is not as marvellous as its own propagandists suggest. '*¡O sea, España es diferente!*' repeats Marga, almost word for word, in a separate conversation. Her tone, however, is opposite. I feel she suspects I am about to badmouth her country – that I will make Spaniards look less like the modern Europeans that they are and, more significantly, desperately want to be. Foreign writers have long been accused of spreading 'black legends' – about a Spanish propensity for violence, anarchy, inquisitions or self-destruction. Few foreigners, however, can match the gloom of late-nineteenth-century Spanish writers like Ángel Ganivet, who deemed Spain 'a cage full of madmen all suffering from the same *manía*: their inability to put up with one another'. I try to explain that, amongst other things, I am looking for things that make Spaniards different to others. One of those, of course, is that many Spaniards – with their avid enthusiasm for the European Union and eager embrace of the latest cultural icons from New York, London, Paris or Berlin – would rather not be different.

Mercedes and Marga had both reached for the 1960s advertising slogan – 'Spain is different!' – invented for Manuel Fraga, Franco's information and tourism minister. The slogan was greeted with black humour at the time. With a dictator in charge, what tourist was going to find it normal? In 2005 the octogenarian Fraga was still the most voted-for political leader in Galicia, one of Spain's seventeen partly self-governing 'autonomous regions', though he narrowly failed to ensure himself a fifth consecutive period as regional premier. Fraga's continued presence in politics is, ironically, another of those things that makes modern Spain 'different'. How many other European nations, after all, entered the twenty-first century with ministers from a right-wing dictatorship still active, and powerful, in politics? Of course Spain is different, I wanted to reply. All countries are. Most, however, are happy – even proud – for it to be that way.

The mass graves of the Civil War were an obvious starting point for my journey into Spanish history. Aznar had refused to pay for them to be found and dug up. These dead did not interest him. An old man in a village near Ávila agreed with his decision. 'If you stir shit, stink rises,' he said. He was not talking about the dead themselves but about the stories they had carried to the grave with them.

The unease caused by these exhumations was palpable. A vow of silence – one that had been adhered to in the years since Franco died – was being broken. People did not know what to make of it all. One of the first reburials of victims from a mass grave was attended by exactly four journalists. These came from the local newspaper, the *New York Times*, CNN and the *Guardian*. The latter three appeared independently. A television cameraman who worked for a national Spanish network, Antena 3, came on his own to film it because he was related to one of the dead. 'I know they won't broadcast it, though,' he said. Spain's national press stayed away.

'I might as well go and dig up my uncles at Paracuellos de Jarama,' one newspaper executive, no Francoist he, told me. It was a reference to his own family members shot by Franco's Republican opponents during the same Civil War. So I went to see their graves, too, in a cemetery by Madrid's airport with a giant white cross laid into the hillside. The long rows of tombstones at Paracuellos de Jarama, with their tragic inscriptions to beloved fathers, husbands, brothers and sons, were eloquent proof that the left, too, had blindly butchered unarmed opponents. Individual headstones blamed *rojos* or 'Marxist hordes' for the killings. On a cold November morning I watched small groups of people scatter pink carnations amongst the crosses. Some stayed for a short ceremony at a small cenotaph. The Falange anthem 'Cara al Sol' was sung. Arms were thrown out in a stiff, fascist salute. It was a rare sighting of Spain's extreme right. It was clear that neither side had clean hands. These dead, however, were in holy ground. They were not in a ditch.

The graves being dug up were a reminder of just how this country had set about making its transformation – *la Transición* – from dictatorship to democracy. After Franco died, in 1975, *la Transición* had seemed truly miraculous. At this point, there had been no falling of the Berlin wall and no full-scale toppling of Latin America's right-wing dictatorships. Nor had Spaniards, unlike their neighbours in Portugal, pushed dictatorship out with a peaceful, carnation-wielding revolution. There was no roadmap for going from authoritarian, dictatorial government to democracy. Spain was unique. It had to find its own way. And it did so by smothering the past. Truth commissions had not really yet been invented. Nuremberg-style trials of the guilty were out of the question. Many of those who would lead *la Transición* had, anyway, Francoist pasts. It was better to cover their personal stories, too, with a cloak of silence. An atavistic fear of the past, of not repeating the bloody confrontation of the Spanish Civil War, was one reason for this silence. Another was not to upset those, especially in the army, who were amongst the biggest threats to the young democracy.

It was unwritten, but known as *el pacto del olvido*, the pact of forgetting. Historians continued their work and, with sometimes limited access to documents from the time, dug and delved. In the early days of the transition there was a sudden thirst for books, in a country used to censorship, on what had really happened to Spain since 1936. But the Civil War and, to a certain degree, Francoism itself became unmentionable elsewhere – in politics, between neighbours and even, in many cases, within families themselves. A senior academic once suggested to me that the whole matter was best studied '*en la intimidad*', in the intimacy of one's own home. It was, in the words of one parliamentarian of *la Transición*, a matter of 'forgetting by everyone for everyone'.

It was also a case of *tapando vergüenzas* – of covering up embarrassments. For, apart from a few Franco nostalgists, Spaniards felt, understandably, shame. They were ashamed of their Civil War and also about the mediocre dictator who emerged from it. Anyway, they said, what mattered was the present, the here-and-now, and the future. The latter was an argument that went down well with a nation bubbling over with optimism for tomorrow and with a hedonistic desire to make the most of today. Spaniards have settled down since the giddy days of Madrid's 1980s '*movida*'. 'Get stoned and stay with it,' aged Madrid mayor Enrique Tierno Galván, affectionately known as '*el viejo profesor*', had exhorted the city's youth. Spaniards generally still believe it is their absolute right – even their obligation – to enjoy themselves. This, researchers have even suggested, may be the real reason why they live so much longer than other Europeans. It may also, however, be why they are Europe's biggest consumers of cocaine.

Once the silence began to break, however, it was unstoppable. Whole tables at El Corte Inglés, the ubiquitous department store, groaned with volumes with titles like *Franco's Graves, The Slaves of Franco, Victims of Victory, The End of Hope, The Lost Children of Francoism* and *Chronicle of the Lost Years.* Spaniards, especially a younger generation whose grandparents and parents had often kept their own silence, suddenly wanted to know more.

Soon, however, it became clear that the silence hid something other than just fear or shame. Spaniards, it turned out, did not agree on the past. History was a political Pandora's box. Once the lid was opened, out flew ancient, hate-fuelled arguments.

A new kind of book appeared. These ones had names like *The Myths of the Civil War, Checas of Madrid: Republican Prisons Revealed* or *1934 – The Civil War Begins, The Socialist Party and Catalan Republican Left Start the Hostilities.* These were often pseudo-history, a prominent historian complained to me. He also believed they were a direct result of the graves being opened. They shot, however, to the top of the bestsellers list. These books, in the broadest sense, accused the people lying in those graves of being guilty of the whole thing in the first place. The left had provoked the Civil War with swings towards extremism, attempted revolutions and leniency with church-burners. And then there were the *checas*, the left-wing prisons and torture cells, and the mass shootings of right-wing prisoners by the Republicans themselves. A left-wing revolution was gathering steam when General Franco and others rebelled, they argued. It was a new version of Franco's old argument. He had saved Spain.

This was the argument that had been disguised by the silence. Spain had two versions of who was to blame for the Civil War. There was one for the old right, and their new apologists, and one for the rest. There was something infantile about the argument that had reappeared. 'You started it!' 'No, you started it!' had the ring of small children arguing. Proven historical facts – and the dispassionate treatment of them – were, sadly, not always a part of the debate.

History, it suddenly became clear, was a Spanish battlefield. There was no generally accepted narrative for what had happened in the 1930s. Nor, I would discover, was there agreement on whole other areas of the past.

The poet Machado had written: 'Little Spaniard who is coming into this world, may God protect you. One of the two Spains will freeze your heart.' Now, some people claimed, the two Spains were beginning to reappear. Ideas of 'them' and 'us', of 'if you are not my friend, you are my enemy' were becoming increasingly powerful. Aznar, especially, seemed to encourage them. There were many on the other side of the political barricades who were happy to return the treatment.

Old fault lines re-emerged. Travelling back to Barcelona or talking to some people in the Basque Country, especially, was becoming increasingly strange. It was not so much a question of entering a different country, as of finding oneself in a different mental space. Opinions rarely heard in Madrid were commonplace in Catalonia and the Basque Country – and vice versa. Spain felt not just divided, but schizophrenic.

Las Dos Españas, the Two Spains, seem to have something to do with the Spanish love of forming groups and clans. Spaniards like to move en masse, to belong to large gaggles. They celebrate, and demonstrate, in huge throngs – their enjoyment increased by the numbers with them. It is one of the great and enviable things about

Spain to an outsider. This is a country where no politician, from left or right, would dream of echoing Margaret Thatcher's words that 'there is no such thing as Society'. Where *anglosajones* do things on their own or with their families, Spaniards often do them by the coach-load. They like the warmth, the solidarity, the sense of belonging that groups give them. That, perhaps, is why their towns and cities pack people together, ignoring the acres of open space around them. Individuality, I discovered when my own children reached school age, can be viewed with suspicion. There is something potentially dangerous, however, about these groups. Individual squabbles can turn into group squabbles. The herd, once roused, can be far more destructive than the beast on its own.

The arguing over history, however, did not end with the Civil War. For Spaniards also had doubts that stretched much further back. Even the question of when Spain came into existence did not seem to have a clear answer. Was it, as one politician on the right proclaimed, 'the oldest country in Europe'? Had an early version of it existed under the Romans or Visigoths as something called Hispania? Or was it Queen Isabella and King Ferdinand, the so-called Catholic Monarchs, who created modern Spain by uniting the kingdoms of Castile and Aragón and completing the Christian '*Reconquista*' in the fifteenth century? Some suggested Spain was much younger, that it did not become fully formed until Spaniards fought together against Napoleon in the early nineteenth century. The argument, once more, had strong political overtones. A Spaniard's idea of history, I discovered, often depended on how they voted. Or was it vice versa?

Even the Moors, who had arrived in Spain in 711 and left five centuries ago, suddenly turned up in political discourse. They were there in Aznar's speeches about Islamist terrorism or in bishops' warnings about attempts to bring a full separation of the Roman Catholic Church from the State. Some saw both Moors and Jews as an integral part of Spanish history and culture. For others, they were still, clearly, an alien, ancient enemy.

The Greek geographer Strabo described the Iberian peninsula – which modern Spain shares with Portugal – as 'like an ox-hide extending in length from west to east, its fore-parts toward the east, and in breadth from north to south'. That ox-hide is now being pulled, stretched and squabbled over. There are warnings that it might tear. A new Socialist prime minister, José Luis Rodríguez Zapatero, is trying to stop that happening. It is a test of the elasticity of the constitution Spaniards wrote for themselves, under the shadow of Francoism, in 1978. Apocalyptic warnings from the opposition suggest the end of Spain is nigh. 'We are witnesses to the dismantling of Spain,' says one of Aznar's ex-ministers.

Spain, a significant number of Spaniards believe, is not really a nation. It is a state that contains – or, even, imposes its will on – several other nations. These have their own names: principally Euskadi (as the Basque Country is now known) and Catalonia, but also Galicia. In these places – which jointly account for a quarter of Spaniards – the word *España* is often unmentionable. It has been replaced by *el estado español*, the Spanish state. This is, sometimes, a country that dares not speak its own name.

Again, history is plundered to support one or other discourse. A Catalan's version of Catalonia's history may have little to do with that of a Madrileño. A Basque nationalist and his pro-Spanish neighbour in Navarre – even though their history has sometimes run the same course – may also disagree on what really happened in the past. From the eighth-century Battle of Roncesvalles, when the Basques fell on Charlemagne's rearguard as it left Spain, to the seventeenth-century Reapers Revolt in Catalonia, the interpretations of what happened – and why – are not just different, but sometimes diametrically opposed. The history young Spaniards are taught at school can often be different too. Iñaki, a Basque history teacher, told me a teenage student recently handed him a drawing – which had been approved by another teacher – in which eighth-century peasants at Roncesvalles carried an *ikurriña*, the flag of modern Euskadi. 'Everybody knows that that flag was invented eleven centuries later,' he said. Another Basque historian, a disciple of Basque nationalism, told me I should never trust historians from elsewhere in Spain when they wrote about the Basques. 'They always twist it to their own ends,' he said.

Spain's Royal Academy of History came to an opposite conclusion. It issued a report claiming that the regional politicians who now control education were making sure schoolchildren received a 'partial, skewed and inexact' version of history. Pupils in some places were learning that their region had been in a state of constant struggle with Madrid. Schools ran the danger of encouraging 'confrontation'. 'In no other European country is the ignorance of history used with the political aim of distortion or creating opposition,' it fumed.

That Spaniards were worried about the integrity of their nation was clear, again, from the bookstores. *Spain, Patriotism and Nation*, *Hispania to España* or *Spain: Three Millennia of History* were a few of the titles produced to apply starch to the ox-hide.

The counter-argument was there, too. *I Am Not Spanish*, read one Catalan-language title in Barcelona's bookshops. In the Basque Country the row was more lethal than that. Separatist gunmen from ETA were still killing, their own version of history helping them pull the trigger. *Why Are We Basques Fighting?* was the title of one book, written from a prison cell, whose justifications stretched back into prehistory.

The great writer and thinker José Ortega y Gasset had warned about all this in the 1920s in his *España Invertebrada (Invertebrate Spain)*. Spain, he warned, lacked a strong backbone to hold it together. It had been falling slowly apart since it reached a height of imperial grandeur – and superpower status – at the end of the sixteenth century. Foreign visitors had already commented on the huge contrasts between Spaniards from different regions. Vast mountain ranges and broad rivers chopped the country up into virtually incommunicable bits. The mid-nineteenth-century traveller Richard Ford called them 'walls and moats'. That meant that Spaniards often knew little about one another. The *pueblo* (home town or village) and the *provincia* (province) were, at that stage, the entire world of most Spaniards.

Yet this new Spain has done much to demolish those barriers. European Union funds have helped bore holes through mountains, running motorways and high-speed trains through them.

Long-distance journeys between places are no longer counted in days, but in hours. Every year they get a little shorter. Nineteenth-century travellers would always remark on how you could tell where a Spaniard was from by their style of dress. Today's Spaniards buy their clothes from the same shops. These are often owned by the same man, Europe's latest retailing billionaire – and Spain's richest man – the publicity-shy Zara founder Amancio Ortega. Spaniards now watch the same TV soaps and the same *galas*, the interminable Saturday night variety shows broadcast from around the country. They are more joined up, and more homogeneous, than they have ever been. They are also more disposed to argue about whether they have anything in common.

When I first lived in Spain, spending the mid-1980s in Barcelona, I had come to admire the way Catalan friends were busy rediscovering their roots – often by studying their own language. I had arrived, fresh out of university, in a state of almost total ignorance about Spain and its different languages. They were an exciting discovery. I went to the theatre in Catalan, I read poetry in the language of the Galicians and was intrigued, on my first visits to San Sebastián, by the unusual and exotic sound of the Basque language, *euskara*. These languages enriched Spain. Instead of celebrating that, however, Spaniards seemed intent on squabbling about them. They were not a cause of common pride, but of division. They still are – more so, in fact, than they were then.

Superficially, Spaniards are good at relating to the past. Few countries hold on to and nurture their traditions so tenderly or so enthusiastically. From the bull-runs of Pamplona to the ku-klux-klan-like *nazarenos* parading through Andalucía's cities over Easter, from the Basque stone-lifting competitions to the Catalan fire festivals – the fiesta remains sacrosanct. One estimate has put annual spending on local fiestas at half a billion pounds. Tradition and modernity somehow manage to fit snugly together in Spain. It is a wonder to those of us from countries, or cultures, where the latter has wiped out much of the former. This strange conjunction of old and new produces some of the most endearing pictures – literally so, in the photographic sense – of modern Spain: the conical-hatted *nazareno* astride a motorbike; the turbanned *moro* from a Moors and Christians festival in Alicante, chatting on his mobile phone; or the woman bullfighter from one of Pedro Almodóvar's films, dressed in a glittering *traje de luces*, a suit of lights.

Tradition and history, however, are two different things. The former is always invented at some moment – and a surprising number of Spanish fiestas are recent inventions – while the latter should not be. Fiestas, anyway, do not seem to me to be celebrations of the past. Some are genuinely spiritual, religious affairs. Others are expressions of local pride or chauvinism. Most, however, are about fun. You only have to see the men of Almonte dressed in their wide *cordobés* hats, their horses tethered to a rail behind the hermitage of The Virgin of El Rocío, swigging back beer or rum and coke, to see that. A million people visit this gleaming white hermitage in Spain's south-west province of Huelva every Whitsun. It is Spain's biggest annual religious pilgrimage. It is also Spain's biggest annual party. Tradition then, like anger, is actually worn quite lightly. There may, or may not, be *gravitas* – but there is rarely the pomposity of its dwindling British equivalents. This, again, has to do with that Spanish love of doing things en masse. It is a reaffirmation of society, of the group, rather than a desperate clinging to the past. It also, of course, has to do with that deeply held belief in the right to have a good time.

Any journey across Spain is, necessarily, going to include a certain amount of having, or watching people have, a good time. But the starting point for my quest was a moment in history when Spaniards got carried away by another, more destructive, sort of emotion. It was time to find those Civil War graves.

Ghosts of Spain

1

Secretos a Voces

Sitting in the late autumn sun, in what had once been the Generalísimo's *plaza*, it was not difficult to imagine what had happened here, sixty-six years earlier. The same crooked, clay-tiled roofs ran down to the wood-balustraded balconies of the buildings around the square. One or two houses were new, and the town hall had been renovated, but the church was, of course, still there. The square remained open on one side, looking out over roof-tops and fields.

I had come here to listen to a story that, were Spain not a country whose history is perforated with holes of silence and forgetting, would have been laid gently to rest long ago. It was a story that had erupted out of the past, spilt over into the present and proved one thing – the sores of the Spanish Civil War could still, even now, be reopened. Two-thirds of a century had gone by, but they were still there, untended and only partially cured.

This was my first visit to Poyales del Hoyo. I did not know then that it would be the first of many trips to the fertile valley of the River Tiétar. At that moment, Poyales del Hoyo was just another Spanish *pueblo* of seven hundred ageing inhabitants. The square was small, neat and, thankfully, unspoilt. Light poured in from the open, southern side and lemon trees peeked around the corner of the church. But, apart from that, the *pueblo* had little special to recommend it. Today was, in any case, a day for the dead, All Saints Day. There was more bustle in the cemetery than in this square, now called the Plaza del Moral. Not so long ago, however, this had been the Plaza del Generalísimo – the superlative title they had given to Europe's most enduring right-wing dictator, Francisco Franco Bahamonde.

So here, more or less, is what happened on 29 December 1936.

The details have undoubtedly been modified over the years in the minds of those who told it to me. The core of it, however, is true. It is a tale that could be told in a thousand *pueblos*. But in most of those places, as they were in Poyales del Hoyo, the shameful events of that period remain *secretos a voces* – 'voiced secrets' that, even today, are only whispered in private.

29 December, 1936

The small lorry was parked in the plaza, *between the village hall, the squat, solid church and a covered walkway propped up by irregular granite columns.* It was a cold December night. Rain was beating down on Poyales del Hoyo, slipping down the cobbles and mud of the steep, narrow streets and into the fields below.

Perched on the foothills of the Gredos mountains in the central Spanish province of Ávila, Poyales del Hoyo likes to boast that it is protected by them from the extremes of the weather of the Castilian plain to the south. But the rain, when it comes, can be relentless. The water shines the streets and puts a dull, matt grey tinge on the tightly packed, white-painted buildings.

The night chosen for killing the three women fell a few days after Christmas and just two before New Year's Eve. A small crowd had formed as the Falangists prepared to carry out their work. There was no lack of volunteers. Only one man, a future Civil Guard officer called Miguel Suárez, protested at what was about to happen. He pulled a young cousin of his out of the crowd and dragged him out of the square, but he could not stop the rest.

The man in charge was Ángel Vadillo. Later to be known by the nickname *Quinientos Uno*, literally 'Five hundred and one', he was the leader of the local Falange, the Spanish Phalanx. This party of the extreme right had gathered just 45,000 votes around Spain (and no seat in the Madrid parliament, Las Cortes) in national elections ten months before. But, as the only party approved by General Francisco Franco, it was growing rapidly in the areas conquered since the military rebellion against the Republic had erupted in July. Vadillo eventually boasted that he had killed 501 *rojos* – thus gaining a nickname which, by most accounts, he was proud of.

In the early months, the shootings were a regular occurrence. *501* and his fellow Falangists would meet in the bars of Poyales or, seven miles (eleven kilometres) away, in Celestino's bar in Candeleda. There they would fortify themselves with *vino de pitarra*, the rough red wine made from the dusty, purple grapes that grow in every garden and smallholding along this fertile stretch of the Tiétar valley. Then, after nightfall, they would go to work.

Tonight it was the turn of Pilar Espinosa, Virtudes de la Puente and Valeriana Granada. The latter, *Quinientos Uno's* niece Damiana agrees today, was only there because another woman in the village was jealous of her. Valeriana, aged twenty-six, had once been the woman's husband's lover. That was before they had married but, in the cauldron of village life, the jealousy still bubbled away. The woman persuaded her Falange friends to add Valeriana's name to the list of those due to be killed. The other two were Republican sympathisers. Pilar was forty-three. She was one of the few in the village who could read. She had subscribed to the newspaper *El Socialista*. Virtudes, aged fifty-three, was not just a Republican but also a Protestant. She used to bathe, immodestly, in a pool in the river that still bears her name. These were all things that marked her as a potential enemy of Franco's National Catholic crusade as it swept slowly but inexorably across Spain.

The night has remained crystal clear in the mind of Obdulia, Pilar Espinosa's daughter. Two-thirds of a century had gone by when she told me what had happened. As soon as she started telling the story, however, she slipped back to that night in 1936 – once more seeing the faces of those around her.

It was the night when she, a fourteen-year-old girl, accompanied her mother in her last hours of life. 'We were already in bed after a hard day in the fields. Suddenly they were beating at the door. There must have been a dozen of them, dressed up in their blue shirts and leather webbing, armed with rifles and pistols. They told us we had to go and speak to the police, that someone had denounced us,' she recalled.

They were taken to a small warehouse, or storeroom, somewhere in the village. But the only questioning they had was from the local priest – who must have known what awaited them. Before the women, together with Pilar's daughter Obdulia and Valeriana's two-year-old girl, Heliodora, were brought out into the square, the priest appeared. He asked whether they wanted him to hear their confession. Perhaps, like Mosén Millán, the priest in Ramon J. Sender's '*Requiem para un campesino español*' ('*Requiem for a Spanish Peasant*'), he consoled himself with the thought that: 'At times, my son, God allows an innocent to die. He let it happen to his own Son, who was more innocent than the three of you.'

The Falangists, meanwhile, had gone to get Feliciano Fraile from the police cells. Feliciano was another Republican, but he was also one of the few in Poyales who knew how to drive. He was forced behind the wheel of the small, requisitioned lorry – which the owner, Rufino, had refused to drive. Then the women were brought out and pushed up into the back of the lorry with the men who would kill them.

Back in 1936, the road out of Poyales del Hoyo hugged the contours of the Gredos foothills tightly, making gentle S-shapes as it travelled slowly towards Candeleda. It snaked its way through pastures, olive groves, and orchards of cherry trees or wide-leafed figs. On the right-hand side the Almanzor, 'The Invincible' – the highest of the Gredos peaks named after the warrior-like hadjib (prime minister) of the tenth-century Muslim kingdom of Córdoba, Muhammad ibn Abi Amir – occasionally came into sight. Snow-capped until late spring, it takes on a hazy blue-grey colour on hot days, its edges blurring into the cloudless sky behind. On the other side of the road, low hills led south to the scorched plains of Castile, to Oropesa and, beyond that, Toledo.

On that rainy night, Obdulia and the three women could not see any of this. They were aware of the lurching of the lorry on the curves, the damp seeping in over the tarpaulin and, I am sure, the fearful certainty of their own deaths.

The women could have been shot anywhere along the road.

But, evidently, the killers wanted to get away from Poyales del Hoyo. The lorry did stop, once, on the way. Obdulia was ordered out. She had time for a quick embrace with her mother. Then she started back through the rain.

'My mother gave me a hug, and that was the last I saw of her. I ran back through the rain and shut myself into the house. I still don't know why they let me get off but I don't feel any gratitude. They killed my mother. I have always hated them for it and I always will,' she recalled, bitterness and defiance still in her face.

The chosen spot was on the final curve just before the road straightens out and runs down the hill into Candeleda, ending under the palm trees of the Plaza del Castillo.

The locals knew it as '*La Vuelta del Esparragal*', 'the asparagus field curve'. Feliciano, the driver, walked off and left the killers to it. Nobody was worried about him running away. There was nowhere to go. Considerable violence was used on Valeriana, the youngest, who was pregnant. Her skull was smashed. They say that her belly and womb were ripped open with a knife. The other two were shot through the head.

All three bodies were left out in the open beside the road. A peasant discovered them the following morning. He dug a grave, placed the three bodies in a Z-shape, shovelled the earth back and marked the spot with a stone. He died of a heart attack a few days later. People said it was *la pena* – the pain of his discovery – that killed him. By that time, however, everyone in Candeleda and Poyales del Hoyo knew the shameful secret of the Vuelta del Esparragal.

A new year broke at the end of the following day. It brought with it more war, and many more deaths like those of Pilar, Valeriana and Virtudes. The victims were buried in roadside graves, hurled into pits, gullies and ditches or stuffed down wells. The violence, once unleashed, reached extremes of cruelty on both sides.

The Spanish Civil War, a bloody curtain-raiser for the global war of ideologies that broke out in 1939, did not end for another two and a half years – until 1 April 1939. The country lived under the absolute control of General Franco, Caudillo of Spain, for almost another four decades. Poyales del Hoyo, Candeleda and the rest of the villages strung along the Tiétar Valley lived under the control of those who killed the three women, and those who supported them, for the same period.

Franco died, still in power, in 1975. The Spanish people, relieved, embraced democracy in record time, consciously fleeing their own brutal past and burying it in silence.

Fear, anyway, has a life of its own. People here kept the secret of the Vuelta del Esparragal for a quarter of a century more.

All Saints' Day, 2002

Sixty-six years later there is freshly dug earth again at the Vuelta del Esparragal. Mariano is down on his knees in the gash of pale, sandy soil opened up by the mechanical digger. He works his fingers through the drying mud and passes a few small, yellowed shards of human bone and tooth into the palm of one hand. With their primitive, heavy-handed working methods, he explains, the volunteers who came here a few days earlier to disinter the three women had not managed to gather everything.

'Look, this must be one of Valeriana's teeth. They smashed her skull. We couldn't find all the bits. We looked for the skeleton of an unborn child, but we could not find all of that either,' he explains.

It is All Saints Day and I have been talking to Mariano on and off on the telephone for several days. His voice had been getting increasingly excited as the date drew nearer. Sitting in a traffic jam outside Madrid – stuck behind family cars packed with people taking flowers to faraway cemeteries on this, the day in which Spaniards so enthusiastically remember their dead – I had called him several times that morning.

Many of those coming to the funeral, he said, were in the same jam on the motorway leading west out of Madrid towards Badajoz and Portugal. Those already in Poyales del Hoyo could wait. 'It has already taken sixty-six years, so a little longer won't matter.

You will be able to recognise me easily. I get *nervioso*, agitated, when things like this are happening,' he explained.

On previous days he had told me of his problems with the *ayuntamiento*, the village council. The authorities there, members of the Conservative right-wing People's Party, wanted nothing to do with the three sets of bones. Mayoress Damiana González was the niece of Ángel Vadillo, the infamous *Quinientos Uno* who was responsible for the killings. She had left town and declined to attend the reburials. She had, grudgingly, left instructions that a reburial should be allowed if it was 'properly' requested by relatives. But the town was to do nothing special for these bodies. They were, the mayoress reasoned, just like any others.

Then, two days before the burial, the deputy mayor – a retired Franco-era Civil Guard officer – had left a message on Mariano's answering machine telling him there was no room for the women in the cemetery. In Poyales del Hoyo, the old splits between left and right were reappearing with vehemence. Here, at least, the accepted wisdom that, twenty-five years after Franco's death, Spain had definitively buried the trauma of the Civil War was transparently false.

'They treated the request with absolute scorn. It was the old right in action again,' said Mariano. He himself was a fully paid-up member of the old left. A former political exile and ex-member of an anti-Franco group, his business card read '*Mariano López – Trabajador y Activista Social*', 'worker and social activist'.

As the battle of the bodies began, the splits became more apparent. For decades the victims' families and their killers had lived cheek-by-jowl. The reburials brought an end to the silence which here, as in much of the rest of Spain, had kept the Civil War out of people's conversations, if not their minds. And, with that, the embers of ancient loathing had begun to glow again.

This was something that, according to the accepted mores of Spain's transition to democracy, was not supposed to happen. At the beginning of the twenty-first century Spain was ruled by the People's Party. It was the first openly right-wing party to win power through the ballot box since November 1933. Spain, it was claimed, had put its self-destructive past and reputation for bloody squabbling behind it. It was proud of its normality. '*España va bien*', 'Spain is going well', was the slogan of the modern, self-confident and fully democratic right-wing party of Prime Minister José María Aznar. Superficially, at least, Spain fitted the phrase. Material progress was visible in a country flooded with new buildings, new roads and new cars. Its young people, taller, stronger and healthier than the older generations, were walking proof of the country's success. Spain had become Europe's model country, a vigorous young democracy with a booming economy and, once more, ambitions to become, however modestly, a player on the world stage.

The mores of this youthful democracy dictated that the bloody, vicious past had been overcome. Nobody was supposed to meddle with it, let alone suggest there were important, unresolved matters capable of re-arousing – even on a small, bloodless local scale and amongst those old enough or close enough to the victims to remember – the destructive passions that drove Spain to civil war.

The Civil War was a series of dates in school textbooks. It was a few lines of information to be memorised at exam time and then forgotten. 'In other countries that suffered similar regimes, such as Italy and Germany, young people have been educated about what fascism was, and they are conscious of the horrors imposed by those regimes. That is not the case in Spain,' Vicenç Navarro, a former political exile turned professor of politics, explained.

Few people, however, seemed worried about that. Had not the left-wing and regional political parties and the trades unions, after much wrangling, been compensated for the property confiscated from them by Franco? Had not the elderly volunteers of the International Brigades been offered Spanish nationality? Had not the *niños de la guerra* – those Republican children evacuated in rusty old merchant ships to Russia at the beginning of the war – been welcomed back sixty years later to a shiny new old people's home built for them on the outskirts of Madrid? Were these not the proper symbols of how Spain had achieved, in the words of psychologists, 'closure' on the trauma of its past?

For some people, the digging up of Civil War victims – such as the three women from Poyales del Hoyo – was a kind of treason. It was a breaking of the pact of forgetting – and silence – that had kept the lid tightly screwed down on the past. That silence had been a cornerstone of the swift, dramatic and successful transition to democracy of which Spaniards were, justly, so proud.

What was clear in Poyales del Hoyo, however, was that reconciliation between the victims of that war had been left out of the equation. The families of those on the losing side were, even now, meant to suffer in silence. They were meant to leave their dead scattered in roadside ditches and, so, play their part in the agreed plan of constructing Spain's future by forgetting their own families' past. In this context the people in Poyales del Hoyo were rebels, breaking Spain's own, unwritten rules about what could or could not be done with its history.

Mariano found a way past the town hall's obstacles. He had discovered that the Poyales del Hoyo gravedigger was a fellow left-winger. The night before the burials, the gravedigger had sworn that, if necessary, he would dig up the patch of ground dedicated to *los caídos por Dios y por España*, those who fell for God and Spain. That was the name given to those who died fighting for Franco's Nationalist forces during the Civil War. Mariano liked that idea.

In the end, a small patch of earth was found in the tight, whitewashed, rectangular graveyard that lay down the hill, beyond the open side of the square. All Saints Day is an important public holiday in Spain. Florists do their best business of the year, selling ten times as many flowers as normal. People flock to cemeteries to honour dead parents, grandparents or other family members. It seemed as though the graveyard at Poyales del Hoyo, with its three or four tiers of niches on each wall, had been specially brightened up with chrysanthemums, carnations and gladioli for the event.

In a ceremony accompanied by poetry and tears, three small, brown caskets were buried side by side. Heliodora, the infant daughter whom Valeriana had handed to a neighbour in the square before climbing into the truck, was there. She was now a woman in her sixties, with neat, short-cut silver hair. She read a simple, self-composed poem over the grave while Obdulia – a squat, olive-faced, healthy-looking eighty-year-old – looked on.

She wanted to tell them, though it was already obvious, that she was pregnant, five months gone./ I was two, held in her arms, crying out 'mamá!', as she implored them to let her live, saying she had done nothing wrong/ Those animals, who had nothing inside, said: 'Let go of her or she will get a bullet too.'

Previously, with the church bells ringing, the coffins had been carried around the village's narrow streets. It was a symbolic act – the first time the losers of a war that had ended more than six decades earlier had paraded their dead in Poyales del Hoyo.

We gathered in the square afterwards. There, Ezekiel Lorente, grandson of Virtudes and now a Socialist village councillor, puffed his chest out and held his head high as a local right-winger walked past. 'He knows what I am thinking. This is our moment,' he told me.

Stories began to emerge of what life had been like in Poyales del Hoyo under the boot of Ángel Vadillo. A teary-eyed woman, Francisca Sánchez, appeared in the square with a list of names, hurriedly scribbled down on a piece of scrap paper, of those in the village who were killed. Her own father, Evaristo, was one of them. Another man, '*El Ratón*' or 'the mouse', she claimed, had his eyes gouged out. In the Tiétar Valley – and elsewhere in rural Spain – many people, entire families, are known by their *motes*, their nicknames. There was the usual struggle to remember people's real names, but soon the piece of paper was being turned over as the list headed past the two dozen.

As people drifted off, a convoy of cars headed for Candeleda for a last look at the former grave. Obdulia waited for us in the Capra Hispánica, the main bar on Candeleda's Plaza del Castillo.

Obdulia was carrying an old, browned photograph of Pilar. It must have been taken when her mother was in her thirties. Like many elderly women still found in *pueblos* around Spain, Pilar was already in that state of semi-permanent mourning that afflicts those whose relations are forever dying. A black shawl has been wrapped tightly across her chest and tucked into a long black skirt. She is, of course, much younger than her daughter is now. But they share the same high, rounded cheekbones, dark complexion and strong mouth. In fact, there is something severe about Pilar as she sits sideways on a wooden chair, one hand holding the back, her hair parted in a razor-sharp line down the middle and staring directly into the lens. Perhaps it is the responsibility of being able to read, or the knowledge that comes from it, that adds the *gravitas* to her face.

After the killing, Obdulia revealed, she stayed locked into her home. A few months later she left for the nearest large-sized town, Talavera de la Reina. Even there, however, the Falange tried to come for her. Franco's repressive machine was in full and bloodthirsty cry in those first few years during and after the war.

But she married young and, by then, had a husband to save her. 'I married a brave man who defended me,' was how she put it. Obdulia's husband had been, like General Franco himself, a '*novio de la muerte*' (a 'fiancé of death'), a member of the country's most famously fearless fighting force, the Spanish Legion. He told them they would only get to Obdulia over his dead body. The small town Falangists, more used to marching unarmed people away at gun-point than fighting, did not test his word.

Obdulia did not set foot in Poyales del Hoyo again for over thirty years. By that time *Quinientos Uno* was dead, having succumbed to a heart attack while in Arenas de San Pedro. (Francisca Sánchez still thinks this was an act of God, even though it happened in the 1960s. 'His sins caught up with him.')

She remembers, however, seeing another of the killers, El Manolo, '*que era malísimo*', 'who was very bad', drinking in the bar. 'I wanted to go and say something to him, but my sister wouldn't let me,' she said. 'I didn't lose my fear until Franco was dead.'

'This thing has stayed in my mind all my life. I've never forgotten. I am reliving it now, as we stand here. All the killers were from the village. They came with the intention of killing, and then they went off to confess.'

She is struggling now, to turn that hatred and fear into forgiveness. Finally she fixes me with a watery stare. 'I can pardon, but I cannot forget. We have to pardon them or it makes us just like them.'

The events of that day were, naturally, moving. But they also raised questions. In the pages of the *Diario de Ávila* – a newspaper normally devoted to recording the proceedings of local councils, the progress of public works and the endless routine of local fiestas – a former mayor of Candeleda had even accused Mariano of belonging to the armed Basque separatist group ETA. A defamation case was pending. For some people, at least, the reburials were a call once more to man – peacefully this time – the old ideological barricades.

Why had such an apparently innocent act provoked such rage and outrage? What other ghosts had been lying under the *Vuelta del Esparragal*? I decided to ask Damiana González Vadillo, the absent mayoress of Poyales del Hoyo.

I went back to find Damiana the following Monday. But she was still away. The man who told me that, it turned out, was her deputy, Aurelio Jarillo. He spoke in the stilted jargon of the military-styled police force, the Civil Guard, he used to serve in Franco's days. The relevant information had already been issued, he said, before adding that journalists had transformed it all into a pack of lies. When would Damiana be back? 'I don't know,' he replied.

Two weeks later I returned again. Damiana was there. Already in her seventies, she was into her last year as mayoress in a village of 700 souls. Like most rural communities in Spain, Poyales del Hoyo has been on the wane since the 1950s. At the time of the Civil War – when most of Spain lived in *pueblos* – it had more than 2,000 inhabitants. 'And it had its own notary,' she told me proudly.

People from Madrid – two hours' drive away – are buying up properties as second homes. Some have even moved here for a quiet life in the country. But Poyales del Hoyo was still ageing. 'Twenty people have died since January,' explained Damiana who, at seventy-seven, was hardly a spring chicken herself.

Damiana claimed there had been no fuss, no objections and no obstruction from the village council to the re-burials. 'I have no problem with that,' she said. But she clearly did.

As we spoke in her spartan office, she first expressed her shock that the church bells had been rung for 'non-believers'. 'How cynical. None of them would have liked that. They used the church here as a prison,' she said.

Then she launched into a tirade against the left and the Republican committee that had controlled the village in the nine weeks between the days that generals Sanjurjo, Franco, Mola and friends had risen up in arms to the moment when Franco's Moorish troops swept into Poyales del Hoyo. Damiana, who was eleven at the time, had no trouble recalling the dates: 'From July 18 to September 8, the day the Moors arrived.'

The killing of dozens of left-wingers in Poyales was, she said, merely the result of the left's own bloodletting at that time. 'One lot finished and the next lot got started. They killed one another as much for village arguments and old hatreds as for anything else,' she said. I heard this version of events in other places, too. The violence was already latent – with each village a ticking time-bomb of angry resentment.

The village was divided into what had already become known as 'the two Spains' – the right and the left – and the bloodletting was mutual. Here, as in nearby Candeleda, the prominent men of the right were rounded up and kept in the church. But here, unlike in Candeleda, nine were taken out and shot. 'The priest was paraded through the village with a horse's bridle tied around his head. They insulted him, blasphemed him and treated him like an animal. They made him drink vinegar and then killed him with two others,' she explained.

Damiana recalled some of the several dozen names which, until Ezekiel Lorente persuaded the council to take it down, had figured on the list of '*Caídos por Dios y por la Patria*' on the church wall. 'A man called Eloy Garrido was one of the first to be killed. He left a widow and three children. They killed him because he was from the right – there was no Falange here then, just "the left" and "the right". Then there were Juan and Isaac. They were father and son. Three sisters were left as widows.'

The three victims in the Candeleda grave, Damiana suggested, were not as innocent as those who dug them up have claimed. 'It was said that these women were involved [in the killings], that they pointed people out,' she said. Lorente's grandmother Virtudes, the mayoress claimed, had once threatened to kill her own mother with a cobbler's spike after an argument over a loaf of bread. The mayor had to organise an escort for her.

In a place this small, the renewed arguing over events of sixty-six years earlier had quickly turned personal. 'The younger generations of the Lorente family and my family are friends. He has told them one side of the story. I never wanted to tell them mine. I never talked about it. But now I have been forced to,' she said. Her own, personal, vow of silence had been broken.

Her uncle had, she suggested, turned to violence only after several members of his own family were killed by the left. 'My uncle fled. He hadn't done anything by then, but they would have killed him if they could. Another uncle hid in the roof of a house. There were many families like that,' she said.

She was unable, or unwilling, to explain, however, the enthusiasm that her uncle would put into his job as the self-appointed avenger of the Tiétar Valley. His nickname of *Quinientos Uno*, she suggested, was an exaggeration.

For every person killed by the left, however, his men killed several times more. That does not mean they were necessarily more bloodthirsty. They did, after all, have more time.

One of Franco's generals, Gonzalo Queipo de Llano, had been explicit about what was expected of the Nationalist forces when the rebellion broke out. 'For every one of mine who falls, I will kill at least ten extremists. Those leaders who flee should not think they will escape [that fate]; I will drag them out from under the stones if necessary and, if they are already dead, I will kill them again.'

When the right started to wreak its revenge, Damiana's mother kept her indoors. Her explanation to her eleven-year-old daughter for what was going on was simple: 'Just as they treated us badly, so they are now being treated badly.'

Damiana really could not understand the fuss about the graves of Pilar, Virtudes and Valeriana. Educated under Franco, she still believed the propaganda of the time. Had not the Generalísimo built, at the '*Valle de Los Caídos*', 'The Valley of the Fallen', outside Madrid, a monument to all the dead of the Civil War, regardless of which side they were on? The common grave of the three women had not been such a big secret. 'If they didn't get them before, it was because they didn't want to. It was always known that they were there. They should do what has to be done, but not go around saying these things. We would be better off keeping our mouths shut, those on one side and those on the other.'

Damiana, like so many of her generation, preferred silence. The stories of who did what to whom, she says, were *cosas del pueblo* – village matters. 'It was all about envies and old hatreds. What was the war for? For nothing.'

Damiana's version of the Civil War, and especially what it was for, is accepted by many of those Spaniards who simply found themselves caught up in history. This is no more so than those with men called up by one or other side, forced to fight and die purely on the basis of whether the area where they lived had fall-en under Republican or Nationalist control.

But the Spanish Civil War, was never about 'nothing'. British historian Hugh Thomas, who wrote the definitive history of the conflict at a time when Spaniards were only allowed to hear the winners' account, declared it to be, at least in its opening days, 'the culmination of a hundred years of class war'. That, however, was just one of the many battles fought out on Spanish soil, and with Spanish blood, between 1936 and 1939.

The Spanish Civil War was many things. A Spain that had stumbled its way through political chaos for more than a century, and where the division between the 'two Spains' of right and left had reached epic and bloody proportions, would fall under the yoke of the former.

The Civil War was the end of the Second Republic. This had

been a well-intentioned, if messy and poorly directed, affair. At its best, the Republic was an attempt to free Spain from the backwardness and moral straitjacket imposed on it by landowners, the Church and a monarchy that had been forced to flee in 1931.

The Republic was born with massive hopes and ambitions, some of which, especially in the field of education, bore early fruit. Had it worked, it might have transformed Spain. In the end, unfortunately, it was no exception in an ongoing history of political tragedy. It had been under assault from all sides, from within and without. Attempted revolutions, military insurrections, strikes, political assassinations, street violence and secessionist moves in Catalonia had left it worn and torn. Franco's latter-day apologists, proponents of a theory that the Generalísimo saved Spain from a workers' revolution, claim that it was already on its deathbed.

The Civil War was also a curtain-raiser for a much greater, global war of ideologies. For this was an early round in the great clash between the fascist ideals being promoted by Hitler and Mussolini and the communism of Stalin's Russia. Hitler's Luftwaffe tested out the carpet-bombing of civilian populations, with infamous consequences, in Guernica. Mussolini also provided abundant troops and supplies. Stalin backed the International Brigades, and eventually ended up with much of Spain's gold. It was also a piece of calculated fence-sitting by Britain, France and the other European democracies. These turned their back on the elected Republican government and remained neutral, partly out of fear that communism might be the eventual winner, but mainly to avoid a punch-up with Hitler and Mussolini. Appeasement had an early outing in Spain.

But the Civil War was, first and foremost, the most important event in twentieth-century Spanish history. It could be argued, in fact, that it was the most important thing to happen for several centuries. A country that had slowly, over several hundred years, lost a once vast empire, finally turned against itself. This loss of empire had reached its final point in 1898 with what became known as *el Desastre*, the Disaster. In that year Spain lost Puerto

Rico, the Philippines and, in a humiliating naval defeat by the United States, the Caribbean jewel of Cuba. Admiral George Dewey sank the Pacific fleet in the Philippines in May. The Atlantic fleet was 'picked off like pigeons in a shoot' near Cuba two months later. Spain's empire was thus reduced to a few poor possessions in Africa. The events of that year provoked a long bout of national soul-searching and self-flagellation led by a group of intellectuals – including Miguel de Unamuno and the novelist Pío Baroja – known as 'the generation of 98'.

The Civil War was also a bloodbath that pitted brother against brother and neighbour against neighbour. By the time the guns had stopped smoking and Franco had signed his final *parte de guerra* on 1 April 1939, some half a million Spaniards were dead. There are no exact figures, but it is thought that some 200,000 were executed by the two sides. There were also thousands of dead Italians and Germans, who fought for Franco, and other foreigners who had volunteered for the International Brigades. One in thirty Spanish men were dead. Some 400,000 went into exile.

The war dragged on for three years. Franco could probably have won it in a lot less time. But he preferred to avoid an early battle in Madrid and, anyway, he was not just after military victory. He wanted more than that. His fellow generals appointed him 'Head of Government of the Spanish State' in September 1936, thinking they were creating a wartime dictatorship. In fact, in the words of one historian, 'They had created a Hobbesian sovereign endowed with greater powers than Napoleon, a sovereign who was to shed few of those powers over forty years.'

It was not, at the very start, Franco's rebellion. The head of the military revolt was the conservative general José Sanjurjo. He was an inveterate conspirator who died in an aeroplane accident on the third day of the war – apparently provoked by the weight of the ceremonial uniforms he was carrying with him. Franco was, at the time, based in the far-off Canary Islands. He started off by taking control of the army in Morocco, moving it across the Strait of Gibraltar and organising a campaign that quickly won much of south-west Spain. A third general, Emilio Mola, did similar work in north-west Spain, while most of the rest of the country remained faithful to the Republic.

Once Franco took control, however, the war had two specific aims apart from military victory. For Franco the war was a *cruzada*, a fundamentalist Roman Catholic crusade against a conspiracy of Marxists (and their 'Jewish spirit'), freemasons and separatists. The crusade's purpose was not just to defeat the enemy but, in good measure, to eradicate it. It was, in that respect, a repeat of what Franco considered one of the most glorious moments of Spanish history – the Christian *Reconquista* of Spain from the Moors. The *Reconquista* had pitted Spain's Christians against its Muslims over several centuries. It led, eventually, to the forced conversion or expulsion not just of the latter, but also, in 1492, of the Spanish Jews.

Franco's victories rarely brought instant peace. They brought, instead, what would later be called 'the politics of revenge'. In its earliest stages this meant retribution, vengeance and more bloodshed in a deliberate and thorough cleansing of all possible opposition. This was made all the more justified, in the minds of those who carried it out, by the fact that some *rojos* had been enthusiastic church-burners, priest-killers and creators of anonymous mass graves themselves. Their victims included thirteen bishops, 4,184 priests, 2,365 friars and 283 monks. Up to 60,000 people were killed by the left, a number probably doubled by Franco's followers. The difference was not just in scale. 'Neither the Republican authorities, nor the political parties of the left sanctioned reprisals,' one historian points out. 'The savage repression perpetrated on the Nationalist side, on the other hand, was an official, systematic and calculated strategy.'

'Everyone who is openly or secretly a supporter of the Popular Front should be shot . . . We have to sow terror. We must eliminate without scruples all those who do not think like ourselves,' General Mola had declared. 'If I found my father amongst my opponents, I would have him shot.'

Franco preferred a slow, thorough war to a lightning victory.

There was work to be done not just at the front, but behind one's own lines – weeding out and eliminating the enemy. 'There can be no ceasefire or agreement . . . I will save Spain from Marxism at any price,' he would tell the American journalist Jay Allen when asked whether he would shoot half of Spain.

That work was, in great measure, carried out by the Falange, a political party which, despite its meagre showing in elections five months before the war, became the only approved party. It quickly attracted the right in all its forms, as well as chancers, opportunists, the vengeful and thugs.

The other aim of the war eventually became to consolidate Franco's own position. Although he initially appeared to be a wary and unwilling plotter, he soon revealed a natural dictatorial bent. A small man with no sense of physical fear and certainly no belief that he might be wrong, he also made sure that, by the time war was over, there was only one person in charge – '*Franco, Caudillo de dios y de la patria*' ('Franco, Caudillo of God and of the nation'). As the title shows, he served God as much as his country.

One reason that Spaniards, especially older Spaniards, do not like to talk about the Civil War is that they still disagree so radically on it. Scratch the surface and most, even those on the modern right who profess dislike of Franco, will find themselves blaming the bloodletting on one side or the other. Better silence, anyway, than an argument that might see the blood of one's grandparents being swapped across the table.

It is a sign of just how much Spain has changed that one of the volunteers involved in digging up graves should be José Antonio Landera – a young member of the same Civil Guard police force that did much of Franco's dirty work. He told me that his schooling had left him with only vague notions of what had happened in the 1930s. 'The Civil War was only talked about superficially. There was no mention of the civilian deaths in virtually every village, of the mass graves or of the disappeared,' he said.

Many books have been written on Spain's Civil War. Few Spaniards, however, have yet managed to write impartially about it. Rafael Borràs Betriu, an emblematic editor who is Spain's most prolific publisher of twentieth-century history books, says the time is not yet ripe for agreement. 'Winners and losers have mostly offered their personal and subjective vision because . . . the Civil War remains alive in the social cloth of family tradition and in the historical memory of Spaniards. Quite a few years will have to go by before what is currently a minority trend can impose itself in the writing of history: seeing the part of the truth which corresponds to the adversary, freed of all connotations of "enemy".'

Film-makers and novelists have, generally, suffered the same partiality. British director Ken Loach cast his eye on the subject with *Land and Freedom* in 1995. 'What shame Spanish cinema must feel. It has to be a foreigner who recovers for us one of the most transcendental pieces of our history,' wrote one critic.

A recent exception to that rule is the novelist Javier Cercas, whose 2001 *Soldados de Salamina* – which fictionalises the story of how a Republican soldier helps a Falangist leader escape execution in the dying days of the war – was a surprise publishing success (even to the author). The novel seemed to tap a desire for reconciliation – or understanding – at least amongst the minority of Spaniards who read books. A notable recent attempt to bridge the divide was, appropriately, called *A History of the Civil War that Nobody Will Like.*

The digging up of graves like that in Poyales del Hoyo has had a galvanising effect on what some Spaniards have come to call their own '*desmemoria histórica*'. This expression was coined to describe an almost deliberate lack of historical memory. Amongst other things, it has set Franco's apologists scribbling. The most popular of these is Pío Moa.

Moa has changed radically since the days when he was a member of the First of October Antifascist Resistance Group (GRAPO) – a left-wing terrorist group that still occasionally rears its ugly head in Spain. He has had a publishing hit with *The Myths of the Civil War* in which, having moved from one extreme to another, he launches a vicious assault on many historians. Amongst his conclusions are that Winston Churchill and Franklin D. Roosevelt were both crueller than Franco, that the Republican loyalists were relatively more bloodthirsty than Franco's rightist rebels when it came to executing opponents and that the generals' rebellion was directed against a revolution brewing within the Republic. His rewards included a top place on the best-sellers list and long interviews on state television when it was controlled by the People's Party.

None of that changes the fact, of course, that Franco had time to hunt down and execute most of those responsible for killing his own supporters. A retroactive law was passed in 1939 which allowed for those deemed politically responsible for political 'crimes' previous to that date to be arrested. The last person to be executed for Civil War crimes was the communist Julián Grimau in 1963.

The killings by *rojos* – especially by anarchists – formed an essential part of the Franco regime's internal propaganda for decades. Hundreds of the priests and nuns they killed have gone down the beatification conveyor-belt at the Vatican in recent years. Pope John Paul II beatified 233 of them in one record-breaking go in 2001. The left's victims were eventually accorded burial in cemeteries, hailed as martyrs and saw their names added to the '*Caídos por Dios y la Patria*' plaques put up in every town and village in Spain. Thousands of the victims of Franco's repression were, however, left in roadside graves or even stuffed down wells (one well in Caudé, in the eastern province of Teruel, is said to be the last resting place of up to 1,000 people).

The full history of the losers – by which I mean the losers' stories rather than the left's version of what happened – is only just being broadcast. The army, which carried out its own executions after summary trials, kept many of its archives on those executed closed until the 1990s. Some files on those executed are still unavailable, piled up in cardboard boxes at the back of military warehouses. Others are simply thought to have disappeared.

There are still thousands of bodies in unmarked graves. The highest estimates talk of 30,000 unidentified corpses. Around 300 have now been recovered. Since the three women from Poyales del

Hoyo were exhumed, two other graves have been identified along the same seven-mile (eleven-kilometre) stretch of road. They are said to contain twenty corpses of men from both Poyales del Hoyo and Candeleda. The rediscovery of the graves caused the author and journalist Isaías Lafuente to pose the following question: 'Can a democratic country allow thousands of citizens murdered like animals by a dictatorial regime to remain buried in its roadside ditches? Can it tolerate this while the man who allowed and encouraged the mass killings rests under the altar of a Christian basilica? The answer is so obvious that is almost an offence to have to ask the question.'

Why had it taken so long to broach the subject, to dig up the dead, to ask the question? Fear is often given as the main reason. Franco's presence made it impossible to talk freely, let alone dig up graves, for almost forty years. That fear lived on into the first years of democracy. It was encouraged by coup rumours and the 1981 storming of parliament by Civil Guard Lieutenant Colonel Antonio Tejero.

Spain's whole democratic transition was, at least publicly, postulated on the stated belief on all sides that, as the returning Communist leader Santiago Carrillo put it, nothing was 'worth a new Civil War between Spaniards'. Even Felipe González, the Socialist prime minister who governed for nearly fourteen years from 1982, heeded the advice given to him by a former general to leave the subject of the Civil War well alone in order not to provoke the ire of the army. Nothing official was done to mark the fiftieth anniversary of the war's start in 1986.

In the graves of Pilar, Virtudes and Valeriana – and in hundreds more like them – there is proof of a silence that has been both collective and willing. One of Europe's most verbose and argumentative peoples has simply chosen to look away from a vital part of its history whose ghastly, ghostly presence is to be found under a few feet of soil.

Not even the family of poet and playwright Federico García Lorca, whose execution by the Franco Nationalists of Granada was explained by Ian Gibson in his 1974 classic *The Death of Lorca*, had tried to recover his body. Gibson's work, specially remarkable for the date in which it was published, was one of the first attempts to counter the Franco-imposed '*desmemoria*' of the time. Lorca's family, despite the popular pressure, still refuses to go any further.

The families of three men thought to have been buried alongside the poet do not, however, agree. Two anarchist *banderilleros* (secondary figures of the bullfight, whose job is to rush out and sticks darts in the bull's back) and a one-legged Republican schoolteacher are said to be in the grave. 'If one side [of the Civil War] can bury their dead with dignity then it is time the other side was able to as well,' the grandson of one of those bullfighters, Francisco Galadí, told me on a visit to Granada. 'The family of García Lorca has to be respected. But my father did not want his father to be left abandoned. Our family were treated as *apestados* – pestilential – for years. My father never got a good job, and we had to go to schools run by priests and *fachas*. I lived under Franco's repression for forty years. After seventy years, now it is time,' he explained.

The grave of the three women was one of the first to be dug up as Spaniards slowly began to look back down at the ground. These early exhumations were interesting, amongst other things, because they showed that Spain actually had a stock of people already experienced in such things. They were forensic scientists, anthropologists and archaeologists who had already worked on similar, if fresher, graves in the former Yugoslavia or Latin America.

One of the early volunteers was Julio Vidal, an archaeologist from the University of León. He was the first to describe these graves as *secretos a voces.* They still, he says, provoke 'a heavy and fearful silence' accompanied by a certain shame. The graves, Vidal says, represent 'the shameful part of our [democratic] transition which, while it keeps its eyes closed, will not allow this page of history to be turned.'

Spain's local magistrates, fearful of a flood of cases, refused to get involved in digging up graves. There were, they said, no crimes for them to investigate. There was no official money for the task of digging them up, either. Aznar's government, which had spent its time studiously trying to show that it had nothing to do with Franco-style rightism, was challenged to act. Emilio Silva took a case to the UN Committee for the Disappeared, more used to arguing over the mass graves of Kosovo or Guatemala than those on western European soil.

As the petitions from relatives of the disappeared flooded in, a national Association for the Recovery of Historical Memory was formed. It tried to stay clear of party politics. It petitioned parliament for help. The petition claimed that up to 30,000 victims of General Franco's supporters were buried in several hundred mass graves – some in cemeteries and others scattered along roadsides, in woods or open country.

'The conflict of the two Spains has not finished, nor will it finish until the truth of what happened is restored and the pain suffered, and still endured, by these families is recognised by handing back the bodies so that they can, at last, be given a dignified burial. Those who lost the war were condemned to silence, imposed on them by the dictatorship and agreed on by the democracy in the Amnesty Law of 1977. That condemnation has now reached the third generation of these families . . . Today there are people who still feel the need to lower their voices or even to close their windows when talking about these events, as if they themselves were doing something clandestine,' the group said in its parliamentary petition.

The group asked parliament to fund its activities, open up all the military archives, exhume and identify the bodies and bring an end to the 'discrimination' against Franco's victims and their families.

The parliament, where Aznar's People's Party held an absolute majority, trod around the subject as if walking on egg shells. Eventually it was agreed that local councils and regional authorities could, if they wanted, set funds aside for exhuming bodies. The same local authorities were ordered, sixty-three years after the war had ended, to avoid 'reopening old wounds or stirring up the *rescoldo*, the embers, of civil confrontation'. The motion was approved, by consensus, on 20 November 2002

– twenty-seven years to the day since General Franco had died.

That a European parliament should, at the turn of the twenty-first century, be passing motions about a war that finished sixty-three years before may seem surprising. That it should include in one of those motions a stern warning about reviving the embers of that confrontation shows that the Civil War still had the power to provoke fear.

The political debate over what to do with the Civil War and its victims continues. A political class which had publicly declared the war to have been overcome has found it impossible to avoid in its own debating chambers. The left found a sudden enthusiasm for the subject when Aznar was in power. It tried, amongst other things, to pass motions that formally recognised the war had been started by an illegal rebellion against the established and elected government. It was an enthusiasm that had been entirely absent when the Socialists were in power in the 1980s and early 1990s.

A significant part of the right continues to insist, however, that the war cannot be blamed on Franco's side alone. People's Party spokesmen at parliamentary debates talked of 'civil confrontation' and 'national self-destruction'. Blame, the modern right insists, should be shared by all. Some believe it should be pinned firmly on the left. Right and left, it seems, are forever destined to disagree.

The Socialist government that has now taken over from Aznar has vowed that it will, finally, do something about the mass graves. It is a sign that something is changing. The plans look set, however, to provoke cries of outrage from the right. More than six decades later there are still political arguments to be had – and, presumably, votes won or lost – on the issue of the Civil War. Spain has yet to put that war to sleep.

What about the killers? No one has ever been tried for crimes like the killings at Poyales del Hoyo or Priaranza. Nor can they be. Most of the killers are dead, of course. But some are not.

In an attempt to find one of them, I travelled back to Candeleda. Here, I was told, an infamous Falangist gunman was still alive. His name was Horencio Sánchez, but like most people here he was known by his *mote*, or nickname – *Sartén*, Frying Pan. The search for him, with Mariano as my guide, proved comical. Candeleda boasts some bizarre nicknames. Amongst those I would hear as we went around the pueblo were *Cagacantaros*, Pitcher-crapper, *Chupahuesos*, Bone-sucker, *Mataperros*, Dog-killer and *Cagamillones*, 'He who craps millions'. (This last *mote*, I was told, was given to a man who boasted about his wealth.)

First, however, Mariano wanted to introduce me to some of those who remembered the Civil War. We started off looking for Feliciano Pérez, who was not at home and, we were told, would be at the funeral of the oldest man in the village, who had died the previous day. We tried the church. This created a serious problem for Mariano. It is quite acceptable to wander in and out and chat to people in church services in Spain, but Mariano refused, on principle, to enter. The priest, he explained, had secretly said a Mass for his deceased father. This had led to a violent argument in the street. A boot, it was suggested, had been applied to the priest's backside. And, anyway, there was the Church's past to be considered. 'You have to understand . . . the Church, the landowners and Franco were one and the same thing,' he explained.

We thought we had the solution to that one when we found the local newsagent chomping on a cigar stub as he stood under the trees outside of the church with a handful of other men. But the newsagent, it turned out, had also sworn never to set foot inside the church, which has a plaque commemorating the local priests killed in the Civil War. 'Not on my life,' he said. So, having discovered that anti-clericalism was still alive and kicking, we gave up.

Eventually we found Feliciano back at home. '*Te cagarás*, you'll crap yourself, if I tell you how old I am,' he said, by way of greeting. Feliciano was in a good mood. With the previous day's death he had, at ninety-six, become the new oldest man in town. Unfortunately his memory was fading and his story of how Franco's Moorish troops took the town was jumbled and confusing.

Felipe Grande Nieto, a gentle old man in his late eighties, had much clearer memories. We talked to him in the back room of a tiny three-room flat. To get to the kitchen-cum-sitting room, we had to walk through the bedroom, where his frail stick of a wife lay shivering with cold. Her small body was stretched out and her arms clasped together on her chest like some medieval figure on top of a cathedral tomb. She moaned softly from time to time, giving every impression of preparing for the other world.

Felipe's father had been relatively well off and had owned a truck. He was, however, a Republican. The Nationalists took the truck away and his family had lived in relative poverty ever since. Felipe apologised as he talked, because, out of his already rheumy blue eyes, tears began to flow. He found two stories especially hard to tell. One was of a man, known as *el Ebanistero*, taken off at night to be shot with five others. 'But, for some reason, he did not die that night. When they sent a man to bury them, he found *el Ebanistero* still alive. "Kill me with the spade, I don't want to be left alive," he begged. So two *guardias* came and finished him off. They were buried down by the river,' he said, the tears running down his cheeks. The other was the story of a man shot as he fled the attacking Moors. His corpse was discovered by a dog. The animal appeared at its master's door with half a human limb in his mouth. 'He killed that dog immediately. It had tasted human flesh,' Felipe said, the tears still flowing.

After hearing the bloodcurdling tales of Falangist violence and humiliation, the idea of meeting Frying Pan – the alleged Falangist killer – was distinctly chilling. I imagined a hard, dry old man, still twisted by hatred or flushed with brutal pride. Or, just possibly, he would be crippled by guilt, ashamed at where the brutality of the time had pushed him and nervously awaiting the final judgement.

I found Frying Pan in the old people's day centre on the palm-lined Avenida de Palmeras. The busty, middle-aged matron, in her blue cardigan, was more than happy to see me. Before introducing us, she made it quite clear which side of the historical divide she sat on. 'This man was one of the ones who killed for cash,' she whispered, surveying a large, open room with tables full of white-haired, fragile bingo players. 'They are all right-wingers in here. There are a lot of bastards loose.'

The matron told me that Frying Pan had got into a bit of trouble recently when another old-age pensioner had thrown his past in his face, spitting at him: 'You should have joined the Civil Guard, given as how you enjoyed pulling the trigger so much.'

She dived in amongst the bingo tables to get Frying Pan. The man who stood up, however, did not fit my image of a bloodthirsty assassin.

Frying Pan was an eighty-six-year-old peasant on his last legs. He hobbled over on two crutches, a bulky, white plastic shopping bag tied to his belt, bouncing awkwardly against his side. The shopping bag held his anorak. Any drama that the meeting might have had was taken away by the matron, who was bobbing around behind his back, blowing imaginary smoke from the end of two imaginary pistols.

Once he realised what was up, Frying Pan did not feel much like talking. He admitted being part of the Falange, but denied having anything to do with the killings. His uncle, he explained, had been 'a man of the right' as well as being the head of the family. 'My mother was a widow and I had four sisters to look after. I was seventeen years old and spent my time working on the fields in my uncle's *finca*. It was my uncle who put my name down for the Falange,' he said. All the killings, he said, had been carried out while he was away at the front in Robledo de Chavela. By the time he came home in 1938, he said, all that was over and done with. And, with that, he excused himself and shuffled off.

José Antonio Landera had better luck at finding killers. A tall, gentle, quietly spoken thirty-one-year-old, José Antonio comes from Fabero, one of the mining *pueblos* of northern León. Fabero lies in El Bierzo, where the plain of Old Castile comes to an abrupt end as it hits the Montes de León and the mountains and steep valleys of the Cordillera Cantábrica. The mountain chain's most spectacular peaks, the Picos de Europa, rear up nearby, ending up just short of the luxuriously green coast of Asturias. The people of El Bierzo are rugged hill-folk or miners, more like their neighbours across the mountains in Asturias and Galicia than their fellow Castilians of the plains.

We met on a humid summer's day in the Atlantic port city of Gijón, where José Antonio was stationed as a member of the Civil Guard. Just as Emilio Silva had done a few miles away in Priaranza, José Antonio had managed to find and dig up a relative assassinated by the Falange. The victim was his great-uncle *Periquete*, a left-wing miners' leader from Fabero for whom José Antonio had developed an almost filial devotion. Despite resistance from his family, who feared local reactions, and pressure from local right-wing mayors and the families of two local doctors – both prominent Falangists who had a hand in the killing – he has pieced together his great-uncle's last week of life.

When José Antonio started his inquiries, two of the killers were still alive. He rang one of them at the old people's home, run by nuns, where he was living. The man, Arturo Sésamo, known as Arturón or 'Big Arthur', was almost deaf but said José Antonio could come round. Impressed by José Antonio's Civil Guard card, and unaware that he was *Periquete*'s great-nephew, he told the story in great detail. He even explained how the great-uncle had, at first, survived being shot. He had eventually been beaten to death by the gang of killers after he disturbed their lunch by sitting up and insulting them when he was meant to be dead.

Eventually, José Antonio could take no more. So he got up and left. 'It was too much for me. I had been thinking about his death for a long time. It was something I felt about strongly,' the gentle policeman, a man too young to remember Franco, explained.

Arturón's reaction was to shout after him, in a hopeful tone of voice: 'So, are they reforming the Falange, then. Are we going to kill some *rojos*?' Three days later, when José Antonio rang back, the nuns told him that Arturón, who was in his nineties, had died of a heart attack

Arturón showed little sign of remorse. Amongst the band of people who have, in the past few years, started the work of finding and digging up the victims of the Falangist *paseos*, stories abound – many undoubtedly apocryphal – of other old Falangists with blood on their hands who are still proud of their work. In Valladolid, there is a retired butcher who reputedly killed people with a *descabello*, the dagger used to finish off fighting bulls who take too long to die in the bull-ring. In a village near Miranda del Ebro there is said to be an old man who used to tie his victims to the front of a car and parade them around town. He still, apparently, claims that he did his country a service by shooting so many *rojos*.

The killers, then, are still out there. They are in their late eighties and nineties now, old men with blood on their hands – but whose time is past. Not one has ever been tried for murdering a *rojo*. The same cannot be said of those on the left who also butchered civilians.

It is true that the far left has latched onto the Civil War, the Republic and the cause of what has become known as the 'recovery of historical memory'. A movement that grew spontaneously has split in two. Spain's communists have taken control of part of it. Keen young radicals will now march with an anti-globalisation banner in one hand and a purple, red and yellow Republican flag in the other. But many, like Emilio Silva and José Antonio Landera, simply see it as an opportunity to right the wrongs suffered by the families of the victims. It is, above all, a chance to put the record straight. They tried, at least initially, to avoid party politics and were annoyed when left-wing parties got involved. Revenge is not in their vocabulary. The justice they seek is historical. There has, therefore, been no pressure to bring the old mass murderers to trial, or, so far, to expose them to public reprobation. That would be pushing the non-aggression pact on which Spain's modern democracy is founded too far. What they demand is the truth, and the right to bury the dead with decency – two rights that were accorded to the victims of the winning side long ago.

Nearly seven decades after the beginning of the war, the truth they seek has only just begun to emerge. Historians are investigating, old people are talking, local groups are taking the matter into their own hands and, with mechanical diggers and shovels, digging up the past. Spain will probably not be fully ready to confront its most bloody episode, however, until all those involved are dead.

Even then Spaniards will be left arguing about what that war brought them. For if the war itself was twentieth-century Spain's most important event, General Francisco Franco, *el Generalísimo*, was its key figure. If Spaniards had tried to keep the memory of the Civil War at bay what, I wondered, had they done with the man who ruled their lives for almost four decades afterwards. The place to find that out, I decided, was in a valley in the countryside outside Madrid – the Valley of the Fallen.

2

Looking for the Generalísimo

The *Valle de los Caídos* is a delightful, shallow dip in the folds of the Sierra de Guadarrama. Overlooked by dramatic outcrops of bare granite, it is populated mainly by pines but punctuated by a scattering of oak, ilex and poplar. Driving up the valley road on a wet, windy November afternoon, I was struck by how peaceful this most controversial of places really was. Dog roses and wild thyme lined the road. Signs warned me to drive slowly and be careful not to run over the wild boar, squirrels or other wildlife that inhabit this oasis of protected parkland. The greedy, growing octopus that is greater Madrid felt far away, though its tentacles of housing and office blocks stretch ever closer.

Juanjo, my barber, used to come here for picnics when he was a boy, back in the 1960s and 1970s. His family would look for wild mushrooms under the fallen pine needles. 'It is a beautiful spot,' he explained. 'Even if you don't like what it stands for.' And therein lies a problem. For Juanjo was one of the few people I had heard speak well of the Valley of the Fallen. Few of my Madrid friends had ever been here, to one of the most bucolic, verdant spots within striking distance of a city that spends half the year marooned in the middle of a burnt, parched flatland. On later visits I occasionally invited someone to accompany me. '*¡Ni muerto!*' – 'Not even when I am dead' – was a typical, and unconsciously ironic, reply. Not even offering to pay the entrance fee charged by Patrimonio Nacional, the state body that owns this and a dozen parks, palaces and monasteries around the country, would persuade them to go.

The reason for this lies at the end of the five-kilometre road that swings up the valley, through the well-tended pines and across a pair of elegant, stone bridges. For here stands the largest, and most recent, piece of fascist religious monumental architecture to have been erected in western Europe. A huge, blue-grey granite cross soars 150 metres into the sky. The base is planted in the Risco de la Nava, an already imposing outcrop of lichen-clad, brownish rocks, dotted with spindly, buckled-over, wind-tortured trees. Down below, a series of vast, austere, arched galleries have been built against the rock. They overlook a wide, Spartan, featureless esplanade. Between the galleries sit two, relatively small, bronze doors.

Stepping through the doors was an Alice in Wonderland experience. An entirely different world lay on the other side. I had swapped the rugged, natural beauty of the sierra for the damp, echoing chamber of what must be the world's biggest underground Christian basilica. It tunnels its way through the rock for 260 cold, still metres. An interior dome, lined in gold mosaic, has been hollowed out to a height of twenty-two metres above the granite and black marble floor. The troglodyte basilica – granted the latter status by Pope John XXIII in 1960, the year after the nineteen-year project was finished – is built to the dimensions of the ego of its creator, General Franco. It is, its admirers point out, longer than St Peter's in the Vatican, and almost as high. Nominally, and according to the literature published by Patrimonio Nacional, it is a monument to all the dead of the Civil War. Damiana González, mayoress of Poyales del Hoyo, had insisted to me that it remained exactly that – a symbol of forgiveness and peace between the two, bitterly opposed, Spains of yesteryear. The bodies of some 40,000 dead were brought here. I could, however, find only two names on the tombstones inside. One was that of the Falange founder José Antonio Primo de Rivera, taken from his Alicante prison cell and shot by the Republicans during the war. The owner of the other one, General Franco, reserved his spot well before his death. 'When my turn comes, put me here,' he told the architect, pointing to the floor behind the altar.

I had come here to witness one of the most remarkable ceremonies to be regularly held in a Christian place of worship. Here, on the closest Saturday to after the 20 November anniversary of

Franco's death, the so-called *nostálgicos* – the few who still feel nostalgia for the Caudillo – gather to pay him homage. I had decided to look for what remained of the most important man in twentieth-century Spain. I should, I had decided, start here. Friends found my interest distasteful, even morbid. Why would I want to go? It would be full of *fachas*, as they call their home-grown brand of ultra-rightists and fascists, or *casposos*, literally the dandruff-ridden, they said. I might as well have been consorting with the living dead. But I wanted to see this unique conjunction of Roman Catholic and fascist ceremonial for myself.

The first surprise was that, on this day, the state waives the fee it normally charges drivers at the entrance gate. Authorities justified this because a religious service was being held. The car park was full to overflowing, even on a rain-drenched, stormy day. 'Silence in this sacred place,' ordered a sign at the basilica entrance. But this was a day of exceptions. Nobody was going to enforce the rule. The basilica was awash with the banners and flags of the Falange and other historic, far-right organisations. Young boys dressed in white cassocks sat primly in the choir stalls. Benedictine monks, also dressed in white, were led by the Abbot in his dazzling mitre.

When I arrived, holy communion was already being offered to, and received by, many of the 1,000-plus people who had come here to pay tribute to the Caudillo. Some were blue-shirted Falangists or young skinheads, but most were not. Place them anywhere else, indeed, and it would have been almost impossible to tell them apart from any other group of Spaniards. There was, perhaps, a higher than usual density of hair oil and Barbour-style jackets – trademarks of the conservative upper-class Spanish youth, the *pijo* – on display amongst the younger men. And there were more pastel-coloured lambswool jumpers and Hermes or Burberry scarves, trademarks of his partner, the *pija*, than the average group of Spaniards might display. But there were also the full range of classes and ages. Small children ran around excitedly, wearing Franco-era Spanish flags decorated with sinister black eagles as if they were Batman capes.

The star of the show, however, was Franco's daughter Carmen, the Duquesa de Franco – a woman once discovered, several years after her father's death, trying to take gold coins out of the country. When the religious service ended, half of the congregation headed for the hole in the rock that would let them out onto the vast, windswept esplanade. The other half, however, crowded forward to where the Duquesa could be found. Banners were held aloft, some adorned with the Cross of St James, known as '*Matamoros*', the 'Moorslayer'. Others carried the Falange's yoke and arrows. Those on the fringes of the crowd clambered up the steps of the choir stalls, craning necks to get a view of the lump of granite in the floor behind the altar that is Franco's tomb. In a question of minutes, the transformation of this Christian temple from place of worship to political parade ground was absolute. Arms were thrown out and held stiffly in place. '*¡Viva Franco!*' came the shouts, followed by '*¡España una, grande y libre!*' ('Spain, one, great and free'). The crowd continued on through the panoply of old Francoist chants. There was a bellowed rendition of the Falange's 'Cara al Sol' anthem, promising that death for the cause will be rewarded by the return of *banderas victoriosas*, the flags of victory.

After a few minutes of this, the Duquesa moved slowly along the tunnel followed by a small court of elderly, diminutive men. Anxious to see her close up, I found myself swept along just a pace behind her. 'Franco! Franco! Franco!' the clutch of excited, red-faced men beside her shouted, their arms raised. Suddenly, as we neared the exit, I found myself accompanying her through a tunnel of raised arms and shouting, chanting voices. The echoes rolled back off the underground walls, multiplying the voices. For a moment, the awe and exhilaration of fascist ceremonialism ran through me. Franco's Spanish brand of fascism differed from those espoused by Hitler or Mussolini and had plenty of time to evolve into something else. His, and the Falange's, sense of ceremony was relatively limited but it came directly from the same school. I felt as though I had time-warped my way back into a black-and-white newsreel to the era of the goose-step, the mass rally and the cult of personality.

I slipped sideways through the raised arms and was just as quickly returned to reality. In fact, there were only a couple of hundred people chanting here. The Duquesa and her little party walked out onto the vast, dark esplanade – distant lightning flashes adding suitable drama to the scenario. They diminished so quickly in size that, within a minute, they looked like a small clutch of elderly pensioners lost in a storm. I wanted to rush over and offer an umbrella, or an arm to hold, in case they slipped on the sheets of water racing across the flagstones or were blown off their feet by the gale. But two minders with Francoist armbands were in attendance. A chauffeur-driven, plum-coloured Rolls-Royce, I was told, waited for them somewhere in the driving rain. The *nostálgicos*, meanwhile, gathered for a bit more singing under the arches outside the basilica. A handful of German skinheads looked on. Then the *nostálgicos* headed for the car park, drove down the road and disappeared out of sight for another year.

That, bar a few small demonstrations and even smaller political meetings, is all that Francisco Franco, *Caudillo de Dios y de la Patria*, gets thirty years after his peaceful, natural death.

The contrast between the Franco regime's view of its own historical import and the way it is treated today could not be greater. The Valley, after all, is an imposing, arrogant reminder of victory, of the Caudillo's visceral sense of the right of conquest. Grey, grim and intimidating, it is designed to inspire awe, respect and obedience. And that – or at least the first part of it – it still achieves. On those crystal-clear days that the thin air of Madrid, Europe's highest major capital, is famous for producing, it can be seen, thirty miles away (fifty kilometres), from the city itself. It is an uncomfortable, and largely unwanted, reminder that Franco may be dead, but his spirit is still out there somewhere.

Just a few miles along the Sierra de Guadarrama, at El Escorial, lies another cold, vast and imposing construction. The royal monastery of El Escorial was built in the sixteenth century by Philip II. V. S. Pritchett called Philip's favourite building 'the oppressive monument of the first totalitarian state in Europe' and the 'mausoleum of Spanish power'. From here the austere and suspicious monarch tried to administer the myriad lands received from his father, the Emperor Charles V. These, with the addition of his own aquisitions, stretched from Holland and southern Italy to North Africa, Latin America and the Philippines. His was the original empire on which the sun never set. That empire, however, did not last. Its gradual decline from the end of the sixteenth century would continue until the days of Franco's own childhood with the disastrous loss, in 1898, of Cuba and the Philippines. To Franco, however, its prison-like walls and monolithic, dull exterior must have seemed the very expression of Castilian military virility and religious might. His own crusade would, he thought, re-establish some of that glorious past. The Valley, too, he decreed, must have 'the grandeur of the monuments of old, which defy time and forgetfulness'.

Franco's court of adulators sometimes compared him to Philip, the counter-reformation zealot and man who sent the Spanish Armada to its stormy, watery grave in the Atlantic. Philip was not his only company. El Cid, Charlemagne, Napoleon, Alexander the Great and the Archangel Gabriel – to mention a few – were all named as the Caudillo's historic equals. Visitors looking for a simplistic psychological explanation for the Valley may be tempted to speculate about small men and large objects. But Franco knew that the bigger and more impressive the monument, the longer his name would last. The Valley was his great passion. It was the not-so-secret other love of a man said to have observed, otherwise, rigorous sexual fidelity. Everything here is built to impress. From the cross and the basilica to the bleak esplanade and a similarly regimented square behind the Risco – home to a Benedectine monastery, a choir school and a large guest house – all here is large and imposing. The scale and drama of the Valley of the Fallen guarantee the name of Francisco Franco will survive for centuries. It was, from the Caudillo's point of view, a good decision. For Spaniards have, otherwise, done all they can to wipe out his imprint.

In physical terms, the Valley of the Fallen is virtually all that remains of Franco. It is an amazing disappearing act, further evidence of the power of forgetting in Spain. For Franco, or, more precisely, Francoism, has been condemned to the ignominy of silent disdain. 'By tacit national consent, the regime was relegated to oblivion,' says Franco's best-known biographer, Paul Preston.

Historians cannot be blamed for this. Dozens of biographies and memoirs of those who knew him have been written. Ever since his death, however, the Franco name has become, in the English sense, an F-word. To be called a Francoist or a *facha* is, almost without exception, an insult. To admit in public to the slightest grain of respect or admiration for Franco is to be a political outcast. This is despite, or perhaps because of, the attempts of a handful of Franco diehards who still see him in terms of the hagiography of his own times. One Benedictine, while I was writing this book, even suggested he should be a candidate for beatification. There can be no real debate about Franco in Spain. He is either black or white, bad or good. There is no grey area in between.

Nowhere is the silence more eloquent than in the state-owned gift shop at the Valley of the Fallen. There are only two guidebooks on sale here. One is a cheap picture book. The other is written by the state body that owns it, Patrimonio Nacional. One does not even mention the fact that Republican prisoners-of-war were used to build the Valley. The other observes, briefly, that prisoners-of-war could redeem part of their sentence by working here. Neither mentions that more than a dozen labourers died here. They also, however, keep mentions of Franco himself to a bare minimum.

The handful of references to him talk, coyly, of 'the former head of state'. Photographs of the tombs of Franco and Primo de Rivera are curiously absent. The books provide, instead, illustrations of the bulgingly muscular set of sculptures known as the Allegory to the Armed Forces or the religious tapestries hanging on the wall. Patrimonio Nacional, explaining its own existence, says it looks after 'palaces, monasteries and convents founded by Spanish monarchs'. It is difficult to see how this place, founded by a dictator, fits.

The gift shop sells Valley key rings, pens, T-shirts, coasters and thimbles. But it does not have any of the books written by, or about, the prisoners who worked and, in some cases, died building the place. Nor is there a single book on Franco or Primo de Rivera.

Unsure what to do with it, successive governments have tried to take the meaning out of the Valley of the Fallen. It is as if the monument had appeared here innocently, and neutrally, out of the blue. There is, their silence suggests, nothing shocking, awesome or even significant about it.

Thirty years after the Caudillo's death, a new Socialist government has finally suuggested it would like to tell the full story of the Valley of the Fallen. It may build a visitors' centre here, devoted to the Civil War. There is no sign, yet, however, of any real change.

I set out to find people who had helped build the Valley. I found two of them. Both, for very different reasons, were sure that it oozed with meaning: malicious for one, glorious for the other.

Diego Márquez Horrillo was a genuine volunteer, a convinced Falangist who would come here during the summer vacations from his university law degree. To him it is, principally, the resting place of José Antonio Primo de Rivera – a man he still reveres as father, in the 1930s, of 'the most modern of all political ideas'. He enjoyed those summers in the hills, where he would marvel at the ingenuity of it all. 'It was an extraordinary project,' he told me in the small Madrid office which is half his law practice and half headquarters of one tiny fragment of what little remains of the Falange. 'I was excited to be involved.'

Nicolás Sánchez-Albornoz was another sort of 'volunteer'. He was one of the political prisoners sent here with the promise of a meagre one peseta a day in a savings account, and the chance of reducing his sentence. He is now an emeritus professor at New York University. I found him at a conference in Barcelona where, for almost the first time since Franco's death, academics were discussing the full extent of a vast prison system though which some 200,000 people – 2 per cent of the male population – passed. Sánchez-Albornoz was sent here in 1948 after being arrested as a student agitator. The cheap labour he and tens of thousands of prison workers around Spain provided would help found the fortunes of several major construction companies. Mussolini's foreign minister, Count Galeazzo Ciano, already shocked by the vast numbers being executed in 1939, found the concentration camps full 'not of prisoners of war, but slaves of war'.

Sánchez-Albornoz saw how food destined for the prisoners never made it beyond the camp gates. The director, like many officials during the first decade of Franco's rule, was getting rich off black-market trading. The state, meanwhile, paid itself for the prisoners' upkeep by taking 80 per cent of an already miserable wage. There were no prison fences here, as there was nowhere to go. Sánchez-Albornoz was one of the few prisoners who dared escape. More than fifty years later, he refuses to go back to Cuelgamuros, the *finca* where the basilica was built. 'I loathe Cuelgamuros. I refuse to put my feet on what, before it was profaned, was a beautiful piece of land . . . unless the crypt is given a different use and now, given my age, that there is also a urinal on Franco's grave so that I can relieve my prostate,' he says. 'With a little more money, and he had plenty of that, he might have hired free workers and avoided the imprint of revenge . . . His remains are buried in a monument to cruelty and corruption.'

The Valley of the Fallen may have survived, but most other physical proof of Franco's, and Francoism's, existence has been wiped from the face of Spain. Major cities like Madrid or Barcelona returned their Avenidas del Generalísimo, their Plazas del Caudillo or their Plazas Francisco Franco to their original names in the 1970s. A single remaining public statue of Franco in Madrid was removed, under cover of darkness, shortly before this book was published. A few months earlier I had gone to look at it. Franco sat astride his horse, but those who did not know who he was could not have guessed. It was a statue without a plaque. I bumped into a Spanish history graduate beside it and asked her whether she thought it should still be here. 'I don't like Franco,' she replied. 'But I think we should remember he existed, just so we do not make the same mistake again.' The Socialist government that ordered its removal obviously disagreed. A triumphal arch and couple of streets named after lesser Francoist generals are now all that remain in Madrid to commemorate that period of history.

When the author and journalist Arcadi Espada went looking for the public remnants of Franco several years ago he found that, with a few exceptions, they had disappeared. Of Spain's provincial capitals only Santander was still festooned with Franco memorabilia, despite pressure from historians for it to be removed. 'Even the whores and beggars are rightists in Santander,' explained the writer Jesús Pardo.

Franco's birthplace of Ferrol, a navy port in Galicia that became known as El Ferrol del Caudillo, waited almost thirty years but eventually also removed its equestrian statue from the central Plaza de España. A People's Party councillor tried to save it, calling for a popular referendum, but had her wrists slapped by party bosses. Not even the party that wins the votes of the old *franquistas* dares show active support for him, or his memory. By the time I visited Ferrol, the statue had gone. The statue, which was later discreetly sent to a naval museum, had been placed in a municipal store.

Espada says that sums up exactly what Spaniards have done with Franco. They have shoved him into storage. He has been placed out of sight and, largely, out of mind. 'In reality, with museums and the street out of the question, the storeroom is exactly where Spain has placed Franco. It is a jumbled, dusty, indeterminate place, somewhere without criteria. Franco showed that the best thing to do with a difficult problem was to shove it into [the back of] a drawer. That is where he is right now.'

Sometimes the solution has been more radical. On a visit to Guadalajara province, I stopped on a road near Torija at a ridge overlooking the plain where the River Henares flows. Here, on the roadside, I discovered a pile of broken, honey-coloured stone, looking like the rubble from some ancient building site. Turning the stones over, however, I found the smashed fragments of a huge, carved Francoist shield. These must have been torn off a local town hall after Franco's death. They had been dumped at the roadside – another anonymous, indeterminate place for the remains of Francoism.

The business of wiping out Franco's physical imprint has been long and slow. There are still a dozen villages, mainly founded during his life near dams or other public works, which will for ever be Franco's. Alberche del Caudillo and Llanos del Caudillo are just two of them – though others, like Barbate and Ferrol, have returned to their original names.

Not everyone, however, embraced the first wave of name-changes and statue removals. A young politician called José María Aznar complained in the *La Nueva Rioja* newspaper in 1979 that town councils were removing the honours and street names of 'the former Head of State who, although it obviously bothers some people, governed for forty years and was called Francisco Franco'.

'Instead of devoting themselves to improving their municipalities, they spend their time rubbing away history,' wrote Aznar. Seventeen years later, as Spanish prime minister, he would avoid, as far as possible, even mentioning Franco's name.

Some right-wing mayors agreed with Aznar and refused point blank to rename their squares and avenues. They can still be found, normally in small towns and villages of what was once '*zona nacional*' – the western half of Spain that fell almost immediately to the right's rebellion.

I only had to travel a few miles south from the mass grave near Poyales del Hoyo to find an example. In the small town of Navalcán, as in many *pueblos*, the contrast between old and new was immediate. Here old women dressed in black still sat out in small groups on the pavements on low, wood and wicker chairs. Broad straw hats kept the sun off them as they sewed or embroidered. The Socialist mayor of this town of 2,300 people was just twenty-five years old. He was not just the youngest mayor in living history, he was also the first left-wing mayor since before 1936. This was a child of Spain's democratic transition. He had no memory or first-hand knowledge of Franco or Francoism.

During the Franco years Navalcán had been governed by a

series of mayors who were the natural heirs of the old *caciques*, the local political strongmen who had traditionally controlled the Spanish countryside. It remained right-wing after his death.

The arrival of a Socialist mayor had been a major event. It was also an eye-opener for the young mayor. 'Some elderly people insisted on congratulating me in private. They did not want others to see them doing it. They still thought there might be something to be afraid of,' he said.

An elderly man with a Valencian accent came and sat with us. He was the town's former bank manager, a former clerk to the local priest and self-appointed local historian. He pointed to a white-painted three-storey building on the far side of the square. 'That is where one of the mayors would rape the girls,' he whispered. 'His illegitimate children are still here. In this town, all we have to do is look into people's faces to know where they come from.' His story may well have been a local myth. It summed up, however, the combined feelings of fear and acquiescence in places where Francoism conferred extraordinary power on its local representatives.

In Navalcán it was still possible, stepping out of the town hall, to go for a circular walk without leaving for more than a few moments the streets with Francoist names. The walk took you through the Plaza General Franco and streets dedicated to General Yagüe, the Defenders of the Álcázar (a fortress in nearby Toledo) and General Queipo de Llano.

Born after Franco died, the young mayor's generation had learnt the basic facts of his life and times at school, but little more. Now, however, he was being forced to catch up on some local history. Several graves of those shot by *Quinientos Uno* had been located nearby and there was talk of digging them up. There were also proposals for changing some, or all, of the streets back to the original names they had borne for centuries. Those proposals had, in turn, caused a stink in the town. It was unclear what would happen. But there was no doubt that, here at least, Franco's ghost was still about.

Santos Juliá, a prominent historian, sums up Spain's attitude to its former dictator like this: 'Spaniards have an ambiguous valuation of

LIBRARY. UNIVERSITY OF CHESTER

Franco. They do not *satanizan*, (literally diabolicalise), him like the Germans do with Hitler. Perhaps that is due to the fact that most living adults do not remember the worst years of the thirties and forties, rather they remember the fifties, sixties and seventies ... And they recall that in the second half of Francoism there was a lack of freedom but also an improvement in the material quality of life.'

When he first attained power Franco embarked on a disastrous drive for autarky, of proud national self-reliance. He blamed the failure of that not on rampant corruption and his own regime but on an international plot of freemasons, communists and so-called false democracies – meaning Britain, France and the US. Eventually, he handed the economy over to technocrats, many of them from the austere Opus Dei Catholic movement. The result was an opening up to the world and a chance to start playing catch-up with the rest of Europe. The economy eventually boomed, giving rise to what became known as the '*años de desarrollo*', 'years of development'. From 1961 to 1973 Spain's economy grew by 7 per cent a year. In the developed world, only Japan was growing quicker. Incomes quadrupled. This, in turn, helped produce what came to be referred to as '*franquismo sociológico*'. In other words, Franco became – admittedly to a degree that was never formally measured – popular in some parts of Spanish society. This was because, in a country which had suffered from famine, hunger, war and need for the best part of two decades, life suddenly, and rapidly, got better. 'After all, Franco did not rule by repression alone: he enjoyed a considerable popular support,' comments Preston. This, he adds, was largely due to 'the passive support of those who had been conditioned into political apathy by political repression, the controlled media and an appallingly inadequate state education system'.

Just how popular Franco was, is, of course, impossible to say. Manuel Jiménez de Parga, head of the country's Constitutional Court, caused a stink by claiming the 'immense majority' of Spaniards were *franquistas*. It was one of the least politically correct – and most debatable – commentaries on the twenty-fifth anniversary of the constitution in 2003. True or not, most Spaniards do not want to believe that about themselves, or about their parents and grandparents. It would imply that, somehow, they had supported or collaborated with the dictator. Judge Jiménez de Parga's view, however exaggerated, would certainly explain why up to half a million Spaniards queued up to pay their last respects to him as his coffin lay in state in 1975.

It also, however, raised a difficult question. If the country's senior judge was right, or even partially so, where were all those *franquistas* now?

If finding physical proof of Franco's existence proved nearly impossible, finding those willing to defend his name – or admit that they themselves had supported him – proved even harder. I had gone to Márquez Horrillo because I thought his branch of the Falange, the long-winded Falange Española de las JONS, might provide some examples. But it turned out that not only did Márquez barely have any support, he did not really consider himself a Francoist either.

In private, Márquez Horrillo turned out to be a lonely, gentle, polite old man still suffering after the recent death of his wife. I was the first foreign journalist to interview him, the 'national leader'and direct heir to José Antonio Primo de Rivera, in over twenty years. That alone was proof of how marginal the once powerful Falange had become. Franco, he said, had betrayed the Falange, using it as an instrument for keeping power and debasing its principles. Primo de Rivera, he insisted, had been a visionary and a revolutionary.

At a campaign meeting for his party at Madrid local elections only one hundred people turned up. A similar number of police stood guard outside the school where the meeting was held. We watched a film of Primo de Rivera giving the 1933 speech, at Madrid's Teatro de la Comedia, when he founded the Falange and warned that it would use 'knuckles and pistols'. The occasion ended, once more, with stiff arms and a rendition of the 'Cara al Sol'. It was distinctly uncomfortable to be the only person in the audience not standing and singing.

Real Falangism, with its talk of nationalising banks and empowering workers, had gone to the grave with Primo de Rivera in 1936, just three years after he thought it up. Falangism, with its ideas of an 'organic democracy' representing families, trades and professsions, villages and towns, had been the last great political theory of the twentieth century, Horrillo said. It is one which, curiously, inspired a political movement in the Lebanon which would also be known as Falangism. Talk of knuckles and pistols, Horrillo claimed, was simply standard for the time and place. It was not relevant to today.

Other Falangist groups I tracked down proved more adoring of Franco, though hardly more popular. Some were barely concealed fronts for right-wing thuggery. These recruited amongst the skinheads of Real Madrid's violent, racist Ultra Sur supporters and other gangs of football hooligans. Others were serious-minded radicals. I went to see a small, rag-tag crowd of them gather on a chilly street corner outside the National Court in the Calle Genóva on 19 November. Here they listened to José Cantalapiedra, a young Falangist leader with a black leather jacket and film-star looks. Cantalapiedra delivered a speech through a crackling microphone. He denounced Spain's democratic governments, Basque and Catalan separatism, immigration, abortion, globalisation, banks and liberal capitalism. When he had finished, the crowd of a few hundred set off on an all-night walk to the Valley of the Fallen, carefully marshalled by several vanloads of police. It was one of the biggest dates in the Falange calendar. Yet, in a city whose streets are daily blocked by marchers of one kind or another, they occupied just a hundred metres of bus lane.

Francoism, as a political concept, is long dead. Some argue that it never really existed as a properly defined ideology. Franco simply amalgamated all the right-wing and conservative elements of Spanish society – be they the army, the Church, the monarchists, Carlists, the landowners or the Falange – and did his best to stop them squabbling amongst themselves. Historians have pointed out that the cause of Francoism is best described 'in negatives – what they were against'. Marxists, freemasons, free-thinkers and separatists formed an eclectic group of enemies. Franco's early admiration for totalitarianism gave way, with the opposition either wiped out or left too cowed to act, to a form of authoritarian pragmatism. The brutal early repression has been described as 'a kind of political investment, a bankable terror, which accelerated the process of Spain's depoliticisation'.

Franco's main achievement was to stay in power, something he managed by force and instinct. His political philosophy, 'National Catholicism', was, as the name implies, mainly about patriotism and God. His main rule was that of obedience, to Church and State. It was hardly a recipe for major change in Spain. Along the way, however, the Generalísimo inoculated several generations of Spaniards against the extreme right. Their parties have never gained more than 2 per cent of the vote in the three decades since his death.

There seemed to be something deeply ironic about the silence into which Francoism had been buried. For the Caudillo was, himself, an expert at silence. 'One is the master of what one does not say, and the slave of what one does,' he once warned his self-designated successor-to-be, the then prince Juan Carlos. This was the opposite of another, much older, Spanish theory on silence. Alonso de Ercilla, in a heroic sixteenth-century depiction of the Chilean natives' resistance to the Spanish conquistadores, La Araucana, noted the tactical usefulness of silence but added: 'There is nothing more difficult, if you look closely, than discovering a *necio*, a fool, if he keeps his quiet.'

This particular facet of the Caudillo's character is attributed to his origins in the wet, green, north-western Atlantic province of Galicia. Gallegos are meant to be famous for something called *retranca*, a sort of deliberate ambivalence or avoidance of committing themselves. Franco was *retranca* personified. He rarely let on what he was thinking, even to his ministers. His mysteriousness kept those around him on their toes. It allowed his propagandists to construct a mythical persona of wisdom, bravery, self-sacrifice and godliness. It also allowed Franco to reinvent himself continually, from Hitler ally to cunning evader of the Second World War or from Crusader to benign and loving patriarch. It also allowed his followers to blame the regime's failings on those around him. Ultimately, critics claim, it allowed him to hide his own mediocrity. He was, one of his former ministers admitted, 'a sphinx without a secret'.

His regime was also a great enforcer of silence. To the silence forced on the *vencidos*, the defeated, was added the silence enforced by the censors, both political and religious. One of the first to fall victim was the seventy-two-year-old philosopher Miguel de Unamuno. He, at the height of the Civil War, told an audience of senior Francoists that 'You will win but you will not convince.' The retort from General José Millán Astray, founder of the Spanish Legion in which Franco had won his military honours as a fearless and ruthless young officer, was '*¡Abajo la inteligencia!*' ('Down with intellectuals!' or 'Down with intelligence!'). Unamuno, one of the few great minds left in Nationalist Spain, was removed from his position as Rector of Salamanca university and died soon afterwards. The British writer Gerald Brenan, travelling in 1949, found much of the country suffering famine, while the regime's apparatchiks got rich off the black market. The press, meanwhile, carried virtually no news about Spain. A newspaper reader 'might well suppose that nothing happens in the Peninsula except football matches, religious ceremonies and bullfights'. Censorship would slacken over the years, but it remained in place – in one form or another – until Franco's death.

The one-sided view of a regime which ruled by right of conquest was reflected, most of all, in schools. Spaniards have recently found a rich, deep vein of humour in the absurd things taught to them by the Franco regime.

In Otones, a small farming village on the parched plain outside Segovia, locals have turned the former schoolhouse into a tiny museum to the education they received under *el Caudillo*. Alicia, a friend from the village, showed me around after one of those traditional Sunday feasts beloved of Madrileños of roast kid and local wine – pointing out the antiquated text books and the propaganda on the wall. The museum is there to laugh at. So, too, are the recently reprinted Francoist school textbooks (which have provided a small publishing boom and spawned films, like *El Florido Pensil*, based on them). These remind Spaniards of how they once learned that Franco was 'a new El Cid, the saviour of Spain'. They contain such edifying teachings as: 'Stimulants like coffee, tobacco, alcohol, newspapers, politics, cinema and luxury undermine us and waste our bodies away'; or 'women have never discovered anything. They lack the creative talent, which God has reserved for men'; and 'a wife has no rights over her own body. On marriage she gives up those rights to her husband. He is the only one who can use those rights and only for reproduction.'

When General Franco died in 1975 the half a million people who queued up to pay their respects were not there, as the joke went, to check that he really was dead. Nor was it simply one of those occasions when Spaniards, often obstinate individualists when faced with authority, indulged their passion for doing things en masse. Bottles of cava, Spanish sparkling wine, were broken open in some homes where the dictator's death seemed long overdue. 'Above the skyline of the Collserola mountains, champagne corks soared into the Autumn twilight. But nobody heard a sound,' writer Manuel Vázquez Montalbán said of his home city, Barcelona. There was also a genuine outpouring of grief. Most of those who mourned, however, reneged on the Generalísimo long ago. The rest have, quite simply, sunk into silence.

I found a few clues as to where they were, however, in my own Madrid neighbourhood. The most startling example came when I was shown an apartment in a street not far from the Retiro park by a smart Argentine woman who said she 'liked to help friends sell their houses'.

'You might not like the decoration,' she warned. 'These are elderly people with elderly peoples' tastes.'

At first sight there was nothing special about the décor, which showed the same taste for heavy wooden furniture, old leather, wooden crosses and fake papyrus lamp shades I had encountered in many other homes. Walking into the sitting room, however, I found myself gasping, involuntarily, with shock. The room was dominated by a life-size oil portrait of a man in a Second World War German military uniform. Adolf Hitler stared out at me, a slight smile under his trademark moustache, wearing a field greatcoat and with something like a map case clutched in his hands.

The effect, for this *anglosajón*, was like being punched on the nose. One of the greatest practitioners of genocide of the past century was a daily companion for the owners of this house. Even more bizarrely, however, the woman showing us around simply considered this a case of 'old-fashioned' décor.

Unable to speak, I looked around me, taking in a glass cabinet containing an Iron Cross and a red (Falange or Carlist) beret and, to confuse me further, a photograph of the current king, Juan Carlos. My journalistic instinct should have led to a thorough quizzing of the 'estate agent' about who her friends were. Instead, I pushed my two small children out of the door and fled onto the street without even bothering to check the names on the mail-boxes in the reception hall downstairs. I was perplexed. It was not just the presence of a symbol which would turn the owner of any house in London, Paris or Berlin into a social pariah, but also the strange mixture of symbols. It was also the casual acceptance that this was just 'old-fashioned décor'. Hitler, Juan Carlos, Iron Crosses and red berets just did not seem to make sense to me. It would take me a while to work out how they might fit together.

A few months later I went to the Gran Peña club on Madrid's Gran Vía, the city's answer to Oxford Street or Shaftesbury Avenue. Roughly equivalent to a traditional London club, its members, many of them former military officers, had erected a bust of Franco in 1992. That was seventeen years after his death and the same year that 'modern' Spain was busy promoting itself at an Expo fair in Seville, at the Barcelona Olympic Games and during Madrid's turn as the European Union's 'cultural capital' for a year. The occasion was a public appearance by Blas Piñar, the virulently right-wing leader (and editor) of Fuerza Nueva, a neo-Francoist party that disbanded in 1982. The recalcitrant Blas Piñar was famous in the final days of Francoism for his denunciations of left-leaning priests. He was also one of the inspirations, if not fathers, of a gang of right-wing thugs called 'The Guerrilleros of Cristo Rey', who had attacked left-wingers in the 1970s (and 1980s). A handful of tall, shaven-headed young Germans stood respectfully in the crowded room as Blas Piñar, a gifted orator, railed against Spain's young democracy. His speech was peppered with references to the saints and quotations from the bible, a large number of which he obviously held in his head.

At the end of the talk I met General Chicharro. He was a polite, pleasant man, the archetype of what I had come to call 'a friendly fascist'. This was a nickname I applied to the impeccably-mannered, if somewhat worrying, old rightists I had started coming across in my own barrio. He was also, at the time, president of the Brotherhood of the División Azul – a division of Franco-sponsored Spanish volunteers that had donned German uniform and gone to fight for Hitler on the eastern front. After a long battle with Spain's defence ministry, the families of the Blue Division veterans were beginning to dig up the graves of their dead and bring them home. The funds given to them by the Defence ministry would become a sore point for those paying from their own pockets for mechanical diggers to find the remains left behind by Franco's death squads.

Chicharro told me about a recent visit to Russia where bottles of vodka had finally broken the ice between the Spanish Hitler veterans, the Germans they had fought alongside and their old Russian opponents. It was a pleasant tale of reconciliation between old adversaries. Before I left, however, he wanted me to know something: 'Those of us who went,' he said proudly, 'we still think exactly the same as we did back then.'

The members of the División Azul won Iron Crosses, admired Hitler and wore the red Falangist beret. Some of them must have been close to Juan Carlos while Franco oversaw his education and he dutifully fulfilled his obligations as the anointed successor-in-waiting. The king probably courted some of them during the transition to democracy – trying to ensure their loyalty to him and to the new Spanish state. They had been privileged members of Francoist society, guaranteed jobs and prestige on their return (though many never returned and some were not freed from Russian prison camps until the mid-1950s, causing Franco to pull Spain out of the first European Nations soccer cup in 1960 when drawn to meet the USSR in the quarter finals). The owner of the Hitler portrait, I suspected, had been one of them.

It turned out that General Chicharro was from my barrio. He was not the only one. Angelines, the bed-ridden old woman who lived opposite us when we moved in, had been a División Azul nurse.

This is not surprising. My building, and many of the neighbouring ones, went up in the 1940s – a period when few of those who were not Franco supporters were in a position to be buying apartments. The original owners are dying off now – Angelines was carried off in a stretcher down the communal staircase and died a few days later in hospital. In the space of just three years she has been followed by Dr Bueno and charming old Paco, who would take his dog out for a walk every night but only, as far as I could tell, to the Bar Goyesca, just a twenty-yard walk away.

The stereotypical elderly, well-off Francoist couple steps out on a winter's day with the lady immaculately coiffured and made up, wearing her fur-coat. The man, his upper lip adorned with a pencil-thin moustache, wears a bottle-green, Austrian-style, pressed wool jacket. Such types can still be found occasionally in my local newspaper shop buying *ABC* or *La Razon*, two conservative Spanish daily newspapers. I suspect some of the surviving older people in my block were, or still are, Franco supporters of some kind. At least one is said to have a Falangist flag on his desk. A Franco portrait appeared on a balcony across the road on the thirtieth anniversary of his death in 2005. The old lady who lived beneath us when we moved occasionally muttered that 'things were better under Franco'. Usually, however, these old Franquistas are silent, and thus unquantifiable. Some see no conflict between Franco and democracy, believing that one was the direct result of the other. Franco, they reason, cured the divide between the two

Spains so that, after his death, they could come together again in peace and join the club of free European nations. He was, they claim, more successful in producing a united country than that other long-lived European strongman and contemporary, Yugoslavia's Marshal Tito.

These were amongst the people who helped place Pío Moa's revisionist *The Myths of the Civil War* on the best-sellers list. 'Franco did not think he had rebelled against a democratic republic but against an extreme danger of revolution . . . Undoubtedly he was right,' Moa argues. 'His regime saved Spain from involvement in the world war, modernised society and established the conditions for a stable democracy.' Moa blames modern right-wing politicians for not defending the Generalísimo's reputation. 'The right will swallow anything, just so that it does not seem itself to be Francoist,' he observes.

Moa, the *nostálgicos* and a handful of neo-Francoists aside, one is hard put to find a Spaniard spontaneously prepared to defend Franco in public – with the eternal exception of the odd Madrid taxi driver. Mostly, they keep their appreciation of the Generalísimo to themselves and their friends. I even know one, a publishing proofreader, who refuses to vote because he dislikes Spain's new democracy, but dutifully turned up when called on to serve at a polling station at election time. Their silence, broken by a handful of mainly elderly writers and historians, is appreciated.

It has also, until recently, been matched by the silence surrounding that other uncomfortable reminder of Franco's existence, his victims – both the living and the dead. As they grow in confidence, but decline rapidly in numbers, the victims have slowly raised their heads in recent years. Their stories, deliberately forgotten and buried during the transition to democracy, are a belated reminder of how the Caudillo ensured he could die, still in power, in his bed.

Mariano called me from Candeleda. He was hugely excited. 'We are going to pay homage to a great freedom fighter, a true hero, one of the few men prepared to risk their lives to fight Franco,' he announced. The hero's name was Gerardo Donate, alias Tito, a local leader of the *maquis* guerrilla movement that, briefly and to no great effect, acted across much of Spain in the 1940s and early 1950s. Tito had led the guerrillas of the Gredos mountains and had died in a shoot-out by the River Alardos, which separates the Extremadura region from Castilla y León. His family, now living in Valencia, had only just discovered what happened to him. The family was on its way – typically, by the coachload – to pay its respects at the place where he died. This was a picturesque pool in one of the mountain streams that bring the snow-melt rushing down through a series of *gargantas* – the streams known literally as 'throats' – cut into the southern slopes of Gredos. The pool has popularly been known as '*El Charco de los Maquis*', 'The Maquis' Pool', ever since.

I was curious. Here, after all, were a group of resistance fighters who had fought a right-wing dictatorial regime run by an ally of Hitler and Mussolini. As a child in 1960s and 1970s Britain, I had grown up enthralled by tales of men and women like this. In comics, trash mags, films and cheap novels the resistance fighters of France, Italy, Yugoslavia and Greece had often been there as the key, heroic supporters to some frightfully brave, and slightly sentimental, British hero. Even today, these loyal partisans occasionally raise their heads in British novels – such as Sebastian Faulks's Charlotte Gray.

In most countries the resistance members remain national heroes. They have medals, monuments and museums. Yet, in the Spanish mind, the *maquis* have largely been forgotten. A handful of ex-fighters, local historians and people on the far left kept their memory from disappearing. They had no place, however, in the pantheon of national heroes. Not even those socialists who had worn their anti-Francoism as a badge of identity and pride in the 1960s and 1970s, and had gone on to run democratic Spain in the 1980s, had bothered with this group of ageing, defeated men and women. Ironically, some of them, exiled from Franco's Spain, could claim hero status in France, having fought with the Resistance there in the Second World War. The tanks that led the Free French into liberated Paris in 1944 bore the names of Spanish cities and *pueblos* such as Zaragoza, Guadalajara and Belchite, and were manned by Spaniards.

Although some Republican fighters had survived in small groups in the sierras as fugitives, they did not become organised until late in the Second World War. Franco's opponents became convinced that, with Hitler and Mussolini on the run, it would not be long before the Allies turned their attention to Europe's other major right-wing dictator. Organised by the Spanish Communist Party, they set up a network whose principal aim was to be in place when the British, French and Americans invaded.

But, just as Britain and the other allies had abandoned the Republic to its fate during the Civil War while Hitler and Mussolini sent troops and money to Franco, so they turned their backs on these appeals for the 'liberation' of Spain. No British heroes would be parachuted in here. The Caudillo, instead, would become an early Cold War winner, a right-wing bulwark against the Communist Warsaw Pact countries. Initially a rabid anti-American, he considered the new superpower 'childish'. But he was wily enough to seal a lifelong grip on power in 1953 by signing a deal that gave the United States air bases on Spanish soil. This, he later observed, appeared to have emptied 'Madrid bars and cabarets of whores, since they almost all marry American sergeants or GIs'.

An invasion of Spain did eventually take place. Led by many of those French resistance heroes, it was launched in the Val d'Aran, a north-facing part of the Pyrenees that is Spanish territory and which boasts its own version of the Gascon language, Aranese. The invasion's planners had hoped the sight of troops coming across the border would encourage a popular uprising. No such thing happened. The Spanish, it seems, were either more tired of war than they were of Franco or were so downtrodden after half a dozen years of vengeful rule that nobody dared lift a finger.

I met Tito's family at a restaurant near the 'Lobera' ('the wolf's lair') – a place where the wolves of Gredos had once roamed freely. They were toying with a paella, wondering why, as Valencians, they were being served up a mediocre dish of what is a speciality in their own region. They had hired a coach and set out at 6 a.m. to get here for an afternoon of ceremonies before setting off again, at nightfall, for the six-hour return trip.

'He was one of three brothers separated by the Civil War who never saw each others' faces again,' said his great nephew Enrique, a paid-up member (and local councillor back in his home town near Valencia) of Spain's communist-led United Left coalition. 'One brother fled to France and was killed there fighting for the Resistance. My grandfather, who died recently, fought for the Republic and was captured and imprisoned. Two of his uncles were Falangists, so they allowed him back to the family village. The war split the family. He had other uncles on the left.'

I had heard many stories like this, of split families with brothers and cousins pleading for the lives of their relatives on the other side to be spared when the death squads and military tribunals of one side or the other came around.

'Before he died, my grandfather said that he never regretted fighting for his ideals. His biggest regret, however, was not knowing where his younger brother, who was only nineteen when the war started, was buried,' explained Enrique, a Republican badge pinned to his chest. 'All he knew was that he had escaped from a prison work camp in Talavera de la Reina and been killed by the Guardia Civil. He did not dare ask any more than that. My father's generation was also too scared to find out, so I started looking myself,' he said. He contacted a historian who had collected the stories of this forgotten group of men and so, eventually, discovered that Tito had died near Candeleda.

Now Tito's great-nephews and great-nieces, and one nephew, were gathering to give him a proper send-off. Mariano had arranged for a local historian, a *maquis* specialist, to give them a talk in Candeleda's town hall. There was standing room only as locals joined the family. Someone placed a republican flag on the dais, thus raising loud complaints from two town councillors who claimed this was an insult to King Juan Carlos. The Spanish monarch's portrait hung on the wall immediately behind them. The historian's tale was a sorry one. The guerrilla movement in

Gredos had survived for about five years from 1942 onwards. It had killed two people in that time, including a noted Falangist in Candeleda. But it had to devote most of its energies to just keeping itself alive, kidnapping people for money and relying on those in far-flung country spots to feed it – either out of solidarity or of fear. Only a handful of people had been involved. They were finished off by a combination of treason from within their own ranks, Civil Guard infiltrators and the use of pseudo-*maquis* groups, the *contrapartidas*, set up by the police to terrorise locals and persuade them that the resistance fighters were really *bandoleros*, common bandits or outlaws.

Tito and his group had been spotted near El Raso, a small village in the mountains above Candeleda. They had hidden in a cave above a mountain pool but had been cornered by the Civil Guard. Tito and one other were killed. Three of his men were wounded, captured, cured of their wounds, tried and shot. Only one escaped.

The Charco de los Maquis, the mountain pool where Tito died, is a magical Gredos spot. The road here from Candeleda twists up-hill to El Raso, passing orchards of fig trees and, in early June, cherry trees weighed down with fat, red cherries. An unpaved track leads out towards the *garganta*. The water here is transparent. Fish dart across a mottled background of large, sunken boulders, their size magnified by the still, crystalline water. Boatmen scuttle across the surface. On both banks there are narrow stretches of green pasture and, higher up, olive groves. A blackened, scorched patch on one hill is a reminder of one of Spain's perennial dramas, the forest fire.

For the last stretch of the road to the *charco* I gave a lift to Benjamín Ruiz. A miner's son from the rebellious northern region of Asturias, he had first seen the inside of a police cell in 1934, at the age of fifteen. An Asturian miners' revolution was put down by Franco on behalf of the elected Conservative government. Some consider this to be the first skirmish of the Civil War. Benjamín would later be Tito's *enlace*, his contact for information and food, in El Raso. He was the last person outside his group to see him alive. 'None of those captured gave me away. If they had ever found out that I was the *enlace* they would have killed me,' he said. Now in his eighties, he had recently suffered a mild heart attack and had trouble walking. But his spirits were lifted by the sight of so many young people. 'Back then there were only a handful of us prepared to do anything against Franco. The young people should know that,' he said.

The valley is fairly steep here and, right above the pool, a narrow crack in the rock gives way to the cave where Tito had spent his last night. I imagined a handful of desperate men, staring at defeat and wondering whether it was better to fight and die or give up and be executed.

The great-nieces and great-nephews read poetry and threw red carnations on the water. Amongst the revolutionary icons dusted off for the occasion was Ernesto 'Che' Guevara. 'Tomorrow when I die, do not come to me to cry, nor look for me in the ground, I am the wind of freedom,' someone read. A wreath of flowers in the purple, red and yellow colours of the Republican flag was cast onto the water and left to float downstream. Curiously distant from the proceedings, however, was Tito's nephew. A man in his sixties, he was Enrique's father and the closest living relative to the deceased 'hero'. I sidled up to him. 'Moving, don't you think?' I asked. 'No,' he replied. 'Just sad. He had no need to escape from the prison work camp. He didn't even have a long sentence to serve. They were three brothers. But, because of politics, they never saw one another again after 1936.'

The person closest to Tito, I realised, was the most reluctant to participate in what had clearly become a left-wing homage to him. Later, the nephew would, once more, stand away from the crowd as Mariano – on crutches, having badly singed his legs a few days earlier while using a blow-torch to make a rough, iron plaque to Tito – harangued the gathering. The nephew's generation had been given the option of being ardent, and privileged, pro-Francoists, downtrodden opponents or simply apolitical. Like many Spaniards of his time, he had chosen the last. He still blamed 'politics' for the tragedy of his father and his brothers. Mariano's words just made him uneasy.

Franco's regime publicly claimed the *maquis* were nothing more than a bunch of rural *bandoleros*. The Spanish parliament belatedly agreed in 2001 that official references to them as *bandoleros* should be removed. It was something, one of the forty aged survivors who turned up said, that happened 'twenty years too late'.

Small stories, picked up along the way, gave me some idea of what it had been like to be on the losing side of the war. In Poyales del Hoyo one woman told me that, as a child, a neighbour had tipped a bedpan of faeces and urine over her head in the street 'for being the daughter of a *rojo*'. Another starving boy, son of a *rojo*, was invited by a local right-winger to dip some bread into a steaming cauldron of stew being prepared for a hunting party, only to have his arm thrust deep into the boiling pot as a cruel joke.

In Palacios del Sil, a small village in the hills of León, an eighty-four-year-old woman, Isabel González, told me she was still bitter about the way her father, whose son was shot and left in a roadside mass grave, was continually humiliated by his Falangist neighbours. 'They would come at any time of the day or night and demand milk from the cow or take whatever they wanted. My father just had to do what they said. It killed him,' she recalled.

The desire to humiliate, terrorise and exact revenge – already apparent at the *Valle de Los Caídos* – was summed up by Franco's chief army psychiatrist, Lieutenant Colonel Antonio Vallejo-Nagera. This man, who went on to be Spain's first university professor of psychology, carried out tests on International Brigade prisoners and Spanish *roja* women prisoners in Málaga in an attempt to prove that Marxists were genetic retards. His recommendations on what to do with those from the other side included that they should 'suffer the punishment they deserve, with death the easiest of them all. Some will live in permanent exile, far from the Mother Country which they did not know how to love. Others will lose their freedom, groaning for years in prisons, purging their crimes with forced work in order to earn their daily bread, and will leave their children an infamous legacy: those who betrayed the Patria cannot leave an honourable surname for their children.'

It was an accurate description of what eventually happened. Some 300,000 people were imprisoned after the war. Tens of thousands were put before kangaroo military courts and shot. Many more went into exile. Some would even lose their children along the way. Even in the later years, when the regime's totalitarian instincts gave way to a form of authoritarian pragmatism, there were usually several hundred political prisoners in jail.

The most shocking recent discovery made by those investigating the excesses of Francoism, made in 2002, has been the treatment meted out to some *rojo* children. Historian Ricard Vinyes, investigating the fate of women prisoners in Franco's jails during and immediately after the Civil War in the state archives, came across a so-called 'red file'. These hold documents covered by a law that protects material on events less than fifty years old in which named people are involved. Curiosity got the better of him. When he opened the file, he discovered, first of all, that the events described in it were more than fifty years old. He read on and so discovered part of the story of what became known as 'the lost children of Francoism'.

These were children separated from *rojo* families and then adopted or handed over to Falange or convent-run orphanages. Some 30,000 children passed through their doors between 1944 and 1955. It was a story that, without realising it, Spaniards had been watching on their television screens for a long time. A popular, American-style live television programme, '*¿Quién Sabe Donde?*' ('*Who Knows Where?*'), had spent several years tearfully reuniting split families and runaway children with their parents. A surprisingly large number of cases dated back to the period following the Civil War.

Vinyes helped turn the story of the children into a two-part television documentary. Most of the evidence, barring the Falange papers found by Vinyes on the campaign to return the evacuated children of *rojos* to Franco's Spain, was given in the form of personal testimonies. What emerged was not a picture of a centralised, organised system for removing children from their parents, but of a sinister atmosphere in which, in case of doubt, the authorities or the Church naturally 'assumed' responsibility for *rojo* children. Vallejo-Nagera had said that saving the *raza*, the race, would require the separation of children from their mothers in places 'away from democratic environments and where the exaltation of bio-psychic racial qualities is encouraged'. It was the kind of idea that Franco, who wrote the script of a film called, precisely, *Raza*, liked.

Two mothers told how their children were taken from them at birth. 'They took my son to be baptised but they never brought him back. I never saw him again . . . I suppose they gave him up for adoption. But they never asked me . . . The *angustia*, the anguish, will stay with me until I die,' said Emilia Girón, considered especially dangerous because her brother was in the *maquis*. Those children evacuated by the Republic to England, France and elsewhere were to be returned, if necessary by force. Vichy France collaborated. The French family of Florencia Calvo tried to hide her, but eventually, at the age of ten, she was shipped back to Spain and sent to an orphanage. 'I cried because I wanted to be back with my family in France. I wet my bed more than once when I arrived and the nuns made me put the sheets on my head. They made me parade through the dining room with the wet sheets so that I would feel even more shame.' Florencia did not find her sister, María, for another fifty years.

In Britain, where more than 4,000 children had been evacuated. The local Falange agent suggested bringing back the well-behaved, very catholic Basque children first. This would leave the British to look after the children of anarchists and communists from the Asturian coalmines who were described as 'wild beasts'. They would thus learn 'what their parents must be like'.

The documentary was shocking. State television, then controlled by the People's Party, declined to show it. The regional stations of Catalonia, the Basque Country and Andalucía – all controlled by opposition parties – did broadcast it. There were record audiences in Catalonia.

Amongst the revelations was evidence that Franco's ultra-Catholic regime had indulged in the shooting of pregnant women at Torrero prison in Zaragoza province. The evidence came from the prison priest, a Capuchin monk, Gumersindo de Estrella, who tried to persuade a judge to desist. 'Imagine if I had to wait seven months for each woman who we have to mete out justice to . . . it is impossible,' the judge had replied.

One testimony, of a seven-day train trip of women prisoners and their children locked into goods wagons, evoked Primo Levi in its detail of hunger, of people forced to live in their own filth, of cold, disease and the death of small children. One of the worst testimonies came from Teresa Martín, who spent her infant years in a disease-ridden women's jail in Saturraran, in the Basque Country. 'The memories are still there. If anyone wants the memory of what happened to continue, all they have to do is ask. I am sixty-two. This is the first time I have talked about it. It is the first time anybody has asked.'

The Catalan broadcaster was inundated by letters. Some correspondents drew perplexed comparisons with Argentina, where the right-wing juntas of the 1970s stole children from prisoners who were secretly killed, the *desaparecidos*. 'Why do we know more about what happened in Argentina or Germany during their dictatorships than we know about what happened here for forty years, even though it ended twenty-five years ago?' asked one viewer. 'I am a university-educated woman. I cannot understand why, after so many years of study, this has never appeared in a history lesson,' wrote another.

Many victims found it hard to break their silence. I saw this at first hand, in Poyales, where people sometimes lowered their voices when talking about the Civil War. The historian Vinyes told me he found ex-prisoners he interviewed sometimes asked him to turn off his tape-recorder, or suddenly changed the subject, if their children appeared. Years of enforced silence had taken their toll. 'They were scared of recounting things that might disturb the family,' he explained. 'Fear remains in the blood.' At an exhibition on the takeover of Barcelona by Franco's army, sixty years after the event, he found one woman sobbing by a board listing the people shot by firing squads. 'That man is my father,' she explained. 'My mother never told me. She just said he disappeared during the war.'

There is also evidence, however, that the generations that lived through both the Civil War and early, extreme Francoism were genuinely fed up with it and had applied their own, voluntary, silence to it long before Franco died. Already, in the early 1950s, V. S. Pritchett found them 'politically tired out'. Gerald Brenan, looking for the grave of the poet and playwright García Lorca, would hear a rightist taxi driver say: 'Between us all we have brought disgrace on Spain. Once it was a happy country; now it is a miserable one, racked from end to end with hatred.' Jane Duran, a Cuban-born, British-based poet whose father had been a senior Republican officer, devoted an entire book of poems to his silence about the Civil War. That silence, maintained in freedom and exile, had started the day war finished.

He lays down his arms./He raises his arms over his head./He will not tell.

In between my visits to the Valley of the Fallen and my other trips looking for Franco, as the comparisons with the Latin American military regimes of the 1970s and 1980s became harder to avoid, I came across a book that had just been published by the Chilean writer Ariel Dorfman. It was called *Exorcising Terror: The Incredible Unending Trial of General Augusto Pinochet*. Dorfman, as a prominent intellectual in the Hispanic world and an anti-Pinochet campaigner, is something of a hero in Spain. In *Exorcising Terror* he asked the following question. 'Pinochet is a mirror . . . Are we willing to judge the country that gave origin to him?' That is a terrifying sort of a question for a country to answer. Had Spain addressed it? Should it have done? Perhaps silence had helped to avoid it.

Some people suggested to me that, indeed, there was a general feeling of shame. Gerald Brenan, during his 1949 journey around Spain, gave more clues. 'Those who let their fanaticism get the better of them in the Civil War are often obsessed by feelings of guilt, for no hangover is worse than that which follows a civil war and a reign of terror.' Perhaps, just perhaps, that is what this silence had really been about. Spaniards were ashamed and embarrassed – some for having supported him, others for having failed to overthrow him and others simply because he existed. It was like a family secret, best not talked about, best shoved to the back of the drawer and left there until it could do no more harm.

The shame, if that is the case, is only now lifting. At the end of the third decade without Franco, the dam holding back the gorier details of Francoism has finally burst. One publishing house has set up an entire series that seems dedicated to nothing else. There is still resistance, however. The People's Party went as far as it would in recognising the Francoist right's historic guilt in the same parliamentary motion in which it permitted local councils to spend money digging up Civil War graves. The motion recognised the existence of victims of 'the repression of the Francoist dictatorship' and denounced 'the violent imposition of ideologies'. But the People's Party – which speaks for more than a third of Spanish voters – has so far refused to go any further. It was the only one of eleven parties in Las Cortes, the Madrid parliament, to boycott a parliamentary homage to Franco's victims in 2003. Its habitual claim is that the left is indulging in 'mothball politics' whenever it brings the issue up.

The details of what happened come, anyway, too late for most of the victims – who are dead. But studying, in any rigorous detail, what actually happened remains a Herculean task. A disturbing number of archives, be they military, prison, police or Church, are an impenetrable mess, with some left rotting, unclassified, in warehouses dotted around the country. Like the statues, they have been shoved to the back of the cupboard by ministries or government departments. In some archives, especially those run by the Church, investigators are not allowed to dig randomly but must say precisely what they are looking for – a question many of them, following vague clues, are unable to answer. Others, such as those of the Francisco Franco Foundation, a drab

Madrid apartment that holds many of his papers and receives state funding, have proven almost impossible for non-friendly historians to access.

How, I wondered as I went seeking the Generalísimo, would a young Spaniard, a child of today, first encounter the man who dominated his country's history in the previous century? An answer to that came from an unexpected source. When he was six, my eldest son came back from his Madrid primary school singing the following ditty to the tune of the Spanish national anthem: '*Franco, Franco que tiene el culo blanco, porque su mujer lo lava con Ariel*' ('Franco, Franco, his arse is very white, and that is because his wife washes it with Ariel'). Children have a special knack for taking the sting out of scary, authority figures by lampooning them. Generations of schoolchildren, I am told, have learnt the same song. Part of the joke, today, is that Spain has one of the few national anthems in the world with no words to it. The old Francoist words were purged after his death, and nothing replaced them.

The fact that he knew the ditty did not mean my son knew who Franco was. We had to explain that to him. It was a rare sighting, though, of Franco in modern Spain. For a moment he had escaped from the storeroom or from the inside of a history book. He had lived on in the playground, a buffoon-like, but still threatening, figure. It was a sign, however, of the old Caudillo's potency that he should survive here as a modern bogeyman, as unrealistic to the children singing about him as Guy Fawkes is to British children.

La Transición – as Spaniards called their transition to democracy – had returned to Spain its pre-Francoist wordless national anthem. It had also laid down, it seemed, many of the unwritten rules of silence that were now being broken. Spaniards, and foreigners who observed this transition, had generally described it in glowing terms. It certainly achieved its overall aim of converting Spain to democracy. I was beginning to wonder, however, whether it was quite as perfect as it had been described. The *Transición*, clearly, was the key to many of the things I was coming across. If I wanted to understand it all, I would have to move on and find out some more about one of the most exciting – and unique – moments in Spanish history.

3

Amnistía and Amnesia: The Pact of Forgetting

I will call him Don Heliodoro, though we knew him simply by his nickname as '*el hueso*', the bone, because, someone told us, he was 'so hard to digest'. He was an elderly Madrileño, an old-fashioned Francoist into whose company I was forced as I set about buying an apartment. He was also a man who, as Spaniards say of those who speak their minds, *no tiene pelos en la lengua* – has no hairs on his tongue. One day, as we shared a taxi, we began talking about Spain's monarch, Juan Carlos I. 'The king?' he bellowed. 'He is a *traidor* [a traitor].'

'You know what I am talking about, don't you, *señor taxista*,' he shouted over the seat at the taxi driver, a man in his late fifties. The *taxista* smiled nervously and kept his mouth firmly shut. It must have been a while since he had had someone like this – one of the last, few diehard followers of Franco and the Falange leader José Antonio Primo de Rivera – in his cab.

Don Heliodoro was a reminder of two things. First, that when Franco died and a young prince called Juan Carlos stepped into the shoes of the head of state, people like this occupied many of the key positions of power. The Don Heliodoros of this world were convinced that democracy would bring with it the evils of communism, divorce, freemasonry, pornography and homosexuality.

The other was that Juan Carlos was Franco's hand-picked heir. Spain has, uniquely in modern Europe, a king elected by a dictator. The rightful heir to the Spanish throne had been the king's father, Don Juan. He had gone into exile with his own father, King Alfonso XIII, when the latter was chased out by Republicans in 1931.

It is questionable, in fact, whether Spaniards would have chosen Juan Carlos, or any other monarch, to lead them had they been given a free choice immediately after Franco's death in November 1975. Spain had not had a king for forty-four years. Neither the political left nor the more Falangist sectors of Franco's regime were natural monarchists. Spaniards generally had lost their respect for monarchs long before. They had not only pushed out Alfonso XIII. They had also forced the abdication of two of his three predecessors.

Juan Carlos felt real affection for the Generalísimo, his biographers say. Don Juan had initiated a tug-of-war with the Caudillo over his son's future by sending him to Madrid on his own at the age of just ten. It was the first time the future king had been to his own country. Franco oversaw his education after that. After thirty years of watchful vigilance, the Caudillo would eventually see in Juan Carlos – as one biographer of both men put it, attributing the observation to Queen Sofía – 'the son that he had never had'.

When the Caudillo publicly named the young prince as his successor, six years before his death, Juan Carlos was effusive in his praise. He also publicly pledged to uphold the principles of Franco's Movimiento Nacional. In his acceptance speech, Juan Carlos lauded not just Franco's dictatorship, but also the 1936 uprising that sparked the bloodbath of the Civil War. 'I receive from his Excellency the Head of State, Generalísimo Franco, the political legitimacy that emerged from July 18, 1936, amidst so much sad but necessary sacrifice and suffering so that our *Patria* could rejoin the path of destiny. The work of setting it on the right road and showing clearly the direction it must go has been carried out by that exceptional man whom Spain has been immensely fortunate to have, and will be fortunate to have for years to come, as the guide of our policy,' Juan Carlos said. 'My hand will not tremble to do all that is necessary to defend the principles [of the Movimiento] and laws that I have just sworn.'

It was reasonable to think, therefore, that Juan Carlos would bring more of the same. 'This is not a restoration of monarchy but the establishment of a new Francoist monarchy,' one of Franco's diehard supporters had claimed. The Don Heliodoros of this world certainly hoped for that. What they got was something completely different. In fact, Juan Carlos had been secretly meeting the pro-democracy opposition for some time. Over the next four years, he would help lead Spaniards to write themselves a democratic constitution, freely elect a parliament and – at a referendum – choose to have a constitutional monarch, himself, as head of state. It was a time of breathless change, intrigue and excitement. It marked the life of a whole generation of Spaniards who, as they now see their children reaping the benefits of what they sowed, are, largely, proud of what they achieved.

Spaniards, mostly, got what they wanted from the *Transición*. Age-old conflicts were resolved with words, not violence. A stable, working democracy was put in place. They can be extremely touchy about criticism of this period, or claims that some questions were left unresolved. 'Spain's *Transición* is envied the world over,' one angry newspaper editorial told Amnesty Internationsl in 2005 when it demanded that justice be handed out to Franco's victims.

The *Transición,* however, was a change in which silence – that apparently alien Spanish quality – would play a key role. Events of the previous fifty years were deliberately pushed into a dark corner as Spaniards observed what came to be known as the *pacto del olvido*, the pact of forgetting.

The only release from Franco was death by natural causes. The Caudillo died in a hospital bed on 20 November 1975. Spaniards did not free themselves, as the Portuguese had done the year before with their peaceful Carnation Revolution. Nor did they achieve freedom with the sort of people's power demonstrations that swept through eastern bloc Communist countries later in the century.

Depending on where a Spaniard lived, the Caudillo had ruled over their life for anything between thirty-six and thirty-nine years. It was time enough for children to become grandparents. I have always found it difficult, despite a recent flood of novels and films on the subject, to imagine the impact he had on each individual Spaniard's existence. I got some idea, however, when I travelled four thousand miles across the Atlantic to report for the *Guardian* newspaper on the world created by another long-living military strongman of Galician origin – Cuban leader Fidel Castro. 'You must understand that it has been my whole life. I haven't had the chance to know or see anything else,' said – in an empty, sad voice – a fifty-year-old woman to whom I gave a lift during a tropical rainstorm outside Havana. A whole generation of Spaniards must have felt the same emptiness, the same sense of waste or lost opportunity.

Even those who, like King Juan Carlos, had spent fifteen years appearing at the Caudillo's side, claimed they had been forced to keep their mouths firmly closed most of the time. 'Why did I never say anything? Because it was a period when nobody, not even me, dared speak,' he said later.

Franco's final message to Spaniards was read out on television by his weeping prime minister, the devoted Carlos Arias Navarro, hours after his death. It called on them to be loyal to Juan Carlos. They were warned not to forget, however, that 'the enemies of Spain and of Christian civilisation are on the alert'.

The message also contained a rare, if perverse, apology to his legion of victims – to that part of Spain known simply as *los vencidos*, the defeated: 'I beg forgiveness of everyone, just as with all my heart I forgive those who declared themselves my enemies.' The apology was offered, as Spaniards describe those talking through clenched teeth, *con la boca pequeña* – with a small mouth. His victims had 'declared themselves' enemies. It was, in other words, their own fault. Franco, of all people, was not about to go to the grave admitting he had been wrong.

Democracy did not appear in Spain overnight – though the period in which it emerged is often viewed through rose-tinted glasses. If Franco expected, or wanted, democracy to happen he forgot to tell anyone. Juan Carlos was, in the words of one historian, meant to 'continue Francoism after Franco'. This proved to be 'the Caudillo's most serious political and personal miscalculation'.

King Juan Carlos's first prime minister was the same Arias Navarro who had wept so copiously for Franco. Arias Navarro – known as the *Carnicero de Málaga*, or the Butcher of Málaga, because of his time as a military prosecutor during the Civil War – vowed he would be 'a strict perpetrator of Francoism'. It took three years of intense and difficult work to get to a point where a new constitution could be written and voted on. Franco may have been dead, but Francoism was still very much present as Spain tottered unsteadily into democracy.

When Juan Carlos was officially proclaimed king he spoke of 'a dynamic moment of change' and of integrating '*distintas y deseables opiniones*' – 'different and desirable opinions'. That could, or could not, have meant democracy. A few days later he issued a royal decree naming the deceased Franco, in perpetuity, general-in-chief of the army, navy and air force.

For fifty hours Franco's body lay in the Sala de Columnas of Madrid's Palacio de Oriente. Hundreds of thousands queued to see his corpse. He was buried at the Valle de Los Caídos after a frantic search for the stone which had been set aside years earlier to cover his grave. One of the waiting mourners fell into the grave a few hours before and had to be removed, unconscious, from what was due to be the Caudillo's last resting place. The ceremony was presided over by a red-eyed, visibly moved, Juan Carlos.

By the time of his death Franco was an international pariah, except to a US which had signed deals for military bases and used him as a Cold War bulwark against communism. The only world leader of any significance to turn up for his funeral was Chile's General Augusto Pinochet – a dictator with similar ideas about his role in delivering the world from communism and atheism. Attempts made, twenty-five years later, by a Spanish court to try Pinochet for genocide, terrorism and torture show just how fast and far the country travelled after Franco had been lowered into his grave. They also highlight, however, the immense contrast between Spain's attitude to those who tortured, killed or repressed in Franco's name and those who did the same elsewhere.

A political prisoner sitting in a Spanish jail could have been forgiven for looking at the future with pessimism at the end of 1975. Franco was dead. But the people appointed by Juan Carlos to run the country were the same lot as before. The Butcher of

Málaga was in charge of the government. The upper echelons of the army, meanwhile, were populated with generals who had earned their spurs fighting for Franco in the Civil War or, later, for Hitler with the volunteer División Azul. The parliament was used to rubber-stamping Franco's legislation, the judges to carrying out his laws and the police to applying them, often brutally. Almost everybody in a position of power was, at least in theory, some sort of Francoist.

In fact, the thirst for democracy was enormous. Fortunately it was, at least by now, shared by Juan Carlos. The undergroundleft-wing press did not, however, see any signs of this. '*¡No al Rey franquista!*', 'No to the Francoist King!', '*¡No al Rey impuesto!*', 'No to an imposed King!' they cried.

There were only two ways of achieving democracy. One was a complete – and potentially violent – break with the past. In that scenario the police and army, where the hardliners were, would have the upper hand. The other was *ruptura pactada* – an agreement, between Francoists and opposition democrats, to break with the past. That, however, meant letting the Francoists themselves, led by Juan Carlos, carry out the changes. For the left, there was no real choice. The Francoists, if they were prepared to, would have to do it. Fortunately, enough of them were. One of the great ironies of recent Spanish history is that many of the fathers of democracy were Francoists. Inevitably, however, they were going to do it their way – or as much their way as possible.

Luis María Anson, a conservative, monarchist journalist, had already spotted the manoeuvres going on in the background before Franco's death. 'The rats are abandoning the regime's ship . . . The cowardice of the Spanish ruling class is truly suffocating . . . Already it has reached the beginnings of the *sauve qui peut*, of the unconditional surrender,' he wrote six months before *el Caudillo* died.

Prominent Francoists reinvented themselves, almost overnight, as diehard democrats. Spain went for what one well-known psychiatrist of the time called 'a world-record in jacket changing'. The jacket-changers were led by Adolfo Suárez, a brilliant young

Falangist who replaced Arias Navarro. He persuaded the Francoist deputies in Las Cortes to commit *hara-kari* by passing a law allowing free elections. He then went on to win those elections with a 'centrist' party that included many former regime *apparatchiks.*

The *Transición* was a time of high political drama. Its protagonists are treated as heroes. Spaniards often forget, however, quite how violent it was. In the five years after Franco's death, more than a hundred demonstrators, left-wing activists, students and separatists were killed by the police or the '*ultras*', the far right. Many more were killed by ETA and other left-wing or separatist terrorist groups.

The people in charge may have considered themselves ex-Francoists, but some of the tactics they used showed little sign of change. Although some of the killing was done by police – sometimes by shooting straight into demonstrations – the men pulling the triggers were rarely, if ever, brought to justice. Five people were killed in one demonstration in the Basque city of Vitoria in 1976 after police had lobbed smoke grenades into a church. The relatives of the dead are still, today, waiting for the killers to be identified. Two of the Francoists-turned-democrats who were in charge of the interior ministry at the time have gone on to enjoy enormous success. Manuel Fraga Iribarne founded what would become the People's Party, which governed the country under José María Aznar for eight years until 2004. He himself was president of the Galician regional government until 2005. Rodolfo Martín Villa served several governments as a minister and went on to become chairman of Spain's main satellite broadcaster, Sogecable.

The negotiating strength of those who held power and those who did not was obviously unequal. Manuel Fraga had opposition leaders arrested. He once boasted to the young Socialist leader Felipe González that it could take eight years to legalise his party while the Communists might always remain banned. 'Remember that I am the power, and you are nothing,' he told him.

Felipe González, who helped negotiate the reforms and would later govern as Spanish prime minister for thirteen years, admits the left had to pay for change with, amongst other things, silence.

'What we have is a change that is agreed between people coming from the old regime and the opposition,' explains González. 'That was very positive but it excluded, for example, an explanation (not to mention any demand that people be held responsible) for what had happened under Francoism, through truth commissions, as other countries have done. There was not sufficient strength to demand either justice or, even, any explanation for the past.'

Within days of Franco's death, demonstrations were being held demanding amnesty for the political prisoners still in jail. These were the days of running battles between demonstrators and the *grises*, the grey-uniformed riot police, which marked the youth of a generation of, mainly, left-wingers. Franco, unforgiving to the end, had ordered the execution of five prisoners in his last year. Political activists were still being beaten and tortured by the police's Brigada Político-Social in some police stations. Asked to order his police to be gentle with amnesty protesters in Valencia, Fraga replied: '*Les voy a moler a palos*' ('I shall beat them black and blue').

The last prisoners were finally released after a general amnesty was granted at the end of 1977. The amnesty was agreed by a parliament elected, a few months earlier, in the first democratic vote for forty-one years. Some of those released were members of ETA and would simply get straight back to the business of terror. Others, though, had spent years going in and out of Franco's prisons for organising peaceful protests. To them, it was a form of victory. Marcelino Camacho, a trade union leader who had spent years in jail, told Las Cortes that the amnesty was the only way to 'close this past of civil wars and crusades'. A Socialist deputy agreed, saying it was 'the fruit of a desire to bury the sad, past history of Spain'. Another deputy gave the best description, however: 'The amnesty is simply a forgetting . . . an amnesty for everyone, a forgetting by everyone for everyone.' The proposal was not just amnesty, but also amnesia.

Spaniards called the unwritten part of the amnesty agreement the *pacto del olvido*. It underpinned the entire transition.

If silence about the past was the price to be paid for the successful self-dissolution of Francoism, the opposition was prepared to sign up to it. Those who negotiated the pact, men like Socialist prime minister-to-be Felipe González, still feel that way. It allowed Suárez to reform the regime from within, using its own rules to do so.

More than twenty-five years later, however, the amnesty law begins to look different to some Spaniards – especially to a younger generation that did not live through Franco's final days. Its second article covered crimes 'against the rights of people' committed – prior to 15 December 1976 – by: 'authorities, functionaries and agents of public order'. Franco's henchmen, in other words, would not have to pay for their crimes.

In an attempt to understand the consequences of that *pacto del olvido*, I found myself walking up the Carrer Josep Anselm Clavé. This leads off the end of Barcelona's famous Ramblas boulevard into what used to be the city's port district. During the 1992 Olympics, I bumped into two lost Atlanta cops here – doing groundwork for their own Olympics four years later – and acted as interpreter. 'I wouldn't go down there, not without my gun anyway,' said one, a big black lieutenant, peering down a dark alley.

Coming back, I found this street had, like so much of this ever-evolving city, changed. Gift shops, including a hammock boutique, gave way to a street of bars and small businesses, with immigrants from Africa, Morocco and China bustling around. Turning up towards Escudellers street, I veered off into a narrow, featureless and slightly sinister alleyway. I had come here to the offices of a group of people who were keeping a small flame alive for the 5,000 Spaniards who died during the Second World War in a Nazi prison camp at Mauthausen, in Austria. A strange piece of news had driven me here to meet the people from a group called the Amical de Mauthausen. For, a few months earlier, I had been surprised to discover that a man called Ramón Serrano Suñer had just died. The surprise was not his death, but the fact that he had still been alive.

Aged 101, the man known to Spaniards as *el Cuñadísimo*, 'the super-brother-in-law', for his relationship with *el Generalísimo*, had proved to be a survivor in numerous ways. For, at one of the bloodiest and most vengeful moments of Spanish history, Serrano Suñer had been his brother-in-law's right-hand man and the second most powerful man in the land. While Spaniards were dying in Mauthausen, Suñer was one of Nazi Germany's most impassioned backers in Madrid. 'Russia is to blame!' he had shouted to the crowds when Hitler invaded the Soviet Union and Franco decided to send his division of volunteers, the División Azul, to help him.

Some of the obituaries I read of him bore little relationship to the picture I carried in my head of an ardent pro-fascist who held such power in the first, and most extreme, few years of Francoism. They were glowing accounts of a charming, intelligent man who saved Spain from the Second World War and went on to oppose Franco. They described him as a fine writer, a successful businessman and a free thinker. Others were not so kind. They used words like *totalitario* and *fascista*. It was difficult to imagine they were writing about the same man.

Serrano Suñer had, I read, spent much of the last few years of his life in the glitzy southern resort of Marbella. A black, chauffeur-driven Mercedes with white blinds would take him almost daily to the same beach. Out would step the chauffeur and a distinguished-looking, very elderly gentleman with a walking stick, a hat, a cashmere jacket and, often, a dark tie knotted around his neck. Serrano Suñer, whose admirers said he conserved a keen eye for young women and who went for his first spin on a water scooter when he was ninety-six, would take the sun for a while. Then he would return to his car and be driven back to his summer house, bought off a former British ambassador, on the hillside above the town.

As a younger man, Serrano Suñer's tall, thin and elegant figure, combined with his stylish, quick-witted manner, provided an unflattering contrast to his ponderous, pot-bellied brother-in-law. 'Beside the Don Quixote of his brother-in-law, the Caudillo often appears to be Sancho Panza,' France's Marshal Pétain once observed. In the bloody, hate-fuelled days of the late 1930s and early 1940s, he helped Franco design his new state. At one point in 1940 he controlled the interior ministry, the foreign ministry and the Falange. Serrano Suñer – whose brothers had been shot by the *rojos* in Madrid – thus helped oversee one of the most brutal, vengeful periods of internal repression. He admired, met and negotiated with both Adolf Hitler and Benito Mussolini. The latter was, he thought, 'a genius' of the kind history threw up only 'once every two or three thousand years'. A man who hated Britain and France, he played host to Reichsführer-SS Heinrich Himmler in Madrid in 1940. The city's streets were decorated with swastikas. The Gestapo chief, not a man famous for compassion, expressed amazement at the scale of the repression unleashed by Franco's Nationalists. He would, nevertheless, agree to send a number of prominent Republicans captured in France back to Spain – where they would be shot.

As foreign minister, Serrano Suñer helped strike a secret deal with Hitler. It was negotiated at a meeting between Hitler and Franco in a railway wagon at Hendaye, southern France. The agreement saw Spain promise to join the Second World War on the Axis side at a time of 'common agreement' and when it considered itself materially ready to do so. Serrano Suñer later claimed personal credit for making sure that never happened. Wild demands made by Franco for a new empire in North Africa were, according to many historians, what really turned the Germans off. Mussolini's foreign minister, nevertheless, considered the *Cuñadísimo* to be the Axis's firmest ally in Spain.

Serrano Suñer, like his brother-in-law, died peacefully of natural causes. Had Franco fulfilled his pledge to join Germany, the two brothers-in-law might have ended up facing some sort of Nuremberg-style trial or, like Mussolini in Milan's Piazzale Loreto, hanging upside down in a public square. But, even though he lived his last quarter of a century in a democratic country, no one ever tried to bring Serrano Suñer to task. Justice was never called for and, some say, was never done.

In fact, he had plenty of time to rewrite his own history, as he was sacked by Franco in 1942. Politically speaking, *el Caudillo* roundly ignored him after that. Some said he got too big for his boots, others that he was punished for cuckolding *el Caudillo*'s wife's sister. One historian claims there were signs that he was trying to turn the Falange into 'a fully-fledged Nazi Party for his own purposes'. Some said that his passion for fascism, Hitler and Mussolini became a problem when the tide of war began to change. Whatever the reason, he went on to paint himself as a force for moderation and, ultimately, as a Franco opponent. 'He could not bear his own past and fought vainly to reconstruct it,' historian Javier Tusell said. The truth was that he had been 'an indispensable instrument in the construction of Franco's dictatorship in its most totalitarian, fascist moment,' Tusell said.

Actually, Serrano Suñer may have had a narrow escape from having his name dragged into court. The people at the Amical de Mauthausen had been plotting to bring him to trial. They could not do so in Spain. So they hoped to have him tried, for crimes against humanity or war crimes, in France. It was from France that thousands of Spanish Republicans, the so-called *Rotspanier*, the 'Red Spaniards' who had fled Spain at the end of the Civil War, were picked up by the Germans during the Second World War and deported to Mauthausen. Here the formula was *Erschöpfung durch Arbeit* – prisoners should work until they dropped. It was, presumably, an idea that Serrano Suñer and Franco were happy to have applied to their own countrymen. Of 7,000 Spaniards, only 2,191 survived. Brutality, overwork, executions, the gas chamber, suicide, hunger and disease all took their toll. Spanish prisoners sent to work at a nearby mine managed to sneak out official SS camp photographs before the Allies arrived and the camp paperwork was destroyed. The photographs showed, amongst other things, visits by Serrano Suñer's friend Himmler. They were later used at Nuremberg, where one of the prisoners forced to work as a photographer, the Catalan Francesc Boix, was the only Spanish witness. They helped secure the death penalty for the Austrian SS leader, Ernst Kaltenbrunner.

Would the French courts, sixty years after the event, really have thought there was enough evidence against Serrano Suñer to try him? In 1998 they had tried and convicted eighty-eight-year-old Maurice Papon, a former senior Vichy official and, later, French cabinet member, for the more clear-cut crime of deporting Jews to German death camps during the Second World War. Did Serrano Suñer know thousands of his countrymen were being sent, mostly to their death, to Nazi prison camps? Did he agree, even suggest, that they should be? Did he care? The questions seem banal when compared to the figures for the number of people killed by Franco's regime while Serrano Suñer was helping run it. Those numbers are constantly argued over, but they are always counted in the tens of thousands. The most recent estimates, starting in 1936, range from 85,000 to 150,000 (with the correct figure, starting in 1936, considered to be up to 100,000).With Serrano Suñer dead, the people from the Amical admit they did not have much evidence, barring the Himmler meetings, linking him directly to Mauthausen. But nailing Serrano Suñer was not the only, or even main, point of trying to put him on trial. 'We always thought that, through him, we could have put the whole dictatorship on trial,' explained one member of the Amical's committtee.

Francoism never has been placed on trial (unless the varied judgements of historians count). Silence was at the heart of Spain's transition to democracy – enshrined in the *pacto del olvido*. The past, and men like Serrano Suñer, were to be left alone. There were no hearings, no truth commissions and no formal process of reconciliation beyond the business of constructing a new democracy. This was no South Africa, no Chile, no Argentina. The mechanics of repression – police files on suspects and informers – would not be made public, as they would be in East Germany, Poland or the Czech Republic. Nor was Franco's Spain a defeated Germany or Japan, forced to confront its own guilty past. In fact, it was Franco's own men who would, largely, oversee and manage the *Transición*. They would do so in a way that made sure neither they, nor those who came before them, could be called to account for anything they had done on behalf of *el Caudillo*. 'The political class turned into angels, proud of the almost mafioso *omertà* when it came to talking about themselves,' wrote one of the handful of critics of that transition, Gregorio Morán.

While the Amical de Mauthausen was plotting to try Serrano Suñer, I found myself, as a journalist, constantly called on to follow the attempts of Spain's celebrated and controversial Judge Baltasar Garzón to pursue other military strongmen who had killed and tortured. The men being chased by Judge Garzón, an investigating magistrate at Madrid's powerful Audiencia Nacional, were not, however, Spanish. They were Chilean, Argentine and from several other Latin American countries. Garzón's pursuit of the military thugs who ruled much of South America in the 1970s and 1980s is a cause célèbre in Spain. He has declared himself competent to pursue them, and is backed by higher courts, because these are 'international crimes'. The alleged perpetrators had declared amnesties for themselves, thus preventing trials in their own countries.

The Argentines, looking for a way to pacify their own military, found a perfect description when they named their '*Ley de Punto Final*', 'Full Stop Law', in 1986. The 'full stop' was meant to put an end to the story of repression and torture started when the military juntas took over ten years earlier (1976). Spaniards, especially those on the left, condemned Argentina's *punto final* law. Few stopped to think, or even realised, that their own amnesty had, in effect, also been a 'full stop' law.

Picking up *El Mundo* newspaper one morning as Garzón struggled to get government approval for his extradition petitions for thirty-nine presumed Argentine torturers, I found an editorial entitled 'The laws of impunity continue to benefit the repressors.' The newspaper was angry that the Argentines might not be extradited, thus 'creating a serious risk that impunity will triumph'. A few days later it repeated the message: 'While the criminals remain free, able to rub shoulders with the victims and their families, we must applaud any initiative that seeks to condemn them and reestablish justice.'

Argentina has since struck down the Punto Final law. Nothing similar happened in Spain. There was no public outpouring of guilt, no formal attempt at naming and shaming – though there is now belated pressure for the creation of a truth commission. The same Brigada Político-Social police agents who regularly beat and tortured their detainees were not only free of any guilt, but could carry on their careers uninterrupted. Infamous Brigada Político-Social torturers – like Roberto Conesa in Madrid or the brothers Creix in Barcelona – continued their careers and went into comfortable retirement. Some even went on to become important police chiefs under Suárez or the Socialist governments that took over in the 1980s. The writer Manuel Vázquez Montalbán was one of those to fall into the hands of brothers Juan and Vicente Creix in the cells at Barcelona's Vía Laietana. 'We, their victims, did not do anything to shine a light on them. The political reforms had already absolved those who owned the Creixes. Would it have been right to pursue their servants?' he asked. In 2001 one of the more notorious Brigada bosses, Melitón Manzanas, was awarded a posthumous medal. This was gained for having been killed by Basque terror group ETA.

In some cases the perceived need for wiping out the past was taken literally. In 1977, Interior Minister Rodolfo Martín Villa, a former Francoist civil governor and Movimiento leader in Barcelona, sent out instructions to some civil governors of Spain's provinces. These were also, still, the regional bosses of the Movimiento Nacional. He told them to destroy the Movimiento's records.

The details of exactly what was destroyed, and how, are sketchy. A Civil Guard officer once told me – on second-hand information – that a team of three officers was sent to the central archive of the Civil Guard police in Madrid, sorting out the documents to be burnt. In Barcelona, a truckload of papers – the entire archive – was taken from the Movimiento's headquarters in the Calle Mallorca to a disused industrial oven in Poble Nov and incinerated. The then civil governor, Salvador Sanchez-Teran, says he contemplated the historical import of what he was doing but decided it was best to destroy the archive. 'Those archives smelt of the remote past,' he explains in his memoir of the time. It was 1977, Franco had died less than two years earlier. The Movimiento itself had only just been disbanded. The paper-burners left behind holes that historians, presumably, can no longer fill. These sorts of decisions were no impediment to career-making. Sanchez-Teran is went on to head the popular, church-owned, right-wing COPE radio station.

I went to Gijón, the port city on the Atlantic coast in Asturias, to hear a story of how some papers had, temporarily, slipped through the net. The man who told the story to me was a retired Civil Guard officer who, from the way he spoke about them, had no sympathy for left-wingers. Fermín had been posted to the Asturian town of Colunga in the late 1980s and had found the records there still intact. His story – uncheckable, but convincingly told – gave me a glimpse of how Francoist repression had worked. There, in different coloured files – white, blue and red – ranking them in degrees of 'danger' were the records on those deemed to be subversive. They were written on super-thin *papel cebolla*, literally 'onion paper', which enabled them to make multiple copies. Leafing through them, even Fermín was amazed at just how much information was kept. 'Some included everything from the person's wedding day to their first arrest,' he said.

There was also a separate section of files on all the police informers, he explained, be they paid *soplones*, snitches, or members of the then illegal parties and trade unions such as the Communist Comisiones Obreras or the Socialist Unión General de Trabajadores. Fermín burned the lot. 'They were meant to have done it years earlier,' he said. I wonder how many reputations he, and the other burners, saved.

The destruction of documents has made reconstructing the mechanisms of Francoist repression much more difficult. It has, especially, helped keep the names of those who took part in it out of the public eye. 'The active or passive participation of sectors of Spanish society in the repression was more important than we care to remember,' recall Nicolás Sartorius and Javier Alfaya, two former political prisoners, in a recent study.

One of the few to have been named as a regime collaborator, however, is none other than Spain's Nobel Prize-winning novelist Camilo José Cela. Cela, the cantankerous and controversial author of *The Family of Pascual Duarte* and *The Hive*, was awarded the Nobel Prize in 1989 for his 'rich and intensive prose, which with restrained compassion forms a challenging vision of man's vulnerability'. He died in 2002. Shortly after his death, historian Pere Ysàs unearthed papers showing that Cela had snitched to the information ministry on those who attended a Spanish writers' conference in 1963. He told officials that 42 of the 102 signatories of a letter denouncing police violence against striking miners in the northern region of Asturias – which he himself had signed – were members of the Spanish Communist Party. He apparently suggested that some dissident writers could be bribed, tamed and reconverted by the generalísimo's regime. Cela's views were contained in an internal report written by an official working for the then information minister. This was the same Manuel Fraga who would become interior minister and, later, head of the Galician government when Spain was a democracy. The novelist claimed, according to the report, that some fellow signatories were 'totally recoverable [for the regime], either through the stimulus of publishing their work or through bribes'. He suggested the regime should target Pedro Laín Entralgo, a leading intellectual, on the basis that he was a weaker character than others in the group.

Spaniards argue over exactly when the *Transición* came to an end. Some say it still has not done so. They point out that the 1978 constitution was written to the *ruido de sables*, the sound of sabre-rattling from army officers threatening to rebel if too much of Francoism was ditched. The *Transición*, they say, will not properly be over until it is rewritten.

One moment that is a candidate for the end of the *Transición*, however, is the day the sabres stopped being rattled and were actually drawn in anger. Spaniards simply call it '*El 23-F*'. Proof that the *ruido de sables* was no joke was provided by the comic-looking, but distinctly unfunny, figure of Lieutenant Colonel Antonio Tejero on 23 February 1981. Dressed in the winged, shiny, tricorn patent leather hat of the Civil Guard, a walrus moustache bursting over his upper lip, Tejero stormed Las Cortes that day with 200 men. The deputies were in the middle of an important parliamentary debate that was due to elect Leopoldo Calvo Sotelo to replace Suárez as prime minister for his centre-right party. They took almost all Spain's deputies hostage.

The American magazine *Time* dubbed Tejero 'the tricorned coupster'. It was a clumsy sort of a coup attempt, and one that has never been fully, or satisfactorily, explained. The 'coupsters' failed to turn off one of the television cameras – thus conserving a valuable record of what happened. Tejero's men peppered the ceiling of the debating ceiling with gunfire while most deputies cowered on the floor in response to Tejero's shouts of: '*¡Al suelo!*', 'To the floor!' They also, however, shouted '*¡En nombre del Rey!*', 'In the King's name!'

In Castelldefels, a beachside Barcelona dormitory town, I met a one-legged musician who told me he had taken part in the events of 23-F. His story added an element of comedy to the coup. The musician still had two legs at that time and was doing military service in Madrid. 'One day we were called out into the parade ground and ordered to get into lorries. We had no idea where we were going. We ended up pulling up in front of Las Cortes. We sat there doing nothing, unsure of what was going on and awaiting orders. I had run out of cigarettes so, when the sergeant wasn't looking, I sneaked off to buy some. When I got back my unit had disappeared. I asked a policeman where they had gone. He pointed a finger to Las Cortes and said: "In there." So I went and joined the rest of them.' I was never sure whether the musician had been part of the coup or part of the forces who took control of the building after Tejero gave himself up. But it was a sign of the confusion that reigned over two days in Madrid, in what was, in reality, a very unfunny episode.

King Juan Carlos stopped the coup. He ordered wavering generals to stay loyal. He told those who had backed the coup to take their men back to their barracks. In a famous broadcast to the nation he wore the uniform of the commander-in-chief of Spain's armed forces. He told Spaniards he would not tolerate 'actions or attitudes of anyone who wants to interrupt by force the democratic process that was decided when, by referendum, the constitution was voted on by the Spanish people'.

Tejero was soon abandoned to his fate by his fellow plotters. He had no option but to surrender. He and two dozen other plotters were sent to jail. These included General Alfonso Armada, who had been one of the king's closest advisers, and General Jaime Milans del Bosch, a swaggering hero of the Civil War siege of El Alcázar barracks in Toledo. As military commander of Valencia, he had ordered his tanks out onto the streets. Milans del Bosch was, thankfully, the only one of Spain's regional military commanders to do so. But it is clear that these were not the only conspirators. A whole raft of other figures, be they military, political or civilian, were simply waiting to see what happened. It was never clear who they were. The plotters obviously believed they had Juan Carlos on their side. There were even rumours that opposition politicians had been ready to form a 'government of national unity' under the guidance of a mysterious, and unidentified, coup leader codenamed *Elefante Blanco* – White Elephant. The coup remains, to this day, one of the great mysteries of recent Spanish history. It has sparked dozens of theories about who was really behind it. 'I do not understand why this has not been talked about in depth, why all the facts on it have not been published. Because the civilian part has remained silenced,' ex-*El País* editor Juan Luis Cebrián says, and Felipe González agrees, in a co-authored book. The Socialist leader, having been held hostage by Tejero, would, indirectly, become one of the greatest beneficiaries of the coup. He won a landslide electoral victory the following year.

Another question that has not been fully answered is why the plotters believed they were operating on the king's orders. Did they delude themselves entirely? Or did the king give them reasons to do so? Armada and Milans del Bosch both seemed convinced they had the king's backing to form a government of national unity led by Armada. 'I had spoken to the monarch by phone several times and had even visited him,' Milans del Bosch later claimed in a prison conversation with a controversial former army colonel, Amadeo Martínez Inglés. 'He always told me I should trust Armada.

Armada's mistake was to let the fanatical and excitable Tejero lead the assault on the parliament. He ignored Armada and, instead of negotiating the formation of a government of national unity, demanded the creation of a military junta. Armada, an old tutor and friend of the king's, was sentenced to thirty years in prison in 1983. Five years later he received a pardon. This was justified on grounds of ill-health. He went on, however, to enjoy a sprightly old age.

Phone conversations between the king and Armada show that, whatever might have been said before, Juan Carlos never wavered in his opposition to the coup once it started. 'I think you've gone mad,' he told him. Juan Carlos told Milans del Bosch the plotters would have to shoot him if they wanted to achieve their aims.

It was one of various coup plots since Franco's death, but the only one to make it out of the barracks. There would be rumours of further, later plots, too, that would only come to light much later. But the 23-F attempt finally spelt the end of the *pronunciamientos* – the uprisings and takeovers by generals – that had wracked Spanish history for 170 years. It is unthinkable, today, that the military could ever rise up in arms again.

The Tejero coup, which also embarrassed much of the army, had one major effect. It helped catapult the Socialist Party of Felipe González into power and, eventually, provoked the disappearance of Suárez's UCD party.

The day Felipe González and his wily, some would say Machiavellian, number two, Alfonso Guerra, leant out of a window at the Hotel Palace, waving a red rose to salute their victory in the 1982 general election, Spanish democracy hit a new gear. González would stay in power for thirteen years. It was a period in which most residues of Francoism were left to die off from natural causes. By the end of it, the *Transición* really was over.

Of all the angry words about Franco poured onto pages and pronounced in speeches in the years since his death, none have come from King Juan Carlos. Some modern-day Republicans see this as proof that he does not deserve to reign. In a country where former Franco officials often either gloss over, or completely ignore, their years of loyal service to the Caudillo, Juan Carlos's attitude is, at least, refreshingly coherent.

Juan Carlos is an outwardly pleasant man and a genuinely popular monarch. He is credited with having converted a whole generation of the Spanish left from republicans into *juancarlistas*, Juan Carlos fans. His opponents are, however, not only those on the extreme right who point out that those 'permanent and inalterable' Movimiento Nacional principles he had sworn to uphold included a pledge to keep Spain in strict observance of 'the doctrine of the Holy, Roman and Apostolic Church'. The anti-monarchical right has its equivalent, more numerously, amongst those who have remained Republicans. These have become increasingly visible in recent years, with the republican flag now a fixture at left-wing demonstrations. These republicans cannot see why Spain, having expelled three of their five monarchs over 150 years, should have replaced a dictator with a king – especially one hand-picked by the same dictator.

Within three years of Franco's death in 1975, the king had not only buried the Movimiento Nacional principles that he had once sworn to uphold, he had buried the Movimiento altogether. By the end of 1978 Spain had become a democracy. Francoism was dead, the Movimiento had been dissolved and the voters were happily piling earth on the graves of both. It was a remarkable transformation. It saw Juan Carlos himself shed almost all his powers to become the largely ornamental head of a constitutional, parliamentary monarchy. He is, in that sense, Europe's last true king – the last monarch to have held the powers of a ruler. No other living European monarch has enjoyed such power, or given it all up. His supporters like to claim that he is also that rare thing, an elected king. When Spaniards approved their constitution in 1978, they voted for parliamentary monarchy.

Yet Juan Carlos himself is also subject to a dose of Spanish silence. For Spanish journalists freely admit that the king – along with his family – is their last great taboo subject. 'There is freedom of speech on everything, except the king and the monarchy,' Cebrían tells González in their book. Journalists talk of *autocensura*, self-censorship. It is not something they are proud of. As one of Spain's most prolific royal writers, Juan Balansó, put it (despite being a fervent Juan Carlos fan): 'There is one thing worse than censorship, self-censorship.' Juan Carlos is not easily criticised. His past in Franco's shadow – even as his temporary replacement when the Caudillo was ill – is glossed over. His finances are not scrutinised. His private life is, well, private.

'There was always a timid editor, prepared to suspect that behind this or that affair [involving royal advisor Manuel de Prado] one might find the king himself,' wrote Pilar Urbano, a prominent journalist, after a financial scandal hit those close to the king in the 1990s.

Spaniards generally give two explanations for this royal reverence. One is that the king deserves it, having seen through the *Transición* and squashed the 1981 coup. Another is that, given its history, the Spanish monarchy needs all the help it can get. 'The fragility of the monarchy is greater than it may seem at first sight,' warned Tusell. 'In the Spanish case, the repetition of cases such as we have seen in other latitudes would have far more devastating effects . . . After all, the interruptions in our tradition of monarchy in contemporary times are far more pronounced.'

In a rare breaking of ranks, Vicenç Navarro made a list of royal-related affairs which television journalism – in a country where only one in ten people buy a newspaper – had chosen to ignore completely. They included four 'economic assessors of the Royal household' who ended up in jail 'without anybody investigating the relationship between them and the king'. There were, he said, a list of presents that went from yachts and palaces to luxury cars from 'business groups and people who try to influence' the king. 'None of them have been commented on by our television stations, which is where most citizens garner their basic information on political life. Such silence would be unthinkable in other democracies.' When the satirical magazine *El Jueves* brought out a book of royal cartoons called *Tocando los Borbones*, the editor complained that two privately owned television stations, Canal Plus and Telecinco, refused to run its advertisements. 'The fact is that we worry that the monarchy is not well enough rooted, and that anything might finish it off,' says a former *El País* editor, Juan Luis Cebrián.

Given the British press's – and newspaper readers' – surfeit of interest in the UK royal family, there is a healthy side to this silence. If Spaniards and their newspapers are not interested in their politicians' private lives, why should they intrude on the royal family's? And if the royal family behaves properly in public, why worry about what it does behind closed doors?

Compared to their British counterparts, the Spanish royals are, at least in public, remarkably modest. When I went to their Zarzuela Palace to see how they lived a few years ago, their press officer proudly showed me the dining room – with seating room for just eighteen. The palace, a former hunting lodge on the outskirts of Madrid, is both relatively small and very unstuffy. Nobody seemed to mind that I took a wrong turning out of the car park and got lost in the royal deer park afterwards. When I eventually found a guard post – pop music wafting out from a radio inside it – I was politely invited to drive myself down a short cut towards the proper exit. The relaxed atmosphere could not have been more distant from the starched surroundings of Britain's royal family.

Trailing the king and his offspring for a couple of days, I found him easy-going and hard-working. His style was more presidential than regal. Hands were shaken and backs, occcasionally, given a manly slap. Women were kissed on the hand. He was rather like a man seeking votes. 'The king says they must go out to work daily, to be with the people,' one staffer explained. The king, in other words, knows he must work to keep his popularity. Given his family's history, that is obviously a sensible idea.

Not all is perfect, however, in the life of a man who – by eschewing ostentation and getting down to street level – has avoided the spectacular own goals of other royal families. Occasionally, newspapers or journalists have broken ranks, running rumours about the king's relationships with a number of women.

Does the king's 'enthusiasm for beautiful women' – as one

biographer delicately puts it – matter to Spaniards? Not really. Gossiping is a national pastime. In the birthplace of *¡Hola!* magazine and a dozen competitors (whose enthusiasm for royal scandals seems limited to those of other countries) it is also a large publishing and television industry. Spaniards enjoy the tittle-tattle but are rarely judgemental. 'A Borbón will always be a Borbón,' they say knowingly, referring to the far more colourful lives of previous monarchs. (Isabel II was said to be a nymphomaniac, while Alfonso XIII had three bastard children, one of whom, Leandro Alfonso, was formally recognised as such by a Spanish court in 2003.) It is a different matter, however, when that enthusiasm encourages, in the words of the same biographer, 'attempts at blackmail by financiers'.

Paul Preston, the professor of Spanish history at the London School of Economics, wrote the biography referred to above. He also sheds light on one of those episodes that Spanish writers generally ignore or skirt around in their – almost unanimously adulatory – descriptions of their king. In one of the most tragic moments of a difficult childhood, Juan Carlos shot his own brother dead. Juan Carlos, then seventeen, and fourteen-year-old Alfonsito were playing with a gun in the exiled family's home in Portugal. No clear account of what happened has yet been given. The gun, it seems, was in Juan Carlos's hands when it went off. The bullet from the .22 pistol either bounced off a wall or simply went straight into Alfonsito's forehead. Juan Carlos' father, Don Juan de Borbón, tried to keep his son alive. The wound, however, was mortal. He died a few minutes later. His father wrapped the teenage corpse in a Spanish flag. The incident must have been a key moment in Juan Carlos's life – both in his relations with a father already using him as a pawn in his games with Franco and in the creation of his own personality, which was still in its formative years. 'The incident affected the Prince dramatically. The rather extrovert figure . . . now seemed afflicted by a tendency to introspection. Relations with his father were never the same again,' says Preston.

On a rainy day in Madrid, I was reminded of the republican

blood that seems to boil under the surface of a significant number of Spaniards. I had gone to hire a car. It was a Saturday and much of central Madrid was cordoned off. The king's son and heir, Prince Felipe, was getting married to a television journalist, Letizia Ortiz. To the disgust of some hard-core conservatives, he had broken ranks with tradition. His bride was not just a commoner – granddaughter of a taxi driver – but a divorcee. The wedding ceremony at the Almudena Cathedral looked set to start under a torrential downpour.

It was a sign of the family's chequered history as on-off monarchs that this was the first royal wedding Madrid had seen since the prince's great-grandfather, King Alfonso XIII, married a British princess, Victoria Eugenia, in 1906. That wedding had been marred by an anarchist bomb attack on their carriage that spattered her dress with the victims' blood. Twenty-five years later, in 1931, she would be forced into exile after the Republic was proclaimed. She did not return until 1968, and then only for the baptism of Prince Felipe. She died the following year. Her remains were eventually taken from Lausanne to the royal *pudridero*, literally the rotting chamber, at the sombre, imposing, five-hundred-year-old royal monastery in San Lorenzo del Escorial – where they still await final burial alongside those of other members of the Spanish royal family.

Security for the royal wedding was tight. Police helicopters clattered overhead. City centre metro stations had been closed. Madrid was only too aware of what a handful of determined terrorists could do. Just a couple of months earlier Islamist bombers had killed 191 people in simultaneous attacks on four commuter trains into the city.

The heavens had opened, keeping most people at home. They would watch the wedding of their future monarch on the television. His bride, a former newsreader whose voice they used to hear on state television every day, had hardly said a word in public since they got engaged and she disappeared off their screens. (One newspaper previously reported that a special safe had been bought to lock up her divorce papers.)

Three young men in green company uniforms were sitting behind the counter at the car hire place. 'It looks like the royal wedding is a washout,' I said, making conversation. They sniggered. '*¡Qué se mojen!*' – 'Let them get wet!' – said one. The others sniggered some more. Spain's royal family, I was reminded, was not universally loved.

A poll published in 2005 in *El Mundo* suggested that trouble might be brewing for Spain's monarchy. Almost a quater of Spaniards declared themselves to be republicans. That was fifty per cent more than five years earlier. Nearly forty per cent of eighteen to twenty-nine-year-olds were republicans – slightly more than those who declared themselves to be monarchists. This was despite the fact that very few said they had a poor opinion of the king or his son as individuals.

Juan Carlos oversaw the *Transición*, stopped a coup and gave up the supremacy handed to him as Europe's last old-fashioned, power-wielding monarch. His personal trajectory – from declared supporter of Francoism and its principles to diehard democrat – sums up the *Transición* itself. The *pacto del olvido* was the price one sector of Spanish society, that of the Civil War *vencidos* and their heirs, paid so that Juan Carlos could pull the Francoists into democracy. If the pact, and the silence, is being broken now, it is – at least in part – because most of the latter were so thoroughly converted.

The mechanism may have worked, but it was hardly fair. 'Cancelling out the past was justified as a way of achieving reconciliation. The division born during the Civil War and boosted during the terrible post-war period had to be overcome. Proof that it had not been overcome, and remained latent, was that one side – that of the losers – was forced to forget as a condition for taking part in the new game,' says Morán.

Most Spaniards now believe democracy was somehow inevitable. Spain had become much wealthier. Its traditional class structure was broken down by the move from the countryside to the city. An urban middle class was in place by the time Franco died, ready to demand democracy and make it work.

Franco's legacy has not fully disappeared, though.

One of the things that helped prepare Spain for democracy was tourism. This took off, and then boomed, under Franco. It made an indelible mark on the country that persists today. The pink-skinned tourists brought with them not just money but the mores and attitudes of democratic northern Europe. The wind of change that blew south with the first package tourists was symbolised by something that, when first seen on a Spanish beach, shocked and delighted people in equal proportions – the bikini. To find out just how those two little pieces of cloth had changed Spain, and how the hordes who arrive every summer continue to do so, I would have to head for the beach. The Spanish costas, in all their terrible, garish glory, awaited.

4
How the Bikini Saved Spain

The route along the lower half of Spain's eastern coast has been travelled many times by invaders and colonisers. They have come south from Europe, north from Africa or, in pirate or trading ships, over the Mediterranean horizon. The place names along the coastline that stretches north from the semi-desert of Almería at Cabo de Gata provide constant reminders: from the Carthaginian Qart Hadast, now Cartagena; to the Romans' Valentia and Dianium, now Valencia and Denia; and, in far greater number, to Moorish settlements with names like Alicante (Al-akant) and Alcoy or Benicassim and Beniali.

Driving north from Almería I am reminded, once more, that this is Spain's driest, dustiest corner. Every time I come here, I am shocked by the harsh, unforgiving nature of the landscape. Even Old Castile, with its parched, yellowed plains, has nothing on it. Water is the local gold, fought over by neighbours, villages and towns. The politicians in Madrid invent, and then scrap, pharaonic systems for diverting the rivers of northern Spain down to this parched corner of the country. Ancient irrigation systems, Roman or Moorish in origin, allow the soil to perform the miracle of growing things. The plants traditionally grown here give an idea of the almost biblical nature of the place. There are acid-sweet medlars, almonds, carobs (which supposedly kept St John the Baptist alive in the wilderness) and, inland at Elche, ancient plantations of date palms that transport you straight to the Arabian desert. The mountains here are all rock. They rear up in great, glinting shards or loom, hazy, grey and menacing, in the distant, pulsating heat.

It all sounds very uninviting. Nineteenth-century travellers were advised to skip this part of Spain. But one adventurous

British lady, Mrs Ramsay, came up this coast by train in 1874 and sternly ticked off fellow travellers for choosing 'to pass this lovely country by night'. She found, at least to the north of Valencia, that 'the railway passes close to the sea, which stretches its calm blue expanse away to the horizon; not a sail breaks the loneliness; the ripple washes lazily into sheltered sandy coves; the rocks are covered with heath, *palmitos* (dwarf palm trees), thyme, and all kinds of aromatic herbs; and the stately pines give a peculiar repose to the landscape.' Certainly, the arid climate did not stop this coast attracting the attention of the great Mediterranean cultures. Four centuries before Christ it produced La Dama de Elche, the most spectacular sculpture of the Iberian, pre-Roman culture. The elegant Dama wears what look like elaborately carved cart-wheels over her ears and boasts what must have been the best lips in antiquity.

This is also one of the far-flung outposts of flamenco, where it was sung in local mines. So, I thought, it was still appropriate to have the full, fibrous voice of singer Camarón de la Isla filling the car with, alternately, his pain or *alegría* as I turned north after a long road trip east from Seville. With Camarón keeping me company, the dusty landscape slid quickly past. A few hours later, I was a quarter of the way up the coast, passing Alicante.

A few miles north from Alicante a thin, mysterious, pole-like structure began to emerge over some distant hills. As the kilometres ticked by, it remained virtually unchanged in size. I realised that I must be looking at something a long way off in the distance. Eventually, the pole began to thicken and, cresting one of the hills along this bumpy coastline, I finally realised I was reaching what the Moors called Beni-Darhim (the son, or followers, of Darhim). The gradually broadening shape ahead of me was Spain's tallest building, the Gran Hotel Bali. It stood like a proud, raised finger on the edge of a place whose current name is not only easily recognised, but has become a modern legend of its own – for this, finally, was Benidorm.

If anywhere in Spain symbolises the country's latest invasion, this is it. A fresh invading horde, sun-hat and sandal-wearing northern European tourists, has rampaged its way along this coast over the past forty years. The horde has made Benidorm its capital. This time there has been no resistance. The burghers of Benidorm have rolled out a welcome carpet of concrete, tarmacadam and brick. Jointly they have vandalised what was once one of the most beautiful spots on the Spanish coast.

Even those of us who are instinctively appalled by Benidorm, however, cannot help but be awe-struck by what has happened here. For locals it is a genuine miracle. The closest thing I have to a Spanish family, one side of my partner's maternal family, comes from Tárbena, a village of six hundred people stuck high up in the mountains above Benidorm. The genetic codes of the peoples who surged backwards and forwards across La Marina – as this part was known until a tourism marketing department renamed it the Costa Blanca, the White Coast – are imprinted somewhere in that of my own children.

Tárbena was once a Moorish village whose inhabitants, given no other option except exile from their home of six hundred years, became *moriscos* – nominally Christian converts – after the *Reconquista*. Even that, however, did not save them. In 1609, Felipe III ordered the *moriscos* out of Spain. Today's Tarbeneros are descendants of the seventeen families imported from the island of Majorca to replace them. They still make the same, soft, paprika-flavoured *sobrasada* sausages of the Majorcans and speak a peculiar dialect of Catalan, which is mainly Valencian, but is still coloured by words of Majorcan.

My children's great-grandfather, Salvador Ripoll Martí, was one of many emigrants who left this stretch of the Mediterranean in 1916. He headed to the Americas, building a life for himself in New York and then in his wife's country, Panama. He returned to live out his retirement and, finally, die here in La Marina.

He was buried in the cemetery at Tárbena, alongside his brothers and sisters and the generations of Ripolls and Martís who had eked out a living from the almonds, the oranges, the lemon trees and the medlars of these austere and desiccated hills. It was from this graveyard, during a night-time stroll, that I first set eyes on Benidorm. This was the early 1990s so the Hotel Bali was still just a hole in the ground. But, there below me in the distance, I could make out the glistening, glaring lights of what one Spanish writer refers to as 'the great touropolis'. Its sudden appearance seemed to me to make a dramatic and violent intrusion on Tárbena's otherwise undisturbed, mountain-top calm.

Few in Tárbena would have agreed with me. For Salvador Ripoll Martí's relatives who still live there, and for those who moved down the hill and into the bright lights, Benidorm is a modern marvel.

There is no better symbol of that Benidorm miracle, with all its glaring faults, than the Hotel Bali. Fifty-two floors, 186 metres high, the Bali is at its most spectacular at night, and from a distance. Then it looks like a massive, silver knife, projecting beams of light up into the clouds. By day, close up, it is a dull, grey, concrete and glass giant. 'We kept waiting for them to paint it,' quipped a drinker at one of the Union flag-bedecked, Sky TV and all-day-British-breakfast bars – with names like the Pheasant Plucker, the Jolly Sailor and The Bridewell – that surround it, when I visited.

The building of the Bali was an epic affair. It was put up gradually over fourteen years by a group of local hotel owners who poured their annual profits into it. No loans were taken. The Bali was built on the back of a boom. On good years it rose steadily upwards. On excellent ones it went still faster. That alone made it, by the standards of the construction industry, one of the strangest buildings to have gone up in Europe in recent decades. It is an accurate symbol of modern Benidorm. The Bali is ambitious but pragmatic, big but boring, great but gruesome. It is, in short, what it, and Benidorm, was designed to be – a vast container for package tourism. And Benidorm is to package tourism what Las Vegas is to gambling – the undisputed capital of the world.

As you draw closer to the town from the south, the Bali is joined in the distance by an army of skinny skyscrapers. They look like a hundred matchsticks standing on end. Some are so thin and tall that one wonders whether a strong gust of wind might not blow them down. A typhoon that blew through this plantation of cement poles might, one imagines, leave it looking like a forest after a violent storm, the buildings uprooted and lying on the floor in a jumble, like so many spillikins or jackstraws.

It is also, however, the high-rise capital of southern Europe. Neither Paris, nor Milan, Rome, Athens, Barcelona or Madrid can compete with its 330 high-rises. No wonder locals have dubbed it, in deference to New York, BeniYork. In Europe as a whole it is out-skyscraped only by Frankfurt, Moscow and Greater London. Paris and London are the only places in Europe with more hotel rooms than Benidorm, which has some 38,000. If Spain is a global superpower in tourism – and it is – then Benidorm is the towering symbol of that status.

Staying in the Bali the night after it had opened, I found myself riding up and down its glass exterior lift, drawn to the nosy-parker view of the front rooms of apartments in a dozen other skyscrapers. The lifts here are, on their own, a reminder that modern Benidorm exists for, and because of, foreigners. 'Stand away from the doors when closing,' the lift ordered me, in an English voice which, in my memory at least, had a light Manchester accent. '*Las puertas están cerrando*,' it repeated – the Spanish vowels mashed flat by the very same English voice. A designer who pitched to work on the lay-out of bedrooms told me he was asked to think of 'an English butcher's wife' when coming up with ideas.

Fifty years ago, this was a modest beach-side village, a place of sailors, fishermen and farmers who patiently tended almond, olive, carob and citrus trees. My children's grandmother first came here, on the way to visit her father's village, in the 1950s. She found a three-mile-long, double crescent of almost virgin golden sand and rolling dunes. In those days, the village sat on and around a rocky outcrop that divided the two beaches, Poniente and Levante. Small fishing boats, the *tarrafes*, hung with four large lanterns each to attract fish at night, bobbed in the water or lay drawn-up on the sand. The men often spent months away from home, as sailors, officers or captains on coastal steamers and transatlantic ships or working the *almadraba*, the complicated maze of nets laid out to trap tuna fish. The system of diverting the fish into a small killing zone, the '*cop*', where they could be killed with iron hooks and harpoons, was perfected under the Moors. Archaeological evidence was once found here of pre-Roman jars for storing the valuable oil in which tuna was conserved. The Iberian settlement where the jars were found has now, inevitably, been buried under concrete. Benidorm, like Spain, would rather look forwards than back. A few archaeological remains were hardly going to survive the gold-rush fever of tourism.

The *almadraba* was a massive, complex task, a piece of maritime engineering with more than 1,000 kilometres of rope, netting and cables, fixed by hundreds of anchors, rings and gates, used to create a single maze covering some six square kilometres of sea. The men of Benidorm were *almadraba* experts. They would be called for from as far away as Tunisia and Sicily to lay the nets as the fish migrated south in the early summer and returned north in the autumn. The women, meanwhile, tended the olives, the almonds, the lemons, oranges and carobs.

Benidorm attracted relatively few visitors. In 1950 there were four or five small *fondas*, *pensiones* and hotels for the odd commercial traveller or for families from Madrid or Barcelona who came to spend the summer. A handful of holiday villas belonged to wealthy families from Valencia, Alcoy and Madrid.

'We didn't call it "*turismo*" back then, we called it "*veraneo*", summering. We got the word "tourism" later, from the Swiss,' the man who was mayor in the 1950s, Pedro Zaragoza Orts, told me when I visited him on his eighty-first birthday in Benidorm.

Zaragoza is the father of modern Benidorm. When I met him, this largely unreconstructed Francoist was still fighting fit and a passionate defender of what had happened to his village. To find him, I had needed to negotiate my way through the town centre's bustling, overcrowded streets, following a man dressed in a flowing, spangled blue cape and glittery top hat. The man was steering a perilous-looking vehicle from a driver's seat perched on top of a ladder some fifteen feet above the wheels. A loudspeaker blasted music and publicity for a nearby water park.

Zaragoza's office was tucked at the back of a nondescript, modern arcade, in the small, chaotic town centre. 'I was born here,' he said, pointing to one corner of the office. 'My mother died there ten days afterwards,' he added, indicating another corner. He was pointing to places that, like most of old Benidorm, no longer existed. His old home had been knocked down long ago to build this drab, functional block and, one assumes, make some money for his family.

Zaragoza's appointment as mayor had little to do with democracy and everything to do with the Franco regime. A certificate showing his appointment as provincial head of Franco's Movimiento Nacional sits on the office wall where, when I went to see him, he still did a bit of lawyering.

What Zaragoza has never been, however, is conservative. He is proud of the Moorish and Jewish blood that, he believes, must run somewhere in his veins. He has an almost Messianic view of tourism as a way of promoting understanding between peoples and cultures.

He is also one of the few Spaniards alive to have had an excommunication process started against him. The blame for that lies with the bikini. 'Without asking permission from anyone, I signed a municipal order authorising the wearing of bikinis,' he explained. 'So the archbishop started an excommunication process. In those days, excommunication was a form of civil death. It meant you could not take entry exams for official jobs, nor become a university student. You became a leper in society.'

This was in 1959, when the first fruits of his dream that Benidorm might become a tourist resort were beginning to ripen. Tall, blonde northern Europeans were arriving in their caravans or off the first package holiday flights to Valencia airport. To the dismay of a clergy which already considered beaches a moral danger to the nation, they also wore the, then voluminous, two-piece swimsuits known as bikinis. The Civil Guard would sometimes order them to cover up, especially if a bikini was spotted off the beach. An English woman was fined for slapping a police officer who insisted she put a shirt on.

Zaragoza's friends in high places turned their backs on him when he took on the all-powerful Church. Two government ministers backed the excommunication campaign. So, one day, he got up at 4 a.m., stuffed some newspaper down his shirt to keep out the cold and got on his Vespa. He rode it for the nine hours it took to get to Madrid and went to see Franco.

'He was the only one who helped me. He asked me how I had come, whether by train or airplane, and I said no, on a Vespa. That surprised him,' Zaragoza explained. 'He told me to go back to Benidorm. Eight days later his wife appeared with the Minister of Governance and his wife. They reconfirmed my appointment as mayor, gave me an insignia to wear on my jacket so that I could enter El Pardo (Franco's Madrid palace) whenever I wanted and stayed for four or five days. After that, Franco's wife, Carmen Polo, would come in the spring or the autumn. She would stay eight days, or fifteen days, in my house,' he said. The Caudillo, or at least his wife, became Benidorm's leading patron.

The archbishop got the message. The excommunication process was dropped. The bikini stayed. Some see this, at least symbolically, as a defining moment in recent Spanish history. It marked the beginning of a timid sexual revolution and helped take the Catholicism out of National Catholicism. The tourists, more importantly, had the power to outface the Church. They brought not just money, but the seeds of change. They also brought the fresh air of democracy. There was no turning back.

General Franco was there at the key moment. Without the bikini there, quite possibly, would have been no modern Benidorm and, in fact, precious little tourism at all. At this stage, had Spain not welcomed it, the nascent package tourism could easily have put its roots down elsewhere in the Mediterranean.

Bikinis would eventually make it past cinema censors in 1964. By 1979, with Franco less than four years in the grave, Spain's beaches – and Spanish women – had gone topless. Today even some municipal swimming pools have nudist zones.

Zaragoza's Vespa trips to El Pardo became regular events. 'I would set off early, do things in Madrid in the afternoon and come back that night. That way I only lost a few hours working time,' he said.

Franco, Zaragoza claimed, understood tourism. He would grill him on his ideas, give him the go-ahead, and then send him packing back to Benidorm. Perhaps the generalísimo was conscious that Spain's previous, though somewhat more benign, dictator – General Miguel Primo de Rivera, father of the Falange founder – had also done his bit for tourism by founding the state chain of Parador hotels, in converted monasteries and castles, in 1928.

'But, *ojo*, watch out, I never once asked Franco for anything for myself or for my family,' said Zaragoza. Franco later made him the country's Director General of Tourism. He also went to be a deputy at Franco's rubber-stamp version of parliament. He does not vote in Spain's modern democracy. 'The political parties are too exclusive. They have some good people, but they also have some complete *hijos de puta*, sons of bitches,' he said. 'I am male, from Benidorm, and a lawyer. Those are the things that define me. Not the political parties. The best politics in the world are summed up in the Ten Commandments. Love God and love thy neighbour as thyself.

'People don't know what Franco was like. He was more humane than people say. He was a good father, a Spaniard, a man with clear ideas who could understand any proposal. He was not a fanatic. He treated me very well and I was not easy because I am rebellious and I do not accept everything I am told. I want to know the truth, I am a fighter,' said Zaragoza.

Zaragoza Orts must be one of the last people on earth to view Franco as a social liberal. 'Franco was liberal. That does not mean he was a libertarian. Libertarianism is creating scandal, it is provocation and filth,' he said.

Franco's decision to back Zaragoza and his bikinis came at a time when he was under increasing pressure to ease the iron grip of both Church and State. That pressure would see some relatively liberal advances, including a relaxing of censorship, during the 1960s – though Franco would later regret much of the latter.

We do not know whether he ever regretted letting the bikini

loose. Years later the revolution that started in Benidorm was still inspiring ecclesiastical tub-thumping. Father Aparicio Pellín put it this way in his 1970 tome *The Problems of Youth*: 'Oh! If they erected a black cross on the beach for every mortal sin committed there, the beach would have more crosses than grains of sand!'

In Benidorm, these days, things can occasionally go so far the other way that they get out of hand. I found this out the day Mercedes, who works in the news department of state broadcaster TVE, called me to say that an e-mail being circulated amongst her colleagues was provoking loud, uncontrollable outbursts of laughter. As it involved my *compatriotas* in Benidorm, perhaps I would like to see it?

And so I came into possession of a news article from *Levante*, a serious-minded local newspaper, the contents of which, I was sure, Zaragoza would disapprove. The article quoted from a report by the town's police. At 3.30 a.m. on a hot August night, they had been called to investigate strange noises emerging from Levante beach, in what was referred to as the '*zona inglesa*', 'the English zone'. There they discovered a group of 200 people cheering on the activities of 'a *señorita* and four men, three of whom were penetrating the *señorita*'. Sexual squeamishness not being a Spanish thing, both the police report and the newspaper explained in precise detail how this feat was being achieved. Ages, names and nationalities were dutifully recorded. The fifth member of the group, I was informed, was filming the others while 'waiting his turn to enter into action'.

The police report identified the woman and one man as British, while the others were Swiss and French. They were persuaded to stop what they were doing. No one in the crowd, however, would admit that they had had their *sensibilidad herida*, sensibilities hurt, or would bring charges. Uncertain what to do, the local police patrol bundled the five into their wagons and took them back to the station. The incident, however, was far from over. When the wagon doors were opened, the *señorita* and the cameraman were found to have recommenced the activities interrupted on the beach. They were reaching the peak of their excitement, thereby, in the official words of the police report, 'bringing to an end their brilliant performance'.

Spain is a tourism superpower. It attracts 53 million foreign visitors a year (16 million of them British and 2.3 million of them Dutch). One in twenty come to Benidorm or the rest of the Costa Blanca. More than 11 per cent of Spain's economy runs off tourism. Some of the credit for that has to go to the old dictator. The same families who turned small plots of beachside farming land into hotels in Majorca, the Costa Brava or the Costa del Sol are now building or running resorts from Cuba and Santo Domingo to Jamaica, Bulgaria and Tunisia.

In 1950, still in his twenties, Zaragoza began to draw broad boulevards on the map where only olive and almond trees stood. Benidorm, like much of this coast from Valencia south, had an ancient agricultural watering system inherited from the Moors. But it had no running, domestic water supply. Drinking water was sold by a man with a mule that dragged a huge cask on wheels. Water wheels were still being used to move water in the fields. Waste was carried out of people's houses in buckets and tipped into the sea or onto the earth. 'We asked ourselves what we had. The answer was not agriculture. It was too dry here. But we had the climate, we had our own, liberal temperament – the result of years of sailing the oceans – and we had the sand on the beach,' he explained. 'It had to be tourism.' Little Benidorm – as neighbouring towns like Alcudia or Denia with Greek or Roman pasts like to remind them – did not even have any significant history to sell. One of Zaragoza's first jobs, indeed, was to invent a town shield. Then he got on with the task of inventing what is, in effect, a new town.

Zaragoza claims the transformation of Benidorm, which followed six years of intense planning, was achieved by consensus. He likes to point to the fact that his original fantasy boulevards, eighty metres wide, were eventually halved in size. These boulevards swept imperiously through small plots of land carefully handed down from generation to generation over centuries. Many people thought he was mad. But he piped water in from fifteen kilometres away in Polop – though that took until 1960 and needed a group of fifty-seven villagers to pledge to pay for the loan needed to buy a distant estate with a good well. He got the imaginary boulevards approved and, most importantly, decided that, when it came to fresh building, height would be no block. A piece of land could get planning permission on the basis of volume, of so many cubic metres of building per square metres of land. Zaragoza picked up a book to explain. 'The building volume could be used like this,' he said, laying the book flat. 'Or it could be used like this, or this,' he said, placing the book first on its spine and then, holding it upright, as if sitting on a bookshelf. 'And if they did it that last way, there was space for gardens, for swimming pools, for tennis courts, or for car parking,' he said. The match-stick high-rise was born.

In fact, this may have been more by accident than design. Zaragoza's dream was of a middle-class garden city with small tourist hotels. In 1950, however, a man called Vladimir Raitz founded a travel company on London's Fleet Street which he named Horizon. It took a group of British tourists to Calvi in Corsica in an airliner which, for the first time, was fleeted especially for the passengers. The package tour was born. Second World War Dakotas, lying around unused, were soon pressed into service. By 1953 he was flying people to Spain and took 1,700 of the new 'package tourists' abroad. 'I am pleased by what I have achieved,' he said in 1993, by which time 12 million British people were flying abroad every year. 'But I am upset by what has happened in some destinations.'

Benidorm's defenders, and there are architects amongst them, say this embracing of the high-rise is the key to its success. It was inspired by the same movement that was replacing the bombed-out streets in London, Paris and Berlin with high-rise blocks of flats. It may seem crowded a hundred metres up, but, by the standards of the rest of the Spanish *costas*, it is light and airy on the ground. It also has the advantage, for a tourist resort, of packing a lot of people close to the beach.

And that, after all, is what Benidorm is about. Its high-rises are so many tourist canisters, filled up, flushed out and filled up again, week in, week out. It is an efficient system.

It may be a massive eyesore, but spread those tourists out horizontally – the way they have done in Marbella or, further down the coast from Benidorm, in Torrevieja and numerous other spots – and they go on for ever. If Benidorm, with its twenty-four square miles and 12.3 kilometres of coastline really does account for 5 per cent of foreign holidaymakers (38,000 hotel rooms of some 700,000) in Spain, then, in theory, the rest could be plonked on an island the size of, say, Ibiza. Alternatively, more of them could still be shovelled into little Benidorm – where building land is by no means all used up.

Benidorm's beach is still beautiful. But now you have to hire a top-floor suite at the Bali if you want to appreciate just how majestic those twin curves of gold are. Most visitors are left to glimpse it through a thicket of buildings. The beach is cleaned every night by machines which churn up and filter the sand. This system is now used all over Spain. A recent newspaper report tells how a woman who fell asleep on a beach was swallowed up by one of the machines. A sign in one, older, beachside hotel overshadowed by the Bali, reminded me that Benidorm's reputation for the cheap and shoddy would never quite go. 'Clients are reminded that reception has a special thinner available to help you remove grease or tar from your feet,' it read.

Zaragoza's dream of a pan-European, middle-class holidaying utopia does not quite live up to closer inspection. For Benidorm is, for British tourists at least, a great, and mostly working-class – or lower-middle-class – institution. This is Blackpool, or Skegness, on the Med. It is a nice, warm, familiar, safe place, full of pies and chips, British cooked breakfasts, English drinking holes, Sky television and the sort of entertainment once provided by working-men's clubs. With time, paella and sangria have stopped being exotic. They have simply joined the list of British holiday staples.

I tried walking down Levante beach asking British people why they were there. 'Because I've been coming for seventeen years,' was one reply. 'The comedians in the clubs are great,' was another, referring to the British stand-ups who come here to work the summer season. And, what is more, they truly loved it. In the mid-1990s the town hall managed to find a British couple who had visited seventy-two times. I have never seen it, but I feel sure that somebody, somewhere is selling long, gooey, pink sticks of Benidorm Rock.

Foreign visitors might be surprised to know, however, that this is also a big resort for Spaniards, with a large community of 'ex-pat' Basques and a large number of second homes for those from Madrid. It also has a reputation, amongst Spanish pensioners, for being the best place in Spain for picking up members of the opposite sex.

Benidorm has also become a huge joke. British newspapers occasionally come here to sneer. I know this because, as a correspondent, I have done it too. But I also have a creeping respect for this carbuncular miracle, this slick, garish tourism machine that sells one thing, and one thing alone – the pleasure of a two-week holiday away from the accounts department, telephone sales or the factory floor. No one is forced to come to Benidorm, yet 5 million visitors do every year. When Spaniards think that someone has spotted an opportunity and made the most of it they say he is '*ni tonto, ni perezoso*' – 'neither stupid, nor lazy'. Perhaps that should go as a motto on Benidorm's fake shield.

I asked Zaragoza what he thought of criticism that Benidorm was an ugly blight. 'I don't know if Benidorm is more or less attractive to look at than it was, but it is definitely more liveable,' he replied. 'We have running water, we have asphalt, we have hospitals. We didn't have them before.'

The thought of criticism, however, soon made him angry. The critics, he said, had mostly never set foot in Benidorm. He had heard, on the radio, a town councillor from Marbella warning that that glitzy rich-man's resort on the southern Costa del Sol was going to rack and ruin. 'He had the nerve to say that it was going to end up like Benidorm. I rang him up, but he would not come to the phone. They've got forty wealthy people who go there, and the day they all go off to Morocco – which they might – they are sunk.'

Were there really only forty families in Marbella, I would not have been sitting, a couple of months later, in the traffic jam on the road that runs east-to-west, more or less along the beach, towards Málaga. This is the old Herculean Way. It was used, in ancient times, by travellers from the south. Now it is clogged up by people from all over the world. It ends, or begins, where the twin Pillars of Hercules rear up at the mouth of the Mediterranean. Legend has it that Hercules, busily completing his twelve labours (it was the tenth), travelled along it on his way to steal the oxen of the three-bodied giant Geryon. He put the pillars up as a memorial to his difficult journey. One version of the tale also has him splitting the mountain between them to let the Mediterranean and Atlantic meet. The Pillars are, of course, the Rock of Gibraltar and, at what sometimes seems like spitting distance, Morocco's towering Jabal Musa, where a last offshoot of the Atlas Mountains runs into the sea.

A new toll motorway was opened a few years ago, further up in the hills, but nothing gets rid of this traffic jam. It is as much a part of Marbella's summer as the constant rumours that Saudi Arabia's royal family has decided to make one of its rare visits. The family owns a huge palace complex, which includes a replica of Washington's White House, on what is known as the Milla de Oro, the Golden Mile. The palaces sit, empty and aloof, with the people of Marbella watching anxiously for signs of activity.

In a way, however, Zaragoza was right about the forty families. Marbella has two kinds of summers. There are the normal bonanza years, when the place fills up with minor Spanish celebrities and politicians, with Scandinavian yachtsmen, British golfers, Dutch tennis players, Russian and Italian mafiosi or those seriously, even professionally, devoted to their own tans and scalpel-aided good looks. Then there are the bonanza years when half a dozen Saudi Boeing 747 airliners touch down at Málaga airport. The monarch descends (the former King Fahd, in his wheelchair, used to be lowered on a mechanical goods ramp) and the deluge begins. The rest of what Zaragoza calls the forty families, the immensely wealthy gulf sheikhs and assorted billionaires with mansions here, are likely to follow suit, if they are not already here.

All, suddenly, is excess. On Fahd's final visit in 2002, a fleet of five hundred brand-new Mercedes hire cars appeared on transporters from Germany, just to cope with the needs of his household. Fahd stayed for seven weeks with a retinue of some 3,000 people. Several hundred five- and four-star hotel rooms were block-booked for the period; half a dozen vast, multi-decked, gleaming, presumably teetotal, gin palaces were moored in the port at Puerto Banús; an entire floor of the local hospital, of which he is a generous benefactor, was reportedly placed on standby for the sickly monarch. His visit was said to have injected some 70 million euros into the town. Unfortunately for Marbella, it was only the fourth time he had come here to the palace complex he named An-nada, The Dew. When he died in 2005, the town hall declared three days of mourning.

Marbella is the other extreme of Spanish tourism. If Benidorm is buckets and spades, fish 'n' chips and stand-up comics, Marbella is designer boutiques, ostentatious wealth and the lap-dancing clubs of Puerto Banús. But if Benidorm is, however horrific, a monument to hard work and determination, Marbella, with its triumphal arches, boastful monuments and brash, ornamental opulence, is a monument to corruption and uncontrolled greed. Benidorm blights the landscape, Marbella simply rapes it. Much the same can be said for the rest of the Costa del Sol.

Unlike Benidorm and the Costa Blanca, the Costa del Sol has always attracted visitors. Well before Britain's criminal classes discovered, in the 1960s, that the lack of an extradition treaty made this the perfect hideaway in the sun, adventurous travellers were making their way to the beaches near Málaga. They were attracted by its port and a climate that rarely sinks, even in winter, to below 13 degrees centigrade, (55 fahrenheit). It was, in fact, during winter that visitors from the north would arrive in the 1920s, fleeing the rain-soaked, chilly weather of Britain and the north. Summer tourism was not really invented until the

1950s when, as one contemporary observer noted, northern Europeans began to 'roast themselves on the beach throughout the torrid August days in a way that fills the local inhabitants with concern'. The first tourists, as tourists do, stuck out like sore thumbs. 'The ladies are conspicuous for their hats, shopping-bags, shapeless coiffures, and resolute expressions, features that are all absent from the Spanish woman,' the same commentator, a British woman who had settled here a decade earlier, observed with obvious distaste.

The writer Laurie Lee arrived here in 1934. He was just nineteen and had reached Vigo, in Galicia, several months earlier by boat with just a handful of shillings and a violin. He wandered across the country by foot, occasionally joined by Spanish tramps, busking with his violin, a remarkable journey set out in *As I Walked Out One Midsummer Morning*. Approaching Málaga from Cádiz, he walked along the coast, sleeping on the beach, occasionally immersing himself in the silent sea.

> The road to Málaga followed a beautiful but exhausted shore, seemingly forgotten by the world. I remember the names – San Pedro, Estepona, Marbella, and Fuengirola . . . they were salt-fish villages, thin-ribbed, sea-hating, cursing their place in the sun. At that time one could have bought the whole coast for a shilling.
>
> Far out to sea, through the melting mist, would emerge a white-sailed fishing fleet, voiceless, timeless, quiet as air, drifting inshore like bits of paper. But they were often ships of despair; they brought little with them, perhaps a few baskets of poor sardines. The women waited, then turned away in silence. The red-eyed fishermen threw themselves down on the sand.

In the late 1950s, Torremolinos – just down the coast from here, near Málaga – joined Benidorm, the Costa Brava and Majorca as one of the Meccas of the newly-invented package tourism. Before the Civil War it had been a hang-out for bohemian British and American artists. A retired British major installed himself in the town's Santa Clara castle, pursuing his own eccentric form of spiritual, contemplative endeavour. He eventually gave all his money to the poor and handed the castle over to his gardener's family on the condition that they let him live his final days in a bare, whitewashed room overlooking the sea.

An idea of what has been lost here can be given by two other British travellers. Writer Rose Macaulay stayed at the major's castle, already transformed into a hotel, in 1949. There she met the only English tourists encountered during a long trip around the country. She swam out to sea at night and looked back to see 'here and there, a light'. Nowadays she would see nothing but light. The economist Marjorie Grice-Hutchinson, who lived here with her German farmer husband, rode her horse along the deserted seafront in the early 1950s. She swam on a beach where 'you never see anyone . . . except an occasional coastguard and his dog, and can float for hours on the calm water, revelling in the spaciousness of sea, moor and *vega*, and exulting in the illusion that this vast world was made for you alone.' It was a time, impossible to imagine now, when the sands were thickly studded with pinky-white, strong, sweet-scented *Pancratium maritimum* lillies.

A few years earlier, in Marbella, a German aristocrat and entrepreneur, Alfonso de Hohenlohe, made a bid for the opposite end of the tourism market. He wanted to attract the type of Rolls-Royce-driving travellers who went to Cannes, Nice or Sardinia. He set up a beach club and hotel. Around it clustered new hotels, shops and restaurants catering for the very rich. Marbella grew, slowly and serenely to begin with, then frantically and uncontrollably.

The arrival of Fahd, and the building of his complex of palaces and mosques at El Rocío, sealed Marbella's status as a Mecca for wealth in the 1970s. Uncontrolled greed, and growth, set in. It is still growing today, a fast-expanding sprawl of *urbanizaciones*, erasing everything in their path. Even Hohenlohe would flee the ensuing nightmare.

'If I could destroy the horrors of Marbella, I would do. But I suspect I would need a lot of dynamite,' he said in one of his last interviews. 'Marbella enjoyed a simple sort of luxury, not at all pretentious, something appreciated by cosmopolitans – which does not mean those with most money. Today there are many rich *catetos*, oafs, who do not understand the meaning of sobriety.'

Sobriety is the last word one would associate with modern Marbella. It certainly does not describe the man responsible for the twenty-first-century version of it, the corrupt, medallion-wearing, millionaire property developer, football club owner and all-round thug, Jesús Gil y Gil. Fed up with paying backhanders to previous Marbella town halls while still having some of his property deals blocked, Gil ran for mayor himself with his Grupo Independiente Liberal, or GIL, party, in 1991. He pledged a heavy hand with beggars, bag-snatchers and hippies. He also promised greater freedom to build. Some expected a 'fairer' system of corruption, too. The people of Marbella liked Gil's offer. They repeated over two more elections. 'I am a liberal dictator,' Gil once declared. If ever a people have deserved what they have got, it is the Marbellís – though the original race is now buried, if not under concrete, at least under the weight of Spanish and other immigrants.

Gil was already infamous in Spain. He first hit the headlines when he went to jail in 1969. A hotel he built near Segovia fell down on a conference of insurance agents, killing fifty-eight of them. Gil had tampered with the architects' plans and skimped on construction materials. He later went down on bended knees to beg clemency from a government minister. General Franco's regime freed him after 18 months. Gil eventually returned the compliment by placing a bust of the Generalísimo in the foyer of Marbella's town hall. His political discourse in the 1990s included occasional references to 'Jewish-Masonic plots'. 'I once said that we lived better under Franco and I am now more convinced of this than ever,' he declared a few years before his death in 2004. At local elections in 1999 Gil won 90,000 votes in the Costa del Sol. His area of control spread to the Spanish north African enclaves of Ceuta and Melilla and to other towns between Gibraltar and Marbella.

Gil perfected the system of running a town, and improving his personal fortunes along with those of friends and collaborators, through corruption and speculation. The more or less colourful Costa del Crime British crooks made way for big hitters from

Russia or Italy. Men like Russian Leonid Terekhov, head of Moscow's hard-nosed Medvekovo mafia syndicate, arrived. Guns appeared. Frenchman Jacques Grangeon, a Marseilles drug smuggler, was gunned down with his wife Catherine in their Marbella villa. Tit-for-tat killings came with the laundered cash and no-questions-asked policy at the town hall.

Corruption spread. The chief judge at the local court was forced to leave after it was revealed that her brother, a wealthy Marbella businessmen, was doing deals with the same Italians whose cases were before the court. Her father, meanwhile, turned out to have been the court's senior clerk. Several British people awaiting trial were among those who claimed during the 1990s that they had been told a cash payment would secure a 'not guilty' verdict.

When 15,000 pages of paperwork relating to seven Gil corruption cases involving 60 million euros of municipal funds disappeared from the local court, police went to visit court clerk Francisco Calero at his suspiciously luxurious apartment. While the police were searching his cupboards, Calero ran out of the apartment and up onto the building's roof. Then he hurled himself off. He took Gil's secrets with him. Fear, or shame? Whichever it was, Calero's demise was an example of death by corruption.

Gil's verdict on the court papers being served on him continually was that they were useful to him as *papel higiénico*, toilet paper. Anti-corruption prosecutors from Madrid eventually put Gil in their sights. But the medallion-wearing man whose size saw him nicknamed 'Moby Gil' continued to duck and dive. He threatened, bribed, cheated or simply defeated his opponents in court. He surrounded himself with loyal thugs. My only brush with him was to park beside his, already double-parked, chauffeur-driven car for a couple of minutes at Madrid's Barajas airport. A large, aggressive chauffeur appeared, a suspiciously baggy jacket covering the bulge in his chest. He suggested I might like to move elsewhere. I ignored him and raced into the airport to grab a waiting friend. The look on his face when I came out, however, told me that only the presence of two small children in the back of my car had saved me from serious reprisals.

Eventually, however, Gil was banned from public office. His reaction was to step back into the shadows and appoint others to represent him. One of these, Julián Muñoz, eventually rebelled. Muñoz had ambitions to become a Jesús Gil himself. He was ousted in a town hall rebellion fixed by Gil in which the political parties of those involved seemed to have nothing to do with the way they voted. Some claimed that a rogue British financier, who fled London in the 1970s and made millions on Marbella real estate, was behind it all.

One hot summer's night, I turned on the television set to find Gil and Muñoz involved in their final showdown. This was not being conducted on a politics or news programme but on *Salsa Rosa*. This late-night TV show is normally devoted, loudly and argumentatively, to updating its viewers on the sex lives, affairs of the heart, broken friendships and plastic surgery of second-rate celebrities. Spain has no muck-raking tabloid press. There is no equivalent to Britain's *Sun* or Germany's *Bild*. But there are at least half a dozen of these shows on Spanish television. A similar number of so-called *prensa rosa*, or 'pink press', magazines are for sale on the news-stands. Here the cheque-book confessions of those famous for being famous are gone over in minute and, often, imaginary detail amid shouted bouts of accusation and counter-accusation. All the so-called 'journalists' on this particular programme really wanted to know was whether the reason for Gil's decision to oust Muñoz had been that he could not stand his girlfriend, the folkloric singer and gay icon Isabel Pantoja. She had previously been known as 'the widow of Spain' after her former husband, the matador Paquirri, was gored to death by a fighting bull. But the battle soon got nastier than that. 'You are a *bandido*,' shouted Gil. 'You are a liar and cheat,' spat Muñoz. 'They are both probably right,' commented *El Mundo* newspaper the next morning.

Gil's Marbella is often held up as an example of the perfection of a system of corruption that is a temptation to all Spanish town halls. Most land needs to be reclassified from 'rural' to 'urban' before it can be built on. The power to do that rests with the town hall, which raises a tax on the new buildings and sells licences. Much building land is, anyway, owned by town halls themselves. They are now so dependent on income gained from construction that, if they stopped building, some would lose between fifty and sixty per cent of their income. There may also be a second, underhand tax. This is the one that must be paid to the mayor, the councillor in charge of urban planning, their political party, their pet project, their wife, children, *testaferro* (front man) or whoever. Nobody can say, for sure, how often this tax is raised. Suspicious Spaniards assume it to be commonplace. If that is really so, then an unbreakable cycle is formed. The personal and political interests of both the developer and the politician meet, as do the spending habits (and funding) of the town hall. All they need to do is keep on building.

Stand on the busy beachfront in Marbella, or anywhere along the Costa del Sol, and this soon becomes apparent. The beachside development is moving rapidly up the hills, devouring everything in its path as the chain of cement joins up down the coast. Year after year I have watched the growth and seen the last few islands of green along the coast disappear. Towns have been joined together, like some giant dot-to-dot drawing, by lines of apartment blocks. Where the beach is already blocked, there has been a steady march inland.

The voices of Spain's environmentalists, meanwhile, are drowned out by the sound of cement mixers and pile-drivers. Golf courses have become the latest drain on already scarce water resources. Some eighty-nine of these are projected along the *costas* over the next five years. Each will consume the water equivalent of a town of twelve thousand people, according to the environmentalists.

The building boom is fuelled, in part, by the proceeds of the drug trade with nearby Morocco and, further afield, with Colombia. A recent 250-million-euro police operation against money-laundering saw entire *urbanizaciones* confiscated by the courts.

The result of the boom is a brand new Mediterranean megalopolis, a single stretch of building extending down the coast for a hundred miles, from Nerja in the east to Sotogrande in the west.

Although 1.2 million people formally live on the Costa del Sol, there are actually believed to be some 3 million residents. Many are foreigners with few interests beyond their own house, the golf course and a handful of friends of the same nationality. There is something very American about this car-dependent ribbon of growth as it defies you, like a small Los Angeles, to discover its centre. If it continues adding, as it currently does, almost fifty thousand houses and apartments a year, it will double its population once more in fifteen to twenty years. There are even predictions that the Costa del Sol megalopolis will, eventually, become Spain's largest city. Unfortunately, as the traffic jams show, it is not something that has been planned for.

Jesús Gil is by no means the only corrupt politician to have disgraced these climes. The clearest proof of a link between drug money, politics and *costas* construction came when the Socialist mayor of Estepona, Antonio Caba, was sentenced to five years in jail for helping launder the money of a Turkish heroin-trafficking syndicate. Caba, elected on the promise of cleaning up the alleged corruption of a previous mayor, had, in his private lawyer's practice, helped Turkish drug smuggler Levent Ucler launder more than one million pounds through local real estate. Ucler, at the time, was also under investigation for the murder of his own wife. Little surprise, then, that the voters of Estepona, at one stage, turned to Jesus Gil's GIL party.

Figures for the amount of black cash being laundered in the *costas*' on-off construction booms are impossible to calculate. It includes not just 'white' cocaine and hashish money, but also the 'grey' money of small European businessmen who buy houses with cash never declared to their own tax authorities. It would be nice to think that all this money, wherever it came from, trickled down to the people of the Costa del Sol. But it circulates, instead, in the upper spheres of developers, construction magnates and the comparatively rich, northern European buyers. 'One wonders how a province with the highest unemployment rates and one of the lowest incomes per capita in the country can have the highest rate of business societies per 1,000 inhabitants and a growth of

1,800 per cent in the construction of new private housing in the last five years,' a recent university study asked out loud. The study, produced by a brave few individuals at Málaga University's criminology institute, pointed out that the *costas* were on a ladder of corruption. If nothing was done, they warned, it could lead to the creation of an established mafia economy.

Their report was, however, greeted with almost total silence. Nothing has been done to end the dependency of town halls on builders and, ultimately, on their clients – the tourists. Indeed, questioning tourism in any way at all is met with almost total incomprehension. To ask a Costa del Sol politician whether they approve or disapprove of tourism and construction is to ask a villager in the sierras of nearby Jaén or Córdoba whether they approve or disapprove of olive trees.

At the provincial police headquarters in Málaga I went to see Chief Inspector Fernando Vives, the man who had been searching Francisco Calero's flat when he hurled himself from the rooftop. Vives headed a team of just eight police officers whose job it was to tackle financial crime on the Costa del Sol. 'It is like fighting an army of elephants with a few ants,' he admitted. Some major money-laundering busts since we met suggest either that his ants are working remarkably hard, or that their numbers have been boosted. The impression remains, however, that only the tip of the iceberg has been dealt with.

Vives was a sensitive cop. 'All you can see along the coast are cranes and more cranes. A large part of that money comes from illegal earnings,' he says. 'The Costa's geography – its hills and woodlands – are being destroyed. Nobody imagined it would be like this.'

Vives said the hashish traffic from Morocco alone was at about 350 tonnes a year. The presence of Gibraltar, with twice as many offshore companies as its 29,000 residents, had helped create the opportunities for crime and corruption. The same routes, and the same international gangs, are increasingly turning to cocaine.

The problem is made worse by British and other expatriate residents. Most cannot be bothered to register as citizens of their new home towns, robbing the area of other funds awarded on the basis of how many people live there. Some 300,000 Britons are estimated to live here. That makes this Britain's fourteenth-largest 'city', larger than, for example, Cardiff, Belfast, Southampton or Bradford. However, fewer than one in ten British residents are registered. *Costa* corruption is as much the result of those who come here, enjoy the Spanish weather and hospitality but refuse to accept any responsibility for the place they live in, as it is of crooked politicians and construction companies.

The *Costa* traffic jam seemed so interminable, that I decided to give up on my attempt to reach Málaga on the coastal road. I turned around. I eventually joined, instead, an even worse jam on the motorway that has been sliced through the hills a couple of miles inland. First, however, I decided to try to find a short-cut through one of the *urbanizaciones* whose often gated and guarded entrances are strung along this road. It was a baffling experience. I recognised little that was Spanish here, except the gardens overflowing with bougainvillea and oleander. The array of architectural styles on display was bewildering. There were Moorish palaces, huge great Basque *caserios*, Mexican *haciendas*, rows of nondescript three-storey terraced hutches, gleaming glass and stainless steel modern apartment blocks, low-slung bungalows and wood-built houses straight out of the Swedish forests or the Canadian prairie. American-style condominiums, and golf courses, were sprouting up in the surrounding countryside. This, one visiting American journalist observed, was a place 'whose gaudy architecture makes Beverly Hills look staid'.

I felt lost. It was not just because I could not find a way back out of this maze – which turned out to have only one entrance, preventing any through road spoiling the residents' peace while making no contribution to unsnarling the chaos on the coastal road. Eventually, I decided that I was not in Spain any more. This was really the outer suburbs of a coastal city in Florida, Australia or any of the white-dominated suburbs along South Africa's Indian Ocean coast. It was, essentially, a new place. It had been invented out of nothing and answered to nothing more than its residents' desire to live a life of leisure.

Spain is a country of small, tightly packed towns, cities and villages. Spaniards like to live piled up on top of one another. Their natural meeting place is the crowded street, the busy bar or the plaza. It is a life of close physical contact, of loud, sociable bustle. Benidorm, at least, has that. But here the only place people can be seen, tanned and blonde, is in their cars, as they head for the tennis club, the golf course or the out-of-town shopping centre, the new Spanish malls. Even the narrow beach, although busy, seems to be a minority interest. Its role has been replaced by tens of thousands of swimming pools – adding to growing problems with water.

This, however, is the new model for Spanish tourism, and not just on the Costa del Sol. Package tourism, the gold mine on which Benidorm was founded, is giving way to budget airlines and on-line booking of private villas. The money that changes hands often does not even come to Spain or pay a tax to help build the roads or water recycling plants. The *urbanizaciones*, some expensive, some full of hurriedly put up, shoddy 'villas', are sprouting up from Majorca to Marbella, from Torremolinos to Torrevieja. Many are ghost towns in winter, their restaurants and shops closed and their houses barred up.

In Benidorm, the editor of the English-language daily newspaper, the *Costa Blanca News*, told me that a friend of his had gone house-hunting to a new *urbanización* in a nearby town. He saw a man working in his garden and stopped to talk to him. The man turned out to be English. 'Are there many foreigners here, then?' the friend asked. 'No, not really. There is one Norwegian, but the rest of us are British,' came the answer. It had not occurred to him that British, in Spain, meant foreign.

I find the package holiday tourist at Benidorm, or the drunken 18–30 revellers battling their way up and down the streets of Ibiza's San Antonio district easier to understand than these new, semi-permanent immigrants to the *costas*. I know package holidaymakers are here for the fun, for cheap booze, to watch their kids play with buckets and spades and to shed their normal skin for a while or, at least, to change its colour. They seek a temporary transformation, a chance to forget the humdrum of their normal lives.

But the residents of the *urbanizaciones* feel to me like a different tribe, as strange as the Visigoths, the Moors or the Vandals must have been when they first arrived on the Iberian peninsula. I realise there is an element of possessiveness, even arrogance, in this. Having, however, made repeated attempts, and repeated failures, at understanding this tribe, I eventually turned to someone better equipped for interpreting the social structures, belief systems and rituals of other peoples – an anthropologist.

It was years since I had read an anthropology book, so I was excited to get my hands on Karen O'Reilly's *The British on the Costa Del Sol*. O'Reilly had followed the great traditions of Bronislaw Malinowski, Margaret Mead, Evans-Pritchard and Pitt-Rivers in immersing herself in the world of her strange and exotic subject. This was to be 'ethnographic research involving long-term participant observation'. But, instead of choosing to live amongst the Trobriand Islanders, the Nuer of the Sudan or the natives of Papua New Guinea, she had disguised herself as an ex-pat on the Costa del Sol. Where others had mud huts, canoes and pig-swapping ceremonies as their raw material, O'Reilly had the Royal British Legion, timeshare touts and the Anglican church coffee mornings in Fuengirola. Her hardships included sitting through an Old Time Music-Hall sing-along and hearing people insist that the ten-year-olds who murdered two-year-old Jamie Bulger should, themselves, be stoned to death.

Her research turned out to be depressing. The Brits came to Spain to get away from a country they saw as rotten with crime, immigration, broken communities and a failing health service. They fooled themselves that they were living a Spanish lifestyle, but spoke little or no Spanish and remained in their ghettoes. Some, after more than a decade, spoke fewer than twenty words of Spanish. 'They . . . retain the Little Englandism, the isolationist tendencies, the island mentality, the "natural" racism or nationalism of *Great* Britain, while denying that they do,' she concluded. They were, she decided, 'betwixt and between'. She might have said 'neither here, nor there'.

Where the *urbanizaciones* are not graveyards in the winter, it is often because those living there are, themselves, close to the grave. Again, Spain has become America or, at least, Florida. It is the last refuge of a greying population, come to stretch their northern European pensions, and their final years, in the sunshine and supermarkets of the costas. In some places they now out number the local population. Whereas those who install themselves in France's Dordogne or Italy's Tuscany often do so in a spirit of cultural inquisitiveness, these people seem to have been attracted only by sunshine.

There are noble exceptions. Spain's first hospice, built outside Málaga, is a tribute to its British founder. Torrevieja football club has a loyal British following, 'the Torry army'. It is almost impossible, however, to find a place where, as a group, the new colonisers have provided anything more than money.

In a last-gasp attempt to find some new immigrants who were actually involved in the place they lived, I went to Teulada, a small town just a few miles from the coast, half an hour's drive north of Benidorm. As I headed for the town hall, I passed a shop front that boldly proclaimed: 'Funeraria, Undertakers, Bestattungsinstitut'. I popped in. These days, owner Pepe Vallés explained to me, people in Teulada and its coastal hamlet, Moraira, die in at least three languages. Shipping corpses home to Britain, Germany and the rest of Europe now accounted for a third of this happy undertaker's income. 'Most are already quite elderly when they get here,' he said. 'Generally they want to be cremated.' It was, he explained, the cheapest option.

In Teulada, more than a third of the 6,000 names on the electoral register are foreign, most of them British. This will soon rise to more than half. As a result, a community whose history can be traced back before the thirteenth-century Christian kings snatched it from the Moors must now learn to cope with a new – some say devastating – sort of conquest. For here, the ex-pat community, tired of their villas overlooking the sea at Moraira being placed at the bottom of the municipal list of priorities, have organised themselves politically. They have, in effect, won control of the town hall.

The villa owners had brought with them a thoroughly British, 'not in my backyard' approach to development. As soon as their own villas were completed, they did not want any more to go up, spoiling the view or the gentle countryside, neatly laid out with low vines, running down to the sea. They had put a massive brake on further development, electing a Spanish mayor who knew his job was to say 'No!' to the succulent proposals put his way by developers. The mayor held separate meetings for them in English, German and French.

Teulada immigrants were obviously getting involved. That, however, did not please everyone. I found a local town councillor, Vicente Marzal, looking depressed. He had just formed the People for Teulada Party to fight the next elections on what could only be described as an anti-immigrant ticket. His complaints were the familiar stuff of changing European communities from Bradford to Marseille. 'People call me racist, but I ask the foreigners whether they would like it if a Turk was running the town hall where they come from and most agree with me,' Marzal said. 'Very few of them speak Spanish, let alone our dialect of Valencian. I don't understand it; they live with us but don't want to speak our language. They don't do anything to integrate.'

The immigrants were setting up English butchers and German pastry-shops. A ghetto mentality had set in, he said. 'They stick together and have their own bars and shops. If you go into one, they look at you strangely. That's not the way we do things here. We leave the door open to everybody.'

Deputy mayoress Sylvia Tatnell, half-British and half-Spanish, defended the immigrants. 'It is very difficult for elderly people to learn a new language,' she said. 'But if you go to the Moors and Christians Festival you will find a third of those taking part are foreign.'

A few weeks later, at midnight on a summer's evening, I was standing amongst a crowd of people looking out at the beach in

Moraira. We were here to watch part of the Moors and Christians Festival that Tatnell had wanted me to see. These are celebrated throughout Alicante and date back more than three centuries in some places. Groups of townsfolk form *filas*, or groups, of either Moors or Christians. Once a year they dress up and 're-enact' the conquest of Spain by the Moors in 711 and the Christian *Reconquista* that ended in 1492.

Tonight the Moors were invading, or at least, a handful were arriving on the beach in a couple of local fishing boats backed up by a small yacht, while a hundred more awaited them on the beach. The Christians, meanwhile, had taken up position on the natural, exposed rock ramparts of the fortress. All were dressed in exotic outfits that seemed to have come from the wardrobe department of the 1961 Hollywood version of *El Cid* – the Christian men doing their best to look like Charlton Heston, the women like Sophia Loren's strong-willed Ximena.

Elaborate firework displays feature heavily in local fiestas across Valencia and up into Catalonia. Tonight was no exception. Nobody in Moraira could have slept as the noisy battle raged. A bloodied El Cid character wandered across the beach on a horse – past the lifeguards' chair that had been left centre-stage – and fell off, mortally wounded, at the foot of the castle ramparts. A loudspeaker played ersatz Arab music full of trumpets, timpani, horns and wailing chants. Not a cliché was missing. The Moors got down on their hands and knees and prayed. Then a troop of dancing girls wearing semi-transparent gauze dresses came on and did a seven veils number that was all bare bellies and gyrating hips. The Christian and Moorish kings exchanged gruff, manly, melodramatic lines over the PA system.

'Identify yourself or I will give you a hiding,' blustered the Christian. 'I am the chief of the all-victorious Moorish horde . . . My hand is impatiently stroking the handle of my sword,' the Moor replied. History never got more kitsch, but the sun-tanned crowd was enjoying it.

A middle-aged British couple beside me were passing comment. 'Oooh! Do we have a disagreement?' the wife said as the protagonists strutted angrily on the sand. Then a dead Christian tumbled down the ramparts. 'Oh dear, is he rolling down those rocks?' asked my neighbour. 'That's not very comfy, is it?'

Eventually, the Moors won their battle amid amplified shouts of 'Ala is great! Ala is victorious!' The Christians shuffled off and the PA system announced: 'Thank you for coming to the night-time invasion of Moraira. Tomorrow at 7 p.m., the *Reconquista*.'

The crowd filed back into town. A pile of fresh vomit on the pavement made me think that the British must be here in force (Spaniards hold their drink). A group of ten-year-old children, meanwhile, threw little bangers at one another and squealed in delight in the square at 1.30 in the morning. They were a reminder that I was in the province of Alicante and was not likely to get much sleep.

Still, I was impressed with the Moraira immigrants. By getting involved with their adopted land, they had ensured that this was a much nicer spot than virtually anywhere else I could find on the *costas*. The new immigrants are lucky that Spaniards show no real animosity. (Marzal's party in Teulada failed to win any seats). This is despite the fact that, at least in the early days, Málaga's psychiatric wing for young people quickly filled up with stressed-out waiters. A 1971 study recorded that 90 per cent of non-chronic mental illness in rural Málaga was amongst teenage boys who had gone to work on the *costas*. In moments of gloom, Spaniards sometimes refer to themselves as 'the waiters of Europe'.

When Spaniards want to laugh at tourists they call them '*guiris*'. One humorous definition described the British sub-species as: 'Famous for their punctuality, they can be counted on to start singing football chants after just five minutes of drinking, and start head-butting everything in sight.' Little has changed, then, since Sir Edward Cecil led an ill-fated strike against Cádiz in 1625. He was forced to flee after his troops got so staggeringly drunk in a particularly well-stocked *bodega*, or wine-cellar, they had captured that they were unable to fight.

A serious study of *guiris* was carried out by anthropologist Nadja Monnet. She found that they 'provoke laughter, are subject to jokes and can be easily fooled'. Perhaps that was what happened to George Sand when she fled to Majorca with her lover, the composer Frédéric Chopin, and her two children in 1838, looking for 'some faraway retreat where there would be no notes to write, no newspapers to peruse, no callers to entertain'.

It seemed to work for Chopin, who completed his Preludes here. Sand, however, never worked up much appreciation for the Majorcan peasant. 'Though he would never rob his neighbour of so much as an olive, he believes that in God's scheme of things the only use for human beings from overseas is to bring the Majorcan nice little profits,' she recorded in *A Winter In Mallorca*. Little did she, early tourist as she was, know that those profits would, eventually, make the Majorcans amongst the wealthiest people in Spain – or turn parts of their island into little outposts of Germany. Nor could she have foreseen that Majorcans, scared by soaring property prices and seeing traditional, rural culture under threat, would be the first Spaniards to take to the streets to protest at some of the results of their self-created tourism boom.

Quite what will happen to the Majorcas, Marbellas and Benidorms of Spain, no one can tell. The package holiday is in crisis. Cheaper rivals, meanwhile, are appearing in Tunisia, Turkey and elsewhere. There is talk of blowing up old hotels, or converting them into apartment blocks. Meanwhile, a whole new generation of euro-Spaniards, children of foreign couples studying at local schools, is growing up on the *costas*. Already one finds them manning bars and selling real estate, slipping easily between one culture and another. Some families moving out of London are choosing Marbella as their base, rather than Essex or Wiltshire. Freelance parents work from home or weekly commute back to the British capital from Málaga airport. Britons own 450,000 properties and are said to be buying upwards of 30,000 *costa* homes a year. One report said to be circulating amongst property developers suggests that 800,000 Germans wish to retire to Spain. The waiters of Europe look set to become Europe's geriatric nurses. Whatever happens, the revolution that started with

Benidorm and its bikinis is bound to bring even more, huge changes.

Dirty money and corruption are part of the price Spaniards pay for the wealth the tourists bring. The danger, as those Málaga University investigators pointed out, is if they spiral out of control and give rise to a mafia economy. Spain has a recent history of flirting with the kind of deep corruption that can shake the state itself. It has also shown, however, that it knows when to pull back. Two contradictory impulses, both very Spanish, are at play. They are anarchy and order. The struggle between the two has, on occasions, been titanic.

5

Anarchy, Order and a Real Pair of Balls

It is August. Most of Spain has shut down for the traditional month of holidays. So we are sitting beside the swimming pool at Carlos's house in Sanlúcar de Barrameda, where the broad, muddy Guadalquivir River runs into the Atlantic near Cádiz. The kids are splashing in the water. There is a bottle of cold manzanilla wine on the table. Several more are chilling in the fridge. The Spanish rap of '*La Mala Rodríguez*', 'The Bad Girl Rodríguez', is blaring out of his music system. A mountain of shrimps await their turn to be torn into with sticky fingers. They are to be dunked into the mayonnaise Carlos is making, the mixer in one hand and the phone wedged between ear and shoulder as his mother gives step-by-step instructions from Madrid. Spaniards, I am reminded once more, take their leisure – and their food – seriously. Their mothers, as always, are on hand to help. Life could not be much better.

Carlos, however, is still working. He has just set up his own company designing, amongst other things, corporate newsletters. The mayonnaise done, his mobile phone goes. He looks happy. A big client has just come his way. The woman in charge of corporate communications at a major company has made clear, however, what she wants in return. 'It's great,' he says enthusiastically, after hanging up. 'I'll do all their magazines. All I have to do is employ her son. He wants to be a designer. I'm sure I'll find something for him to do. Even if he's useless, it will be worth it.'

They call it *enchufe*. It is the art of being 'plugged in' – of having, cultivating and using contacts. It is not generally as crude as this. At its best, in fact, it is invisible – a subtle and apparently inoffensive use of one's address book, or especially, one's network of siblings, cousins, aunts and uncles.

I have tried to resist it, but either it is not that easy or I am not that strong. A residual and, friends assured me, absurdly exaggerated sense of fairness initially held me back from full use, or abuse, of my contacts in my early days in the Spanish capital. In Madrid, they insisted, only losers try to remain above it. This, after all, was the capital of *enchufe* – a place that had centuries of experience of handing out, or demanding, favours from kings, ministers or governments. What is more, they added, I was a journalist. I had *enchufe* by the bucketful.

Then we bought our flat, installed a new gas boiler and waited for the gas company to switch on the supply. An inspector came. There were new regulations, he explained. We would have to knock a larger hole in our kitchen wall – a place for excess gas fumes to escape from – if we were to be connected. Our existing hole was now too small. That afternoon I got a chisel and hammer and widened it myself.

I rang the gas company and told them we had fixed the problem. When could they send the inspector back? 'Soon,' they said. We waited, and waited. Days went by, then we started counting weeks. The weather got cold. Both the boiler and the cooker worked off gas. Our children's baths got colder. We lived off microwaved food. The children's noses ran. As Madrid's icy winter set in, I rang daily. 'You are on the priority list,' a voice repeated down the phone. I tried losing my temper. I demanded to talk to a superior. But to no avail. The voice just hung up. The inspector never came.

I finally recalled that journalists, the sort of people whose written words might affect a company share price, have *enchufe* at stockmarket-listed utility companies. I rang the gas company's press office. I made it sound as innocent as possible. I was only looking for advice, I said. Could they suggest how I might set about solving my problem?

Two hours later the doorbell rang. The inspector, and his assistant, had come. 'We're here to connect you,' they said cheerily. Within minutes the job was done. I do not remember them looking at my carefully widened hole. I was pleased with myself, though. I had solved the problem. My partner, however, was not so happy. 'If it is that easy, why didn't you do it earlier?' she asked.

That was my conversion to *enchufe*. I tried saving it for emergencies, but after a while it just came naturally. A few weeks later I found myself standing at the Iberia airlines desk at Málaga airport after a long, difficult day's work. I wanted to get home to Madrid. I had, foolishly, lost the return half of my ticket. The clerk behind the counter, I soon realised, was not going to give me a new one. I rang a contact at head office. A few minutes later the clerk was obligingly issuing the ticket.

So I found myself asking people to put a word in for me here or ring friends of friends for favours and introductions there. I, in turn, would offer up – or be asked for – my help. A word with the headmaster, to see if a friend's child can get into our over-solicited school? Seats at the theatre when it is sold out? Just pick up the phone and ask. Sometimes it works, sometimes it does not. If you do not try, however, you will never know.

Enchufe is not without its enemies. One Spanish website, run by the so-called Publicity, Equality, Merit and Capability group, PIMYC, as it is known for short, roots out *enchufe* in the jobs-for-life world of public employment. For every person who gains by *enchufe*, it points out, there is another who loses. It lists offspring, friends and relatives of politicians who do surprisingly well when sitting *oposiciones*, the exams that are set for everyone from library assistants to judges. Even the armed forces are, according to one current case, suspected of it – the sons of several air force generals being unfairly booted up the ranks, according to the complainants.

Is *enchufe* a form of corruption? In the strict, moralistic, *anglosajón* sense, it is. It keeps those already in the loop, inside it. It stops those outside from getting in. When outright cheating is involved, it is obviously corrupting. 'The tradition of nepotism, cronyism and of a subterranean market in mutual favours is one of the features of the lowest Spain,' says *El País* columnist Rosa Montero.

Not being given to moral absolutes, however, a little bit of cheating does not generally rate high on the list of things Spaniards care about. It is there at bullfights, where rumours of doped animals with their horns shaved off abound. It is a feature of exam time, in the form of the *chuleta* – the crudely hidden list of vital facts. It is there, too, when parents fill out their application forms for school places. These are said to be full of borrowed addresses and fake, point-winning illnesses diagnosed by friendly doctors. It is, of course, also there in the *declaración de la renta*, the annual tax return. Even literary awards (and Spain has some of the biggest, with the Planeta prize handing out 601,000 euros) seem to be affected. Like *enchufe*, however, all this is not really frowned on. It is, rather, seen as a bit of sporting rule-bending.

Chancers and adventurous rule-breakers have always intrigued, or been admired by, Spaniards. A whole genre of writing, the picaresque novel, emerged in the seventeenth century with stories of heroes who had managed to cheat their way through life – with Francisco Quevedo's *La Vida del Buscón*, usually translated as *The Swindler*, the most famous example. '*Queremos comer sin trabajar*', 'We want to eat without working', was how one writer expressed the *pícaro*'s dream.

As I thought about corruption one day, a Barcelona woman came on the radio to talk about why her apartment block was about to be bulldozed. The building, along with several others, was threatening to collapse into a new metro tunnel dug underneath it. It seemed that not enough cement had been used. This, in turn, was because project money had allegedly been raked off to pay bribes. The Catalan regional premier had already claimed that builders routinely paid a 3 per cent commission to his predecessor. Asked if she believed that, the woman gave an answer many Spaniards would have provided: 'I always assumed that people took a cut.' Even she did not seem scandalised.

The main corrupting power in Spain is what, generically, has become known as '*el ladrillo*' – 'the brick'. The phenomenon is by no means restricted to the *costas*. As Spain's economy booms, towns and cities have been turned into vast building sites. The building of new homes, office blocks, EU-funded motorways or other public works is being done on a scale unthinkable in cluttered northern Europe. Everywhere you look in Spain, the city skylines are crammed with cranes. Vast new barrios appear almost overnight in Madrid, complete with their shopping malls, sports centres and underground stations. Tiny satellite *pueblos* become, in the space of just a few years, busy new towns. Massive bulldozers push new motorways through olive groves as bewildered elderly villagers look on, and their grandchildren calculate whether they can now go for nights out in the nearest city.

The People's Party regional government that came to power in Madrid in 2003 owed its existence to a scandal – and internal split – which prevented the Socialists from forming a government. Many people in Madrid are convinced that the succulent profits and under-the-counter payments for building licences provoked an otherwise inexplicable rebellion by two newly-elected Socialist deputies. As is usual in these cases, however, nothing was proven. In Seville, meanwhile, the Socialist mayor is trying to explain how a major builder close to his party managed to be paid for several public buildings that were never erected.

Catalonia, Madrid, Seville and the Costa del Sol account for much, if not most, of Spain's new building work. Where politicians are builders, as they often are in the Costa del Sol, corruption seems inevitable. Where they are also football club owners, as some also are, then corruption, for some reason, seems even more likely.

Things could be a lot worse, however. Compared with the deep, institutionalised corruption in, say, Italy, Spain is a clean country. For while corruption – or the popular belief in it – floats freely around regional and local government, it has not settled in the core of the Spanish state.

It could, however, have been all so very, very different. For there was a time when corruption came close to tearing the country apart. It was a time when Felipe González's Socialist governments – in so many other ways a shining, brilliant success – began to split at the seams. Socialist corruption was not just a question of a few missing millions. It was also, as the victims of police-backed death squads operating against Basque radicals would find out, a matter of lives and deaths.

The fact that this corruption never became institutionalised was due to the combined efforts of judges, journalists and straight cops. One man, however, stood out. Baltasar Garzón, known as the *superjuez*, the super-judge, is Spain's most controversial, crusading magistrate – the country's answer to the Clean Hands judges of Italy. He is a distinguished, if self-loving, torchbearer for those other Spanish values – nobility, fairness, valour and justice – that, in a somewhat more deranged fashion, Don Quixote de la Mancha preached. He is, like all heroes, imperfect. Vanity, arrogance, ambition and a weakness for the eye-catching gesture all contribute to a large Achilles heel.

The son of a small farmer turned petrol-station attendant from Jaén, Garzón became one of the youngest magistrates of the all-powerful Audiencia Nacional court in 1988. A meteoric and controversial career has seen him take on everything from state-sponsored terrorism and ETA to international drug-trafficking and former Latin American military strongmen like Chile's Augusto Pinochet. An ability, often deliberate, to get himself into the limelight, means that his name is familiar to Spaniards of all origins and classes. A devoted following fights, yearly, to get him awarded a Nobel Peace Prize

Perhaps his finest attribute, however, is to generate the sort of bile and anger that Spain often reserves for its greatest sons. He is, in a great Spanish put-down that has much to do with envy, accused of the cardinal sin of *buscando protagonismo,* seeking to be a protagonist. The fact that this accusation comes from across the political spectrum – in a country where the tendency to join one political tribe or another leaves few true independents – only adds to his allure. Envy is one of those features that Spaniards, in moments of introspection, consider one of their worst weaknesses.

'I will never join in the Gregorian chants intoned by the high priests of envy. This is a sly country where we not only mind doing things but we mind other people doing things too, because they show us up,' the writer Francisco Umbral said, defending

Garzón. 'So what if he seeks *protagonismo*? Only those who seek to be protagonists move history.'

Garzón's greatest service to preventing the spread of corruption through official Spain was his determination to prove state involvement in a police-run dirty war that claimed twenty-seven lives. That dirty war was fought against ETA, though a third of the victims – who included an elderly French shepherd, a teenage girl and a couple of gypsies – had nothing to do with the group. It was carried out by an outfit that called itself the Grupos Antiterroristas de Liberación, popularly known as GAL. The group was founded and funded by the interior ministry under Felipe González's Socialists. It used Portuguese and French mercenaries to carry out the attacks. González professes that he was never told what was going on. His most famous comment on the affair was: 'The rule of law is defended in the courts, and in the salons, but also in the sewers.' There was, he implied, nasty work to be done down there.

An investigating magistrate is someone who, by British standards, wields extraordinary power. He does not conduct trials, but prepares them. It is his job to help co-ordinate the police inquiry, decide whether there is a case to be answered, decide which suspects should be jailed or bailed and, eventually, whether they should be charged. To that extent he is, in the initial stages of a case, not just judge but also prosecutor and policeman. An appeal process is there to make sure the *magistrado* does not abuse that power.

For a *magistrado* in the Audiencia Nacional – an unremarkable looking modern office block across from the Supreme Court – the power is even greater. For this is where Spain's biggest cases end up. It has always given me a thrill to visit it. Sitting around in its nondescript landings, waiting for a chance to speak to this or that judge or public prosecutor, I have rubbed shoulders with some of the nation's greatest villains. Drug barons, crooked bankers, British murderers awaiting extradition, Italian mafiosi and ETA gunmen wander by with their handcuffs and police escorts. The more interesting trials happen in a basement courtroom shielded off from the public by bullet-proof glass.

The Audiencia Nacional is where the young Garzón, still just thirty-two years old, began an inquiry in 1988 into two police officers, Michel Domínguez and José Amedo. The two officers were involved in hiring mercenaries to carry out bomb attacks, shootings and kidnappings of suspected ETA members. The killings had mainly taken place on French soil, and in the first few years of the Socialist government.

Garzón was a new kind of *magistrado*: an outsider, working-class, instinctively left-wing and arrogantly aware of his own abilities and the importance of his job. The Audiencia Nacional had, in 1977, replaced Franco's Tribunal de Orden Público – the court that gave the persecution of political opponents its legal gloss. TOP's remit had been 'to try crimes which show a tendency to subvert, to a greater or lesser degree, the basic principles of the state, disturb public order or sow anguish in the national conscience.' Some of the Audiencia Nacional's first judges and prosecutors moved straight from one court to another. 'They didn't even wait the usual three days to rise from the dead,' according to one observer. The new democratic regime, however, needed judges and prosecutors to administer justice. It had to turn to those who knew how. People who had once pledged to 'serve Spain with absolute loyalty to the Caudillo' and observe 'strict loyalty to the principles of the Movement and other Fundamental Laws of the Kingdom', joined the new upholders of democracy. Several would later reach the Supreme Court.

Garzón was the latest shot of fresh blood to be introduced into the system. If his superiors expected another 9 a.m. to 3 p.m. functionary of the '*Vuelva Vd mañana*', 'Come back tomorrow', bureaucratic fashion so caustically described by the nineteenth-century Madrid chronicler Mariano José de Larra, they could not have been more wrong. Garzón's father had driven into him the idea that, to get on, 'you have to see the sun rise'. Garzón was not just ambitious and clever, but hard-working and obstinate. Even now he is by no means typical. Some judges still work mornings at their court and then earn money, cash in hand, in the afternoons – coaching people for law exams. 'They never ask whether this is compatible (with their role as a judge) or declare what they earn to the tax authorities . . . These are *secretos a voces* that nobody tries to do anything about and, presumably, nobody will,' says Garzón. A little bit of rule-breaking, it seems, can be tolerated, even amongst those who watch over the nation's rules. Perhaps that is why, as Garzón also says, there is still a worrying amount of '*desidia, desinterés y desmotiviación*' – 'laziness, lack of motivation and lack of interest' in a sluggish court system that can take more than a decade to resolve a case.

When Garzón eventually took evidence from Domínguez and Amedo, they appeared with a lawyer paid for by the Interior Ministry. Garzón shocked the González government by jailing them.

The GAL scandal was slowly exposed by a number of newspapers and by a handful of police officers working with Garzón. The Socialists fought dirty, however, and not just against ETA. The controversial young editor of *Diario 16* newspaper, Pedro J. Ramírez, was sacked as a result of his newspaper's GAL coverage.

After both had appeared on television, Interior Minister José Luis Corcuera issued the following warning, according to the version provided by Ramírez's new newspaper, *El Mundo*: 'You feel sure of yourself because you are the editor of a newspaper – but you may stop being so very soon.' Corcuera was right. *Diario 16* bowed to government pressure and sacked him – a move that started a decline that would eventually see it disappear altogether. Ramírez went on, within just a few months, to found *El Mundo*. From there he doggedly maintained his pursuit of GAL and the Interior Ministry. One of the highlights came when two of his reporters dug up a GAL arms cache in a place known as the Col de Corlecou, in south-west France. The cache included pistols, photographs from police archives and ammunition used by the Spanish police.

The GAL campaign was, at least partially, paid for with *fondos reservados* – a multi-million-peseta secret fund with no accounting. Money was handed out, in brown envelopes or by the briefcase, at the discretion of senior ministry officials. The funds were, it turned out, not just used to pay for a dirty war but also to provide double salaries to some ministry officials. Jewels and gifts were bought for their wives. In generous monthly payments, it was also buying the silence of Amedo and Domínguez. Some lined the pockets of ministry officials. The GAL affair, in fact, was just the visible part of an iceberg-full of corruption in the interior ministry.

The mid-1990s was an extraordinary period in Spain. The scandals came so thick and fast – each one seemingly more incredible than the one before – that it became difficult to keep up. Amongst the most startling revelations was that one of the biggest thieves in the land was none other than Luis Roldán – the Socialist chief of the Civil Guard police. Roldán had bought himself apartments, country estates, cars and girlfriends with money from *fondos reservados* or with bribes from builders wanting contracts for new Civil Guard barracks. 'How could anyone have suspected that the parish priest would have turned out to be a brothel owner?' Corcuera commented, in his party's defence, when the Roldán scandal broke. Soon after that it was revealed that the governor of the Bank of Spain was keeping secret, tax-opaque bank accounts. Even the *Boletín Oficial del Estado* – where the formal decisions of government are published – was being printed on corrupt paper, its director having taken bribes from paper suppliers. At the same time the Socialist party was shown to be taking – or demanding – illegal contributions from major companies. A network of front companies helped launder these 'contributions'. The party's finance chief kept some for herself. The money helped build a refrigerated wardrobe for her fur coats. In a sign that all parties were involved in the same dirty game, there were calls from all sides for the first Socialist to be caught in a two-million-dollar illegal funding scandal to be immediately pardoned. 'The sooner we turn the page on this matter, the better it will be for all of us,' said one Basque nationalist politician.

Some blamed the political version of *enchufe* for this. In 1988 the Socialist party estimated that forty thousand of its members, one-third of the total, occupied 'institutional posts'. Most of these were elected officials, but the rest were simply political appointees. It is a system, still in existence today, that makes for uncomfortably intimate links between politics, careers and personal wealth. The election of a new regional government of Galicia in 2005 was expected, for example, to lead to 2,000 jobs changing hands.

To add to the confusion, military intelligence was found to be listening in to the mobile phone calls of everyone from businessmen and journalists to King Juan Carlos himself. A rogue former intelligence officer, Juan Alberto Perote, meanwhile, threatened to release files he had taken home with him. There were even allegations that military intelligence had been kidnapping tramps off the streets of Madrid and experimenting on them with home-made knock-out drops. One tramp was said to have died.

It was the GAL campaign, however, that broke all the boundaries. Amongst the most shocking cases was the kidnapping of a Spanish exile, Segundo Marey, who was mistaken for an ETA leader. Marey was kidnapped in 1983 as he prepared to watch a Benny Hill film at his home in the French border town of Hendaye. He was released ten days later. A note placed in his pocket claimed the previously unheard-of GAL was responsible. Interior Minister José Barrionuevo and ten other ministry and police officials were eventually jailed. 'I don't think I can forgive them. They destroyed my life,' Marey said afterwards. The court was clear about what had happened. 'It was precisely those given the task of watching over the freedom and peaceful exercise of people's rights . . . who committed the crime of robbing him of his freedom, in subhuman conditions,' the judgment said.

Then there was the death of Juan Carlos García Goena in 1987. A bomb exploded under his car as he left his pregnant wife and two children to go to work in the border town of Hendaye. It was yet another case of mistaken identity. García Goena had moved to France years before to avoid doing military service. He had nothing to do with ETA. I have visited his wife, Laura Martín, several times. She has never given up trying to find out what really happened that fateful morning. 'Is there no one, not one of them, who suffers remorse that does not let them live?' she asked when interviewed by Paddy Woodworth for his book *Dirty War, Clean Hands*. 'Someone should call me on the phone and say : "Look, Señora Martín, I can't live. I am eaten up with remorse . . ." and I would forgive him.'

Finally, there was the case of two young ETA members, José Antonio Lasa and José Ignacio Zabala – both aged twenty – who were kidnapped in France. They were held, and probably tortured, at a government house in the Basque city of San Sebastián. Then they were taken halfway across Spain to Alicante, forced to dig their own graves and shot. Their bodies were only found more than a year after their deaths. They were not identified until a decade later. They had been blindfolded with insulating tape, gagged, shot in the head and their bodies buried in fifty kilos of quicklime in a remote spot near the town of Busot, near Alicante. A man out shooting with his dogs found bits of one of their skeletons spread around by animals that had dug them up. Bandages covered what, presumably, were wounds received when they were kidnapped or, possibly, when tortured. An anonymous caller had, in fact, rung a local radio station in Alicante on the day they were killed. 'They died crying like cowards. They asked for a priest but we refused because they did not deserve one.'

GAL was, however, anything but efficient. In Guethary, southwest France, I visited a restaurant whose owners had seen their previous establishment wrecked by GAL members who tossed in home-made hand grenades. The brothers Ibarboure told the tale as a funny story. It was recounted with waving arms and full sound effects. 'Boom!' went the grenades, 'Ping!' went the shrapnel. A mysterious woman, known as *La Dama Negra,* the Black Lady, or *La Rubia de los GAL*, The Blonde from GAL, was suspected to have thrown the grenades in. The results were anything but funny, though they could have been worse. When the smoke cleared, one brother was deaf in one ear. Another member of the family had managed to save himself by diving behind a fridge. Were they involved in Basque separatism? '*Non monsieur*, we have nothing to do with that!' It was another GAL mistake. This time, fortunately, it was not lethal.

A Civil Guard general, a former Socialist civil governor and three Civil Guard officers would, eventually, go to jail for the Lasa and Zabala murders. The man who ordered their murders, Civil Guard general Enrique Rodríguez Galindo, served just five years of his twenty-seven-year sentence. He was allowed home after that for 'reasons of health'.

No one in Spain has gone to jail for García Goena's death, however, or for most of the others. There simply was not enough evidence to prove who had been involved. At least one potential witness disappeared and then reappeared dead.

A Civil Guard colonel, José Lull Català, explained to Garzón how ETA had been fought during the 1980s, when he was a senior officer in the Basque Country. 'There were massive round-ups in which many abuses were committed, without restriction of violence. One of the practices was what was called *sacar al monte* – taking out to the mountain. It involved taking suspects to some wasteland or the countryside and giving them a thorough beating . . . If a Guardia went too far – some broken ribs, a leg or arm fractured – they would invent an accident.' General Rodríguez Galindo, the senior Civil Guard officer in the Basque province of Guipúzcoa, expressed his priorities like this: '*Coger etarras como sea, aunque matándolos*', 'Catch ETA members whatever way possible, even if it means killing them.' Those who caught them would receive cash premiums out of the *fondos reservados*. 'I do not regret anything that we did,' a Civil Guard officer posted in San Sebastián at the time told me years later. Many Spaniards were not that bothered either. The only good *etarra*, they believed, was a dead one. In the news room of a Madrid newspaper I once saw the death of two ETA members in a police shoot-out greeted with a gleeful cry of: 'Two-nil!' The GAL campaign also achieved one of its aims – better co-operation from France in the fight against ETA.

Garzón drew a diagram of who was who in GAL, and the connections between them. At the top of the structure he wrote an 'X'. It was clear that someone high up was in charge. Mr X remains a mystery today. González's enemies, and some of the victim's relatives, pointed their fingers at him. The courts dismissed their allegations. 'It is an accusation that I have never made, because I am unaware of his participation,' says Garzón.

The official response to Garzón's investigation was to bang doors closed in his face. 'We should . . . destroy all reports that make a direct or indirect reference to GAL,' read one military order.

When that failed to work, González tried another tactic. He appealed to Garzón's vanity. It worked. In 1993 he was invited by Felipe González to stand as an 'independent' Socialist candidate in the general election – as number two on the party's Madrid list behind González himself. Garzón accepted. Ambition, vanity and what the judge admits his main weakness – *soberbia*, or arrogance – led him to make a huge mistake. As one, otherwise fawning, biographer put it, explaining why this married but popular *magistrado* did not have any known lovers: 'The only person he really loves is himself.'

It was a brilliant, if cynical, move by González. Garzón was a star. Corruption was the Socialists' Achilles heel. By signing the campaigning magistrate up, he had shown he was serious about dealing with it. One Socialist leader claimed Garzón added so many points to the PSOE's poll rating that it instantly drew level with their right-wing opponents in the People's Party. González, against the odds, won a fourth term. Garzón expected a post as an anti-corruption supremo. He was made, instead, Spain's anti-drugs czar. He was being sidelined. His new job did, however, make him part of the Interior Ministry. There he soon found how money was, literally, lying around the place. 'There was a room full of watches, ties, scarves, pens . . . that were for giving away as presents; and there was another room full of paintings. The truly amazing thing, however, was that it all disappeared in twenty-four hours,' he told one biographer. One day a cleaning lady brought him a million pesetas (six thousand euros) she had found lying in the drawer of an unoccupied desk.

Garzón eventually told González that Barrionuevo, still a deputy in parliament, should be sacked if the Socialists were serious about cleaning up their act. The answer, according to Garzón's biographer, was: 'I can't . . . I've told him to go and he said no, that if he went, I would go with him.' Barrionuevo, in other words, thought he could bring down the government. Garzón resigned his seat a year later. Under the rules governing the Spanish justice system, he was allowed back to the Audiencia Nacional.

One of his first moves was to return to the GAL case. The dirty tricks department of the interior ministry now went into full swing. He was followed, his phone was tapped and his house broken into – twice. Once the visitors left a banana skin on a bed. It was a sinister calling card, a deliberate sign that they had been there. He went on a radio show to denounce what was going on. 'If you don't show cowardice, if you keep going . . . they end up assassinating you. That is what they did to judge Giovanni Falcone [the Italian anti-mafia magistrate who is one of Garzón's heroes]. But they are not going to get rid of me with these tricks. The more pressure they put on . . . the more determined I get. They'll have to kill me, because I am going to keep fighting until the end,' he said.

In fact, it seems, the list of those with a motive for killing Garzón is so long that – had they carried out the threat – it would have been difficult to prove who had done it. This is the judge, after all, who tried to extradite General Pinochet from London. ETA, Galician drugs clans, Turkish heroin smugglers and a few Latin American generals would all like him dead. The first three, at least, are known to have expressed a desire to wipe him out.

The reaction from the government was to move a team of police officers from Barcelona to Madrid to dig up dirt on the judge. 'It was Kafkaesque, they were seeking some sort of stain on my private behaviour. They investigated to see whether I snorted cocaine, if I had orgies with champagne and prostitutes, if I was in charge of a network of police corruption or money laundering, or if I was inclined towards paedophilia or homosexuality . . . More than anger, it made me sad to see how far our democracy had degenerated,' he says. 'A judge could have his phone bugged, his house broken into, be spied on by police and attempts made to dishonour or scare him . . . All because I had reopened a case that pointed at people close to the government.' It was a game, however, that Garzón would win.

The Socialists' final downfall did not happen until González, struggling to keep a minority government afloat in a storm of scandals, was forced to call early elections in 1996. It is said that a democracy is never properly installed until there have been two peaceful changes of government. This, at last, was it.

In most other countries the Socialists would have gone long before. But an atavistic, Franco-inspired fear of the right – and González's undoubted charisma – kept them hanging on. The Socialists had, in fact, done much to bury the Franco inheritance. They had also – despite the corruption, the death squads, the meddling in the judiciary, the blatant party control of state media and the arrogance of those who believed they were there for life – driven the country forward. González steered them into the centre ground, doing a U-turn on pulling out of NATO and calling a referendum to ratify membership. He pursued the sort of mild, market-driven, privatising, deficit-cutting economics that were a precursor to the 'third way' of later European socialists. That approach even saw the Socialist-supporting Unión General de Trabajadores (one of Spain's big two trade unions, led by Nicolás Redondo, who had helped him to the party leadership) call a general strike against him. For the part of Spain that felt an instinctive fear of the left, it was a relief. Not only was no one going to be forced to pay for Francoism but big money could still be made. Only a right-wing democratic government – something Spain had not had for sixty years – could confirm, however, that the country really had become a 'normal' democracy.

Although it was both the well-overdue end of a cycle and the inevitable fall of a rotten apple from the tree, some Socialists refused to see their defeat like that. They blamed, instead, judges like Garzón, newspaper editors like Ramírez and a number of prominent journalists and others whom they called 'the syndicate of crime'. The latter had orchestrated their downfall. The plot, they claimed, had been not just to oust the government but to shake the very foundations of the state.

There were two major pieces of fallout from the Socialists' corruption scandals. One was the Socialists' absolute refusal to admit they had done anything wrong. They defended Barrionuevo to the hilt, claiming he was innocent until proven guilty. When he was finally proven guilty, however, they claimed it was all a plot. It had been cooked up by journalists, judges and the People's Party. 'How is it possible that some judges dare to find the innocent guilty?' was González's reaction to the sentence.

It had all been an attempt to rubbish 'the Socialist Party and Felipe González, with the aim of achieving his political annihilation,' new party leader Joaquín Almunia declared. 'This trial was instigated in the context of a political operation to oust the Socialist Party from power after the 1993 elections. Its preparation [*carried out by Garzón*] was plagued by irregularities that robbed the accused of their legal rights and it ends as it started.' The Socialists preferred political suicide to an admittance of guilt.

Observers speculated that Barrionuevo knew too much for the party to cast him off. The former minister, GAL and corruption were to be the party's curse for the following years. Barrionuevo, meanwhile, continued protesting his innocence. He eventually wrote a book comparing himself to great Spaniards who had been cruelly persecuted – from the sixteenth-century *conquistador* Hernán Cortés to Falange founder José Antonio Primo de Rivera. Rosa Montero, writing in *El País*, gave a succinct explanation of how far Barrionuevo and others had dirtied the Socialist stable. 'Don't tell my mother I'm the interior minister: she thinks I work as a piano player at a brothel,' she said.

The importance of this case – and the other Socialist corruption scandals – was that even those in the highest positions of the state could be forced to pay for their crimes. Justice, in this instance, was done and seen to be done. Spaniards knew that those in power under Franco were pretty much exempt from the law. They were not sure, however, how much the same rule applied in a democracy. It was a crucial moment. The courts, people discovered, could protect them from the government when it broke the law.

It was by no means perfect, however. As often happens, good intentions were later dissipated. Barrionuevo spent exactly 105 nights in jail. First he was given a partial pardon by the Aznar government which saw his ten-year sentence reduced by two-thirds. Then he was accorded the right 'on security grounds' to sleep at home, reporting twice a week to the prison until his time was served. It was as if, having proved that the rules worked, there was no need to stick by them any more. 'Murder is seen as a lesser evil,' commented one Communist politician.

Spain's main parties have, so far, proved bad losers when ousted from power. The second piece of fall-out from this particular loss was a shambolic and crude dirty-tricks campaign. This time the target was Ramírez. *El Mundo*'s increasingly powerful editor was caught up in a sordid tale of sex games, hidden cameras and videotapes. Copies of a short video starring married Ramírez and an amply proportioned woman called Exuperancia from the former Spanish colony of Equatorial Guinea turned up in the post-boxes of Madrid journalists. It was, by all accounts, strong stuff, though drama was lost by the fact that the cameraman's hand shook as he filmed through a roughly drilled hole in a cupboard door.

Ramírez, to his credit, fought back. 'What could be seen there, starting with her huge rear-end and followed by mine, was, thanks to some rudimentary sex-shop games, not going to improve my social prestige,' he says in his own account of the episode. Prison sentences would eventually be handed down to, amongst others, a former Socialist provincial civil governor who had taken part in the plot. It showed how low the party of González – once the bright torchbearer of Spanish hopes – had sunk. It also proved, once again, that sex scandals just do not wash in Spain. Ramírez won. He still edits *El Mundo*. It is now the second newspaper in the land, after the mildly socialist *El País*.

Seeing the words that Spaniards have used to describe themselves in the past, it is surprising that corruption is not more widespread. They have a self-proclaimed reputation, after all, for being natural anarchists. 'Every Spaniard's ideal is to carry a statutory letter with a single provision, brief but imperious: "This

Spaniard is entitled to do whatever he feels like doing," wrote Ángel Ganivet. In the mid-nineteenth century, the catholic, conservative thinker Juan Donoso Cortés had claimed that 'the dominating fact of Spanish society is this corruption that is in the marrow of our bones . . . in the atmosphere that surrounds us and in the air we breathe'. Ortega y Gasset said that '*el encanallamiento*, the debasement, of the average man in our country makes Spain a nation which has lived for centuries with a dirty conscience'.

There is, however, an equal but opposite force in Spain. This comes from a deep vein of austerity. Its spirit might be associated with the arid plains of Old Castile or the strict silence of the increasingly under-populated, enclosed convents and monasteries. Historically, it can be seen in Philip II's sixteenth-century obsession with kingly duty. He failed to visit his imprisoned, though beloved, son Don Carlos on his deathbed only by, in the words of one historian, 'ruthlessly suppressing personal joys and sorrows' when royal duty called. It can be seen in his solitary rule from the palace-monastery at El Escorial. 'Simplicity in the construction, severity in the whole; nobility without arrogance, majesty without ostentation,' he had ordered his architects. His father – the Emperor Charles V – was similarly obsessed by duty and also retired to a small palace adjoined to another one, at Yuste. It is a spirit that crops up in surprising places. It is there, for example, in the strict lay Catholic orders like Opus Dei. This powerful and growing movement has added Calvinist touches to Roman Catholicism, embracing both the work ethic and the use of *cilicios* (barbed metal chains that dig into your thigh). A similar interest in austerity and order can be seen, too, in the purer proponents of both the hard political left and the old Falange. In geographical terms, Basques and Catalans might claim a love of industry and order is theirs too. None of Spain's democratic prime ministers has shown any wish to accumulate money while in their posts. The great obsession of José María Aznar, Spain's last Conservative premier, was '*las reglas del juego*' – 'the rules of the game' – as he called the Spanish constitution. It is this spirit of legality and order, exemplified by Garzón, that has, so far, won out at the core of the Spanish state.

There was one more battle to be won during the socialist period, however, for it to stay that way. This time the Socialists were on the side of good, as the upholders of order. Their major target was financial corruption. On the other side, representing me-first anarchy, were certain wielders of big money who thought cash could buy them everything from immunity to prosecution to the loyalty of King Juan Carlos.

Some blame the Socialists themselves for, at first, encouraging financial corruption as a way of allowing the economy to slip past the bureaucratic obstacles left over from Franco's day. 'Corruption is the oil of the system. It lubricates the wheels so that they turn smoothly and do not screech. It is only necessary to make sure that it does not go beyond a certain level,' was the theory that novelist Juan Benet later said he had heard in Felipe González's Moncloa offices.

It was a time when money, politics and, perhaps inevitably, football became a battlefield of court cases and private detectives. Brown envelopes full of allegations against politicians and business rivals were deposited regularly in the mail boxes of journalists. This was also the era of the *pelotazo* – the get-rich-quick schemes that saw millionaires appear out of nowhere, often for doing nothing more than being the middle men in dubious commercial transactions. It was also the time of '*los beautiful*'. These were the champagne socialists who swapped their ideals for cash and celebrated in an ostentatious fashion. Their leader, still an adored role-model for millions of gossip-magazine readers, was Isabel Preysler. Her main feat was to marry both singer Julio Iglesias and González's finance minister, Miguel Boyer.

The scandals they produced were complex, murky affairs. They featured some of the noisiest men in Spain – men such as Jesús Gil, mayor of Marbella and owner of Atlético de Madrid football club, or José María Ruiz-Mateos, owner of a giant industrial and financial conglomerate that emerged from the sherry town of Jerez. Ruiz-Mateos famously dressed up in a Superman costume.

He also once tried to land blows on Boyer, after the latter had intervened in his Rumasa empire, to the cry of 'I'll punch you, *leche*!' (The last word in this phrase means, literally, milk, though it also refers to semen.) Gil was also keen on fisticuffs. 'You are a pile of shit!', the president of Compostela football club, José María Caneda, shouted when they exchanged punches in front of the television cameras.

Both Gil and Ruiz-Mateos sought political power as they tried to avoid court cases and attempted to exact revenge on 'the politicians' who were their enemies. Natural populists, they had their small successes. These were men who, in the language of the football terrace or the bull ring, believed that what really mattered was to have *un buen par de cojones* – a real pair of balls. They were examples of what the comic film-maker Santiago Segura – in two hilarious films based around a character called *Torrente* – termed *casposa* (dandruff-ridden) Spain.

As the owner of first division Atlético de Madrid football club for his last twelve years, Gil was disciplined several times for insulting referees, including accusing a French referee of homosexuality, and inciting the club's followers to violence. One black player, the Colombian Adolfo 'El Tren' Valencia, was a particular obsession. 'I'll kill that black man!' he once spluttered. His contributions to racial harmony included 'Spain stinks from so many blacks'. Even the paid-up *socios*, or season-ticket holders, of Atlético were not safe from his bilious comments. 'The *socios*,' he declared, were from 'a low social stratus'. But that was not all. 'Whoever doesn't have a drug addict in the family, quite possibly has a prostitute.' Gil was the archetype *casposo*.

Both he and Ruiz-Mateos survived their multiple confrontations with mainstream politicians, though not without spending time in jail or losing their bigger battles. Gil died in 2004. Ruiz-Mateos's family, meanwhile, has built a new empire – including the Rayo Vallecano football club that is presided over by his septuagenarian wife – but is keeping quiet. '*Por la boca muere el pez*,' – 'the fish dies through its mouth' – is the new family slogan, according to one of his daughters. They are only missed, I suspect, by foreign newspaper correspondents. They were fantastic copy.

While Gil and Ruiz-Mateos made the noise, the real danger lay in some more silent, subtle and powerful players. The corruption battle reached a peak when two of Spain's biggest deal-makers, the oil-haired banker Mario Conde and Catalan businessman Javier De la Rosa fell into disgrace. For they were not content to go down alone.

De la Rosa was the son of an infamous fraudster who disappeared in the 1970s with the police on his heels. The son presided over Spain's biggest-ever bankruptcy as head of the Spanish portfolio of the Kuwait Investment Office (KIO), grouped together in a company called Grupo Torras. Amongst those to go to jail as a result were De la Rosa himself and Manuel de Prado y Colón de Carvajal, one of King Juan Carlos's closest friends and his personal ambassador.

Mario Conde, meanwhile, was a clever Galician who planned to be Spain's Silvio Berlusconi. He got worryingly close. A brilliant lawyer turned banker, he planned to form his own party. Then, however, the Banesto bank was taken out of his hands following the appearance of a 3.6 billion euro (605,000 million pesetas) hole in its accounts. He had pocketed at least 50 million euros for himself – and ended up in jail.

What seemed like straightforward cases of bent businessmen, however, soon became more complex. For De la Rosa and Conde both used their cash for more than just financial corruption. One of Conde's allies, for example, turned out to be Colonel Juan Alberto Perote. He was the former military intelligence officer who had stolen 1,240 microfiches containing thousands of top-secret documents.

The most obscure moment of all came when Conde's name was attached to a series of attempts, led by Javier De la Rosa, to blackmail King Juan Carlos. The two men threatened 'to use part of their immense fortunes to oblige the monarch to abdicate under the pressure of the numerous scandals related to the people surrounding Juan Carlos', according to the authors of a book that exposed the blackmail attempt. The two multi-millionaires were going around claiming that 'the Head of State had allowed himself to be corrupted and they had given him billions of pesetas', according to the same book. The blackmail did not work. Both men went to jail. The 'material' never appeared. Considerable doubt was cast, however, on the king's ability to choose his friends.

This became even more apparent when Prado y Colón de Carvajal also ended up in jail. He had also taken a large slice out of the money that Kuwait put into, and lost in, Spain. The king's ambassador, who referred to Juan Carlos as his '*patrón*' and claimed to be his main financial advisor, had pocketed 11 million euros. De la Rosa claimed Prado y Colón de Carvajal had been given the money 'at the request of a high institution of the state'. In fact, one observer said, Colón de Carvajal had hidden behind 'a cloak of disloyalty, which covered him, but had left the king naked'. A royal spokesman declared that: 'From now on there will have to be more care about who uses the king's name.'

Even in jail Conde continues to leave behind him a trail of corruption. In 2003 a judge was suspended for six months after trying to pressure colleagues into allowing the banker out on day release. His prison governor, meanwhile, was sacked after the millionaire ex-banker was found to be enjoying family visits every five days instead of the regular monthly visits given to his fellow inmates. It will be interesting to see what Conde – still rich, still clever and possibly keen to get even – does when he gets out.

Garzón believes that the corruption that marred the Socialist era had much to do with the nature of the *Transición* and Spain's refusal, or inability, to make a clean break with the past. As a young man, he had wanted not *reforma*, but a complete break. He had opposed Suárez's political reform referendum in 1976 (which an incredible 95 per cent of voters backed in a 78 per cent turnout), thinking it did not go far enough in burying the old regime. 'I still think that way, even though history has run a good course and we have the constitution and our democracy. But there is too much encumbrance, too many bad habits from the past that should not have been kept. And there are blankets of silence . . . Look no further than GAL, which is an *intragolpe*, a self-inflicted strike against the state.'

González himself argues that the Socialists inherited a dirty war whose roots stretched back into Francoism and put a stop to it. 'People do not understand that the state apparatus was retained, in its entirety, from the dictatorship,' he once explained.

Given the extent to which his last two governments were marred by corruption it is remarkable that González, when he finally lost, only did so by 300,000 votes. Had the Socialists kept their noses clean, they could have run Spain for twenty years or more. Some clearly thought they would. With the appearance of José María Aznar – a tax inspector, no less – it seemed as though the much-needed clean-up in public life would finally take place. Aznar's glaring lack of charisma was one reason why González hung on so long. Aznar clearly belonged to the legalistic and austere vein of Spanish life. During his eight years in power, corruption all but disappeared from central government. It appeared to follow the flow of money, however, to where it was being spent – by regional and local governments.

It is in the construction companies that deal with these governments that the major fortunes of modern Spain are being made. The coming men of Spanish business – with the exception of Amancio Ortega, owner of the successful Zara retail chain – are those who place brick on brick.

If the relationship between *ladrillo* and corruption is tight, then the one between *ladrillo* and football has been even tighter. It reached its peak in the bulky, gold-adorned shape of Jesús Gil. Until recently, builders were to be found running or owning many of the clubs in the Spanish league's first division. This is a generation, however, that is disappearing.

It is a sign of the times that the new football bosses are not the sort of men to indulge in the fisticuffs and foul-mouthed slanging matches of their predecessors. Nor would anyone accuse them of outright corruption. Spain has become too sophisticated for that. Real Madrid, for example, has become a huge, slick industry under Florentino Pérez, head of the mighty ACS construction empire. Under Pérez it signed many of the planet's most marketing-friendly stars. From Beckham to Zidane and Figo to Ronaldo, Pérez's earliest signings set the club up as a shirt-selling machine. It also produced what became, when its multi-millionaire stars decided to play their best, an electrifying sight. It is now the second richest club in the world after Manchester United.

Even Real Madrid's success, however, was due to a large dose of *enchufe*, this time of the legal kind. The signing of these players, or at least the first ones to join the firmament of what Madrid supporters call *galácticos*, galactic superstars, was possible due to a massive injection of cash into a club that was tottering on the brink of bankruptcy. That cash came from one of the most spectacular real estate deals – a true *pelotazo* – Madrid has seen.

Four new skyscrapers, bigger than anything ever seen in the Spanish capital, are soon set to dominate the city's skyline. They are being built, one beside another, on the site of Real Madrid's recently demolished training ground. This is a former greenfield site conveniently located on the fringes of Madrid's business district, known as '*la City*'. At around forty-five storeys each they will rise up above the Picasso Tower, a gleaming white and glass structure that currently holds the city's record with forty-three floors.

Madrid's local authorities conveniently reclassified the training ground's status so that the construction teams could move in. Real Madrid kept ownership of two and a half of the new towers. Local authorities got the rest. In a single stroke, Pérez netted some 390 million euros for the club. At the same time, the local authorities gained seventy floors of prime office space. The circle of private and political interest was, once more, closed around real estate. Environmentalists complained. A Barcelona-football-club-supporting Euro MP even asked the European Commission in Brussels to investigate. It declared that nothing untoward had happened. The deal, not surprisingly, led to cries of 'foul' from other clubs – notably cross-town rivals at working-class Atlético de Madrid. 'They would kill us if we behaved the way they do,' complained Gil.

Real Madrid has always been the nearest thing Spain has to an official, state-sponsored club. Five European Cups won in the late 1950s were treated as proof of Franco's muscular national Catholic principles at work. The club's 'virile' technique was meant to reflect the qualities of the diminutive dictator's own regime. Even then, however, the big stars were imported, foreign players like Argentine Alfredo di Stefano. As a result, a whole new category of football supporters evolved. They are the so-called *antimadridistas* – whose guiding passion is to see Real Madrid lose. Chief amongst them are Barcelona and Atlético de Madrid fans. *Antimadridistas* claim that Real Madrid success in the 1950s was due to the Caudillo's support. In fact, it was probably Franco who used Real Madrid, rather than the other way around. It is, however, still the favoutite club of the political right. With both the city hall and the regional government of Madrid in the hands of the Conservative People's Party, therefore, Real Madrid was on strong ground when it tried to cash in on its land. Madrid's Socialist leader Rafael Simancas claimed the deal was a massive gift to the People's Party club – which gained 150 times more than the amount agreed with the Socialists for a similar deal when they ran the city. 'They have just let Pérez have whatever he wanted,' he complained.

Real Madrid had been spending more than it earned for years. When Pérez signed his deal in 2001 the club reportedly owed nearly 270 million euros. He turned it into a smooth machine, raking in merchandising money. Cash, however, is what drives the machine. Coaches, some fans suspect, field players who make the club money rather than those who play best. With money the dominating concept, the superstar players were not always interested in sweating out there on the pitch. When they did all decide to make an effort, however, even a Barcelona supporter and natural *antimadridista*, such as myself, had to admit that something special was happening.

Football, of course, is one of the great Spanish passions. At a time when players, coaches and even fans come from all over the world, however, it is increasingly hard to identify anything different about the football played in Spain from that played elsewhere. In fact, many of the things that once made Spain different – from siestas to multitudinous families – have all but disappeared. Bullfighting remains. This, the *fiesta nacional*, still gets written up daily on the culture pages of newspapers (it is considered art, not sport). It does not appal me, the way it does so many of my compatriots – and some Spaniards. I can see courage in it, but not art. It is not, in short, something that interests me.

There is, however, something recognisably artistic that remains distinctly Spanish. Flamenco, be it music or dance, has attracted the curious gaze of foreigners for more than a century. This *anglosajón* is no exception, though I am no expert. If I was to travel across modern Spain, I decided, I should take the opportunity to find out more – and have some fun doing it.

6

The Mean Streets of Flamenco

I have come to Seville on the AVE, the high-speed train that links the city to Madrid. When it began operating in 1992, the AVE slashed the overland travel time between the two cities by more than half. It did this in uncharacteristically smooth-running, gleaming, punctilious style. Benito Mussolini would have wanted one of these – a nation's glory encased in a 300 kilometre per hour train. But here, too, is a monument to *enchufe*. Who, after all, doubts that the reason Seville got Spain's first high-speed train was because a Socialist prime minister and his deputy, Felipe González and Alfonso Guerra, both came from here. It remains the envy of virtually every other major city in Spain. Not even Barcelona is connected to the capital like this, the job of shifting 5,000 business executives back and forth each day being done, instead, by fuel-guzzling, cramped and crowded shuttle jets. There is a whiff of corruption to the AVE too. A dozen years after it was completed, court cases are still pending to determine where all the money went.

Seville is the most seductive, sensuous city in Spain. Some complain that nothing of great import has happened here since the city lost its near monopoly on trade with Spain's colonies in the seventeenth century. Drenched in New World wealth – in silver and gold from Peru and Mexico or Caribbean pearls and precious stones – Seville must have been one of the richest places on the planet. Visitors do not generally care that this all came to a rather abrupt halt. They may, in fact, like the idea. For they have been left the sixteenth- and seventeenth-century baroque architecture, the slow, charming pace of life, the broad Guadalquivir river lined with the terraces of bars and cafeterias, and the white- and ochre-painted charm of the old Jewish Santa Cruz district.

Everything here – from the perfume of the orange blossom to the lisping, lilting Andalusian accent – seems to insist that you acquiesce and give yourself up to its charms. 'Don't fight it,' Seville commands, as you are lulled into a sensual stupor. 'You are here to enjoy.'

Narrow, chaotic streets hide a multitude of secret places – squares, fountains, gardens, churches, *palacetes*, bars – allowing everybody to discover, and claim for their own, some favourite, hidden corner. Mine is a bar just around the corner from the Bridge of Triana. Here, at a shiny stainless steel counter, a team of hard-working waiters serve stewed bull's tail, tomato soaked in oil and herbs, cubes of marinated, battered dogfish and glasses of cold *manzanilla* sherry. Also, though, there is the chapel at the Hospital de La Caridad. The prior, and chief benefactor, here was once the infamous, if reformed, seventeenth-century philanderer Miguel de Mañara. This prototype Don Juan asked for the following words to be inscribed where his ashes were put to rest: 'Here lie the bones and ashes of the worst man the world has ever known.' The dark, cruel paintings here by Juan Valdés, with their disintegrating corpses of finely dressed bishops, seem to accuse this overstuffed city of being obsessed with mundane brilliance. The chapel is so full of saints, virgins, tubby, winged cherubs and the inevitable, in Seville, paintings of Murillo that, as one local writer told me, 'There is simply no room for anything else.' Then there is the broad boulevard known as the Alameda de Hercules at night, with its bohemian, slightly shabby, air. Around the corner, prostitutes sit out on chairs in the street, fanning themselves in the heat. Even they are not in a hurry to hustle. Once you start making the list of personal jewels, in fact, it is hard to stop. Seville, like a haughty Andalusian beauty, simply demands your attention.

It seemed a shame, therefore, to be stashing my valuables in a lock-up at Santa Justa railway station, keeping just a small amount of money in my pocket and preparing to turn my back on the more obvious delights of the city. This time, however, I had not come here looking for baroque Seville. I was not here for the spotted dresses and handsome, oil-haired *jinetes*, horsemen, of the April Fair. Nor was I coming to see the spooky Easter Week processions of the ku-klux-klan-hooded *nazarenos* as they parade their statues of the Virgin Mary and Jesus. Attractive as these things are, they sometimes feel like part of a fossilised, if lovingly-maintained, Seville past. I was, instead, on a quest. I wanted to find the raw, unadulterated soul of modern flamenco. For that, I needed to find Seville's live, beating, musical heart. I knew I was not going to find it in the city-centre tourist shows, the flamenco *tablaos*.

I took a hire car – insured against all eventualities – and drove out past the tropical-looking gardens of the Parque María Luisa and the pavilions left standing from Seville's first international expo, held in 1929. From here, the broad and elegant Avenida de la Palmera, with its tall palms and purple flowering jacarandas, pointed me out in the direction of the sherry town of Jerez. Elegant, turn-of-the-century mansion houses lined the road, though most seemed to have become offices for international accountancy firms. Then came the imposing stadium of Real Betis Balompié, one of the city's two eternal rivals in the country's soccer first division (the other is Sevilla FC).

Here, rather than continue towards the promised land of Jerez or the delights on the coast at Cádiz, I took a sharp left. The urban landscape went rapidly downhill. The car ducked under a railway line and there, easily recognisable by the junked cars, the patches of balding wasteland and the colourful rubbish piled about, was the most infamous barrio in Seville, '*Las Tres Mil Viviendas*', 'The Three Thousand Homes'. I am glad, at this stage, that nobody had told me, as I sat waiting at the traffic light, that some local citizens were, at that time, raising their own particular tax for visiting or leaving the barrio. A brick through the windscreen as you waited at the lights, a wrench on the car door, a wave of a knife and the highwaymen of Las Tres Mil would snatch whatever they wanted.

There are monuments to the failure of 1960s planning all over western Europe. Las Tres Mil is Seville's offering. This is where the gypsies of the riverside neighbourhood of Triana, once the cradle of flamenco, were moved. They were sent here together with *chabolistas*, shanty-town dwellers, from the outskirts of the city, some of whose homes had disappeared when a tributary of the River Guadalquivir, the Tamarguillo, overflowed its banks. They were, according to the jargon of the time, '*la gente del Aluvión*', the 'people of the flood'. Las Tres Mil, The Three Thousand Homes, was to be their Ark.

Perched on the west bank of the broad River Guadalquivir, their original barrio of Triana looks across its murky waters at old Seville. From its riverside cafes you look out at the splendours of the Torre de Oro, the white walls of the Maestranza bull-ring, the palm-lined Paseo Cristóbal Colón and a city skyline crowned by the twelfth-century minaret turned cathedral bell-tower, the Giralda. For several hundred years this was part of Seville's docklands. It was famous for its artisans. Their reputations spread, in the wake of the Spanish galleons, across the New World. Fifty years, or a century ago, this would also have been the place to look for the raw substance of flamenco. Théophile Gautier, the French Romantic, came across a group of gypsies camped out beside a bubbling cauldron. 'Beside this impoverished hearth was seated a *gitana* with her hook-nosed, tanned and bronze profile, naked to the waist, a proof that she was completely devoid of coquetry . . . This state of nudity is not uncommon, and shocks no one,' he said.

In the 1950s, flamenco was still part of its everyday life. 'In the afternoon one could hear the tune of *bulerías* and *tangos* (two flamenco styles or *palos*) coming from a cluster of houses. A baptism, a wedding, a request for a woman's hand in marriage, a son returned from military service, a woman who had just won the lottery . . . any event set the tribe into action. Triana still had melody,' recalls Ricardo Pachón, a flamenco producer who grew up there.

From Triana the gypsy singers and dancers would be called across the river for the *juergas*, or parties, of wealthy *señoritos* and bullfighters. They would come, too, to the popular *cafés cantantes* of the late nineteenth century and, in the twentieth century, to the *tablaos*, the tourist shows. Then they were dispatched back across the bridge to their own side of town. Spaniards as a whole have never learned to love their gypsies – who are estimated to number some 650,000. Even today polls show that many would rather not live beside them.

There are gypsies left in Triana, but nothing like there used to be. The melody has gone. Las Tres Mil was an excuse for a huge real-estate scam. The gypsies were lured away from their forges and houses in the Cava de Los Gitanos and the *chabolas* on the edges of Triana.

They were promised brand new, 'modern' housing. Orders were issued for the demolition of their old homes, many with shared patios that acted as the centre of social, and cultural, life. The Cava de Los Civiles (literally 'the civilians'), the *payo*, non-gypsy part of Triana, remained relatively untouched. Gleaming new blocks – their unimaginative name of 'The Three Thousand Homes' a giveaway to the bureaucratic nature of the project – way to the south of the city would keep them happy. It would also keep them out of sight and, by extension, out of mind.

In the tower blocks of The Three Thousand, one of Spain's most enduring urban legends was born. An old gypsy, at a loss about what to do with his mule in a fourth-floor flat, made him a stable in the spare room. By day the mule would work or, simply, feed on the grassy verges of Las Tres Mil. At night, however, his owner stuck him in the lift and took him home. A local photographer snapped the donkey peering out of a window. Ever since then, first-hand sightings of donkeys have been made, almost always falsely, in the flats of gypsies wherever they settle in high-rise Spain.

Las Tres Mil is part of a vast collection of similar estates properly known as the Polígono Sur. The latter houses some sixty thousand people, 20 per cent of them gypsies. They are hemmed in on three sides: by the railway tracks to Cádiz; by the busy *Carretera de Su Eminencia*, the Highway of His Eminence; and by the high walls of what used to be the Hytasa textile factory. One in every twelve Sevillanos live here. That is 1 in 700 Spaniards.

The rudimentary four- to eight-storey blocks drip with colourful washing. Self-built walled or fenced gardens eat up the wide pavements. Some are outdoor cages, covered in wrought iron bars to keep out the junkies who come to shop in the city's drugs supermarket, a desolate corner of the barrio known as Las Vegas. Immortalised in a song, '*En la Esquina de Las Vegas*', by the flamenco-blues guitarist-singer Raimundo Amador, this wretched, abandoned section of Las Tres Mil is home to thriving communities of rats and cockroaches.

The first time I drove in here, I had not yet worked out quite how bad Las Vegas was. On two visits, separated by a year, the talk each time was of a shoot-out as the drugs clans fought their turf wars. The odd police car cruises by. But Las Vegas is a place without law. The occasional shiny Mercedes or huge white van are a sign that, despite the trappings of poverty, large sums of money run through the barrio. Three gypsy clans are said to rule the place.

My first guide to Las Tres Mil was a man I will call Rafael, a local gypsy musician and producer. Driving through Las Vegas with him was a disturbing experience. Bonfires blazed on strips of wasteland, gypsy youths gathered around them. There used to be traffic lights here. Now there are decapitated posts with jagged, rusting tops. Rafael showed me a rough, hand-painted sign pointing to some kind of chapel. The sign pointed to a hole in a wire fence which, in turn, only gave access to the back of a semi-abandoned building and the waste ground around it. 'That is where they go to do their *culto*, to worship, after they shoot up,' he explained. 'They have a little room down there somewhere. They say there are pictures of Christ on the walls.'

Skeletal junkies, the war-injured of the narcotics trade, shuffle backwards and forwards. Poorly bandaged wounds are evidence of the daily damage they inflict on themselves. 'I call them *mutilados* – the mutilated ones,' explained Rafael.

Some of the *mutilados* are themselves gypsies. Heroin has scythed its way like a grim reaper, syringe in hand, through one generation of Spanish gypsies. It now threatens a second one. Many junkies, gypsies or *payos*, have come to live here, scraping a living from the drug trade in order to fuel their own addictions.

Some blocks are half abandoned. Flats change hands for as little as 150 euros, with no paperwork and no proof of ownership – just a roof and little else except a ready supply of heroin or cocaine.

Groups of dealers hang out by the wrought-iron cages that have been put across the entrances to each of the apartment blocks. A permanent layer of rubbish lines each street and the big green rubbish containers are burned out heaps of twisted, molten plastic. We passed an almost completely abandoned eight-storey block. A curtain of rough material hung across the entranceway, giving the smack addicts a bit of privacy as they hunted for undamaged veins. 'Look!' said Rafael, pointing to a gushing sewer pipe. 'The shit is just falling into their back yards.'

The rest of Seville is frightened of this place. 'Don't go there,' they told me in a Seville production company that had made a film on the barrio's flamenco talents. 'You won't find a taxi driver ready to take you.' In fact, I have never found a taxi driver who refused to go to Las Tres Mil or most of the rest of Polígono Sur. Las Vegas, however, was out of bounds. 'They have car races there – and they don't care about looking before crossing a junction,' apologised one driver. A young French photographer I ran into here was greeted afterwards in a bar in central Seville as if he had returned from the front line of a war. The waitress almost fainted with relief when he reappeared. She did not know that we had spent the afternoon with José Jiménez, 'el Bobote', a flamenco dancer who travels the globe accompanying some of Spain's greatest dancers. He had chosen to continue living in his flat here, despite also owning a house in a middle-class district of town.

The first people I spoke to in Las Tres Mil were three local Spanish Jehovah's Witnesses – inheritors, if you like, of the bible-selling tradition of that nineteenth-century British eccentric George Borrow who befriended gypsies and wrote extravagant travel books. 'Are you carrying anything valuable? Don't let them know you are foreign. It's dangerous,' they warned. In fact, if you discount Las Vegas, Las Tres Mil is no worse than many inner-city estates in Britain. With its streets alive with people, it is, in some ways, a lot better.

The first time I came here, Rafael was still trying to get something done about Las Vegas. He wanted a police station here, but suspected his efforts would not work. The police, and authorities, he had concluded, preferred to have Seville's 'drugs supermarket' here in a corner of Las Tres Mil than elsewhere in town. The barrio's grim statistics are, as a result, nothing short of spectacular. One in three children do not even make it through the school gates in the morning. 'We get people who are sixteen, eighteen or twenty turning up here who have never stepped inside a school,' explained one teacher at an adult education centre. Some residents do not, officially, exist. 'They have no ID card, no social security number. It's as if they had never been born,' a social worker told me.

I had not come to Las Tres Mil, however, to see its miseries but, instead, to discover the miracles that burst from its asphalted-over soil. For, if Triana, along with Jerez, the Bay of Cádiz and a handful of other spots strung along the line connecting them, was once the cradle of flamenco, Las Tres Mil can claim to be a new repository of that tradition. It is also the birthplace of some of flamenco's newest, most surprising, offshoots. Flamenco is by no means an exclusively gypsy music. Many of its greatest exponents, however, are gypsies.

Triana's gypsies brought their music with them. The new generations from the barrio have flamenco in their veins. But these are modern, urban gypsies. They have also grown up with rock, pop, punk, hip-hop and the influences of 'world music'. They have fused flamenco with modern urban sounds, or with music and instruments from far away, adding to the continued expansion of Spain's unique contribution to the worlds of music and dance.

Flamenco and its new bastard varieties, which stretch from flamenco-rock and flamenco-rap to easy listening *flamenquillo,* is everywhere in Las Tres Mil. It spills out of kitchen windows, hammers out of car sound systems and plays on people's lips. In bars and on street corners, it can suddenly appear. A man draws the first few phrases of a song out from deep inside him, and suddenly his friends are *tocando palmas*, beating out a complex, staccato, machine-gun rhythm with their hands. This, along with a dancer's stamping feet, is the traditional source of flamenco's percussion. If the song is successful, that might just be the start. The *juerga* – the partying – begins. Nobody can predict when it will end. That, anyway, was what I had been told – though the reality, in my brief experience of the barrio, did not quite live up to the description. This, though, was why I had come to Las Tres Mil. A decent flamenco *juerga* in the barrio, I was told, was something that should not be missed.

The barrio's list of flamenco artists is long and glorious. This is the home of Farruquito, the latest dance phenomenon to start touring the globe, and the rest of his clan. His family's flamenco pedigree stretches back several generations. From here, too, come the Amador brothers, guitarists Raimundo and Rafael, who fused flamenco with the blues. With a group called Pata Negra they proudly declared that '*todo lo que me gusta es ilegal, imoral o engorda*' – 'everything I like is illegal, immoral or makes me fat'. Rafael Amador has fallen victim to the barrio's worst side. Drugs and alcohol have spoilt, if not his talent, then at least his ability to use it. Raimundo, meanwhile, has pursued a highly successful solo career. He sometimes plays with his blues idol, B. B. King.

Some of the best-rated singers, men like the mysterious Pelayo, a Las Vegas gypsy who has spent many years in jail, refuse to sing professionally. They will only sing if they feel *la gana*, 'the urge'.

El Esqueleto, a civic centre just around the corner from Las Vegas, is a prime example of the surreal, absurdist sense of humour of Las Tres Mil. Like much of what has happened in this neighbourhood, it was started in a burst of enthusiasm but was abandoned when only half built. What was left was a jumble of beams, pillars and girders, a skeleton of a building which soon became known in barrio jargon as just that, '*el esqueleto*'. By the time the building was restarted, the name had stuck. It now bears the grandiose name of The Skeleton Civic Centre.

My search for a decent *juerga* did not start successfully. Rafael told me it was impossible to predict where and when one might happen. I could hang about the barrio for weeks without getting lucky. On a warm summer's evening, however, he called me to meet him at El Esqueleto. A working musician, composer and enthusiastic promoter of local talent, he wanted me to witness the public presentation of his latest musical discovery. '*Es un monstruo*' – 'He is a singing monster,' he insisted. A local Andalusian television station was devoting an arts show to Las Tres Mil. Rafael's newly found young talent, a teenage gypsy boy, was to sing.

Among the crowd gathered here at the door to El Esqueleto was *el Indio*, The Indian. A former *novio de la muerte* (fiancé of death), or member of the Spanish Legion, *el Indio* is a Seville eccentric. He dresses as a Red Indian brave, complete with a homemade bow and sheath of arrows. If this was Seville's Wild West, *el Indio* played the part of its downtrodden native.

Today he was bereft of his bow and arrow – they had been confiscated, once more, by the police – and was dressed just in shorts. His weathered, sagging body was criss-crossed with scars that welled up over a patchwork of fading tattoos. A white feather was stuck through a hole in his left nipple. A single spike of hair pointed up to the sky from the centre of an otherwise shaved head. *El Indio* is a *payo* – a non-gypsy – who knows how to make the gypsies laugh. They salute him with that time-honoured, hand-raised Indian greeting – 'How!'

A scar on his stomach was the result of an operation on a burst gut. 'I drank too much beer,' he explained. No reason was offered, however, for another set of scars, which poured off his right shoulder like molten wax. They ran in raw, red dribbles of raised skin down his arm and chest.

Two gypsy brothers, Juan and Rafa Ruiz, joined us, hoping to get on the show. They had been singing and dancing on the streets of Seville for years but dreamt of becoming real, professional artists. They get occasional invitations to play at *romerías*, the festive pilgrimages of the summer months in Andalucía, or for parties of huntsmen, modern-day *señoritos* who like to end a day of blasting at wild boar or deer with music and *juerga*. 'When the party is on, everyone wants to be a gypsy, but when it is over, they don't want to know anything about you,' explained Rafael.

Juan began to strum a rhythm. *El Indio* broke into dance, his body curving around his flabby, exposed belly as he stamped the tiled floor with his dilapidated sneakers, beat his thighs and threw himself into a clumsy spin. The gypsies cracked up with laughter.

The television studio was in a small theatre in the centre of Seville. I took Juan and Rafa and a couple of teenagers from a music workshop at The Skeleton, who were also due to play, in my car. They wanted the air conditioning on full blast and the windows closed. 'The wind will wreck my hairstyle,' explained one. Juan spent the journey fiddling with the radio trying to find a station playing decent *flamenquillo*.

At a traffic light, Juan wound down the window and, for no apparent reason, started shouting to a Japanese girl. 'Hello *guapa* – good-looking – don't you remember me?' Words and smiles were exchanged. The window was rolled back up. 'I know her,' he explained. 'She sings *bulerías*.' Even the Japanese, he said, were hung up on flamenco.

At the television studio, Rafael introduced me to the 'monster'. Carlos was seventeen years old, pouring with sweat, but already affecting a star's disdain for lesser mortals. He instructed a photographer not to take pictures of him. 'You can do the others,' he said.

As it got closer to his performance, Carlos's already considerable range of nervous tics and twitches increased. He pinched his nose, scratched his chin, craned his head forward to stretch his neck muscles and, with both hands at once, tried to fan himself. An hour before it was time to go on stage, his shirt was already drenched through. His cool, clean 'look' was getting increasingly wrinkled. Occasionally he let out a thin, clear, falsetto note and loosened his throat with the first few bars of the purest-sounding flamenco, his voice gliding through the quarter tones. The boy obviously had talent.

A production assistant came backstage carrying a form. It was Carlos's agreement to cede his performance rights for the evening. He looked at it in panic and handed it to Juan. He, in turn, looked at it in panic and handed it to me. It was my job to fill it in. As I asked Carlos to spell out his name, I realised why I was doing this. Carlos could only just spell. The speed with which Juan handed the form over made me suspect he could not read either. Little surprise, then, that the constant lament of the artists in Las Tres Mil is that they are 'being ripped off'. Finally it was time for the *monstruo* to appear on his television debut. Rafael had invented a twee stage name for him. He has a surname, however, that would ring bells amongst the local flamenco cognoscenti – that of a family of Triana singers.

The performance, when it came, was a disaster. Carlos was being launched, not as a flamenco singer but as a sort of pop balladeer. He sang a middle-of-the-road, instantly forgettable ditty penned for him, I suspect, by Rafael. This is an old trick. Pure flamenco is hard work, with a small, intense, knowledgeable, and highly critical, hard core of buffs. If you want to make money, sing something else. To make things worse, Carlos did it to playback and did it badly. His lips and contorted, pop-star body movements were badly out of sync with the words being sung.

Afterwards, we congratulated him effusively. He thought he had done well and there, out on the street, as the boys and girls from the music workshop were packing their percussion in the back of the van, he broke into true song. It was the same high, clear, pure flamenco voice he had warmed up with. Shed of all pressure, and of the baggage of pop culture, he was a flamenco thoroughbred. The boys from Rafael's workshop could not help but reach for their instruments and start beating a rhythm. I tried to work out what form of flamenco he was singing. A high-pitched *tanguillo* perhaps? I wished I knew more.

By now, however, it was 2 a.m. We were in a narrow, residential street in the old quarter. The security guards came rushing out of the theatre, trying to shush everybody up. A few minutes earlier the show's production team had been treating the Tres Mil gypsies as artists, plying them with drink, slices of cured Serrano ham and canapés. Now they were out on the street again and not needed. Guillermo, a music producer, looked on. 'If they do that in their barrio, people just say: "Hey, look. He's in a good mood." But you can't do that here, not in the centre of town.'

The kids from the Tres Mil piled back into their van and were gone, singing their way home. We were not invited to the *juerga* which, I suspected, would carry on back in the barrio. A line still separates *gitano* from *payo*. I was not going to force my way across it. I was, however, enviously aware of missing something. I realised I would have to look elsewhere for my raw, pure flamenco.

My next stop, I decided, should be a place where gypsies have plenty of time to sing and nowhere to escape to. That meant taking the road out of Seville towards Mairena, to a building whose purpose could be recognised by its high, modern brick walls and even higher watchtower – Seville's jail.

The relationship between jails, gypsies and flamenco is as old as flamenco itself. At the base of the family tree of flamenco styles lie the *tonás* which are, in turn, divided into the *martinetes* (originating from the blacksmith's forge), the *deblas* (from the gypsy word for goddess) and the *carcelera*, the prison song. The words to these songs speak of five hundred years of persecution of gypsies and their culture.

The *carcelera* predates the introduction of musical instruments into flamenco, throwing it back, at least, to the mid-nineteenth century when the first written accounts of the music appeared. It may come from even earlier, perhaps to the time in the eighteenth century when Fernando VI ordered Spain's gypsies to be jailed if they refused to give up their *caló* language and way of life.

It is a pure lament of prison hardship – a sub-genre of the global experience of gypsy pain and suffering that has fuelled, and continues to fuel, much of flamenco. The words to one typical *carcelera* go like this:

The bell for silence has rung already/Now they order quiet/And when the bell rings again, mother/They will tell us to get up.

When I was in prison/All I could do to pass the time/Was count the rings/That made up my chain.

Flamenco has dozens of styles or types of song, known as *palos*. They have all been carefully categorised and placed on a 'family tree'. These are sometimes reproduced in flamenco books as just that, though no two trees seem to fully coincide. The tree's roots are buried somewhere in the eighteenth century or earlier. The *palo* families appear along its branches. Here are the *rumbas*, *tanguillos* and *alegrías*, the songs of partying and dancing, or the complex *siguiriyas* and *soleas*. There is even a branch known as the '*palos de ida y vuelta*', the 'round-trip *palos*', brought back from the Americas by musicians who travelled west to the long-disappeared Spanish empire. These last ones bear the names of Latin American musical styles such as *milongas*, *tangos*, and *guajiras* – though they often bear little relationship to the Cuban, Argentine or Mexican music of the same names.

The origins of flamenco are lost in history. That does not stop the cognoscenti, a passionate, opinionated and nit-picking bunch, from spending much time disagreeing on them. The Romans were said to be fascinated by the dancing girls of Cádiz, though they predate flamenco and Spanish gypsies – by centuries. Records show gypsy dancers from Triana being hired for parties in the 1740s, though they were also generally deemed to be pre-flamenco. Early nineteenth-century travellers would watch *fandangos* being danced. My preferred version of the story is of a series of musical forms brought by the gypsies in their exodus from India and their slow crossing, over several centuries, of the Middle East and Europe. They crossed the Pyrenees into Spain in the fifteenth century. They were noted musicians whose services could be bought for weddings and celebrations. Spanish culture was itself a melting pot at the time, with Arab and Jewish music adding to a stock of *romances*, traditional poetry, occasionally set to music. Flamenco, it seems, emerged from this stew over the centuries – appearing in a recognisable form in the early nineteenth century. The rhythms inherited from all sides, be they the metre of medieval poetry or the beat of Indian music, created what is, at times, an extraordinarily difficult structure. It is not, and never has been, a purely gypsy music. Some of the best exponents have no gypsy blood at all in them. Gypsies, however, have always been at its centre.

Difficult, or not, the best-known *palos* came naturally to the crowd of *gitano* prisoners I found gathered for a flamenco workshop after the gates had clanked shut behind me in Seville's jail.

Spanish jails are remarkably modern, well equipped and tolerant places. Some boast glass-backed squash courts, swimming pools and theatres. Most of the British prisoners in them do not apply to serve their time back home in Britain's run-down, aggressive, Victorian-built prisons. 'I've seen the inside of Brixton, the Scrubs and a couple of others,' a prison-hardened East End drug trafficker in Salamanca's Topas jail told me once. 'This is a million times better. I miss my mum, but I'm not going back.'

'A country's health can be measured by how it looks after its weakest members,' a Spanish prison governor explained to me. If that is so, Spain is in fine fettle. Amongst other things, prisoners get private conjugal visits from their wives or girlfriends in rooms equipped with double beds. This jail, and others, are mixed, though the different sexes live in separate wings. Some couples even meet and get married in Spanish prisons.

I had come to Seville's jail to meet competitors in what must be one of the most specialised, but also one of the most passionate, musical competitions of all times – '*El Concurso de Cante Flamenco del Sistema Penitenciario*', 'The Flamenco Song Contest of the Penitentiary System'. It is against prison etiquette to ask why people are inside the *talego*, as Spanish jail argot calls a prison. So I had no idea why Rafael, a fifty-three-year old with flowing grey locks, shiny leather shoes, a choker of wooden beads and a massive gold ring on one finger was here. He was, respectfully, referred to as '*tío*', 'uncle' by the younger Silva and twenty other men, almost exclusively gypsy, in the prison's flamenco workshop. Murderers? Thieves? Drug dealers? Petty crooks? It did not matter. Prison is a leveller. Everybody here was sharing the same fate.

Silva was a Tres Mil boy, and the most thoughtful and serious singer. He was the jail's chosen representative for the sing-off at Granada prison a few weeks later. He belonged to the same clan, or extended family group, in the barrio as my musician friend Rafael. 'When I am singing I stop feeling the pain. Only song, and tears, can get rid of it,' he explained.

Pain and joy, *pena* and *alegría*, are the two emotional motors of flamenco, but here, they explained, only one was available to them.

Flamenco had been with them since the day they were born. It had been there at parties, baptisms, weddings and, often, in their parents' voices around the house for as long as they could remember. 'Sometimes I sit in a corner of the exercise yard and start singing. When I look up there are half a dozen gypsies there with me, *tocando palmas*,' one explained.

They were pleased with their workshop. Many had only known the three or four *palos* that were sung at home. Here, in a jail that houses gypsies from across Andalucía, they had extended their range. Most of all, however, this was an opportunity to unburden themselves through song and dance.

Rafael had brought with him the songs of Algeciras and La Línea, the area of Cádiz around Gibraltar. 'When I listen to Uncle Rafael, it breaks my heart,' said Silva. Uncle Rafael was, indeed, extraordinary. His voice was all mud and gravel, so deep, thick, rough and heartfelt that Alfonso declared the style to be *rancio* – literally rancid, but somehow appropriate for a voice as thick as churned butter.

They took turns to sing, twenty of them standing on the prison's rudimentary theatre stage, beating out rhythms on their hands. Suddenly, there was something very feminine about this bunch of crooks. 'Your voice sounds like peaches in nectar,' shouted one in a fit of enthusiasm for a fellow inmate's singing. '*¡Hermoso mi primo!* Beautiful, my cousin!,' shouted another. Occasionally one stepped forward, arms elegantly raised, wrists cocked, delicately pacing out the first few steps of a dance before launching into a joyful, if somewhat out of control, moment of heel-drumming, hopping and spinning. A handful of the glassier-eyed prisoners looked as though they had no trouble finding drugs in jail, but there was no alcohol here to drive the *juerga*. It was not needed. The music itself was enough to carry them off.

There was no sheet music. 'No one would be able to read it,' explained Alfonso, a professional flamenco singer and volunteer worker at the jail. Some had nevertheless mastered, without studying, the complex structures of *soleás* and *siguiriyas*.

A few weeks after visiting Seville jail, I found myself in the visitors' bar at Granada jail – a shiny, modern building sticking up, incongruously, out of fields of olive trees twenty miles from the city. I was here waiting to see the prison flamenco song final. A British photographer had asked to come along. 'Wherever I go they have a bar,' he said. And he was right. That morning we had had breakfast – freshly squeezed orange juice and thick, toasted rolls drowned in a garlic-flavoured olive oil and tomato pulp – at the bar in the Renault dealership in Seville. There are said to be more than 138,000 bars in Spain. This is as many as the rest of western Europe put together. The prison was doing its bit to keep the numbers up. The visitors downing *café con leche* and pastries, while waiting their turn to see inmates, were mostly gypsy families.

'My husband is going to sing,' one hefty matron – black dress, large bosom and a single gold tooth punctuating her smile – informed me. 'Why can't I watch?'

They had brought the competitors in from a dozen jails – from as far away as Valencia and Extremadura, as well as from each of the eight Andalusian provinces. The presidents of all the Andalusian provincial associations of flamenco *peñas* – the flamenco clubs which were funding the prizes – were here to act as judges. These were mainly round-bellied, self-important men in jackets and ties. They were also sticklers for the proper observance of flamenco tradition or, at least, for their version of it. There was no gypsy amongst them, as far as I could tell. Nor were there any women. Ten out of the twelve finalists, however, were gypsies.

I found Silva backstage, looking serious and feeling out of his depth. 'I caught a cold in the police wagon on the way here,' he complained, pointing to a throat that, he said, was now too sore to win prizes.

The performers had rustled up their best clothing. There were, amongst the jeans and T-shirts of regular prison wear, a smattering of shiny, Cuban-heeled ankle boots, spotted cravats, waistcoats, black shirts and clanking medallions. In one case, a cream suit had even appeared. Despite the banter and desperate dragging on the flamenco voice's greatest enemy – the Winston cigarette – most looked tense. It was hardly surprising. This was a serious event. Many had no real experience of singing in public.

'This is not charity. We will judge them the way we would any other competition,' the jury's chairman told me. 'We are looking for someone who might become one of the great voices. There are no concessions just because they are prisoners.' He knew, however, that Spanish prisons were a secret repository of flamenco talent. Gypsies who would never enter a competition outside the prison walls would, in this unique competition, suddenly find their voices exposed to, and appreciated by, more than just friends or family. Here, perhaps more than anywhere else, a secret jewel could turn up.

The nervousness of the competitors, then, was hardly surprising. When this competition was first launched, the prize included not just a small amount of money but a recording contract, a concert tour and, it turned out, early exit from jail. This time only the money and contract were on offer.

The singer in the cream suit was a wiry, angular man. He could have stepped out of an El Greco painting. His hooked nose, beard and attitude of artistic superiority also gave him the air of a tenth-century Moorish Caliph.

'I am a nightingale, kept behind bars,' he said, in a conspiratorial tone. 'This is a competition to the death. There are people here, inside prison, who sing much better than those outside.' The Caliph later raised some of the loudest applause of the day from the audience of fellow inmates by singing: 'They put me in jail just because I tried to defend myself.'

Flamenco, one contestant explained, was pain and *quejío,* a flamenco word to describe the outpouring of that same pain. 'When you sing in jail, blood comes out of your mouth,' he said.

Most of the contestants had similar stories. Their music came from their families. Drugs or violent feuds between gypsy clans had brought them to jail. The prison walls pushed them deeper into themselves and deeper into their song. I was struck by the similarities to that other jailhouse music par excellence, the blues. Men with recording machines made the pilgrimage to the state penitentiaries of Mississippi as long ago as the 1930s in order to capture the music being made there. It is not surprising that, at the hands of that Tres Mil Viviendas family, the Amadors, blues and flamenco had finally met. 'They are both about suffering and sentiment. Our peoples, gypsies and *negros*, have suffered a lot, or our ancestors have. We both, also, manage to wring a lot out of just a few notes,' Raimundo Amador explained to me once. 'Gypsies and *negros* both like gold, and giving away money to children, because we both believe in luck.'

A jolly, round-bellied priest introduced the singers one by one, throwing the audience prison jokes and reading out the little biographical notes the prisoners had given him. 'Manuel loves women and bulls,' he declared, bringing cackling and catcalling from the ranks of the women prisoners in this mixed-sex jail. A burly female guard dived in amongst the rows of red plastic bucket seats and ordered the loudest offenders out of the theatre.

For years I had had a love–hate relationship with flamenco, turned on by its recorded, studio-mixed output and especially by its more popular, but impure, versions. Camarón de la Isla, especially, had captured me with his pure *cante jondo*, the so-called 'deep song', and the records he made with guitarist Paco de Lucía. I had, however, almost always been disappointed by public performances. Only rarely did I find anyone who seemed to have been gripped by *duende*. Early trips to watch imitators of the great Camarón had a purely soporific effect on me. Yet I knew that, at its most passionate and profound, flamenco was meant to provoke extraordinary emotions. For some fans it is virtually a religion. There are tales of people ripping their shirts to shreds in excitement or being moved to tears. Camarón de la Isla even gained the nickname of *acabareuniones* after apparently provoking some visiting Galicians – hardly the most 'flamencos' of Spaniards – to start tearing up their own shirts. Good flamenco, I was constantly told, would make the hairs on my arm stand on end. And that, I discovered, was finally happening to me in Granada jail's concert hall. It started with el Chanquete, a big, bearded *payo* from Marbella with a gentle, sweet voice. 'I have a past in drugs that I now regret. Really, they ought to be letting me go home,' he told me.

Things got better as the afternoon went on. Backstage, guitarists and singers were indulging in bouts of spontaneous musicality, groups forming, breaking up and re-forming. On stage, soloists were being joined by other competitors to provide a backing chorus and *palmas*. Some ended up dancing their way up and down the stage to wild applause from the mainly gypsy public.

The defining moment came with the appearance of a small, quiet man with a broad, nervous smile. In his black clothes and shiny boots, I had barely noticed him backstage. He came, anyway, from Valencia – hardly the cradle of flamenco. The stage, however, transformed him. He sat down beside the guitarist, stared down at the floor and steadied himself. Then he began pawing the floor slowly with one of those shiny, Cuban-heeled boots. His body tensed, a heel clicked against the floor, he reached out a hand to the audience, lifted his face to us and began to sing.

He was called Ángel. He had a powerful, rich voice that Victor, the prison officer in charge of the show, compared to that of a once-famous singer of popular *coplas*, Rafael Farina. 'In fact,' said Victor, who obviously knew a thing or two, 'He is probably even better than that.'

Already excited by what was going on, both backstage and front, I found myself transfixed by this Ángel. A tingling, euphoric sensation came over me. It appeared to sweep through much of the audience too. The female prisoners jumped to their feet as the little man reached his peaks, then sat as he drew back into soft lament. Occasionally, a voice from the crowd would shout praise or encouragement. He got a standing ovation and I, finally, got the flamenco epiphany I had been seeking. I have never looked back. Ángel opened the door to a whole world of music – which I am only just beginning to explore.

Afterwards, the jury and singers gathered beside the star attraction of any modern Spanish jail – the outdoor swimming pool. One jury member told me that the top four in the competition could all sing professionally. That provoked the fourth-place winner, a nervy, speedy gypsy from Madrid, to ask me to 'have a word with the governor. See if you can get me a weekend pass. But what I really need is a manager. I've been going on stage since I was a child. I can sing anything.'

Ángel came second. I would have chosen differently, but the jury had its rules. Ángel wore his talent lightly and was immensely, childishly pleased. The prizes were handed out by a once-famous female flamenco dancer whom I had never heard of. She gave the winners prints of herself dancing. The Valencian brought his over to me and, once again, I found myself doing the writing for a gypsy. 'To María Heredia, *con todo mi afecto*!' I scribbled on it. 'I'm giving it to my girlfriend here in the jail,' he said, winking. News of his triumph had probably already reached her. One of the women's modules overlooked the swimming pool. A running commentary was being relayed from block to block via the peculiar Spanish prison language of hand signals. Manicured hands with long, crimson-painted fingernails poked out from behind the bars, gesticulating and wagging fingers in a private language far more complex, but just as secret, as the old fan language of Spanish courtiers. 'I certainly don't understand it,' the prison's deputy governor said.

The prison flamenco contest has a chequered history. It started off with a bang, after the son of the great Agujetas won first place, tying with an expert in *camaroneo* (as singing in the style of Camarón de La Isla is known) called José Serrano. Both men were let out early and their record was released in the US. Later editions were far more modest or, simply, failed to happen, drowned in prison bureaucracy. With this edition, it was picking up again.

I wanted to track down Antonio Agujetas, the son, and José Serrano to find out how the jail competition had changed their lives. My attempts to get hold of the former came to nothing. I called the local newspaper in Jerez, a town that is considered one of the last repositories of traditional, authentic flamenco. 'I saw him in the street the other day, with a group of so-called friends. It was, I'm afraid, a pathetic sight,' the newspaper's flamenco expert confided to me. 'He is in and out of drug rehabilitation programmes and argues with his father all the time. He's in no state to be interviewed. It's a sad story, but all too common.'

Tracking down Serrano was similarly complicated. Eventually Antonio Estévez, a local builder and small-time flamenco patron in the industrial town of Dos Hermanas, just outside Seville, found him for me. 'He's a difficult man. I don't know if you have been warned, but he is going to ask you for money,' said Antonio. I had not been told. We had an uneasy meeting in a bar. Serrano was there with his wife – large, dark and frowning with suspicion – his trousers clumsily darned and several days' stubble on his face. At forty-two, he was my age but looked a decade older. I refused to pay for an interview. Then, as his wife looked sternly on, he pleaded on behalf of his children. A twenty-euro note exchanged hands. His wife gleamed happily. It was a mistake. After that, Serrano gave whichever answer he thought I wanted to hear.

We drove up to Cerro Blanco, a gypsy barrio of crumbling, one-storey houses in Dos Hermanas. Serrano ushered us into a dilapidated, single-bedroom house furnished with nothing more than a bed, a kitchen table, a few plastic chairs, a loudly humming refrigerator and a rusting sink. 'What was the best thing about winning the prison flamenco contest?' I asked. 'Getting out of jail early,' he replied with great conviction, as a six-year-old son clung to his leg. 'I saved myself three or four years inside. I couldn't believe it when I got out. I kissed the ground, just like the Pope.' He repeated the now familiar explanation about how prison added 'sentiment' to a flamenco voice. 'Singing outside jail is not the same,' he said. 'You don't get the same feeling.'

Serrano had grown up in Las Tres Mil. He had started off as a child doing the rounds of Seville's tourist cafes in the company of the Amador brothers, singing, dancing and passing around a hat. The Amadors had gone on to enjoy phenomenal success. Serrano had served eighteen years of a sentence for murder.

He occasionally sang professionally, but winning the jailhouse flamenco contest had obviously not made him a star, or produced wealth. Dishevelled drunks and junkies wandered the barrio. The neighbouring houses, looking out over a patch of wasteland, were no better than his. Antonio, who dripped with gold accessories himself, had warned us not to bring any valuables. 'They know me, so they won't rob me,' he said. 'But you should be careful.' Once again, however, the gypsies were more friendly than threatening.

'He can't be bothered to look for performances,' explained Antonio, as we left. 'If you don't make an effort, people forget you. You know, I wanted you to do that interview, and I was about to give him money myself. But he'll only spend some of it on food, the rest will probably go on cocaine.'

Serrano, however, has not gone back to jail since he left it half a dozen years ago. Nor has he got hooked on cocaine or any other drug. He is not interested in travelling, even if that means he can never expect to have a proper career as a singer. 'I like my home. I like being with my family,' he says. A gypsy man who can earn enough to keep his family going, without working too hard, still gains respect from his peers and family. By those standards, Serrano's voice has been a success. And that is impossible to begrudge.

Persecution and jail have been part of the culture of Spain's gypsies almost ever since they first crossed the Pyrenees in the fifteenth century. They arrived in groups of up to a hundred each led by a man using the title of count or duke. Often they claimed to be pilgrims, or said they had been expelled from their former homes by Muslims. In fact, this was the final stage of a slow migration over five centuries in which they had crossed Persia, the Middle East and Greece after leaving India several hundred years earlier. Their skills with horses and, it is said, their music, meant they were initially welcomed. But, like the Jews, the Moors and the Moriscos, the gypsies were ordered out of Spain. They stubbornly refused, however, to budge. The first expulsion order came in 1499, signed by Isabella and Ferdinand, the same Catholic monarchs who had thrown the Jews out seven years earlier. Camarón de la Isla, like his brother Manuel, had a Star of David and a crescent moon tattooed together above his right thumb. This was, the latter once explained, meant to be a symbol of the shared history of persecution of Jews, Muslims and gypsies in Christian lands.

Over several centuries Spain's gypsies were repeatedly ordered to change their ways, stop using their language and stop even calling themselves *gitanos*. They were threatened with expulsion, with galley-slavery on the Spanish treasure galleons and with transportation to the New World.

But the gypsies, who were largely sedentary from early on and sometimes based themselves in so-called *gitanerias* in or beside major cities such as Madrid and Seville, simply never obeyed the expulsion orders. They also roundly ignored the commands to 'mend' their ways. One royal order explicitly excluded them from the right of avoiding arrest by seeking refuge at a church altar. The Inquisition had its turn with them too. The Church was especially worried about gypsies who married their cousins. In 1745, Fernando VI succumbed to a strange fit of 'enlightenment' thinking and had them rounded up en masse. Some nine thousand were sent to jail.

Gypsies were, as now, widely blamed for things they did not do. In *The Life of Lazarillo de Tormes and His Fortunes and Adversities*, a sixteenth-century Spanish novel, the hero asks whether a group of bandoleros are 'all gypsies, from Egypt'. The answer was a resounding no. 'They were all clerics, friars, nuns or thieves escaped from jails or convents,' the anonymous author wrote. The worst 'were those who had left their monasteries, exchanging a passive life for an active one'.

Not all was hardship, however. Gypsies have always had their patrons, supporters and defenders. These included lords, priests and ordinary folk ready to stand up for 'good gypsies' and protest or intervene when the entire community was punished for the sins of a few.

The roguish British bible-seller George Borrow, who wandered Spain in the 1830s, was just one of many travellers to fall under their spell. He even devoted a book to them, *The Zincali, or an Account of the Gypsies of Spain*. Others, he noted, were similarly captivated. These were 'individuals who have taken pleasure in their phraseology, pronunciation, and way of life; but, above all, in the songs and dances of the females . . . In the barrio of Triana, a large *Gitano* colony had flourished, with the denizens of which it is at all times easy to have intercourse.'

Borrow can be taken with a large pinch of salt, but his description of the moment a gypsy wedding party starts dancing in a room piled three inches thick with sweetmeats gives an idea of the wildness of *juergas* past. 'In a few minutes the sweetmeats were reduced to powder, or rather to a mud, the dancers were soiled to the knees with sugar, fruits and yolks of egg. Still more terrific became the lunatic merriment. The men sprang high into the air, neighed, brayed, and crowed; whilst the *Gitanas* snapped their fingers in their own fashion, louder than castanets, distorting their forms into obscene attitudes, and uttering words to repeat which were an abomination.' Yet, still he loved them.

Those old gypsy protectors and enthusiasts have their modern equivalents. They include the social workers of the Tres Mil and those of the jails. There is something deeply attractive about the naivety of some gypsies, about their simple, yet historic, refusal to sign up to the modern world. Those who have won their trust were, I found, highly protective of them. Then there were the legion of *payo* flamenco buffs. These were often the first to say that, although there are many great *payo* flamenco singers, you could not do it properly unless you had gypsy blood in your veins. Access to *duende*, the mysterious, magical force that inspires the best flamenco, was, I was told, available only to true gypsies.

Gypsy-chasing was not the exclusive domain of absolute monarchs, however. General Franco ordered the militarised rural police, the Civil Guard, to keep the gypsies under control, specifying it as a task in the force's 1943 code. The generalísimo's regime patronised what some people have, only half-jokingly, referred to as '*nacional flamenquismo*', a folkloric accompaniment to the '*nacional catolicismo*' ideology of his regime. The popular *copla*, which many flamenco artists turned to, was the radio music of the regime. Franco, in short, was happy to see the spotted shirts, tight waistcoats and the broad Cordobese hats of what might be described as musical-hall gypsiness. There were no lack of gypsies and other artists prepared to play ball. Spain's gypsies have always known how to adapt. It was under him, though, that the gypsy families were cleaned out of Triana.

Despite all this, the Spanish gypsies' culture and social structure, already different from other gypsy groups around the continent, held strong. They remained stubborn, sometimes rebellious and always proud. They saw off, in short, every threat that came over the horizon, except drugs.

Gypsy culture is slowly being diluted. Some gypsies are now unrecognisable from other Spaniards. Life expectancy, however, is reported to be almost ten years lower than for other Spaniards, while only 1 per cent of gypsies go to university. Traditions remain strong. The checking of a bride's virginity by searching for blood on the sheets used on her wedding night is still practised by some. The gypsies kept their own laws and, until recently, still turned to their own elders, the so-called *tíos*, or uncles, to mediate in blood and honour disputes. But the rise of drug barons, gypsy politicians and, some say, evangelical pastors, has shaken their authority, if not the respect with which the elderly are still held. The *tíos* often established frontiers between competing groups so that they should not need to sort out questions of honour by turning to violence. It is something prison governors are still careful to do.

Separation, however, does not always work. The flamenco workshop group in Seville jail, for example, had recently seen its numbers reduced by one. A participant, serving time for a stabbing, had returned home on his first weekend out of jail. He had immediately been stabbed to death in a bar. Everybody was convinced it had been a revenge killing. 'It should not have gone that far,' commented Silva, shaking his head. 'More violence is not a solution.'

I should admit here to a long-standing penchant for some of the stranger bastard offspring of flamenco. It is the sort of stuff that sends serious-minded purists reaching for their guns. I learned to love groups such as Los Chichos, Las Grecas and Los Chunguitos when, on long journeys, I stocked up on cheap tapes and CDs at roadside bars.

These groups can only be described as the Status Quos of the flamenco world. The Chunguitos had the bad hairstyles, gold chains, medallions and 1970s dress sense of the worst of northern Soul. On older record covers they boast a passing resemblance to the Bay City Rollers. They took the simpler flamenco rhythms, especially *rumbas*, and turned them into electronic, urban pop. Their lyrics do not pass even the most basic mores of political correctness. 'You were so beautiful that I felt a desire to kill you, because I realised you were no longer mine,' they sing, or, quite simply: 'Pass me the joint, I want to get stoned . . .'

The women in these songs are mothers, virgins, whores, junkies, whipping posts and, especially, traitors to their men. '*Papá*, don't beat up *mamá* . . . because *mamá* is a good person.' The men, in turn, are poor, violent, bitter, drugged and, often, in jail. 'I would never have imagined/ that you might cheat on me/ my love was so blind/ that, for you, I killed,' Los Chichos sing in '*Mujer Cruel*', 'Cruel Woman'.

Liking these groups is roughly equivalent to being hung up on 1970s British pop-rock, with the added disgrace of lyrics that would put the most violent rappers to shame. It is not a recognised sign of high cultural standards. They do represent, however, a moment when flamenco began to mix with the world of rock and pop – as it continues to do. Unfortunately, this new wave of flamenco *rockeros* were also amongst the first wave of victims of the heroin explosion. The Grecas fought so badly that one of them, Tina, eventually stabbed the other, Carmela. An emaciated, peseta-less Tina could be seen wandering the Madrid barrio of Lavapiés in the early 1990s. She went on to spend time in jails and psychiatric units before the drugs finally killed her in 1995. One of the Los Chichos, in a deranged moment, managed to kill himself by throwing himself from a first-floor window.

What these groups did was a travesty to flamenco purists. But, just as the nineteenth-century *café cantantes,* the *coplas aflamencadas* of the mid-twentieth century and the Catalan *rumbas* of the 1960s had done, they opened flamenco back out to the world. A deluge of flamenco rock and pop has followed since then. The latest generation, brought up on hip-hop, acid house or rap, is producing its own potent, rhythmic mixtures. From the flamenco-blues guitar of Raimundo Amador to the Moroccan or Berber fusions of El Lebrijano and Radio Tarifa to the eclectic rap, hip-hop and everything else mix of Ojos de Brujo, the fusion continues. Spain is virtually unique, in western Europe, in having such a strong motor of autochthonous music. For flamenco is the bright, burning force behind a flow of popular music that is recognisably Spanish.

One man has done more to popularise flamenco in the past twenty years than anybody else. He was, of course, a gypsy. His name was José Monge Cruz, better known as Camarón de la Isla, the Shrimp of the Island. The Shrimp was a man with Mick Jagger lips and one of the worst, most bouffant, hairstyles since James Brown. He also possessed the best, most tragic, flamenco voice of the past quarter of a century.

Camarón was an intense introvert – a man of profound, hermetic silences. He lived in a period when young singers, thanks to the influence of pop and rock, could become living legends. It was also a time when flamenco itself opened up, incorporating new instruments and allowing itself to be influenced by the turbulent popular culture of the 1960s and 1970s. Camarón himself would lose from this meeting, dying a rock star's early death. Along the way, however, he ensured himself the same kind of mythical status of fellow tortured, 'live fast, die young' stars like Jimi Hendrix or Jim Morrison. He died in 1992. Some say that flamenco has yet to recover.

The Iglesia Mayor, the main church, stands on the Calle Real, the Royal Street, of the southern town of San Fernando. Perched on a flat 'island' called La Isla de León it overlooks the salt flats, muddy wetlands and still waters of the Bay of Cádiz. A plaque on the church reminds those present that this is where, in 1812, one of the key events in Spanish history took place. For it was here that a rebel parliament, fighting the French rule imposed by Napoleon, wrote the first Spanish constitution to enshrine popular sovereignty (male suffrage excluded monks, criminals, servants and those with no income). It was a time when Spain was adding new words to the international lexicon of war and politics. A new species of fighters, dubbed '*guerrillas*', harried the French. A new political label, meanwhile, was invented for those behind the constitution. They were the world's first '*liberales*'. Their battles with Catholic traditionalists, and the continued coup attempts, or *pronunciamientos*, of both sides, would dominate a politically chaotic nineteenth century but, also, bring universal male suffrage in 1891 (though elections were still manipulated by the interior ministry).

The liberal ethos of the constitution would later be betrayed by the man its authors had wanted to come back and run the country, Fernando VII '*el Deseado*', 'The desired one'. After winning, with the help of Wellington, their battle against Napoleon, the liberals saw their constitution declared null and void by Fernando.

In the Calle Carmen, one of the narrow streets leading down to the bay from the Calle Real, a second, more recent, important event in Spanish history took place. Here, in the shabby end of the shabbiest part of town, in a two-room house that shared a small patio with several neighbours, José Monge Cruz was born in December 1950. These were still the grey years in Spain, the years of hunger that followed the Civil War. José Monge was born at the bottom of the social and economic ladder – an Andalusian gypsy. But San Fernando, with its shipping and salt industries and its naval barracks, was relatively prosperous. And José's father, like many gypsies, had a forge which his elder brother Manuel, eighteen years his senior, took over when the father died in 1966.

The Monges did not starve. A blacksmith was near the top of the gypsy social order. One of José's brothers still lives in the handful of rooms where the eight Monge brothers and sisters grew up. When I visited it, the paint was peeling off the walls and the tiny, shared patio was run down and shambolic. A plaque on the outside wall reminded visitors that this was where José Monge Cruz was born and that his uncle had, because of his relatively pallid skin and his *rubio*, light-coloured, hair nicknamed him 'Camarón de la Isla', the 'Shrimp of the Island'. Camarón de la Isla, the plaque insisted had been 'a gypsy through and through'. He was 'so slim that he was almost translucent . . . and, instead of walking, he seemed to spring from one side to the other.'

José's mother, Juana, was a *canastera*, a basket-maker. After her husband's death, however, she kept the family afloat by cleaning bars and cafés. Few of those who met Juana remember her for how she earned her money. What they remember, instead, is how she sang. Camarón's father sang too. That early flamenco *palo*, the *martinete*, is a forge tune, traditionally accompanied only by the clink of a blacksmith's hammer. But it was Juana who the great names of flamenco – Manolo Caracol, La Niña de los Peines or La Perla de Cádiz – would come and listen to when they passed through town. Juana's children would all inherit some of her talent. Manuel, the eldest brother, began earning extra money by singing to the *señoritos* – rich men out on the town – at the Venta de Vargas, a local restaurant. But it was Camarón who, by the time he was twelve, was already the star.

I met Manuel in San Fernando's cemetery, where he goes daily to tend Camarón's huge marble tomb. I handed him a thick bunch of red and white carnations, a gift from two ardent Camarón admirers in Madrid. Manuel spends his time here arranging the fresh flowers that arrive continually and sometimes shooing off the fans who want to clamber up beside the seated statue of Camarón. 'Someone turns up virtually every day. From Seville, from Barcelona, from France or Germany,' said Manuel, still amazed at just how far his brother's name has travelled. The Shrimp sits atop his tomb with his trademark long, curling locks – responsible for an entire generation's worth of bad gypsy hairstyles – brushed up from his forehead and dripping down onto his shoulders. A dandy's handkerchief sits in his top pocket. The tomb is a piece of drab kitsch. Covered with slabs of black shiny marble, mottled with brown, it looks out of place in a cemetery where virtually everything else – except for the fresh carnations and roses, the paper flowers and a handful of mangy cats – is a brilliant white.

The greatest fanatics are the gypsies themselves, for whom Camarón is, quite simply, *El Príncipe,* The Prince. When he was alive, gypsy women would bring their children up to him and beg him just to touch them. He knew the myth was going too far when that happened. 'I don't like it,' he told his friend, later biographer, Enrique Montiel.

Manuel sticks my carnations in a pot, busily fluffing them up, fussing around with others that are already there. 'The other day I found some gypsy children here. They could only be about ten years old. They must have been here selling flowers at the *feria,* (the local fiestas). One of them said: "I am going to curl up here tonight beside my cousin Camarón and sleep next to him." "You can't do that," I said. "Nobody is allowed in here after the gates have been shut and, anyway, you'll get scared amongst all the dead." "I'll be all right. My cousin will look after me," the kid said.'

Camarón provoked a rare phenomenon in Spanish culture – public displays of gypsy pride. Entire families of gypsies would appear at his concerts and, while the *payos* looked on in amazement, let rip the full passion of flamenco. Fat matrons danced with beautiful, bejewelled and untouchable granddaughters. Tears were shed. The gypsy *juerga* was there for all to see.

Camarón's funeral in San Fernando saw coach-loads of gypsies bussed in from around the country and scenes of mass hysteria. Fifty thousand people arrived in a town of eighty thousand. Spain had rarely seen such a concentration of its gypsies. This was not just the death of a star, but the funeral of a prince, a demi-god, a man whose voice and hands were thought to contain magic forces that came from beyond the normal world of human experience.

Enrique Montiel, a writer who came from the posher end of town, had played with Camarón and his friends in the streets of San Fernando or jumping off the town's bridge into the river below. Enrique remembers, as a boy, drifting towards a noisy crowd gathered in a makeshift bar in the city's old, semi-ruined Moorish castle. 'It was where the town's cockfights were held,' he told me as we picked at *tortillitas de camarón*, fried shrimp pancakes, in the Venta de Vargas. Stars of bullfighting, flamenco and *farándula*, Spanish 'showbiz', stared down at us from photographs. A stunningly beautiful, bare-shouldered starlet with cleanly chiselled features and wide eyes turned out, to my amazement, to be Carmen Sevilla. I only knew her as the ageing television star who presented the lottery results.

Enrique continued his story. 'But when I got there, it was not cockfighting that people were fussing about. A ten-year-old blond gypsy boy was standing on a table singing. People were going crazy. It was Camarón,' he said.

His brother recalls how, when Camarón was still just a child, the *señoritos* who gathered at the Venta de Vargas would insist that he came to sing. 'After a while they always asked for Camarón, and we all knew we would earn more money that way. I would have to crawl on to the bed above all the other sleeping bodies and prod him awake. Often he would tell me that he didn't want to come.'

It was the start of a story of genius and tragedy, of the first flamenco star of the media age. Just as Camarón was often unwilling to sing for the *señoritos*, so he was an unwilling star. Quiet, introverted, uninterested in the trappings of wealth and stardom, he was a mystery to most people – even to the legion who claimed to be his friends. Rafael, my friend from Las Tres Mil, recalls meeting one of the shyest, quietest men he had ever seen: 'He would wrap his arms around his body and sink into himself when he was in company,' he said. 'You had to pull the words from his mouth. But he was a beautiful person.'

Camarón de la Isla died in 1992, aged just forty-two. A cancer caused by four packets of Winstons a day finished him off. Years of drug abuse, of heroin and cocaine, had already drained the resistance out of a body that produced a sound which revolutionised flamenco. With his death, Camarón's mythical status was ensured for ever. It continues to grow.

I asked Enrique about the drug abuse. 'I am not going to talk about that,' he said. Nor would most other people. Drugs were an intruder, something none of his friends or family will ever discuss. To some, especially the gypsies, mentioning the smack habit, the cocaine – snorted and smoked – the experiments with LSD, the days on end when he just disappeared with junkies, sleeping out in the rough if necessary as he consumed and consumed – even his wife, *la Chispa*, 'the Spark', could not persuade him home – is to show a lack of respect. The *payos* who inhabit the flamenco universe are just as careful, wary that the gypsies who hold the key to flamenco's magic garden may shut them out. Those prepared to talk about it ask not to be quoted by name. 'He was a multiple drug user. His consumption was extraordinary,' said one friend who should know. 'In the same time that you would do a single line of coke, he could shove grams of it up his nose.'

Camarón's first dozen records were made with the guitarist Paco de Lucía, under the benevolent dictatorship of the latter's father. They are serious, straight flamenco albums – part of a total output of some twenty records which, in life, only sold around 360,000 copies.

Camarón's final albums took ages to record. He would, occasionally, slip off into a state of numbed semi-consciousness. His penultimate album was called, simply, *Soy Gitano*, I am a Gypsy. Even when he was off the drugs and battling cancer, he had his own mixture of favourite prescription drugs – rohypnol and other downers – that he would put together to cope with the pain and withdrawal.

Camarón toyed with his body the way he would muck about with the recording machines that he collected, but never really mastered. Just as he saw the machines as practitioners of some sort of musical alchemy, so he gave his body over to the alchemy of powders, pills and liquids. He was, eventually, out of his skull much of the time.

In the end, he needed a personal nurse to help him manage his habit and point him towards various cures. At one stage he suffered temporary paralysis to a hand. At the nurse's house he would chase the heroin dragon and then turn suddenly, uncharacteristically, loquacious. When the nurse and his wife finally went to bed, a puppy-like Camarón occasionally turned up in their room saying he was lonely. Paranoias crept in. He disliked solitude. And nothing is more lonely than the road. Towards the end, all he wanted was to be with la Chispa and his children. 'I'll study a lot and make a record every couple of years,' he told friends. Tobacco, inhaled deep, held down, smoked with a profound and needy pleasure, stopped that happening. In fact, by the time he died, tobacco had already done serious damage to the quality of that voice and, especially, the lungs that drove it. Camarón, unbelievably, had begun to lose that remarkable control of pitch and breathing that was part of his uniqueness. He could not control his breath sufficiently to sing the more difficult *palos* as he would have liked to. Some of the posthumous releases of his music have used the artificial wonders of recording studio machines to improve the mythical voice.

Sung flamenco is a complex, difficult thing. There are strict rules about rhythm. And there are dozens of *palos*. Each has its own rule-book and, often, exacting demands on the singer's ability. By the time he was fifteen, when Antonio Vargas recorded him at the Venta de Vargas – the noise of the occasional lorry coming down the road audible in the background – Camarón had a virtuoso's control of many of them. But he also had a distinctive voice which, magically, tapped the raw, emotional depths of *cante jondo*, while still retaining a master's control. 'He improvised often without adulterating the essence . . . He searched for points where he could twist and tease the traditional styles so as to make the resulting song his own,' the critic Manuel Ríos explains.

It was when he went to Madrid and met up with an extraordinary young guitarist called Paco de Lucía, that the amazing things began to happen. A whole school of flamenco had grown up with the rule-book as written by Antonio Mairena, a singer and academic of flamenco who died in 1983 having 'recovered', and written down, many of the older *palos*. Camarón and de Lucía were part of a new generation which gradually introduced changes.

New instruments appeared. The old formula of guitar and voice was widened out. The guitar itself went from being principally an instrument of accompaniment to having a strong voice of its own. De Lucía brought in a percussion instrument from Peru, the *cajón* – a wooden box that the player sits on and beats – which is now an accepted part of flamenco. Flutes, bass instruments and string sections also appeared. The Royal Philharmonic Orchestra even played on one album.

The break with orthodoxy came after Camarón split, not so much with Paco de Lucía, but with his father. The father, Antonio Sánchez, produced Camarón's first eleven records, with his son always on the guitar. When Camarón changed producer in 1979, he turned to Ricardo Pachón. The result was *La Leyenda del Tiempo,* a record which scandalised purists. Even some gypsies returned it to the shops, claiming 'this is not Camarón'. The poetry Pachón and co-composer Kiko Veneno turned to for the words to their music was not the old romance stuff but later Spanish classics like Lorca and, even, the Persian Omar Khayám. They also brought in instruments as foreign and bizarre – to flamenco purists – as keyboards, electronic bass and, even, a sitar. It was, according to one biographer, 'the most important flamenco record of recent decades'. Camarón himself was scared by the reaction of the purists, and asked to tone things down in later albums, but a mould had been broken. Spanish geniuses, however, famously take a long time to achieve recognition. The record sold only 5,482 copies before his death.

It was enough, however, to take flamenco to a new audience. 'Suddenly the people who liked what he was doing were the same people who liked rock or who liked jazz,' Pachón told me after waving me into his Seville townhouse in what looked like a Japanese kimono. Camarón started appearing at international festivals. The world's musicians began to fall in love with him. 'He was a musician's musician. Those who knew, could tell he was doing something extraordinary. It didn't matter what their own musical background was,' explained Montiel. The list of admirers was long, from Mick Jagger to Quincy Jones.

A would-be young Spanish rock star known as El Gran Wyoming (who would go on to be a motor-mouthed, satirical television presenter) was dragged, unwillingly, to a Camarón concert and remembered it like this. 'This wasn't a show, it was something else. That man was not going through a memorised repertory. He wasn't pretending. I saw my idols of that moment. *El Camarón* was like Janis Joplin, like Joe Cocker, like Jimi Hendrix. He wasn't good or bad. He was, as the saying went back then, "strong stuff".'

Camarón's rise coincided with a special period in Spanish history, a sudden explosion of freedom released by Franco's death. And here was flamenco, stripped of its tacky, folkloric, flag-waving adornments. It was, if you like, a people's music, at a time when the people were, once more, in control.

Flamenco's continuing development is best summed up in the words of one nineteenth-century *soleá*. 'How are you going to compare/ a pool of water with a fountain?' it asks. 'The sun comes out and dries the pool/But the fountain keeps on flowing.' Flamenco has kept on flowing, and changing. Spain is the wealthier, and luckier, for it. It boasts one of the Continent's few, living, evolving home-grown music and dance forms. It is a vivacious beast that time, fashion, the disdain of some and the over-enthusiastic embrace of others have all been unable to put down.

On the tenth anniversary of his death, I took my partner – a die-hard Camarón fan – and children to a flamenco mass in Camarón's memory at the church on the Calle Real. My partner soon proved that Camarón, even from the grave, could exert a star's debilitation of his fans' nervous systems and mental composure. There were tears in the car, outbursts of rage at the idea that we might arrive late and a jumpy desire to see la Chispa and Camarón's children – would they look like him? – in the flesh. A priest, well-known for his love of flamenco, had come from Madrid to take the service. He sang much of it himself, mostly off-tune, to flamenco *palos* and, eventually, in a very un-priestly moment, shed tears for Camarón. At the door afterwards we thanked him, saying we had never seen a priest cry in church before. 'Some priests are very roguish . . . but we are also good people,' he replied. It could have been an epitaph for Camarón himself.

On a Sunday evening in Seville, I followed another Tres Mil gypsy, Amaro, and his family in their huge green Renault Master van out past the rubbish and bonfires of Las Vegas. We crossed the wide Avenida de la Paz to a street of warehouse units and workshops, appropriately named Las Herramientas, the Street of Tools. Here, squeezed between a frozen foods warehouse, a metal-beating workshop and a place selling second-hand fridges, was a unit that had been turned into a chapel of the Evangelical Church of Philadelphia.

Popularly known as the 'Gypsies' church', the evangelicals have captured some 100,000 Spanish gypsies – some 15 per cent of the total – since the first few gypsy pastors were recruited while picking grapes in France in the 1960s. As flamencoised music blasted out from the unit that housed the church, Melchor, the pastor, explained why it has done so well. 'The gypsies have, historically, been ignored and forgotten, not just socially, economically and politically but in the religious sense as well. The Catholic priests never explained the Gospel well,' he explained. 'I feel proud of my culture, of who we are. The evangelical church does not ask you to change your culture. It embraces it. We write our songs and use our own rhythms, with all their strength and ability, to express our feelings. Here it is gypsies who do the singing and who do the preaching,' he said.

Although the church also welcomes *payos*, I found it hard to spot any amongst the two hundred people sat on the hard wooden benches, women on the left and men on the right. Wind whistled through the warehouse roof, clad in rainwater-stained chipboard, and strip lights hung from bare metal girders.

The contrast with the overstuffed baroque churches of old Seville could not have been greater. The walls of the gypsy chapel were of rough-painted breeze-block. A couple of posters provided the only decoration. One, bearing a photo of a waterfall in green woodlands, exhorts: 'To all the thirsty, come to the waters.'

There were babies in pushchairs and kids running backwards and forwards, fighting over crisps, or taking messages from their mother to their father and vice versa. There was music, too, and *palmas*.

The message from the preacher struck at the hearts of a people used to living on the margins, suspicious of a world ruled by ambition, frenetic work and money. 'The system of this world is "Have, have and have more". It produces hate and enmity. It brings chaos and death,' the preacher, a large gypsy man in a beige suit and tie with his top button undone, said amid loud cries of 'Amen!' 'Alleluya!' and 'Blessed be God!' 'The system of God is to forgive, to forget and to live in delight. It says: "I am happy with what I have and will give what I can." It brings love and a chance to live in delight and full freedom.'

Melchor explained that the church was also heavily involved in drug rehabilitation and education. I had already been told that ignorance was largely to blame for heroin's success amongst gypsies – with one group of women in Algeciras getting hooked after using it to deal with period pains. 'Drugs are a social problem that affect the poor especially and, within the poor, the gypsies. We have to educate our young,' he said. 'We ourselves have had problems and the Gospel helped us. Many gypsies have been rehabilitated this way.'

There was a strong sense, despite the apocalyptic, fundamentalist rhetoric, of honest men (for this was a male-led affair, though the women's pews were fuller) determined to lead their families through the dangerous waters of a world into which Spain's gypsies, by choice or not, sometimes find it so hard to fit. I am no church-lover. Stepping out of the industrial unit at the end of the service, however, amid hand-shaking and back-slapping, I found myself wishing these Philadelphians well. I was concerned, too, for the children here and their worried parents.

Camarón, a man whose clanking neck jewellery could include, at the same time, chains and medallions bearing images of the Virgin of El Rocío, the Star of David, the Christ of San Fernando or the anchor of the Brotherhood of Esperanza of Triana, was never much interested in the evangelicals – though his wife, la Chispa, was. His chosen delights were, in the end, his ruin.

Rafael told me a story, one which Camarón's brother Manuel did not recognise and Enrique Montiel thought could be another myth to have emerged around his figure. 'Two days before his death, a doctor who was treating him in Barcelona found a note he had written on the bedside table. The man kept it. Now he feels guilty about it, and wants to get it back to the family,' said Rafael, who claimed to have read a copy. 'The letter said the following: "To all the young people. Life is beautiful, but it is also bad. I, who am telling you this, am almost free."'

Rafael, unfortunately, did not seem to have grasped the message. Driving around Las Tres Mil one day I saw him striding off towards Las Vegas. He was a man obviously looking for a deal. He had admitted to using coke a bit, but swore there was nothing untoward in an occasional habit. 'When you have children you have to start acting responsibly. You have to know how to control yourself or you are lost,' he had said.

On my return several months later, however, he failed to answer my phone calls. I wondered whether I had offended him. Eventually a mutual friend explained. Rafael had been swallowed up by Las Vegas. It was time to move on, to leave Spain's gypsies and their remarkable music behind. I wanted to stay away from politics and history, however. The country's endless roads, and their bars, had introduced me to some of the stranger offshoots of flamenco. Now it was time to turn off them to visit somewhere else. I wanted to find out what lay behind the colourful neon signs that, so loudly and obviously, decorate a different kind of roadside establishment.

7
Clubs and Curas

I have retired to my local bar to leaf through the morning newspapers. Breakfast is served without any words being exchanged between myself and the waiter, beyond a brisk '*buenos días*'. He knows my order. It appears automatically, the clanking, bashing, steaming and sizzling of coffee machine and *plancha*, the hot plate used for frying and toasting, starting as soon as I am spotted walking through the door. This can be a complex business. How do you keep your fingers clean when the toasted roll you have been given has a large pool of olive oil washing over its crusty banks? And, once the oil is on your fingers, how do you stop it sticking the pages of your newspaper together? The little, square, tissue serviettes, grabbed from the plastic container on my table, pile up in front of me.

When it comes to sex surveys, I am used to turning to *Cosmopolitan* magazine or its glossy equivalents. Spain, however, has the august Instituto Nacional de Estadística, the state-run National Statistics Institute. So it is that, between sips of *café con leche* from a small glass that burns my finger-tips, I am informed that the *instituto* has discovered the following: more than one in four Spanish men under forty-nine have had sex with a prostitute during their lives, while one in seventeen have done so over the past year. 'Both figures are noticeably higher than those observed in other surveys in Europe,' the investigators comment. The *instituto* did not dare say it directly, but it was calling Spanish men the most enthusiastic brothel johns of Europe. Could that be true?

I looked around the bar, with its varnished, cork-tiled walls and strange 1970s decor. I wondered idly about the people here. Which of the men was a brothel regular? Could it be the blue-overalled painters and decorators renovating some apartment in our block?

Was it the insurance-salesman type, frowning over his copy of *El Mundo*? Could it be the old man with the small moustache, leafing through the conservative *ABC* newspaper? Or would it be the chain-smoking 'intellectual', one eye on the National Geographic documentary showing on the television set perched high above the door, the other watching the nurses file in from hospital for breakfast? And what about the nurses, or the elderly, carefully made-up ladies who gather here to swap tales of ailments and operations while updating their oral births and deaths column on the barrio. Were their husbands, boyfriends, sons or brothers brothel-goers? Did they care? Did anybody? Should I? Did the *instituto's* figures say anything about Spanish society? Or was this another bizarre, even prurient, subject that only an *anglosajón* would consider interesting? There was only one way to find out. It was time to let some neon into my life. I would have to visit one of those gaudily lit *clubes de alterne*, the brothels that dot Spain's main highways.

Which is how I ended up at El Club Romaní, a huge, neon-lit pile of granite and slate – half French chateau, half Galician country *pazo* – in an industrial estate beside the motorway running south from Valencia. This was my first-ever visit to a brothel. I was trying hard to remember that the only way you could shock a certain type of Spaniard about sex was, well, by being shocked by it. So, as a young man in a black leather jacket and a friendly, wrinkled old doorman showed me around, I adopted what I hoped was a worldly, nonchalant personality.

I had spotted these clubs before. Who could miss them? Lit up with multi-coloured displays of neon, they shout their presence out loud. Newcomers wonder what these fanfares of pink, red, green and blue light that they see up and down Spain's highways mean. Spaniards, however, know that much neon can mean only one thing.

I am not sure what I was expecting, but it certainly was not this. It was early afternoon and the club was still empty. We had wandered through the bar area and into a small corridor. A sliding door had been pushed aside and I was staring at a large, round bed covered with a bright yellow bedspread. Some colourful, crocheted cushions and stuffed scarlet love hearts were scattered on it. Circling the bed was a sort of padded crash bar. In fact, lined up below the erotic prints on the walls, there were a whole variety of bars and handles. Some were recognisable as the sort that elderly people put in beside their baths so they can haul themselves out of the water.

'This is the room that has been adapted for *discapacitados*, for the disabled,' announced the man in the black leather jacket, half-proud, half-amused. There was an en suite bathroom, with a ramp into the shower. The toilet had all the bars and extra bits a disabled person could hope for. But the *pièce de résistance* was sitting in the corner. 'This is a very special wheelchair,' black leather jacket, a former Moscow correspondent for a Spanish newspaper group turned PR man for brothel owners, explained. 'You press a button and it stands itself, and whoever is in it, almost upright. That means they can go to the bar and have a drink too,' he said, chuckling.

I was not sure whether to believe this. The room, I thought, must be a publicity stunt, something mocked up to win a bit of sympathy for his boss's trade. But then the old man piped up. 'In the old days we had to carry them upstairs to the bedrooms in our arms,' he sighed. 'It was hard work. It was pretty humiliating for them, too.'

What is interesting about Spanish brothels is not so much that they exist, but that they are so blatant. This, in turn, reflects Spanish attitudes to them, and to sex. Where *anglosajones*, for example, would be shocked, Spaniards are blithely indifferent. The *instituto's* findings provoked no commentary – and no debate – in Spain. Newspapers reported, and then immediately forget about them. As an experiment in contrast, I ran the figures past a class of New York University students who I taught on a Masters' course in Madrid. 'Gross!' came the unanimous reply from the front-row women. A wide ocean, clearly, separates one idea of sexual morality from another. In fact sex and morality are two words that a certain kind of Spaniard does not think should be uttered together, especially if other people's sex lives and other people's morality are being discussed. This did not mean Spaniards were wild sexual inventors. The American postgraduates would have won hands down on real experience if they had been compared to Spaniards of the same age. The *instituto's* own figures confirmed that.

Before coming to the Club Romaní, the PR man had taken me to see José Luis, the lawyer for the brothel owners' association that employed him, at the headquarters of his private security firm in Valencia. The lawyer had a Franco-era Spanish flag behind his desk. He was an *ultra*, a Spanish right-wing extremist.

Mariló, a Spanish prostitute, joined us. A single mother and former squatter, she was twenty-nine years old, cheerful and chatty. Mariló was introduced as the spokeswoman for a prostitutes' lobby group, though it looked decidedly as if the group had really been formed by José Luis, who fed her lines. Mariló is, in fact, one of the minority of prostitutes in Spain, fewer than 5 per cent, who are actually Spanish.

'What I really want is for people to stop looking down at me and treating me like a *bolsa de basura*, a rubbish-bag. It is time people recognised that we provide a social service,' she said. Mariló was convinced of this last point. She adopted the professional lingo of the social worker to explain it. 'We help get rid of depression and stress, and we help people communicate. Those are important things.'

The social-worker jargon slipped, however, when she mused on the only way to stop men going to prostitutes: 'You would have to cut off their *pililas*, their little pricks.'

Mariló knew exactly why she was doing this. 'It's a way of getting money. Who else is going to pay my daughter's nursery school?' she asked. 'I am not exploited. If anybody is exploited, it is the men. We exploit their sexual desires for money. And if anyone fails to show me respect in the bedroom, then they don't get it. I am the one in charge.' Occasionally, however, she expressed doubts about her career choice. 'That's because you lack self-esteem,' José Luis told her. 'Yes, it must be,' she answered.

The association, José Luis wanted me to know, did not consider its members to be running *burdeles*, as brothels are properly called. It was called the National Association of Owners of '*Alterne*' Places. He gave me a glossy magazine listing its members, places with names like S'candalo, Kiss Club, Falcon Crest and Hotel Elvis.

The clubs, he said, were places men went to *alternar*. The verb itself was a clue to the ambiguity with which the whole topic is treated in Spain. We struggled to come up with a definition. José Luis offered '*trato y amistad*', 'socialising and friendship'. It was such a uniquely Spanish word that I later looked it up in the dictionary of the Real Academia Española, which has the final word on the Spanish language. The Royal Academy, in a long-winded definition, said it was actually the women who were practising *alterne* as they 'stimulate clients to spend money in their company, thereby obtaining a percentage'.

Whatever the exact definition, '*alterne*', José Luis insisted, did not mean buying sex. Up to two-thirds of clients were only after a drink and a scantily clad woman to listen to their opinions, laugh at their jokes or make them feel attractive. 'It is easy to calculate, because you may sell 1,200 tickets at the door – but only get 400 *subidas* – goings-up – to the rooms,' said José Luis.

Mariló explained that the sex side of the game normally followed a heavily over-priced drink or two, for which she got a commission, and some chat. 'I am told that in northern Europe things are much colder. The clients come in, point to a girl and they are off. Here, at least, you get a bit of conversation,' she said. It somehow seemed very Spanish to put talking on a par with sex, even if both were paid for.

José Luis admitted that the confused nature of the law, which banned people from making money off prostitutes but did not make selling sex illegal, effectively allowed prostitution to flourish. Spain, he said, was probably the most permissive country in Europe (though Germany and Holland may dispute that). It even attracted sex tourists to clubs along its borders. 'There is a lot of legal *nebulosidad*, haziness, and therefore there is great freedom . . . Prohibition would turn off the neon and bring in the mafias,' he said. In fact, the mafias moved in long ago. Most of Spain's more than 2,000 clubs are not members of José Luis's association. An indeterminate number are in the hands of mafias and pimps who 'own' immigrant girls.

The association's members had got around the law on not living off prostitution by only charging the girls 'rent' on the rooms they used. 'These are hotels. They provide rooms for the girls, who work for themselves,' Jose Luis said. 'No laws are being broken.'

Reliable figures on Spanish prostitution are hard to come by. A Civil Guard report in 2004 counted 20,000 prostitutes working in clubs in a geographical area that contained 38 per cent of the Spanish population. It was, the same report said, twice as many as in 1999. José Luis claimed that *alterne* and the sex industry turned over 18 billion euros a year (and could, potentially, pay 3 billion euros in tax). That seemed a wild exaggeration. With just over a third of Spain covered by the Civil Guard report, however, and many prostitutes working the streets or out of city apartments, this is obviously a huge, and lucrative, business. And lots of people share in the bonanza.

A few hours later, after black leather jacket had scared the living daylights out of me in his powerful Audi, we were in Sollona, the small town that boasts El Romaní as one of its major businesses. This is where Valencia's industrial suburbs meet the countryside. A Ford car factory, turning out Fiestas, Focuses and Kas, lies not far away. Around the corner, swallowed up by the industrial units, lies a tiny, well-cared-for, yellow-painted chapel dedicated to the Virgin of Aguavives. The industrial estate gives way to orchards of fruit trees that stretch out towards the old rice fields and wetlands of the Albufera, the large lake that runs up to the Mediterranean seashore.

In the car, the PR man told me of a minor-division football team from Albacete, which was saved from bankruptcy by shirt sponsorship from the Night Star, a local brothel. 'One of the bonuses for not being relegated was a night at the club,' he confided. Some *alterne* clubs were a key part of the local economy.

One former health spa with a chapel for celebrating 'weddings, christenings and first communions' had become a club called 'Madam's'. It was said to contribute 30,000 euros a year in municipal taxes to the frontier town of Capmany, in Catalonia – enough to employ a road-sweeper or two. Some clubs in Galicia, he said, even managed to get local mayors to the openings.

The only legal problems the clubs got, he said, were raids from Labour Ministry inspectors. They shut the clubs down for a day or two and fined them up to 6,000 euros per girl. I never properly understood why. If *alterne* was a confusing word to define, then the laws that ruled it were, quite simply, crazy. On the one hand, it was illegal to make money off prostitutes. On the other, it was not illegal to have them working in your club. Then again, it was wrong, according to the Labour Ministry, not to give them proper work contracts. But giving them work contracts would, formally, mean making money off prostitutes. The law meant there was no straight answer to one of the questions I was asking myself. Was Spain formally in favour of (or, at least, not against) prostitution, or not? Perhaps, I thought, nobody wanted the question asked, or dared take a public stance on it.

My tour of El Romaní revealed just how big a business this was. On the upper floors there were huge, luxury suites with saunas and six-seater jacuzzis. There was a small, well-equipped gym for the 60 to 100 girls who lived here in shared rooms. In the attic I was shown a fully-equipped hairdressing salon and sun-bed. Downstairs there was a boutique selling, amongst other things, miniature bikinis and pairs of platform shoes with impossibly high heels. The prostitutes had their own canteen. A cork board informed them about medical tests and gave addresses of local Western Union branches, so they could send money home. Globalisation, I realised, was firmly entrenched in the Spanish sex trade. A global need for money met a local demand for sex.

The owner's son, a young man whose expensive black leather jacket matched that of the PR man, showed me a file full of photocopies of the girls' passports. They came from at least two dozen countries, stretching from Poland, Portugal and Paraguay to Lithuania, Nigeria or Brazil. 'We send copies of their passports to the Guardia Civil,' he explained. 'That way they can check if any are false.' The local police, in other words, far from being a threat, were punctually informed of exactly who was working at the club.

The owner's son said the club filled up with eighteen- to twenty-five-year-olds on Saturday nights, some dropped by girlfriends who met them later at a nearby macro-discotheque. 'There are things you just don't believe until you see them,' he said. Many prostitutes took Saturdays off. The youngsters were not big enough spenders for them.

An hour or so after my tour of the empty club we came back. Men were coming off shift, or finishing a day at the office. The car park was almost full, though the owner's son insisted this was a quiet afternoon. He was still hopeful that the crews of three Nato frigates docked in Valencia – from Britain, the US and Italy – would show up. The bar was now packed with girls in micro-bikinis, tottering around on towering platforms with transparent, stacked heels. Some were already draped around clients at the bar. Others were leading men upstairs to the rooms.

'*¿Fumas?*', 'Do you smoke?' asked a Moroccan girl, apparently looking for a cigarette. 'No, I'm afraid not,' I replied. '*¿Y follas?*', 'Do you fuck then?' she added.

After the initial shock, and the problem of where to rest your gaze, the inside of a *club* pretty soon turns mundane. The clients were an average cross-section of adult Spanish men or, at least, of those who could afford to drop twenty euros on a drink or anything from 60 to 600 on sex. Curiously, many really did look as though they were trying to chat up the girls – as if the credit card was not the key part of the deal.

What, I wondered, did the people of Sollana think of having El Romaní, that temple to commercial sex, in their backyard? In town I found another building with bright lights on the front. A figure of Christ decorates the front of the Santa María Magdalena church in the Plaça Major. It is surrounded, not with neon, but with a ring of clear light-bulbs. I found the priest in his parish house just behind the church. He opened the door, but did not invite me in. 'Does anybody in Sollona ever complain about El Romaní?' I asked.

'Not really,' he said. 'Some people complain in private. But it is out of the way in the industrial estate.

'Whoever goes, goes, and whoever does not, does not,' he added, somewhat enigmatically. '*La gente pasa.* People can't be bothered.' The priest himself only went to the industrial estate to officiate at the fiestas for the Virgin of Aïgues Vives in August.

There is no sign of forced exploitation in El Romaní. But this is the high end of the sex market. Only eighty clubs belong to the association, with its rules about medical check-ups and telling police who is working in them. Catalonia, where local authorities have introduced a form of registration, has some 270 clubs. The vast majority, however, make up their own rules. Some have thugs on the door and debt-laden illegal immigrants working, in effect, as sex slaves. What, I wondered when I drove past it outside Toledo, would a club called 'Cow Woman' be like?

I was still perplexed. If it was illegal to make money out of prostitutes – even if it was not illegal to be, or go to, a prostitute – how could the clubs be so brash about their business? And, if prostitution really did turn over that much money, who was getting the cash? One obvious place where the money was going was to Spain's major newspapers.

In my highly conservative neighbourhood of Madrid, a peculiarly shaped newspaper is stacked high every morning at the newsagents. Called *ABC*, it is little more than the size of a magazine. Old men with bottle-green woollen overcoats or Burberry macintoshes queue up at my local newspaper shop every morning to buy this, the voice of traditional, Roman Catholic Spain – though, I notice that, after a recent revamp, it is also gaining younger readers. Every Thursday a religious supplement, *Alfa y Omega*, gives voice to the concerns of the archbishopric of Madrid – including, for example, warnings about the dangers of gay marriage or single parenthood.

Flick through the pages of *ABC*, however, and you will find its readers are no strangers to prostitution. For here are several pages covered with hundreds of small advertisements from prostitutes. 'Eva, 19. Upper-class girl from Salamanca neighbourhood, so insatiable that my parents threw me out of the house after catching me in bed with lots of boys. I am pure *vicio*, (vice). Now I live on my own . . . and can do all the *guarraditas* (dirty little things) I ever dreamed of,' runs one. It is by no means the most explicit. All Spain's 'serious' newspapers run advertisements like this. *El País*, *El Mundo*, *La Vanguardia*, *El Periódico*, *El Correo* . . . All the worthiest publications boast pages of advertisements that, in some newspapers, can be accompanied by photos of scantily clad women and descriptions of the world's more bizarre sexual practices. The advertisements are placed by male, female and transvestite prostitutes. Like all established small-ads columns, they have their own argot. There are promises of sexual practices from across the world – Greece, Thailand, Japan, even Burma – in 'private apartment, hotel or at your home'. Credit cards, some advertisements reassure readers, will be accepted. The Comisiones Obreras trade union claimed in 2005 that one newspaper, which it did not name, was gaining 6 million euros a year from these advertisements.

The contrast between a country which, when asked by pollsters, describes itself as 80 per cent Roman Catholic and its generally laissez-faire attitude to all things sexual is one of Spain's great paradoxes. That contrast reaches its zenith in the pages of *ABC* and – lest you think that this is a last vestige of 'old' Spain – in its new, successful, even more conservative rival, *La Razón*. The Pope inspires the editorials but it is prostitutes who service the small-ads pages. The left-wing and liberal press is, in a convenient combination of commercial and moral interests, laissez-faire on sex and, by extension, prostitution, almost as a matter of identity. Searching through the archives of the left-wing *El País*, for example, I find precious little room afforded to the kind of feminist thinking that says prostitution gives men the wrong idea about women.

Prostitution, then, is a sort of open secret. It is there for all to see, but is surrounded by either silence or indifference. Spanish friends, of both sexes, enjoyed my tales from El Romaní. Few made any comment, however, except to say that the disabled room sounded like a good idea. Most did not realise that Spain had far more, or at least far more visible, brothels than other places. Some agreed that prostitutes provided a social service. The contrast with my class-full of New York University students could not be greater. That is not to say that some Spaniards – mostly traditional, Catholic conservatives or feminists – do not want to get rid of prostitution, but they remain largely silent or unheard.

The problems with the *anglosajones*, several Spanish newspaper columnists had already informed me, was that too many of us were *moralistas*. Although the translation, 'moralist', often sounds harmless enough, in Spanish it brought connotations of extreme puritanism. *Moralistas*, they suggested, were moral fascists, out to control the private lives of others.

Spaniards seem genuinely unconcerned about sexual morality or, more accurately, other people's sexual morality. A recent glut of open-to-air, late-night porn on local television channels – peppered with advertisements for chat lines – has been greeted with either jokes, or resounding silence. I once walked into a bar in a small Andalusian town to find it playing on the television set in the corner. The customers, male and female, continued their conversations as if it was just another bullfight or football match rather than a stew of naked, ejaculating bodies. Turning on the television while sitting up late one night working on this book in a small hotel in a lovingly restored old building in Granada's Albaicín district, I was given my introduction to gay porn. Two men were mechanically sodomising one another on what appeared to be some local broadcaster. Are the conservative burghers of Granada, or any other city whose local television stations are, like the local newspaper, making money off prostitution or pornography, up in arms? Not at all. It is not just that nobody is, or is prepared to admit to being, scandalised. Sex, paid for or otherwise, just seems to be a matter-of-fact sort of business. Puritanism, it seems, really does belong to Europe's north.

I was reminded of this by Alex Ollé, one of the directors of the avant-garde Catalan theatre group La Fura dels Baus, as we sat at a café table in the main square of the small Murcian farming town of Lorca. I had just sat through his play *XXX* at the town's quaint, turn-of-the-century playhouse. La Fura have gained themselves an international reputation for sensorial bombardment, for getting in their public's faces. *XXX* was no exception. It featured a live internet link to a Barcelona peep-show as well as simulated, or filmed, threesomes, foursomes, blow-jobs, cunnilingus, spaghetti sex, sodomy, rape, S&M, incest and, to finish it all off, genital mutilation. At one stage the play had invited me to contemplate the non-dilemma of whether pornography or war was more shocking, as if the two things were somehow comparable. More seriously, it was also an invitation to think about where the limits were. I had to close my eyes for most of the last five minutes, the rape and mutilation scene, so my personal answer was obviously somewhere before that. But none of the dapper elderly gents or fierce-looking matrons, fresh from the hairdressers for their night out at the theatre, appeared, at least on the surface, terribly disturbed. Certainly none accepted the invitation to leave if they felt shocked.

'This show would cause a scandal in a small British town,' said Ollé, accurately predicting what would happened when it travelled to a London stage a year later. 'The British are very conservative. When it comes to sex, there is not too much prejudice here in Spain.'

I am not sure, however, whether he was completely right. There still seems to be something very male-centred and, one young *Madrileña* woman suggested to me, slightly seedy about this attitude. Certainly, she assured me, young men still had different ideas about what was acceptable sexual behaviour for them and what was acceptable for young women. That form of prejudice at least had not disappeared.

Only a handful of voices on the Catholic, conservative right or the feminist left seem to get worked up about prostitution or pornography. Shortly after I had visited El Romaní, I came across a long report in *El País* newspaper on the country's status as Europe's largest consumer of cocaine. A psychiatrist suggested that one reason for that was that a defining trait of modern Spaniards was that they were radically opposed to banning anything. 'Anything that smacks of restriction or prohibition in this country is considered immoral, old-fashioned and fascist,' the psychologist, Carlos Alvarez Vara, said. Spaniards, in short, do not like being told what not to do.

To be scandalised about sex is to be '*estrecho*', 'narrow' or prudish – something associated with the repressive, and hypocritical, time under General Franco when the Church really did set the rules. His death set Spain on a delayed sexual revolution that was grasped with fervour. But it would be wrong to blame all this on *el Caudillo*. Too many years have gone by. The pendulum has had plenty of time to swing the other way.

One measure of Spaniards' attitudes to the rules that govern sex is the age of consent. This was raised from twelve to thirteen in 1999 by Aznar's government. Other European countries place that age at anywhere between fourteen and seventeen. In the US it goes as high as eighteen in some states. Only a handful of countries – mostly Latin American or African – have a similar, or lower, age. In practice, however, Spaniards start their sex lives later than in other European countries. Most young Spanish men remain virgins until after their eighteenth birthday while most women wait until they are nineteen.

There can be a brisk, often amused, frankness in the way Spaniards discuss sex. On several occasions I have been caught out, and thrown into tongue-tied episodes of embarrassment, by sudden, graphic confessions of peccadilloes or amatory experiments. What, after all, do you say to a neighbour who apologises for not answering his doorbell because he was 'snogging the babysitter' while his wife was out? This attitude is reflected on television. One advertisement, for a chocolate bar, starts, as a joke, with a young man waking up with a tent-pole-sized erection in his boxer shorts.

This sexual frankness, apart from being ever-present in the films of Pedro Almodóvar and others, is also evident in the literary world. Most bookshops can be counted on to stock a few of the mauve-spined works put out by Tusquets publishing company in the *Sonrisa Vertical* – the Vertical Smile – collection of erotic writing. The Vertical Smile has been one of Spain's most popular literary prizes (and there are almost 3,000 of these each year), though it has recently suffered from a paucity of entries. Nobel prize-winner Camilo José Cela once sat on the jury. The contrast with Britain, where it is a prize for bad sex writing that gets all the attention, could not be greater. Some of Spain's best contemporary writers, including Almudena Grandes and her *The Ages of Lulu* – later translated into twenty languages – have walked off with the 20,000-euro prize. The jury praised one winner for 'the richness of scenes that, aside from being fresh, turn out to be perverse, fetishistic and transgressive'.

All this frankness and unshockability might make one think that Spaniards were avid sexual adventurers, leaping from bed to bed and experimenting with every single possible sexual variety like characters from an Almodóvar film. But the Instituto Nacional de Estadística, with its *Cosmopolitan* hat on again, says that is not true. Half the women under forty-nine that it surveyed, and a quarter of the men, had been to bed with just one person.

A survey carried out in the mid-1990s by government-funded investigators at the Centre for Sociological Research found that only 41 per cent of Spaniards aged between eighteen and twenty-four had initiated their sex lives in a bed. With most still living at their parents' homes, the others had resorted to cars, the great outdoors or anywhere else they could find a moment of privacy. 'Parents are confused and out of touch. Most are convinced that their children do not have a sex life,' a sociologist quoted by one newspaper explained.

This problem has led to some ingenious suggestions from local politicians. The southern seaside town of Velez-Málaga, for example, considered turning off the seafront lights for an hour every night so couples could 'release their sexual desires'. 'It has always been traditional for young people to use the dark and the low tide for a roll in the sand,' a town councillor explained. Granada's

Green Party, meanwhile, suggested handing out a hotel voucher, called a *bonosex*, to young people living at home. In the regional government of Extremadura, one functionary proposed setting aside 'sex zones' for young couples. None of these suggestions prospered. The last one was slapped down by Juan Carlos Rodríguez Ibarra, the Socialist regional premier. 'I am not about to turn the regional government into some sort of *madame*,' he snorted. 'They will just have to find somewhere themselves.' They do.

In the elegant, if crumbling, Madrid apartment block where I lived before buying my own flat, I was given a great lesson in Spanish sex education over the decades. I had been called to a tenants' meeting which was to be held around the marble coffee table of Doña Rafaela, a smart and exquisitely mannered seventy-year-old who lived on the fourth floor. A rebellion had broken out against our landlord, who also lived in the building. At the appointed hour I crept furtively down the darkened staircase and rapped on Doña Rafaela's door. She ushered me into a neat drawing room where half a dozen grey-haired ladies sat waiting expectantly. '*¡Dios mío*, it's a man!' one exclaimed. With the exception of our landlord, they pointed out, I was the only adult male in a building where most people had lived for more than thirty years. Many were still paying minuscule rents, frozen, if index-linked, back then. We, relatively recent arrivals, were paying twenty times more than some of the others. As the building gave him so little income, the landlord refused to invest in it. So it was that chunks of masonry were falling off the front of the building – requiring the fire brigade to cordon off the street one day – while the stairwell ceiling had also come crashing down.

I knew most of these *señoras* by sight, of course. Pleasantries had been exchanged at the doorway. Our two small children had been admired. One had even been presented with a bright yellow plastic cosh by Doña Adelaida from the second floor. But our short, shared trips in the groaning wood-and-glass lift had left time for little more than this.

It would have been rude to get straight down to business, so we chatted. Unexpectedly, the conversation turned to sex. The subject was brought up by Raquel, a chain-smoking granny-of-two from the first floor, who burst into the room clutching two bottles of wine and a box of books.

Raquel had just written *The Address Book of Lost Friends*, a publishing success which told of her daughter's heroin addiction and subsequent death from AIDS. It is a startling tale of degradation amongst the *niños bien*, the rich kids, of the haughty Madrid barrio of Salamanca, in the dizzying first decade of the transition to democracy. Raquel had been at the journalistic forefront of the *Transición*, logging the amazing self-transformation of the Spanish parliament. While she worked, and drank, her daughter – a frightening, siren-like Lolita – descended into heroin addiction. She pulled cousins, friends and other neighbourhood kids along with her. Most were long dead. Two young grandsons, and the deep lines scoured on Raquel's face, were all she left behind.

The grandsons were handsome young teenagers who, in an attempt not to repeat mistakes, had been sent to the local church school. Raquel was worried about AIDS. She had been trying to explain the importance of condoms to the eldest grandson, she said, but he had cut her short. 'They think they know it all because they get sex education at school,' she sighed.

'Well, thank God they get that,' snorted Doña Adelaida, a no-nonsense, Miss Marple figure with sensibly cropped grey hair. 'I remember when my professor of natural sciences at the university announced that our next lecture would be on human reproduction. "So there will be no need for the young ladies to come," he told us!'

'Oh, there was none of that silly stuff when I was a student,' remarked Doña Rafaela. 'We heard it all.'

'That, Rafaela, is because you went to university before me, during the Republic. I had to put up with Franco!' snorted Doña Adelaida, now a university professor herself.

The arrival of Franco's regime was one giant step backwards in social progress. Brothels survived, even thrived in the *barrios chinos*, the red-light districts in the old city centres.

Elsewhere, however, Franco set about abolishing the Republic's liberal rules. Divorce was abolished, except where permitted by the Church. Civil weddings were only allowed between two non-Catholics. Abortion, of course, was illegal. A Supreme Court Prosecutor's Office report in 1974, however, put the number of abortions at the amazingly high rate of 300,000 a year, or 40 per cent of live births.

Franco's new Civil Code ordered that: 'A man must protect his wife, and she must obey her husband.' A husband's permission was needed for women to sign all sorts of legal documents. Under this *permiso marital* system, she could not take a job or open a bank account without his go-ahead. Adultery by a wife was always a crime. Adultery by a husband was only one if it happened in the family home, if he lived with his mistress or if it was public knowledge.

'When you are married, you must never confront him, never use your anger against his anger, or your stubbornness against his. When he gets angry, you will shut up; when he shouts, lower your head without reply; when he demands, you will cede, unless your Christian conscience prevents you . . . To love is to endure,' a Church guide advised brides-to-be.

Old ideas of honour, shame, virginity and jealousy, some still deeply rooted in rural Spain, were dusted off and given a fresh shine. These were, anyway, enough to allow British anthropologists such as Julian Pitt-Rivers (in the mid-1950s) to evolve theories on the importance of honour, shame or grace in Mediterranean societies that were required reading on my social anthropology course at Oxford University. Change was slow. By the end of the regime, supposedly risqué films were made in which, according to the writer Rafael Torres, 'a fat, ugly, stupid Spanish man would be pursued by beautiful half-naked women simply because he was a *macho español*, a breed of man supposedly much valued by Scandinavians and, in fact, by most women in the world.'

The worst thing, however, was that, as Torres puts it: 'Women disappeared from the scene, except as passive objects. *Machismo* was radicalized.' This meant women were not allowed to flaunt themselves, but men could harry them as they walked down the street. José Ortega y Gasset coined the phrase '*violación visual*', 'visual rape'. '*Piropos*', words of 'flattery' shouted at girls as they walked down the street, reached their zenith. These are dying out. At their worst, they were straightforwardly crude. At their best, however, they could be highly amusing. My favourite, brought off the street by a *Madrileña* friend, remains: '*Pisa fuerte niña, que paga el ayuntamiento*'. 'Tread firmly, *niña*, the town council's paying [for the paving stones]!'

The Church became, once more, one of the major powers in the land and a constant chaperone for Spaniards' private lives. In 1958 the Bishops' Conference's Committee on Morality and Orthodoxy warned that unmarried couples who promenaded arm-in-arm were placing themselves in *peligro grave*, grave danger.

In 1963 the *Boletín Oficial de España* published rules for film-makers which prohibited, amongst other things, 'the justification of divorce, adultery or anything that attacks the institution of marriage or the family'. Criticism of the Church's 'dogma, morality or worship' was banned in the same order, as was anything that provoked 'low passions' or was 'lascivious, brutal, gross or morbid'.

Film censors committed some celebrated faux pas, including turning two of the protagonists of John Ford's *Mogambo*, Grace Kelly and Donald Sinden, from husband and wife into brother and sister. An attempt to stop Kelly's on-screen affair with Clark Gable becoming adultery thus saw her marriage turned into incest. Even the political censorship reached moments of sublime stupidity. Bogart's lines about the Spanish Republic were expunged from *Casablanca* while, in Robert Aldrich's *Dirty Dozen*, a no-good character called Franko was renamed, because his name sounded too much like that of *el Caudillo*.

Sometimes it was the censors themselves who inflamed imaginations. Spaniards imagined, for example, that in *Gilda*, Rita Hayworth did not just peel off her long glove to the tune of 'Put the Blame on Mame', but stripped for the cameras completely – and that this sight had been denied them by the censor's scissors.

An obscure German documentary, *Helga*, became a surprise hit when put on show at one of the Arte y Ensayo, art-house, cinemas that were opened in the later, more liberal, days of the regime. Extra showings were required to cope with those desperate to see a heavily censored film on sexual education.

The back rows of cinemas, the darker corners of parks and the doorways of streets such as Madrid's Calle Echegaray, meanwhile, were the working places of women known as *pajilleras*, literally masturbators. They came equipped with a handkerchief and a vigorous wrist action. Some, according to Rafael Torres, would, for a little extra, sing a *jota*, a traditional folk-dancing song, while they performed their task.

If women's sexuality scared Franco, his regime's views on homosexuality were wholly predictable. Browsing through my local second-hand bookstore, I found myself confronted by a book entitled *Sodomitas*. It was a 1956 tome, which put homosexuality into the same bag of 'enemies of the state' as Marxism, freemasonry and Judaism. 'This book was written to demonstrate the danger that the sodomite poses to the *Patria*, the fatherland,' its author, one M. Carlavilla, proclaimed. 'The herd of sodomite wild beasts, thousands strong, has invaded the busy streets looking for its young prey . . . Your son may return home, corrupted, hiding his shameful secret.

'There is an undoubted affinity between the sodomite and the communist, both being aberrations against the family,' Carlavilla added, before launching into a 300-page investigation of the subject.

Homosexuals were a threat to the regime's ideal of a virile Spain. 'Any effeminate or introvert who insults the movement will be killed like a dog,' General Queipo de Llano once threatened. Introversion, it seems, was a thoroughly unmanly, un-Spanish, suspicious attribute. When the country's greatest twentieth-century poet and playwright, Federico García Lorca, was shot by a Falangist death squad in the hills outside Granada, one of his assassins later boasted that he had 'shot him twice in the arse for being a poof'.

Thousands of homosexuals were jailed, put in camps or locked up in mental institutions. Prison terms of up to three years were imposed under laws covering 'public scandal' or 'social danger'. Homosexuals were packed off to mental hospitals where some were given electric shock treatment.

Even, then, however, an underlying seam of social tolerance appeared to co-exist with the regime's homophobic rantings. As always, the gap between the rules and what people actually did was huge. Aristocratic and pro-regime gays carried on pretty much as normal, with some even recalling the Franco period as a glorious time of illicit sexual encounters, according to one historian, Pablo Fuentes. Young men, some barely more than boys, who had come to Madrid to escape hunger or seek adventure would gather around the Las Ventas bull-ring. Many dreamt of becoming matadors, but ended up selling their bodies as *chaperos*, rent boys, instead.

For those who fell foul of the regime's laws, life was hell. Antonio was sent to prison at seventeen in the early 1970s after he told his mother that he was gay. She asked a nun for advice. 'The nun went straight to the police and I was arrested and sent for trial,' he told me. 'I spent three months in prison. I was raped there and in the police cells.'

When Franco died, however, there was no immediate change. In fact, when thousands of political and other prisoners, including terrorists, were pardoned the year after Franco's death, homosexuals were left to serve out their sentences. They could still be jailed until 1979.

In the late 1990s, when stopped by police officers who checked his identity with the precinct, Antonio discovered that his homosexuality was still registered on a police file. 'Watch out, that one's queer,' one of the police officers said. It was not until 2001 that Spain's parliament finally pledged to erase the criminal records of gays locked up by Franco's regime. But Spain, as ever, changes quickly. A police officer stopping a man wandering around Madrid's 'pink' barrio of Chueca today would probably expect his victim to be gay. He might, in fact, be openly gay himself.

When Spain changed governments in 2004, one of the first things the incoming Socialists of Prime Minister José Luis Rodríguez Zapatero did was to stick to a pledge to give equal rights to gays and transvestites. Spain, suddenly, became the third country in the world to introduce gay marriage – after traditionally liberal Holland and Belgium. The government had done its homework. More than 60 per cent of Spaniards were actively in favour of gay marriage. They were, in fact, more tolerant about it than, say, Swedes. That did not stop the church bringing half a million demonstrators onto Madrid's streets to complain about it.

At heart, most Spaniards are highly tolerant of the sexual choices of others. Even before the new gay marriage law, the Civil Guard, that symbol of Francoist repression, had begun allowing gay officers to cohabit in its barracks.

I decided to test just how deep Spanish tolerance was by going to Villalba, a traditional, conservative town in Galicia, on the day Zapatero's government announced it would legalise gay marriage. This country town of just 15,000 was the birthplace of Manuel Fraga, founder of the People's Party and, at the time, premier of the Galician regional government. He had been known to declare that those favouring gay marriage were 'vandals' and 'anarchists' who were 'seeking to destroy the family'. It was also the home town of Cardinal Antonio María Rouco Varela, Spain's senior bishop, whose officials had warned that it was 'a virus in society'. I had expected the town, dotted with granite *cruceiro* crosses and signs pointing pilgrims along the Way of St James, to be foaming at the mouth with indignation. But the People's Party deputy mayor, a country vet, said local farmers were beyond surprise. 'Different sexual expressions have always existed in the countryside. People have always known that,' he said. 'There have always been priests in these parts with children, too. Nothing shocks people around here.'

At dinner that same night in a classy Santiago de Compostela restaurant, a senior, if urban, executive of a Spanish company seriously suggested that, when thinking about sexuality in the countryside, one should not forget a farmer's relationship with his livestock. More pertinently, a gay activist in Santiago pointed out that Spanish homosexuals had no need to hide or close themselves in. 'Spain has always been more open. That is why we do not have gay ghettoes like you get in Britain or other countries,' he said.

As Franco headed for his deathbed, Spaniards began to party. When he died, they, or some of them, went wild. It was, according to Rafael Torres, a question of 'a mass negation of what had come before, without concession to shame, to feelings or to intelligence.

'Given that hunger is resolved by eating a lot, not by sampling small rations of delicacies, Spanish society tried to rid itself of its starvation with an uncontrolled, if inevitable, sexual revolution, which tore down the whole absurd edifice of repression and censorship,' he explains. 'But, just as happened in politics, there never was a true revolution of the affairs of the heart . . . The long, interminable Franco years left behind them a wilderness, a land sown with salt, a space that has simply been burnt out.'

It was an exciting time, and one of dizzying choices. Carmen Maura, the actress who was Pedro Almodóvar's first muse, described it to me this way. 'These were the silly questions of the time: Do I want sex, or don't I? If I don't, does that mean I am not *moderna*? Am I political, or aren't I? Right or left? You might suddenly find yourself trying to learn the words to "The International", because the following day there was a political meeting.' It was an atmosphere reflected in film director Fernando Colomo's 1977 *Paper Tigers*, which starred Maura.

When Franco died, the Roman Catholic Church finally lost its grip on Spain. Some priests had supported the illegal democratic opposition, spawning a group of revolutionary 'worker priests', otherwise known as the *curas rojos*. These had gone to work on building sites and in factories. A special priests' prison had, in fact, been opened in Zamora. A 1973 police report catalogues 10.6 per cent (exactly!) of the country's 23,971 parish priests as *activistas*. Some bishops had also pressed for reform, but many Spaniards had, with reason, come to think of the Church and Francoism as one thing. Was his doctrine not called, after all,

National Catholicism? Franco had signed a concordat with the Vatican that gave the Spanish church money, censorship rights and media powers – but gave him power over the appointment of bishops.

Spain is, formally, now a secular state. Despite this, however, the Church's claws are still sunk into government. When I fill out my annual tax returns I, along with all tax-paying Spaniards, am invited to tick a box saying that I want to contribute a small part of my taxes to the Roman Catholic Church. Some 40 per cent of Spaniards do, while a similar number mark a box giving to charities. In fact, the state continues to subsidise the Church, making sure it receives a fixed sum every year, regardless of how many people 'volunteer' to help it out with their taxes. A 'temporary' agreement signed in 1979 was meant to end in 1985 when the Church would become self-financing. It is still in place. Taxpayers, including non-Catholics such as myself, thus pay out 140 million euros extra each year to pay priests' salaries. One estimate puts the amount of public funding received by the church at almost one-third of its total spending.

The Church also controls many private schools and, in the State sector, appoints the country's 13,000 religion teachers. It requires them to impart 'proper doctrine' and bear 'testimony of Christian life'. It can, and does, sack them on 'moral or religious grounds'. Examples included sackings for marrying a divorcee, going on strike or refusing to pay part of their salary back into a 'voluntary' Church fund.

It is difficult to tell how religious Spaniards really are. One recent poll saw more than 80 per cent say they were Catholics, while 48 per cent admitted to being 'practising' Catholics. The proportion of Spaniards who define themselves as religious is, according to a different poll, no different to the proportion of Germans or Dutch who do so. It is significantly smaller than their southern Catholic neighbours in Portugal or Italy. Only the British and French consider themselves less religious. In fact, the Franco period now looks more like a last-gasp attempt at hanging on to already waning Church powers.

Strong, anti-religious sentiments of *anticlericalismo* also existed. These reached their violent zenith with the church-burning and priest-killing of the Civil War. Hatred of a powerful Church, however, went back much further. Barcelona's so-called Semana Trágica, Tragic Week, in 1909, saw plumes of smoke dotting the city horizon as church after church was set alight. This mirrored similar episodes from earlier in the century. 'Destroy its temples, tear aside the veil of novices and elevate them to the category of mothers,' the populist demagogue Alejandro Lerroux had urged.

In 1835 a progressive liberal, Juan Mendizábal, came to power. He confiscated much of the Church's landed property, selling it off at auction. The liberals' enemies, a group of conservative catholics known as the Carlists, not only supported a rival dynastic line for the Crown but also rallied to the battle cry of 'the church in Danger'.

While the bishops huff and puff, the gulf between the Vatican's teachings and what Spaniards do continues to widen. Rebellion, meanwhile, has also come from within. Spain boasts the Roman Catholic church's first avowedly gay and sexually active priest, Father José Mantero. I met Father Mantero at the offices of a glossy gay Spanish magazine, *Zero*, on whose front cover he had proclaimed that, 'Being gay is a gift from God.' Father Mantero, from the southern town of Valverde del Camino, was a thirty-nine-year-old bearded man with a silver earring. 'The Church says we must have compassion for homosexuals, which means it thinks there is something wrong with us. For many gay priests this is a personal hell. They see themselves as defective beings,' he told me. 'This Church should be about love and justice. Now it is just worried about sex.'

Sick of seeing straight priests get away with breaking their celibacy vows, Father Mantero eventually broke his. In his parish he was 'Don José' or, to the young, 'Pepe'. In gay internet chat rooms he was 'Kyrlian'. He would travel to Madrid, visit gay bars and go to 'hairy bear' parties (a sub-genre of the gay scene, whose clientele consists chiefly of big paternal men with beards). There were, he insisted, hundreds, if not thousands, of gay priests in Spain. Spanish bishops declared him 'sick' and suffering from 'moral disorder'. A Vatican spokesman talked of 'a sceptic boil'.

Mantero was by no means typical of Spanish Catholics, or of their clergy. But, after meeting him, I found myself wondering why a practising gay Spanish priest, rather than, say a Pole, an Italian or an Irishman, should be the one to come out and rebel in such a public, defiant fashion. I wondered, also, why I was not surprised. Was it because I thought of Spaniards as naturally rebellious? Or because they were so often convinced they, personally, were in the right? Perhaps it was that he knew there was no need to fear social rejection? Or, simply, because other Spaniards were so rarely shocked by sex? The answer, I decided, was somewhere in a mixture of all those things.

As time goes by, the Church is losing all its battles, bar the money one, with the Spanish state. Abortion, already available practically – but not quite – on demand, is due for further liberalisation by the current Socialist government. Some British women now travel to Spain for later-term abortions that they could not legally get at home. It is a reversal of the once traditional traffic of young Spanish women travelling to London clinics. Here, again, Spaniards are deaf to the Vatican. Not even the Conservative People's Party, during its eight years in power until 2004, dared turn the clock back.

Divorce was legalised in 1981. It was a moment of true liberation for many women, but still one that came a full six years after Franco's death. Carmen Maura had first-hand experience of what life was like for the 'separated' woman under Franco. Born into a conservative family, she was educated by nuns, married at nineteen and became a full-time actress at twenty-four. She paid a huge, unfair cost for that decision. Her husband took her two children. In Franco's Spain, having agreed to separate, she was in a no-win situation. Her own family also disowned her. Her emblematic status as Almodóvar girl and, therefore, icon of the *movida* is somewhat ironic. She lived little of the fervour of that exciting period in Spanish history when everything was changing at breakneck speed. 'I was too busy trying to get my children back,' she explained.

Franco's death would, eventually, bring Spanish women legal equality. A new law approved in 2005 even obliges men to share domestic work and the care of children and elderly dependants. What is written in the law books, however, is still clearly not matched by what happens in most Spanish homes or, especially, workplaces. Feminism, the writer Tobias Jones said about Italy recently, passed that country by. That is not true in Spain. Spanish women have grabbed, if not militant feminism, then at least its fruits, with fervent relief. They have one big problem, however. Spanish men, as I was to discover when my children were born, have not.

8

Men and Children First

After five years living in Spain I had thought I was immune to culture shock. Proudly integrated, linguistically adapted, accepted by friends and neighbours, I felt I had cracked Madrid. Like many foreigners who establish themselves in a new place, I had at first tried to become like my hosts, a pseudo-Spaniard. But that did not really work. My *anglosajón* soul was obviously too hard set. So I finally settled for an in-between status as an integrated outsider – half inside and looking out, half outside and looking in. It was a comfortable, liberating sort of position, fixed neither to the rules of one culture nor to those of the other. I was, literally, living the best of both worlds. Then parenthood struck.

This was a collision with the best and worst of Spain. On the one hand, I was to discover the glorious existence, and hallowed status, of the Spanish family and its adored and spoilt star-turn – the child. On the other, I was to find out just how, as Spanish society has rocketed forward in so many ways, its women have been left trailing – and toiling – in the slipstream.

Madrid is a wonderful place for children. Society, a maligned concept in the *anglosajón* world, is alive and well in Spain. Families are at its heart. A barely concealed frisson of excitement ran through our barrio when my partner became visibly pregnant. The butcher's '*filetes*' got fatter and the breakfast rations at the Bar Urbe got longer. In the winter months pregnancy was one of the few things that could dislodge Cati, the door-lady, from the warmth of her windowless, three-room, ground-floor flat. She emerged daily from her hideaway, wrapped in a fleecy, green dressing gown, to demand her regular bulletin, with as much medical detail as possible, on the pregnancy's development.

There is nothing quite so personal, particular and culturally conditioned as the way people have babies. Elsewhere, the natural childbirth revolution was in full gear. At kitchen tables from Manchester to New York I had listened to women talk, boast even, of rejecting pain relief, of giving birth in water tanks, and of men who massaged, soothed or even chanted their partners through the hours of childbirth. The stories were often inspiring, sometimes hilarious and occasionally appalling. But this was the way we expected to go.

For the first pregnancy we had been given a whole library of *anglosajón* and French natural birthing books. They included a rather scary one in which West Coast hippy women and their very hairy partners got off on the 'rush' of childbirth. The essence of their message was this: women give birth; their husbands, or partners, are handy as cheerleaders, comforters and confidence builders; doctors, meanwhile, are useful, occasionally vital, but are generally extras in the drama. The obvious protagonists were the mother and her child.

It was at our first prenatal class that I realised the childbirth revolution and, with it, a large chunk of feminism, had not reached Spain. We arrived early, sat down in the front row and began chatting with Encarna, the midwife. As we talked, and the seats behind us filled up, I began to get an uneasy feeling. When Encarna stood up to start the class, I swivelled slowly, surreptitiously around and looked back. Yes, I was the only man.

Over the coming weeks, barring an occasional, one-off showing from a nervous-looking fellow father-to-be and a single 'bring-your-partner-or-else' occasion, it was me and a dozen pregnant women. Occasionally I, too, joined the male flight. Encarna, with her husky smoker's voice, hangover eyes, an empty plastic cigarette holder clamped between her teeth and a box of Marlboro peeking from her gown pocket, was a lively representative of the earthy, carefree side of Spain. She made us moan, groan, push, shove, soothe and laugh. Smoking, she agreed, was a bad thing. But, this being Spain, there was no moral prohibition, no disapproval of those who could not give up. Who was she to tell anyone off? Instead, she gave advice about how long to leave between a cigarette and the next round of breast feeding. Encarna wanted to talk about sex. Her basic message was to have as much as possible, both before and as soon as possible after childbirth, because it made you feel good. She recommended washing babies' bottoms in public drinking fountains (Madrid has a lot, though fewer every day). But no, she was sorry, men were not allowed to be present at the birth, at least not at the hospital we were meant to go to. And no, nobody had home births. Things were changing, but not that quickly. Giving birth meant stepping onto the conveyor-belt and letting the doctors take charge.

Spain's state health system is a command economy. My view of it is of course, largely subjective. Once you have got beyond primary care, you are there to do as you are told. You fill out this form, stand in that queue and remember that '*el doctor*', or '*la doctora*', knows best. Spaniards are normally wonderful, imaginative abusers of bureaucracy or rules of any kind. Given the chance, they will charm, cheat or bulldoze their way through them. Stand them in front of a man, or a woman, in a white coat, however, and they go meekly wherever they are led. Doctors, pharmacists and even the owners of health food shops – who have adopted the uniform to hide their quackery – are all treated with a degree of respect, even awe, that their counterparts elsewhere could only dream of.

The long, complex words of medicine are magical to Spaniards. Their ability to discuss illness, in a combination of detailed medical jargon and vivid, no-holds-barred descriptions of symptoms – pustules, bowel movements and genital itches included – is prodigious. In newspapers and radio programmes footballers' injuries are described in minute, loving detail. One player, I read in today's sports daily *As*, has a fracture to the *escafoides carpiano* of his hand. Another has torn the *cápsula posterior* of his knee. Does your average Spanish soccer fan know what these remote corners of the body are? Or is it just that, as I suspect, the medical words are too mysteriously impressive to miss out? The magical remedies spelt out by their doctors, and the machines used on them, are named, word-by-staggeringly-scientific-word, as if they were the potions of ancient alchemists – *electroencefalografía, resonancia magnética, artroscopia.*

Spain has a historically high caesarean rate. One study, from 1998 and concentrating on Catalonia, showed 26 per cent of births were done by Caesarean. This was two and a half times, for example, the rate in Holland or Sweden. Numbers were rising rapidly. One hospital reached 38 per cent. Some other western countries are now beginning to catch up with that figure, but others have kept them down to around 10 per cent. Medical intervention, in Spain, does not end there. Episiotomies are performed on nine out of ten first-time mothers. Enemas and pubic shaving are also a routine part of the mother-to-be's trip down the birthing production line at Spanish hospitals. All this, the report pointed out, contravenes a World Health Organisation (WHO) resolution on the rights of pregnant women. The fact that the rate of caesareans surges on Friday and Saturday mornings suggests some are performed for the convenience of doctors keen to get away for the weekend (though some mothers are also keen on 'convenience' births). Private hospitals are the worst, performing 30 per cent more caesareans. One child I know was, her parents now suspect, delivered several days early by programmed caesarean just so a doctor could get his bill in before the end of the second quarter. I would like to think that was not true. But a theatre nurse said she once threw a doctor's surgical instruments to the ground – so they would require re-sterilising – because he was trying to rush an operation so he could get to a Real Madrid game.

Spanish women rarely complain about any of this. Respect for the man, or woman, in the white coat is absolute. Only 1 in 4,000 births takes place outside a hospital (compared to more than a quarter in Holland). Doctors say Spain has cut its perinatal mortality rate considerably over the last couple of decades, thanks to hospital births. It may just be, however, that Spaniards are not squeamish about the scalpel. This is estimated to be the country with the highest plastic surgery rate in Europe. It also has one of the highest rates of organ donorship.

Spain's public primary health care is especially good. Wherever you are – even in remote country towns – there is a doctor on hand twenty-four hours a day at the local *centro de salud*. Spain, unlike other European countries, has too many doctors. It currently exports them, especially to Britain and Portugal. This surfeit means there is a large pool of semi-employed, part-time doctors. They are still willing to sit up all night for not very much money. The primary health care they offer is one reason, along with a Mediterranean diet heavy in fresh fruit and vegetables, fish and olive oil, why Spaniards outlive almost all other Europeans.

Our patience with public health ran out, however, with the preparation for childbirth. We had found ourselves locked into a dreary routine of seeing *tocólogos*, specialist doctors who monitor pregnancies on a monthly basis. They performed this task with all the zest of bored mechanics forced to check the oil, filters and tyre pressures of two dozen cars a day. So we went to see a private gynaecologist who was one of the few survivors of the first women's clinics that emerged in the 1970s. These had been places where contraception was not a sin and women could talk freely about abortion. She kept her medical implements wrapped up in silver foil on a shelf, like so many take-away *bocadillos* – the plump, bready sandwiches of the Spanish emergency lunch. We had gone from one extreme to another, for the new gynaecologist was an impassioned enthusiast. She gave me long, ecstatic descriptions of my partner's cervix. 'What beauty!' she exclaimed. Invitations were even issued to join her at the viewing end of the examining table. But no, she could not recommend a hospital in Madrid, private or public, that specialised in natural birthing.

So we did our own market research. And that is how we ended up at the Ciudad Sanitaria Doce de Octubre, the Twelfth of October Health City, a huge public hospital covering Madrid's southern neighbourhoods. This we picked because it allowed a partner to be there at the moment of birth. It was not our designated hospital, but we applied the logic of Spanish rule-breaking and reasoned that they would not turn away a woman in labour. We also organised some *enchufe*, swapping the private services of the enthusiast for those of one of the hospital's chief gynaecologists, a youngish man we had met at a dinner party. That way we could drop his name at the admissions office.

At first sight, this vast medical 'city' looked like some remnant of a five-year plan in an ex-Communist state. It was a jungle of drab high-rise buildings and low, square, concrete blocks tucked between the warehouses and working-class housing estates of southern Madrid. Closer up, it turned out to be like a small, self-contained Spanish town. There were bars, restaurants, a bank, double parking, car thieves and tow trucks.

Appearances can deceive, however. Inside the tower blocks are some of the best facilities and finest researchers in Spain. More importantly, the Doce de Octubre had the best maternity ward in the city. It owed this honour to the fact that it was also the busiest. Spain may now have one of the lowest birth-rates in the world, at 1.3 children per woman of child-bearing age, but the country's immigrants and gypsy families who populate the south of the city do not know that. In fact, Spain's suddenly burgeoning community of immigrants, attracted by a dozen years of strong, constant economic growth, have already turned around a declining birth-rate that hit a low of fewer than 1.2 children in 1998.

The day the waters broke, we sat nervously in the back of a big, white Mercedes taxi bumping our way along the hospital driveway while the *taxista* informed us excitedly just how wonderful his own two children, born at the same place, had turned out. Our experience of the joy, humiliation, anger and wonder involved in having a baby in Spain was about to enter its final, and defining, stage.

We had wanted this to be a natural birth, but recognised it was unlikely to happen. The baby was already two weeks late. Scans showed he was also very large. Connected to a drip, hours of exhausting contractions were gone through without any result. In the meantime, a constantly changing cast of doctors, nurses, cleaners and assorted others in green or white coats, wandered in and out.

A surgeon was, eventually, called. My request to be present during the caesarean was turned down. This was not unexpected.

Surgeons and anaesthetists are by no means all keen to have visitors in the operating room. It was not, however, a strange request. Some Spanish surgeons, as we would discover when our second child was born, are quite happy to have the father there. Our mistake was to ask why, in this case, the answer had been no. '*¡Porque lo digo yo!*' – 'Because I say so!' came the imperious reply. It sparked an unseemly row – involving surgeon, mother-to-be and myself – in which British phlegm, that alien characteristic that so intrigues Spaniards, went out of the hospital window. The anaesthetist had to act as peacemaker.

All that was, of course, forgotten when I found myself, an hour later, holding the little fingers of a puce-coloured baby as he lay in an incubator in the neonatal ward. With his mother still out from the operation, I was tolerated as a visitor but sent home at 'closing time' that evening. He would have to spend his first night on his own.

Beside every bed in a state hospital in Spain sits an armchair, which also folds out into a bed. This chair, and the bed, are expected to be occupied twenty-four hours a day by a relative of the patient. Spaniards find it indignant, inhuman in fact, that these do not exist in all British hospitals. The relative is there to entertain, fuss, receive visitors and act as an extra, no-cost nurse, watching the drip and relaying messages to the hospital staff. He or, normally, she is joined during visiting hours by reams of other relatives and friends who, in the maternity ward at least, could be counted on to switch the television on full blast and start watching the football, especially if Atlético de Madrid – this end of town's team – were playing.

The Doce de Octubre maternity ward was a riot, in the best sense of the word. It was also where, as we stayed a week while my partner recovered from the caesarean, we had our first lessons in being parents under the gentle guidance of the nurses. Our company included several gypsy women who seemed half our age but were already onto their third or fourth. Their other children occasionally ran wild, despite one mother's threats that if they didn't behave, '*la paya te va a pinchar*' ('the non-gypsy', as the nurse was known, 'will stick a needle into you'). It remains one of my favourite spots on earth. I could think of no finer place to start looking after a child, and no stranger place to go through the process of getting it out.

That said, we were back eighteen months later, with another large, very late baby looking set for a caesarean. This time we were better prepared. We had worked up our *enchufe* with the young chief gynaecologist further. He would perform the operation and, if he could persuade the duty anaesthetist, I would be in the theatre to see my second son being born. Permission was obtained after he had assured the anaesthetist, turning one brief experience in Bosnia into a lifetime of dodging bullets, that I was a hardened war correspondent with long experience of blood and gore. It was my responsibility to live up to the description, and not faint.

Even then, it was touch and go. At the last minute, I was handed a green hair-net and some green doctor's pyjamas. I was told to sprint down a corridor, go into one of the doctor's dressing rooms and put them on. This was a worryingly easy thing to do. The other doctors offered a polite '*buenos días*' as I slipped on my disguise. To them, I was just a new doctor on the block. I found myself wondering how many other frauds there were wandering the hospital corridors. My mind went back to the dozens of sets of green pyjamas that had wandered through the labour room on the previous occasion. 'Just checking!' they had said cheerfully, before doing exactly that. If there was a next time, I decided, I would demand ID cards at the door. This time, in the neonatal unit, I was reminded how deep bull culture ran in Spain. My second son was '*un torito*', a little bull, a passing doctor said.

Birth, we had already discovered, was about a woman and her doctor, not about a woman and her partner. Occasionally, it seemed to be about the doctor and little else. The gynaecologist's other patients looked at him in a state of near adoration. It was hardly surprising that it seemed to have gone to his head. Our final goodbye to the Doce de Octubre, in a treatment room a few weeks later, was a reminder of how some doctors peered down at patients from their personal Mount Olympuses. He removed the last few staples from the caesarean wound – and arranged a golf match on his mobile phone as he did it.

All that happened in the late 1990s, and Spain will have changed since then. It seems, however, to be moving uncharacteristically slowly. One recent father-to-be told me he was just one of two prospective dads to turn up at prenatal classes. That is, I suppose, a 100 per cent increase on my experience. It is not, however, a revolution.

If the basic idea that women might want to be in control of how they gave birth to children had not taken off, it was hardly surprising that, when it came to looking after them, Spain had not moved on very far. The only man at the prenatal class soon became one of the handful of fathers at the playground in the Retiro park on weekdays. I was not there every day, as others were, but thank you Chema, Julio, Santi, Ramón and Marcelo for the male company. We were heavily outnumbered by mothers and the middle-class replacement for parents, *la chica*, 'the girl'. *La chica* is an Ecuadorian, Peruvian or Colombian immigrant who, despite the name, may be aged anywhere between eighteen and sixty. She is the cleaner, nanny and, sometimes, cook in a middle-class, urban household. In posher parts of Madrid, and one apartment in my building, she must wear a maid's uniform. Middle-class Spain would fall to pieces without her.

Spain, on paper, has managed all the advances of feminism that have been achieved elsewhere in Europe. Equal rights, equal salaries, equality itself, is enshrined in law. Women are in government. They accounted, in fact, for half of the Socialist cabinet appointed in 2004. That is a feat only previously matched by Sweden and Finland. When it came to celebrating their achievement, however, the *ministras* chose to do a spread for *Vogue*. The Spanish *progre*, progressive, woman may believe in boldly advancing forwards, but she is not going to ditch her attachment to glamour.

On Franco's death on 20 November 1975, Spanish women's lives were governed by what, for most of the rest of Europe, were 1930s rules. The *permiso marital* was proof of that. Progress, then, has been remarkable. Spanish feminism, however, did not appear entirely out of nothing. As with so many other things, Spanish women seeking role models had to look back to the 1930s and the sudden, remarkable burst of reforming energy provided by those who got rid of the monarchy and founded the Second Republic in 1931. The Republic had set about reforming a Civil Code which declared, for example, that 'the husband who, catching his wife committing adultery should kill her in the act, or the man . . . will be punished by banishment'. Even this minimal form of punishment, however, did not apply 'should he cause them only lesser wounds'. In that case, it stated, 'there will be no legal sanctions'.

A home-grown breed of feminist pioneers won women the vote in 1931. That was only three years after full women's suffrage in Britain and more than a decade ahead of France, Italy or Belgium. 'The concession of the vote to women caused considerable scandal in the debating chamber . . . The blue bench [of the ministers] was almost assaulted by deputies who argued with the ministers and gave signs of great exaltation,' one contemporary newspaper report recorded. Women such as Victoria Kent and María Martínez Sierra drove through reforms. A year later they also gained divorce by mutual consent – almost forty years before this appeared, for example, in Britain and Denmark. It would be one of the first laws that Franco overturned.

One of the most remarkable of this new breed of progressive, reforming women was Hildegart Rodríguez, sometimes known as 'the Red Virgin'. Her tragic story sums up the conflicting visions of women at the time. Hildegart, a child prodigy born in 1914 but dead at the age of eighteen, was the ambitious project of her mother, Aurora.

Aurora's view of her own sex was decidedly warped. 'Women, in general, lack souls. There are animals who have more delightful souls,' she believed. 'They are, it is painful to admit, the worst of the human species.'

Despite this, Aurora decided to create her own super-being. She already had money, so, 'with no pleasure', she found, and spent three nights with, a man to set the project going. The result, a baby girl rather than a baby boy, must have been something of a blow, but that did not hold her back. The programme of genius creation started during pregnancy, with Aurora changing position every hour in bed, in order to stimulate the foetus. Proper training started as soon as the baby had popped out of the womb. Hildegart could read and write by the age of three. She was speaking French, English and German by the age of eight. Philosophy and sexual education, almost unheard of at the time, were high on Aurora's list. The latter was there because 'women lose themselves because of sex'.

Hildegart joined the Socialist Party at the age of fourteen. She started to publish in the newspaper *El Socialista*, without the editor knowing how old she was. When he found out, he declared she might become 'one of the great figures of world socialism'. By the age of seventeen she had a degree in law, was studying medicine and was vice-president of the Socialist Youth Organisation. A controversial book entitled *Did Marx Get It Wrong?* saw her expelled from the party. By this stage the Second Republic had been born. Spain was experiencing a dizzying, if short-lived, burst of social progress. The teenage Hildegart was caught up in the excitement. She published more books, gave speeches, became famous and founded a League for Sexual Reform. She corresponded with, amongst others, the writer H. G. Wells, the British sexologist Havelock Ellis and, in the US, birth-control campaigner Margaret Sanger. At all times, however, she was chaperoned by Aurora.

Hildegart eventually decided to break free. She told her mother she was planning a trip to London to see, amongst others, Wells. Aurora was fiercely against the idea and they argued long and hard. One night Aurora sat beside her daughter for several hours, watching her sleep. Then she fetched a pistol and shot the teenager – one bullet through the head, three in the chest – as she slept. Aurora was carted off to the lunatic asylum. She remained stubbornly, deliriously proud of her crime. Hildegart, she claimed, had begged for death saying: 'You who created me must destroy me. Punish me severely.'

Spain's statute books have, once and for all, put paid to her mother's ideas about women's position. But changing laws is one thing. Changing mores is something else. And, when it comes to families, Spanish men show little sign of wanting anything, except their size (smaller is better), to change. This, to a greater or lesser degree, is a problem everywhere. But a single statistic suffices to show how much worse it is here. Only some 5,000 men a year currently take up their right to up to ten weeks' paternity leave in Spain, compared to 250,000 women who take maternity leave.

When our eldest son turned two, we started looking for a nursery school for him to attend for a few hours every day. We wanted a place where he could discover that other children were useful for more than just infant martial arts. So it was that we began to visit the barrio's nurseries, almost all of which are private. With 95 per cent of children going to nursery school by the age of three, there was no lack of choice. Our first surprise, however, was that we had arrived late – by about two years. In every nursery there was a room, or two, devoted to rows of cots. Many children, it was explained, started here at sixteen weeks – exactly the moment at which their mother needed to be back at the workplace.

When we finally made our choice, we would find out for ourselves how this system worked. Anxious mothers, or watch-glancing dads, would appear at the door with a small bundle in a pram. The baby would be handed over, the pram shuffled off to the pram car park. Sometimes the child would be brought by *la chica,* other times by a grandmother. The latter would be treated with a respect that the former was seldom accorded. The bundle may, or may not cry. Medicines would, if necessary, be discussed. And off they would go, like so many pampered battery hens, to the room with the cots.

A separate door might then open and a swarm of slightly older, crawling infants appear through it. The crawlers would be shepherded this way or that like a gaggle of slow-moving geese. If they had to go upstairs, they tackled the staircase like professional climbers determined to conquer Mount Everest, a mass of bobbing, well-padded bottoms heading for the peak.

And so it went on. A couple of hundred children aged between zero and six, all encased in neat, green-and-white checked gingham pinafores, came here every day. Some started at 8 a.m. and were given breakfast. One of the most startling things about these children was the tweeness with which some were dressed. We had spotted the specialist children's shops full of powder-blue boys' outfits and pink girls' outfits before becoming parents ourselves. But it was when a delicate, powder-blue, knitted-cotton, ribboned baby suit arrived from an acquaintance who was not only meant to be a prominent feminist but was also a Socialist minister, that we realised this was not just a fashion for 1950s nostalgists. At the nursery school and in the park, we would see parents who looked and dressed like us, parading children dressed in elaborate knickerbockers, smocked dresses, sashes, bows, Peter Pan collars, pin-tucks or matching knickers and bloomers. Often these children would come in matched pairs, their clothes identical or, if boy and girl, made of the same material. The occasional family of three or four kids might be identified by the fact that they were all, despite the age spread, wearing the same clothes, just in different sizes.

The children at our nursery school were, it was argued, here to learn to socialise. In reality, however, the youngest were here because their fathers would not have dreamt of stopping, or reducing, their working hours, and it was time for their mums to take up their posts at work again. There were exceptions, but mothers basically kept – and keep – all the responsibilities of the household and children's welfare, despite having working hours that might stretch until 7 p.m. or later. One study shows that, if you combine their hours at the office with the work they do at home, Spanish women work an average of an hour a day more than their men. The normal ratio of housework between one sex and the other eleven to one (4.4 hours to thirty minutes a day). An alarming statistic from the same study was that they were, jointly, the hardest workers in Europe. The sociologist who presented the study, María Ángeles Durán, said that young Spanish women had opted for the easiest 'solution' to the problem of squeezing children into their busy timetable. 'Given that they take up so much time, we have decided not to have them,' she said.

Socialisation has remained an obsession for our children's teachers. In the first years of infant school, the teachers seem to care more about '*formando el grupo*', 'forming the group', than, for example, maths. Reading is good, but can be viewed as a suspiciously solitary occupation. A child who seeks only their own company is deemed strange. They may find themselves up before that figure who looms large, the school psychologist. There is no white coat here, but there might as well be. Most parents meekly accept their judgements in the same way they obey their doctors.

One thing none of my children's friends belong to is something that could, in any way, be described as a large family. Running through my mind, I can, indeed, think of only two or three who have more than one sibling. The huge families of the past, beloved by the Franco regime and its Catholic sponsors, are just that – of the past. Three siblings walking down the street in a chain are a strange, remarkable sight. Officially this is a *familia numerosa*, with special welfare and education rights. Have four, and people will immediately suspect you belong to Opus Dei – the ultra-strict, mysterious Catholic group who many Spaniards see, as they once saw freemasons, lurking secretly in the shadows of power.

Some of my children's friends' parents, however, can tell you what it was like to be one of six, seven, eight or twelve brothers and sisters. These were encouraged by Franco, who saw the number of families with four or more children rise from 116,000 to more than a quarter of a million during his period in power. The general verdict seems to be that it was not so wonderful to be lost amongst so many siblings.

If life has been getting better continuously, and rapidly, for Spaniards over the past three decades, one type of Spaniard has done even better than the rest. That Spaniard is a child. The imperious little princes and princesses of the, now typical, one or two child Spanish family are a wonder to behold. The centre of attention of parents, grandparents, neighbours, aunts, uncles and an endless list of admirers, their life is as golden as it can get. They issue instructions to adults in loud voices. A cry of '*¡Agua!*', and water is brought. '*¡Galletas!*' and biscuits appear. '*¡Cola Cao!*' and the chocolate drink that appears at almost any time of the day is brought out. '*¡Quiero ver la tele!*' and the television is switched on. There are, of course, many exceptions but it seems that childhood is often an obligation-free experience. Adults tidy toys. Adults get food. Adults are there, in short, to serve. One of the Spanish words for spoil, *mimar*, hints at the idea that this may not be such a terrible thing. It also means to pet, coddle or pamper.

This is not to say that Spanish children lack manners, just that they have a different concept of them. Place a piece of chocolate cake in front of them and they will stare at it blankly until you have provided a spoon or fork to eat it with. Like their parents, they would not want to dirty their hands. In fact, like their parents again, they are acutely aware of cleanliness and tidiness – even if they may be blissfully unaware of how the latter is achieved. My office at home, for example, is an object of awe for some of the visiting six-year-olds. Piled high with newspapers, magazines and books, chaos and mess are an inherent part of its life. It is a very homely sort of a mess. One regular visitor, however, had obviously never seen anything like it in his six years of life. '*¿Qué ha pasado aquí?*', 'What happened here?' he asked in a shocked, high-pitched voice on one visit. '*¿Quién ha sido?*', 'Who did this?' he asked on another. When I gave the office a massive spring clean, I invited him in. There was no comment. Normality had obviously been achieved.

Spanish visitors to Britain are often shocked by what they see. No showers, carpets on bathroom floors – a sure-fire focus for infection-bearing germs – and untidy clutter are alien and worrying characteristics. Spain, after all, must have a per capita consumption of bleach – applied daily to tiled floors and liberally sloshed around bathrooms and kitchens – that is amongst the highest on the planet. One playground discussion at our school saw a mother regretting having put wooden skirting boards, rather than a row of easily bleach-cleaned tiles, into her apartment. The problem, she explained, was the fluff that got stuck behind it. 'There is only one way to get it out,' she complained. 'You have to use toothpicks.'

Her children, however, were unlikely to be wielding the toothpicks. Spanish children already watch as much television, and suffer from nearly as much obesity, as those arch juvenile couch potatoes – their British and American counterparts. But what, in Britain and the US, is laziness is, in Spain, indulgence. If prohibition, saying 'no' to someone, is already broadly unacceptable when that someone is an adult, then it is doubly so if they are a child.

This is not, however, without its benefits. This was driven home to me one day, on a return visit to Britain, in a Devon pub. The landlord not only refused our infant children entry but, as we ate his wretched food in a light drizzle in the pub garden, he stood in his doorway and regaled us with stories about why pubs were better without kids. The sign outside his door, 'no dogs, no children', just about summed up the status of British children and, by association, their parents.

Whereas small children turn British parents into social lepers, they elevate Spanish parents into privileged human beings. You, the parent, have achieved a sublime status. You have created your own family and your reward is to have some of the absolute indulgence shown to your children rub off, also, on you. In restaurants, for example, rather than be shown the door or taken off to a 'families only' quarantine zone, you find the waiters' attention and efforts doubling. There will be crayons, colouring books and delicacies for the kids. And when your child karate-chops his glass of *mosto*, sweet grape juice, onto the tiled floor, the waiter appears not just with a mop, but with a smile and a new, full glass. If the children then choose to roll around the floor practising infant all-in wrestling, well that is just a sign of robust, endearing good health. Other diners are likely to agree.

My own children have grown up crawling over bar tops, being manhandled by waiters – even, in one regular watering hole, encouraged by the owner to pound away at the till to make it go 'ping' and send the money-drawer shooting out. How could one explain the 'no children' rule to Jesús, the owner? And what would one say to a stranger who wandered in and exclaimed, as he helped one of my muddy-footed boys walk up and down his suited trouser leg: 'Aren't children wonderful?'

You have to accept, of course, that your children are in some way public property. A father out on his own with a baby on a winter's day will, almost inevitably, be told by some busybody grandmother that he has not wrapped the child up well enough. Strange men not only expect to be able to talk to your children, they may want to touch them too.

In *Prospect* magazine, Bella Thomas told the story of an elderly Spanish man, resident in Britain, who had spontaneously befriended some children on a Surrey high street. A cheek was pinched here, some hair ruffled there. This is standard, affectionate behaviour in Spain. The dynamics of what is a simple, virtuous circle are easy – and should be unnecessary – to explain: the elderly man is indulgent to the children; the children bask in his admiration; and the man goes away with a warm glow, feeling he has done a good thing. In Britain, the police were called. The old man was taken to a police station and made to explain himself. Not surprisingly, unable to understand a world where male strangers are suspected paedophiles and single women are potential baby-snatchers, he decided to move back to Spain.

There is a central enigma to the way Spaniards bring up their children, which I have never been able to solve. How is it that the spoiled, rude under-tens later turn into such polite, agreeable and self-confident teenagers? The surly adolescent is a relatively rare sight in Spain. Teenagers may grumble about their parents, but they do not go for full-out generational hatred. Teenage rebellion, in fact, seems virtually non-existent. Spanish teenagers, when polled, have no trouble pointing out that family is the most important thing in their lives.

If a Spanish childhood is such an indulged, golden thing, then it is no surprise that young Spaniards should try to stretch this stage of their lives out. What it does not explain, however, is why so many of them are determined to stay living with *mamá* and *papá* for as long as possible. Most remain at home into the second part of their twenties. A significant number are still there after their thirtieth birthday. It is difficult to decide whether it is Spanish parents who do not want their children to grow up, or young Spaniards who dislike the idea of becoming independent adults.

As Spain progresses, socially and economically, at a dizzying rate, one might expect all this to be changing. But the figures show that, rather than move out earlier, Spanish children are now staying even longer at their parents' home. In 1990 a quarter of twenty-six- to twenty-nine-year-olds were living at home. Within a decade that figure had risen to a half. Women leave slightly earlier than young men, presumably because they know how to cook and do their own laundry. By 2000, 50 per cent of men were still living with their parents at the age of twenty-nine. New figures suggesting a fall in the age at which people leave home are, I suspect, largely a reflection of the fact that many immigrants are in this age group.

Young men and young women remain at home, if they can, until they are forced out by circumstance – often by marriage. Personal, and unscientific, observation makes me think that the higher up the class scale, the more likely they are to stay. It takes a job in the US, Paris or London to prise young merchant bankers, doctors or engineers from the parental home. The bigger the apartment or house is, after all, the more facilities it offers. It is those squashed into the tiny flats in Madrid's working-class suburbs who are most keen to find their own place.

Even legally, it seems, a Spanish childhood can last well into a person's twenties. Occasionally, reminders come from the newspapers. Barcelona's *La Vanguardia*, for example, informed me one day that a judge had ordered a divorced man to pay his ex-wife 225 euros a month to cover his twenty-five-year-old son's upkeep while he did postgraduate studies. The judge ruled that the son was 'not at such an advanced age for finishing his academic studies' and had 'not yet gained his own financial independence'. Another case saw a fireman from Lleida forced to pay similar upkeep for a twenty-seven-year-old who had still not managed to finish his degree. 'When is a father allowed to stop supporting his children?' he asked.

Young Spaniards complain that a lack of jobs, cheap housing and university grants are to blame for this situation. But, with Spaniards getting wealthier at such a dizzying rate and new jobs attracting millions of immigrants, that does not wash. The truth is that most only leave their parent's home when they think they can move into something as good, or better. One betrothed couple, a television cameraman and production assistant from Barcelona, proudly announced to me one day that they had bought themselves a car-parking space near the apartment they were buying together. The apartment had, like many of those that spring up around Spain's cities, been bought on an architect's plan, but they had put down a deposit and were already paying a mortgage. It would take several years for the building that houses it to go up. In the meanwhile, it was more important for them to secure, for several thousand euros, a spot to put their car when they got there, than to pay for a rented flat away from their parents.

Some desperate parents have gone to court to evict children in a bid for what has been billed 'parental emancipation'. María and Mariano Giménez convinced a judge in Zaragoza that their two sons, twenty and eighteen, had forfeited the right to live at home by treating them abusively. The couple's lawyer warned, however, that eviction was not generally an option. 'The law establishes that the parents' obligation to feed and house can only be suppressed under extreme circumstances,' he said. That obligation only disappeared when a child moved out or started earning their own money, he explained. (The state, which has never been generous with unemployment pay, also benefits from this system whenever recession strikes. The young unemployed usually have someone to look after them.) Children's rights over their parents do, in fact, continue until these are in the grave. A Spanish parent may not write children out of their will. A rule known as the *legítima* establishes that children are *herederos forzosos*, 'forced inheritors' – automatically sharing out a large part of the estate when the last parent dies.

Again, however, there is an upside to this endless Spanish childhood. Young Spaniards also stay at home because they either love, like or tolerate their parents. A recent poll, in which even Spanish researchers defined 'young people' as being anything between fifteen and twenty-nine years old, saw 96 per cent state that they were happy with their families. The feelings are, obviously, reciprocated. The children are protected from the sometimes brutal rites of passage of eighteen-year-olds in other countries, where they are forced to fend for themselves in some alien or new environment. Most will remain close to their parents even when they do move out. Those still lucky enough to enjoy two-hour lunch breaks may turn up for lunch several times a week. And their children, too, will come to see their grandparents as a natural, and close, part of their family.

Tradition and huge taxes on buying and selling houses mean that many people only ever buy one home, and stay in it until they die. In our building, for example, the appearance of a 'For Sale' sign on the front door often means that another neighbour has passed away. Mostly they died in their apartments, or within hours or days of the ambulance being called.

The routine of death in Madrid, and elsewhere in Spain, is a well-trodden path. The dead are carted off to the *tanatorio*, the city's official morgue. This is perched above the ten-lane inner ring road, the M30, between the mosque and an ugly, concrete and glass hotel. Beautified by morticians, they are laid out in their coffins and put on public display so friends and family can make a final, posthumous visit while giving the immediate family their condolences.

Over the years the *tanatorio* has become a sadly familiar place. When a friend's close relative dies, you are expected to appear, offer condolences, take a peek at the cadaver and stay for a chat.

One might expect this to be a solemn place. But, with vigils going on for up to twenty-six dead, all neatly arranged in adjoining cubicles, the *tanatorio* bustles like a railway terminus. First-timers might think they have stepped into a small airport terminal. Groups of people mill about. A TV monitor tells you which corpse is in which cubicle. A cash dispenser sits in the middle of the foyer. Another machine produces prepaid phone cards. There is, inevitably, a large bar-cum-restaurant doing brisk trade. I even have friends who, because of its extended opening hours, have used it for the last drink on an evening out. A new *tanatorio*, I notice, has just been opened in Madrid. It advertises on the radio with the slogan 'the most modern *tanatorio* in Europe'.

These *velatorios* do not have to be deeply tragic. I remember, for example, a friend's grandfather, his head wrapped in a white shroud. His peaceful, nonagenarian face gave him the look of a sixteenth-century Spanish mystic. I also recall, however, Juan Carlos's eighteen-year-old, and only, son. On that occasion, no condolences could possibly come close to easing the pain. But, at least, a grieving single father had company for the first twenty-four hours after death.

Madrid burials normally take place the day after death in one of the city's handful of vast cemeteries. At the newest one, the Cementerio Sur, a priest stands at the gate, providing a drive-in rites-of-committal service. The hearses that roll through stop briefly and open their doors for him to say the words over the coffin before heading off to the appointed burial niche.

Inside the cemetery, the burial niches are lined up, like so many apartment blocks, in long walls, six tiers high. The niches must be paid for and rental is for a limited period, unless it is renewed by future generations. When your time is up, and if your family declines to pay, your bones are removed and tossed into a communal ossuary.

Gerald Brenan, travelling through Spain in 1949, came across a large pit of bones in the cemetery in Granada as he searched for the grave of the poet and playwright Federico García Lorca – shot thirteen years earlier. Mostly, the bones belonged to some of the thousands of *Granadinos* given death sentences by Franco's kangaroo courts and shot during the Civil War. But one, older, body drew his attention. 'Stretched across the rubble of bones, in an attitude of rigid attention, was a complete and well-preserved corpse, dressed in green and black-braided uniform,' wrote Brenan. 'Its face, a little greenish too with dark markings, as though the flesh were trying to take on the colour of the uniform, had the severe, self-concentrated look of a man who is engaged in some self-important task.'

The local gravedigger explained that the body belonged to a Civil Guard colonel who had died fifty years earlier. He had been well preserved because he had lain in one of the higher niches. 'We took him up the other day because his family have stopped paying the rent,' the gravedigger explained.

Brenan's own death, in 1987, caused Spanish authorities considerable headaches. Don Gerardo, as he was known, may not have been famous in Britain, but in Spain he was an icon. He had already starred in a bizarre episode in which he left his home in Alhaurín el Grande, near Málaga, and checked into an old people's home in Pinner. A somewhat confused Brenan was deemed to have been taken there against his will, provoking the local mayor to fly to Britain and bring him back, pledging that the town would look after him. On his death (soon afterwards), it was discovered that he wanted to leave his body to medicine. It went to Málaga University's Faculty of Medicine, where it stayed for the next fourteen years. The faculty's doctors never dared mutilate the corpse for research because, they said, Don Gerardo was too important. 'I had hoped that, with time, people would forget that we had his body,' José María Smith Ágreda, the professor to whom Brenan had personally entrusted his body, said. 'It did not seem decent to put the author of *The Spanish Labyrinth* on the dissecting table.'

Eventually it was agreed that he should be buried. The body was incinerated, and the ashes placed in an urn mixed with earth from the two Andalusian towns where he had lived, Yegen and Alhaurín el Grande. It was buried in the British Cemetery in Málaga, beside Gamel Woolsey, his American poet wife. The cemetery is an extraordinarily beautiful and tranquil spot in the heart of old Málaga. A small, honey-coloured stone Anglican church stands in the midst of a garden full of thick Mediterranean vegetation and plumbago flowers. It had been set up in the mid-eighteenth century by a British consul appalled that Protestants were not allowed to be buried in Catholic graveyards. Their coffins had, instead, to be left, during the night, standing feet-first on the seashore at a spot where the city tipped its rubbish – and where the corpses were at the mercy of scavenging dogs.

Even in death, then, Spaniards' innate ability to operate as a social mass helps turn tragedy into occasion. This ability to shed, for a moment, their personal, liberal agenda and instinctively incorporate themselves into a social group is, perhaps, the secret to Spanish communal living. Perhaps that is why they work at it so hard at school. At moments of great political tension, they show an unmatched ability to pour onto the streets en masse and protest. The great demonstrations in Madrid over the past twenty-five years – against killings by the Basque terrorist group ETA, Islamist bomb attacks, coup attempts or, even, the Iraq war – each gathered more than a million people together.

The friction between a Spaniard's liberal desire to do whatever he or she wants and their need to live in a mass with others of a similar disposition emerges in that troublesome institution known, often inappropriately, as *la comunidad*, the community of neighbours. This brings the owners of all the apartments in one building together to run its common affairs. Although there has recently been a move towards *urbanizaciones* of terraced or detached homes on the outskirts of cities, most Spaniards still like to live piled up atop one another. Small towns, as a result, often start in a startlingly abrupt fashion. There are fields or open countryside and then, suddenly, there is the bare brickwork flank of the first apartment block. Another is attached to it next door, and the whole medium-rise townscape can continue like that until, just as suddenly, you are back out in the countryside.

This cheek-by-jowl living is the natural state of the inner city, where I live. It is continued in many of the new barrios that emerge out of nowhere in the country's rapidly expanding cities, where huge blocks of apartments, some with their own communal swimming pool, are sprouting up. With almost four out of five homes owned by the people living in them, Spaniards outdo even the British – leave the French and Germans trailing – as property owners. That means that they own their flat, but also co-own the building it is in with their neighbours.

Meetings of the *comunidad* are, traditionally, where you learn the ugly truth about your neighbours. These quarrelsome, heated assemblies are often held in a smoky back room of the local bar. Hours are spent angrily debating mundane matters – such as whether the lift floor should be covered in lino or rubber. Votes are sometimes cast not on the merits of argument, but to even old scores.

It was our downstairs neighbour who plunged us into the affairs of our own *comunidad*. The man we bought from had warned us that the elderly woman downstairs was '*como una cabra*' – 'as mad as a goat'. She soon informed us that the tenants who had been in our apartment before had played nasty tricks on her. They had spotted her ceiling with black dots. They had managed to make smoke and fumes travel downstairs. They had also, she claimed, sneaked dead birds into her apartment.

Things started more or less well. She would bring us letters, written in English, from a foreign bank where her ex-husband had left her money, so we could translate them. She would tell us how evil the rest of our neighbours were. She would refuse to go away.

Then, one day, she sent the police round. I had almost killed her, she claimed, and ought to be locked up. Two armed police officers arrived at our door to deliver her *denuncia* and tell me I should go down to the police station and give my version of events. A long, rambling note written in her spidery handwriting on the back of a piece of scrap paper was pushed under our door. 'If you try to fool the judge, you will go to prison,' she warned.

Our downstairs neighbour had some reason for complaint. The false ceiling in her dining room had fallen down, showering her mock-Chippendale furniture with sodden plaster and bringing down a chandelier. She, fortunately, had not been in the room when it happened. But she still considered this a case of near homicidal negligence on our part.

The cause, it turned out, was a leak from our roof terrace. In Madrid it had rained for weeks. Across town a couple of semi-abandoned buildings had already collapsed under the weight of it. My terrace, bizarrely but fortunately, turned out not to be my legal responsibility. As part of the outside fabric of the building, it was the *comunidad* that was meant to pay for its upkeep. The judge shelved the case against me. The *comunidad*, after a couple of years in which her dining room stayed in its semi-ruined state, eventually struck a deal.

Film-maker Alex de la Iglesia made a film which he called *La Comunidad*. It was an Ealing-style comedy, in which the neighbours try to bump off an estate agent, played by Carmen Maura. She, according to the plot, had discovered a treasure trove of cash in a dead man's apartment. It was a spoof on the underlying tensions that lie in all *comunidades*. One of the most popular series on Spanish television now follows a similar formula. But the truth is that, hard work as it is, *la comunidad* succeeds as an institution. A Spaniard's social agility is, in the end, superior to their fierce feelings of personal independence.

Over time I have watched as my own children, mostly British by blood but mostly Spanish by culture, learn to belong to those huge groups that Spaniards find one of their most natural habitats. 'Just imagine,' said one mother, watching a gang of six-year-olds play. 'They'll still be friends when they are our age.' Only if, I was tempted to say, they never move out of the barrio, like you.

But I realised she might be right one day as I watched my younger son and other four-year-olds from his infants class climbing noisily into a coach. They were going away to spend three days with their teachers and lots of farmyard animals at a '*granja escuela*' – 'a school farm'. This had been sold to us as a further, intensive round of group-formation training and, therefore, key to their education. I felt a pang of envy as I watched my child go. He already belonged to that noisy, congenial mass known as Spaniards in a way that I – with my innate, sometimes awkward, *anglosajón* individualism – find impossible.

9
11-M: Moros y Cristianos

The road south from Granada towards the Mediterranean rises gently uphill as it rounds the western fringes of the snow-capped Sierra Nevada. As you crest the rise, the *sierra* swells upwards on the left, a first, dramatic rampart towards the Mulhacén, mainland Spain's highest peak. This is where the rivers start running south, rushing for the nearby sea. It is, however, the name of this pass – rather than the countryside around it – that impresses. For this, a modest sign indicates, is the '*Puerto del Suspiro del Moro*', 'The Pass of the Moor's Sigh'.

It was here, according to legend, that Boabdil, the last Moorish ruler of Granada, looked back for the final time towards the city. Boabdil, whose Mediterranean kingdom had stretched west to Málaga and east to Almería, was a sentimental man. Standing here on a January day in 1492, the story goes, he wept. It was not just the end of his personal reign, but of 781 years of Muslim kingdoms in Spain. The Granadinos still celebrate the *Fiesta de la Reconquista*, of the Reconquest, every 2 January. They are not always keen to recognise it, but a century and a half must still pass before their city can claim to have been Christian for longer than it was a place where, principally, Mohammed was revered.

Boabdil was on his way to La Alpujarra, the steep, south-facing foothills of the Sierra Nevada. Queen Isabella of Castile and King Ferdinand of Aragón had left him a small fiefdom in return for his capitulation. As he stood looking back towards Granada and his recently abandoned Alhambra fortress-palace, his formidable mother, Ayxa, is reputed to have scolded him. Washington Irving, the American writer who was so entranced by the Alhambra when he arrived here in the 1820s, put her words this way: '"You do well," said she, "to weep as a woman over what you could not defend as a man'." Irving did not invent the story himself. Well before he arrived here on his horse, this had been known as 'The Moor's Sigh'. The road he took from the city was known then as '*La Cuesta de Las Lágrimas*', 'The Slope of Tears'.

The year Granada was taken, bringing almost eight centuries of Christian *Reconquista* of Iberia to a formal end, was extraordinary. It is hard to overestimate the importance, not just to Spain but to the world, of the events that unfurled under the joint flags of Castile and Aragón. This year still conjures up a one-line childhood rhyme which I used to memorise dates. 'In 1492,' I learnt, 'Columbus sailed the ocean blue.' On the far side of the Atlantic, indeed, Christopher Columbus 'discovered' the Americas, creating a colony on the island of Hispaniola – now home to the Dominican Republic and Haiti. Spain's Jews, meanwhile, were expelled on the orders of Isabella and Ferdinand. This couple, known as the Catholic Kings, had, by uniting their realms, effectively founded modern Spain (though it would take until 1512 to fit in the last piece of the puzzle, Navarre). Today's Sephardic Jews, clustered in communities from Los Angeles to Paris to Tel Aviv, are the descendants of that diaspora. Legend has it that some families still conserve, five hundred years later, the old iron key to their house in Toledo. At a synagogue in the besieged Bosnian capital of Sarajevo I was once able to converse, in an admittedly stuttering fashion, with an elderly man using two similar languages that we could both understand – his Ladino and my Castilian Spanish. The old man's Ladino – a quaint, time-warped version of Spanish conserved over centuries by the Sephardic community – might have been even more easily understood by Miguel de Cervantes, the creator of Don Quixote and a contemporary of William Shakespeare. The expulsion of the Jews was just the first stage in a process of ethnic and religious cleansing. The Moors themselves were also gradually obliged to convert to Christianity and, when they refused or only pretended to do so, eventually expelled.

Boabdil's melancholy trip into the Alpujarra led him to one of the most beautiful spots in Spain. The steep slopes of the Alpujarra hills are covered in scrub, deciduous woodland, olives or small orchards of apple, cherry, fig, pear, orange, lemon, medlar and almond trees. Deep gullies cut into the hillsides which, in places, are stripped nearly bare by erosion. All is bathed in that special, clear, whitish light of south and central Spain. Watered by snow-melt and springs from the Sierra Nevada, this was the 'desert island' discovered by writer Gerald Brenan. His Bloomsbury friends, Virginia Woolf, Lytton Strachey and Dora Carrington, rode mules up through the valleys to stay at his home in Yegen in the 1920s. Brenan was struck here by the stillness and the quality of the thin air. Sounds from a village four miles away – barking dogs, men singing flamenco's *cante jondo*, even the noise of running water – would travel crisply across the valley. There was 'a feeling of air surrounding one, of fields of air washing over one that I have never come across anywhere else'. Woolf recalled 'scrambling on the hillside among fig trees and olives . . . as excited as a schoolgirl on holiday'.

In those days the tightly huddled houses in the *pueblos* were a drab, unpainted grey. The standard of living for some had not changed for centuries. Poorer families boasted just one possession – a cooking pot. There were no metalled roads and no money for whitewash. Now there are not only roads – though these are still bone-rattlers in places – but the white-painted villages gleam like Christmas decorations scattered down the steep hillsides. Visitors like to think they have always been like that. In fact the Alpujarra villages, like so many places and people around Spain, only became wealthy enough to pretty themselves up later in the twentieth century.

Driving towards Yegen from the Pass of the Moor's Sigh on the high road towards Trevélez, which some claim is Spain's highest village, another roadside sign gives a clue to the history of Spain's Moors. More particularly, it tells of the *moriscos*, the Moorish population that nominally converted to Christianity after Boabdil's defeat and his subsequent move, a few years later, to north Africa. Here, cutting under one of the tight curves that look down into the precipitous, bare valleys where the Trevélez, Poqueira and

Guadalfeo rivers flow, is the *Barranco de la Sangre*, the Gully of Blood. The *moriscos* of La Alpujarra, in a last-ditch attempt to hold on to the customs, language, clothes, veils and even bathing practices that had been banned by decree, rebelled in 1568. A plaque on a house in the nearby village of Válor, erected recently by a group of Spanish converts to Islam, marks the site of the home of Aben Humeya, the leader of the revolt. 'To Aben Humeya and the *moriscos*, the height of freedom for Al Andalus,' it says.

Rather than the height of freedom, however, the rebellion was part of the death throes of Moorish Spain. One of the worst battles was here, in the Gully of Blood. Legend has it the blood of the Christian soldiers flowed uphill in order not to mix with the Moorish, crypto-Islamic blood of the *moriscos*.

Forty years later the *moriscos* – who still accounted, for example, for a third of the population of the Valencia region – were forced to leave. Some 275,000 of them were ordered out in 1609. Many died of hunger or exhaustion. Others were massacred on their arrival in North Africa, or were killed even before they had managed to leave Spain.

The *moriscos*, and the Moors themselves, had always seemed to me just another quaint, if important and romantic, part of Spanish history. Their presence in modern Spain (except in language and place names) was solely architectural. Here, after all, were the splendid Alhambra palace, the vast *mezquita* in Córdoba with its 580 columns and the hilltop Alcazaba fortresses overlooking Málaga and Almería. They had left, too, some uniquely Spanish architectural forms, where east and west overlapped to produce the hybrid *mudéjar* and *mozárabe* styles in churches and monasteries.

Occasionally, Al Andalus would reappear in the news. Muslims, for example, tried to gain access for themselves and other religions to pray at the Córdoba *mezquita* – which now houses the city's cathedral – but were turned down by the Vatican. Those who prostrate themselves before the *mezquita*'s sparkling, golden *mihrab* can still be thrown out. In Granada, meanwhile, a group of European converts eventually got money out of the United Arab Emirates to build a smart, gleaming new mosque on top of the Albaicín. It symbolically overlooks the Alhambra from a charming barrio of winding lanes and cypress-filled gardens that once boasted twenty-eight mosques. That, I thought, was it. Al Andalus was a great tourism draw. Granada, with its Moroccan gift shops and restaurants offering *couscous* and *tajines*, had even become something of a Moorish theme park. Here was one piece of history that Spaniards were not about to argue over.

I could not have been more wrong. Late in 2004, José María Aznar, the former prime minister whose Conservative People's Party (PP) had been ejected from power in favour of the Socialists of José Luis Rodríguez Zapatero at elections that March, gave a lecture at Washington's Georgetown University. His party's defeat had come three days after 191 Madrid railway commuters were killed in the west's worst Islamist terror attack since September 11. It had been the most traumatic moment in recent Spanish history. To understand the circumstances surrounding that defeat, Aznar told the Georgetown students, they should wind the clock back to 711. This, Spanish schoolchildren are meant to know, was the moment when a Berber called Tarik Bin Ziyad crossed the Mediterranean with a small army and began a swift invasion of Iberia (whilst also leaving his name behind at the large rock known as Jabal-al-Tarik, the Rock of Tarik, now Gibraltar).

'Spain's problem with Al-Qaida starts in the eighth century . . . when a Spain recently invaded by the Moors refused to become just another piece in the Islamic world and began a long battle to recover its identity,' Aznar said. 'This *reconquista* process was very long, lasting some eight hundred years.'

Aznar was widely ridiculed for his words. They were an attempt to relate the train attacks to Al Andalus. Christian Spain, he meant, had long been a target for Islamic crusaders. An old enemy, in other words, had returned.

Few people agreed. One who might have done, however, was a bearded and robed man then believed to be hiding out somewhere in Pakistan. Osama bin Laden had shown a personal interest in Al-Andalus, signalling it to his followers as an apostate territory and lamenting its loss to Islam. On the day in October, 2001, that the United States began its campaign against the Taliban in Afghanistan, the Al-Qaida founder issued one of his famous videotapes. He was followed by his number two, the Egyptian Ayman al-Zawahiri. 'Let the whole world know that we shall never accept that the tragedy of Al Andalus should be repeated,' al-Zawahiri said. Two months before the Madrid attacks, Bin Laden himself returned to the theme, lamenting the weakness of the Arab world. 'It is enough to know that the economy of all Arab countries is weaker than the economy of one country that had once been part of our world when we used to truly adhere to Islam. That country is the lost Al Andalus,' he said on a tape broadcast by Al Jazeera.

A newspaper editorial summed up the feelings of those Spaniards who had angrily rejected Aznar's policies and his disastrous handling of the bombings at the polls that March. 'In their reinvention of the past, and their vindication of the crusades between Islam and Christianity, there is a disturbing similarity between Aznar and Bin Laden,' huffed *El País*. Spain's Muslims, be they immigrant Moroccans or local converts, agreed.

Aznar was not the only outraged Spaniard talking of a conspiracy to turn the clock back several centuries. A few weeks earlier, Spain's leading clergyman, the arch-conservative Cardinal Antonio María Rouco, had trodden a similar path. 'Some people wish to place us in the year 711,' Cardinal Rouco said. He was complaining about rumours that the Socialist government planned to put other religions or denominations, be they Islam, Judaism or the Protestant churches, on the same footing as Roman Catholicism – which, amongst other things, has a near stranglehold on religious teaching at schools. 'It seems as if we are meant to wipe ourselves out of history.'

Once again, I found, Spaniards were bickering over the meaning of their own history. Only this time it was about a period that stretched back, in British terms, to even before the days of the Vikings. It seemed that the country's self-image was somehow at stake. Should Spain be defined as a proudly Roman Catholic nation that emerged, or re-emerged, from a valiant eight-century battle against Islam? Or should it, as the historian Américo Castro first proposed decades ago, think of itself as being forged from a historic encounter between religions and cultures, including both Islam and Judaism? For a country of inevitably intimate relations with a Muslim world that is clearly visible across the Mediterranean from its southernmost shores, these are important questions.

This latest row had been sparked by the tragic, dramatic events of those four bitter, yet historic, days in March 2004. These were the four days bracketed, at one end, by the train bombings and, at the other, by the surprise ousting of Aznar's party from power.

Early on the morning of 11 March, Luis Garrudo, the doorman of a small block of flats close to the railway station in Alcalá de Henares, a Madrid dormitory town, noticed a white Renault Kangoo van parked across the street. It was a bright, spring morning. Three men busied themselves around the van. They seemed dressed for the coldest of winter days. Their heads and faces were all but hidden behind scarves, hats and hoods.

'When I saw them I thought they looked like armed robbers or something like that, though it didn't make much sense at that time of the morning,' Luis told me when I went to see him twenty-four hours later. 'They were all covered up around their heads and necks, and it wasn't even cold.'

At just before 7 a.m. Luis walked the 200 metres to the railway station to pick up a copy of *Metro*, a free daily morning newspaper. He found himself walking behind one of the men from the van. 'He seemed to be in a hurry,' he told me. 'He was walking very quickly, carrying something and, again, I could hardly see his face at all.'

Luis thought, from the white scarf tied high across his neck and chin, that he might be a Real Madrid fan. 'All I could see was the scarf and something covering the top of his head. You could only really see his eyes. By the time I got back, the other two men had gone. The van was still there.'

Luis was walking behind one of the worst mass murderers in recent European history. For this was one of several young

Muslim radicals and small-time crooks equipped with thirteen bombs. A few minutes later they started hopping from carriage to carriage, and from train to train, across platforms packed full of early morning workers – builders, office cleaners, electricians and schoolteachers. This was the 8 a.m. start crowd, those who had to be at building sites and warehouses well before most office workers had even left their homes. Many, more than a quarter, were immigrants, attracted by the cheap rents this far out of the Spanish capital. The man Luis Garrudo followed would place at least one of thirteen cheap sports bags in at least one of four different trains. Each bag contained a mobile phone, a copper detonator, nuts and screws to act as shrapnel, and some twelve kilos of Spanish-made Goma 2 Eco explosives.

The bombers targeted four separate trains which passed through Alcalá de Henares between 7.00 a.m. and 7.15. In some cases they may have ridden them for the first few stops as they headed in towards Madrid's Atocha station, distributing the bombs amongst the packed carriages. Within half-an-hour, Europe's initiation into the new tactics of radical Islamist terror was complete.

The bombs were detonated by the alarms in the mobile telephones. They started going off at 7.37 and had wrought their full destruction by 7.43. In some trains those who went to help the wounded from the first bomb were caught by a second or third. By the time they finished exploding, there were four trains each with immense, jagged holes blown through several carriages. The smoking hulks were strung along the line between Atocha, where one train had just arrived, and the working-class barrio of El Pozo del Tío Raimundo. The latter's name was once synonymous with the poverty of immigrant workers arriving from other parts of Spain. One bomb had exploded in a wagon known as 'little Romania' because it was where immigrants from that country gathered every morning. Fifty-four of the dead were immigrants.

There were Muslims, too, and schoolchildren, babies, pregnant women, young couples and parents with their young children. All of these, and more, would die, their bodies peppered with shrapnel or the breath squeezed out of them by the blow and suck of the blast.

Those who survived recall the ghastly silence that followed immediately after. Some will never forget. 'It still flashes through my mind continuously . . . The silence, the dust and the things I saw that I can't bring myself to describe to you,' Clara Escribano, a survivor from the train at Santa Eugenia, told me months later.

The first emergency workers to arrive were also struck by the stillness of this tableau of horror. 'It was the silence that made it so different from other attacks,' Dr Ervigio Corral, a veteran of ETA attacks, told me. Dr Corral was the man in charge of Madrid's ambulance services. He had rushed to Atocha station and was the first to enter some coaches. The dead, or their remains, were everywhere. 'The only living people left inside were those who could not move. They were almost all suffering from burst eardrums, which meant they could not hear you. When you asked what was wrong with them, they did not answer. They asked you for help only with their eyes.'

Europe had only seen one attack on this scale before, in 1988, when 270 people were killed by a Libyan bomb on Pan Am Flight 103, forcing it to crash into the Scottish town of Lockerbie.

Dr Corral would see some eighty corpses in that first hour, in Atocha and 500 yards up the track where a second bombed train had ground to a halt after bits of carriage had been blown into apartments overlooking the track. Over the next thirty-six hours he would personally give the news of death to some 130 bereaved and distraught families.

The death toll could have been higher. Of the thirteen bombs, only ten exploded. Madrileños found out that day, to their surprise, that they had one of the best-equipped ambulance and emergency services in Europe. Two field hospitals were set up, hundreds of volunteers called in and, of the 400 injured rushed to hospital, only one died on the way. Fourteen more died after they got there. The timing of the attacks helped, too. Hospitals were just changing shifts, so had twice the normal number of staff at hand. Operating theatres were empty. 'If it happened again, I would just ask that it happen at the same time,' a doctor who treated the injured told me.

My apartment lies just a block from the Gregorio Marañón hospital, which took most of the injured. That morning my children waited ten minutes to cross the road on their way to school. The stream of ambulances tearing past made their usual zebra crossing impassable.

Spain had not lived a moment of such enormous drama and tension since Civil Guard lieutenant colonel Antonio Tejero and his men stormed parliament in their failed 1981 coup attempt.

A massacre of this kind was simply of a different scale to the Basque separatist ETA bombs that had killed and maimed with frustrating regularity on Madrid's streets for three decades. Madrileños had marched in their millions to protest against some ETA killings. They were rarely, however, touched by them directly.

There was nothing anonymous about the death and carnage on what soon became known as 11-M or '*el Once M*'. Everybody, it seemed, had been directly or indirectly affected. If they had not seen it, survived it or had to work in the middle of it, they knew someone who had. My own, not terribly large, network of friends and acquaintances soon turned up half a dozen 'somebody who' stories: a schoolteacher lost a former pupil and spent the day trying to prevent her teenage pupils rushing home to see if parents, relatives and friends were okay; a psychologist worked all night as a volunteer helping families identify bodies at a huge morgue set up in the city's exhibition centre; a fireman long ago retired into an office job put on his helmet once more, went to Atocha, wept, pulled himself together and got to work; and a doctor, arrived at the gates of Atocha to catch her morning train, saw the crowds running, threw up and fled in terror.

Perhaps I should have expected it, but it was shocking to see how quickly the narrative of what had happened that day – and over the next three days until the general election – split into separate, conflicting and angrily confrontational strands. If Spaniards can argue over historic events of thirteen centuries ago, perhaps it is inevitable that they should do so over history as it happens. *El 11-M,* with its horror and the chain of political events it set off, now looks set to be one of those events on which Spaniards will never agree. The division, unfortunately, is on sadly familiar political lines. On this matter, *las dos Españas*, the two Spains, of history are once more at loggerheads. The twin versions often rely on putting belief above proof, on turning to those you trust rather than the evidence presented.

There was nothing casual about the timing of the attacks. It was two and a half years to the day since the 9/11 attacks on the Twin Towers in New York. It was also, more importantly, three days before a general election. If the bombers aim was to influence the course of those elections, they were highly successful. Even they, however, could not have foreseen exactly how, or why, over the next three extraordinary days, they would do so.

It took just a few hours to add political confusion to human catastrophe. Most people immediately suspected ETA. The magnitude and style of the attacks, however, left sufficient room for doubt. ETA, after all, had never acted on this scale, or with this degree of wanton, arbitrary barbarity. The first authoritative voice to publicly point the finger, however, came from the Basque Country itself. Basque regional premier Juan José Ibarretxe denounced the work of 'vermin' and 'murderers'. 'ETA is writing its last, disgraceful, pages,' he said. If Ibarretxe said it was ETA, it was reasonable to believe he would know. The Basque government's police, after all, had its own units specialised in fighting ETA. Nobody realised at the time that this was simply one of the first knee-jerk political reactions of a day laden with them. For his own political reasons, Ibarretxe wanted to be the first to heap shame on ETA.

The government soon followed suit. Their front man for this was Interior Minister Ángel Acebes. The strings, however, were being pulled directly from the Moncloa Palace where Aznar had set up a crisis committee. This excluded the political opposition. It also, to begin with, excluded the country's intelligence services, the Centro Nacional de Inteligencia (CNI). If any minutes or notes were taken at that committee, they were later destroyed.

Aznar's team at the Moncloa Palace prime minister's office wiped computer records, including security copies, of their eight years in power before leaving a few weeks later. Aznar only left paper copies of official, legal documents – and the 12,000-euro bill for erasing the computers.

'The government does not have any doubt at all that ETA is responsible,' Acebes said. 'ETA was looking to commit a massacre in Spain and it has managed it.' It was a line that, with only slowly waning levels of insistence but rapidly evaporating levels of credibility, the government would stick to for most of the next four days. ETA's favourite explosive, Titadyn 30 AG had, they initially said, been used. Basque terrorists had, three months earlier, been caught smuggling bombs onto trains into Madrid. Just a few weeks earlier an ETA van-bomb packed with explosives, apparently heading for the same Madrid suburbs where the bombs were planted, had been captured. One of the terrorists arrested that day said there had also been a failed attempt at planting thirteen rucksack-bombs at a ski resort. These were all reasons to suspect ETA. They were not, however, proof.

Before Acebes spoke there came a denial from those normally damned as ETA's mouthpieces – the leaders of the banned Batasuna party. 'This attack is not the work of ETA. This is an action carried out by the Arab resistance movement,' said Batasuna leader Arnaldo Otegi. Otegi, who left jail in 1990 after serving half of a six-year prison sentence for his part in an ETA kidnapping, had never before condemned the group's attacks. This time he publicly expressed 'absolute repulsion' for a 'massacre . . . that was indiscriminate and affected mainly working-class people'.

'We want to make it absolutely clear. The *izquierda abertzale* (the patriotic left) does not even consider as a hypothesis that ETA is behind what happened in Madrid. Neither the target nor the modus operandi allow one to say ETA is behind it,' he said.

His denial acted like a red rag to the government bull. Aznar harboured a blind hatred for ETA. He was now convinced they were trying to wriggle off the hook. Aznar personally rang the most important newspaper editors, the first time some had received a call in eight years. 'What Otegi is trying to do is pass the blame onto the Islamists in order to gain time,' he told Pedro J. Ramírez, editor of *El Mundo*.

'He guaranteed to me that it was ETA,' Jesús Ceberio, editor of *El País*, said afterwards. 'It was an assurance given in absolute terms.'

Aznar's calls produced opposite reactions. Ramírez, realising Aznar had failed to give concrete evidence, took the word ETA out of the headline of his special mid-afternoon edition. *El País*, by contrast, added it in, declaring 'ETA slaughter in Madrid'. 'I clearly made a mistake,' a bitter Ceberio admitted later.

In the past, however, it had been unthinkable for Batasuna politicians to condemn ETA's acts. Batasuna had, in fact, recently been banned. Otegi's denials were just one more element that made doubt obligatory – at least until the smoking gun, the killer piece of evidence, could be turned up.

The more ETA protested it was not them, the louder the government insisted it was. They, and anybody else who gave public credence to their words, were involved in 'an attempt by malicious people to divert people's attention', Acebes said.

As I hurtled back along the motorway towards Madrid that morning, having been caught working out of town, I recalled how the People's Party had sold a very different line on ETA just a few weeks earlier. '*ETA mata, pero no miente*', 'ETA murders, but it does not lie,' the former interior minister and party boss in the Basque Country, Jaime Mayor Oreja, had said. Major Oreja, a political heavyweight and former candidate to succeed Aznar as party leader, had produced the phrase after ETA called a regional truce in Catalonia. That truce followed a secret meeting with Josep-Lluís Carod-Rovira, leader of a Catalan separatist party. Mayor Oreja's phrase was his way of accusing Carod-Rovira of lying when he claimed not to have done a deal with ETA to stop it killing in Catalonia. It was also an attempt to hurt the Socialists, who had Carod-Rovira as a coalition partner in the Catalan regional government.

The phrase was a reminder of two things: first, that the People's

Party was prepared to change its interpretation of ETA's reliability as a source of information about its own actions depending on the circumstances; and, secondly, it had fought a significant part of the election on the issue of ETA. This had been the most brutal and divisive part of a bare-knuckle People's Party election campaign. There had been repeated attempts to paint the Socialists as weak and woolly. Nationalist and separatist parties, meanwhile, were presented as, at least morally, swimming in the same gutter as ETA. It had widened still further the chasm that opened up under Aznar between his own side and the rest of the political spectrum. That, in turn, had set some commentators talking, once more, about that historically spine-chilling phenomenon of *las dos Españas*.

Under Aznar, the People's Party had been immensely successful against ETA. Police action had reduced it to a shell of its former self. Aznar could have campaigned on his great feat of reducing ETA to an increasingly insignificant rump. He went, instead, several steps further. ETA became an electoral cosh to bludgeon others with.

The previous weeks had been a reminder that, well before George W. Bush made terrorism a major part of a political campaign, José María Aznar had discovered it for himself. Not surprisingly, Aznar was Bush's most fervent European ally – even more so than Britain's Tony Blair. He had backed war in Iraq in what was, depending on your point of view, an act of considerable political courage or of immense stupidity. Polls showed more than 80 per cent of the country disagreed. Aznar balked at sending troops to invade Iraq. As soon as the first part of that war was over, however, he had sent enough troops to make Spain one of the biggest forces on the ground after the US and Britain. They wore the cross of Santiago, otherwise known as 'the Moorslayer', on their uniforms. Going on about ETA had, deliberately or not, been a useful way of diverting attention from his unpopular, unilateral decision to go to Iraq.

I reached Madrid late on the morning of the train bombings to find this noisy city in a state of stunned silence. Streets were eerily empty. Everything seemed dulled. I saw the charred carcasses of trains, the fire officers still extracting bodies from the mangled wreckage. The occasional carload of people with shocked, pallid faces drove around in circles as they sought news of the missing. There was weeping, hysteria and anger outside the hospitals.

The cavernous IFEMA exhibition hall was turned into an impromptu morgue because its refrigerated air could stop bodies decomposing. Forensic scientists and doctors did a macabre jigsaw puzzle, trying to match the body parts of the 191 dead. It was a difficult task. They began thinking they had a dozen more bodies than they ended up with. The victims' families sat around in grim, grieving groups, waiting for Dr Corral and his colleagues to call them to view the dead.

The government's loud insistence that it had been an ETA attack reached full volume that first day. A motion was forced through the United Nations in New York, blaming the Basque terrorists. Spanish embassies were instructed 'to make the most of every opportunity encountered to confirm ETA's responsibility'.

There were other spill-overs too. In my local greengrocers the hatred was palpable. Accusing fingers pointed not just north to the Basque Country, but east to Catalonia. 'They will be happy about this in Catalonia,' said one client. It was as if Catalans were synonymous with the violence generated by a Basque Country that lay a thousand kilometres away on the other side of Spain. It was also a sign of how deep the divisions in Spain had become over the previous few years. Two days later a row between a policeman's wife and sixty-one-year-old baker Ángel Berroeta, who refused to put up an anti-ETA sign in his bakery window in Pamplona, would see the policeman and his son burst into the baker's shop and shoot him dead. Berroeta was a victim of the hysteria that the government's response helped provoke.

An honest and responsible reply from the government would have required it to admit doubt. With the red rag of ETA dancing in front of their noses and three days to go before an election, that was not possible. Doubt was summarily banished.

Spaniards were getting used to the virulence with which Aznar's government defended the indefensible. Aznar had been absolute in his insistence that weapons of mass destruction existed in Iraq. His reaction to previous disasters had been to retreat into defensiveness or denial. When the *Prestige* oil tanker had gone down off the coast of Galicia a year earlier, the government had assured everyone that the oil would not be swept onto Spanish beaches. It would later take months to clean them. When sixty-two Spanish United Nations peacekeepers died in a rickety, Yak-42 Ukrainian charter plane that crashed into a Turkish mountain on their way home from Afghanistan, the government ferociously denied that thirty bodies had been wrongly identified by Spanish military doctors. Eventually, all would have to be exhumed except those who, mistakenly and against their real families' wishes, had been cremated. An aggressive bunker mentality had become a mark of the Aznar government.

Later that afternoon, as I was hammering out my own, written version of the day's events, the telephone rang. It was the spokesperson's office at Aznar's Moncloa Palace headquarters, calling out of the blue. The woman at the other end of the phone, who I knew, had been instructed to give me the reasons why the government was convinced it was ETA. These included: that ETA had planned to attack trains before; that the explosives used were of a kind it had previously used; and, lastly, that ETA did not always give warnings before its attacks. The first two seemed good arguments, though it later turned out that the police knew by now that Titadyn had not, in fact, been used. The last excuse, an attempt to head off the Batasuna arguments that ETA did not attack randomly, smacked of panic. Of course ETA did not always give warnings. How else could it have killed 800 people over thirty years? The call rang warning bells. The government not only thought it was ETA. Its cold-calling and panicky arguments showed it wanted, or even needed, everyone else to think so too.

Within a few minutes, however, the tale began to unravel. News came on the radio about the van that doorman Luis Garrudo had reported to the police. It contained copper detonators of a kind not used by ETA. There was also a Koranic tape. Doubt was no longer reasonable. It was actively required.

The next day, however, with forty-eight hours until the voting stations opened, Aznar and Acebes continued to spin the ETA line. The prime minister insisted Acebes had been right to blame the Basque group. 'There was no reason to think that it was not the same lot who had tried before, and there still is not,' Aznar said.

That evening, Acebes compounded his mistake further. 'There is no reason, at the moment, for ETA not to be the main line of investigation,' he insisted. Mariano Rajoy, the People's Party candidate taking over from Aznar, told interviewers from the *El Mundo* newspaper that he was 'morally convinced' it was ETA. Moral conviction seemed the strangest, and least trustworthy, argument of all. Where were the facts? There was still no smoking gun in ETA's hands.

More than a million people packed the centre of Madrid that night to demonstrate against the attacks, despite steady rainfall. Most walked, or stood in the choked streets, silently. Only one phrase seemed to bring the protesters together. 'It is not raining, Madrid is weeping!' someone said. The great rift, however, was already opening up. '*¡ETA no! ¡ETA no!*' read some banners. '*Otegi, cabrón, súbete al vagón*', 'Otegi, you bastard, get yourself into the railway carriage,' some chanted. Or, joining together, in order, peaceful Catalan separatists, pro-ETA Basques and Pasqual Maragall, the Socialist party leader in Catalonia, they cried: '*Rovira, Otegi, Maragall,* They negotiate, we die.' Zapatero found himself confronted by demonstrators loudly protesting at his party's alleged softness on ETA. But the old anti-war signs calling for '*Paz*', 'Peace', were also there – blaming Aznar for making Spain a target. Some shouted '*¡Aznar asesino!*' By the end of the demonstration there were loud cries of what was to become the angry, resounding question of the next 36 hours: '*¿Quién ha sido? ¿Quién ha sido?*', 'Who was it? Who was it?'

State television TVE, a faithful slave to whichever government is in power, ignored those who protested against Aznar or war. It zoomed in on the anti-ETA signs. Later it programmed a documentary about the February 2000 ETA murder of Basque Socialist leader Fernando Buesa and his bodyguard, Jorge Díaz Elorza. Buesa's family protested at what it saw as cynical use of his death by the People's Party. 'We cannot remain silent when, in such an artful form, attempts are made to make the truth another casualty of this barbarity and, less so, when they try to make electoral use of the memory of two terrorist victims.' But the People's Party had decided, long before, that ETA's victims somehow 'belonged' to them.

The divisions that, over the next days, would make one friend's grandmother recall the frightening, hate-filled weeks of 1936 when the Civil War broke out, were out in the open.

Across Spain, the demonstrations were repeated. Eleven million people, a quarter of the country, reportedly took to the streets. Figures on marches like this are routinely exaggerated but this was, once more, an outpouring of that great Spanish virtue – *solidaridad*, solidarity. The splits, however, were obvious across the country. Tension ran high in those places already angry with Aznar. In the Catalan capital of Barcelona, Socialists and People's Party leaders refused to walk together. *Barceloneses*, whose newspapers and Catalan-language television broadcasters had been more sceptical about the ETA line than their Madrid counterparts, had shouted '*¡No a la guerra!*' – 'No to war!' Deputy Prime Minister Rodrigo Rato was forced to take refuge from the angry crowd in a car park. 'It [the demonstration] left me worried. I saw scenes of tension and intolerance ... more appropriate to a divided society than that of a display of unity,' José Antich, the editor of Barcelona's *La Vanguardia* newspaper, said the next day. In Bilbao, Basque nationalists walked separately from non-nationalists.

While Spain marched, police were already tying up the Islamist connection. The clues came from the trains themselves. Three bombs had failed to explode. Two were blown up on site. The bag containing the other, however, was not recognised immediately. It was taken, along with other abandoned luggage, to the mass morgue set up at Madrid's exhibition centre. It remained unclaimed by the families there, so it was sent back to a police station near Santa Eugenia railway station – where it had first come from. It was not until a police officer there opened the bag, that the key element of the future investigation was found. Two wires were sticking up from a mobile phone and a detonator. This was bomb number 13. A courageous bomb disposal expert called Pedro Lorente drove it to a nearby park and defused it. The mechanism for detonating the bombs, it was discovered, had been the mobile phone alarms. These had triggered the detonators, blowing up the twelve kilos of explosives and scattering the shrapnel packed around them.

Lorente was able to extract the mobile phone. Its SIM card led police to the wholesalers and people they had sold on to. Moroccans Jamal Zougam, Mohamed Bekkali and Mohammed Chaoui, all in their early thirties, jointly ran a *locutorio*, a shop equipped with cheap-rate telephone lines for calling abroad. Their shop was in the central Madrid neighbourhood of Lavapiés – a melting pot of the capital's immigrants. They also sold, on the side, mobile phones which they illegally altered so they could be used without payment.

Only a teenage petty crook, who acted as a messenger boy bringing the explosives to Madrid from Asturias and returning with the hashish that helped pay for it, was the first person convicted. But two dozen people were arrested over the following weeks as the mobile phones led police towards the bombers. The night after the attacks, Bekkali had joined the protest marchers in Madrid, lighting a candle for the dead. That is what his younger sister, Charafa, told a journalist from the *Guardian*, Owen Bowcott, when he went to visit their well-off, carpet-trading family in Tangier that week. 'His voice was a bit taut,' she recalled. 'He said he had been on the march against terrorism and lit one of the candles. He said he felt very sad for the victims. He was arrested that evening.'

On the surface, at least, this was exceptionally good police work. It should have made Aznar's government look good. Instead it made it look foolish.

Even then, however, nothing was clear. If the phones used in the attacks were supplied by Moroccans, it did not necessarily mean they were the bombers. 'They were nice people, very friendly,' the Spanish man who sold crisps, nuts, sweets and dried fruits in a tiny shop right in front of the *locutorio* told me. 'They weren't fundamentalists,' a couple of their Lavapiés immigrant friends swore.

Zougam was, in fact, well-known to police. Police in Madrid, acting at the request of a French judge, had raided the Zougam family apartment in 2001. They found videos of his Moroccan friends fighting as mujahedin in Dagestan, Russia. Also, in a clear sign that he was, at the very least, intrigued by the fundamentalist creed, they also found a videotape containing an interview with Osama bin Laden and several books on global jihad. Zougam's address book included the numbers of several men awaiting trial in Spanish prisons on al-Qaida-related charges.

Zougam had moved from Tangier, where two of the passengers killed in Madrid on 11 March also came from, with his mother, Aicha, and older half-brother, Mohammed Chaoui, in 1983. He was ten and an early immigrant at a time when Madrid and Spain were still remarkably homogenous places. Back in the Tangier kasbah, however, he had aroused suspicions on family visits home. He sometimes stayed with the Benayiche family, alleged members of the Groupe Islamique Combattant Marocain (GICM). This was part of the Salifiya Jihadia movement. It had been blamed for the suicide bomb attacks which had killed forty-five people, including many at the Casa de España social club, in Casablanca in May 2003. Through the Benayiches, there were links to Al-Qaida. One brother, Abdellah, had been killed by an American bomb at the Tora Bora cave complex as Osama bin Laden and other Al-Qaida fighters fled from Afghanistan. Another, Abdelaziz, was under arrest in Spain for alleged membership of an al-Qaida cell. The third, Salaheddine, was in a Moroccan prison for the Casablanca bombings. They possibly took Zougam to see their fiery preacher Mohammed Fizazi, who was given to urging the 'assassination of the impious'. Fizazi is now serving thirty years in jail for the Casablanca attacks. Under interrogation Fizazi allegedly declared: 'I love death as much as the impious love life.' It was a phrase that would reappear in the mouths of the Madrid bombers, who did not consider their campaign to be over.

The three arrested men, like many of those picked up after them, had never looked the part. Zougam wore jeans and had a fashionable haircut. Bekkali was a graduate from Tetouan University. A Real Madrid fanatic, he owned a David Beckham shirt. 'He seemed a completely normal person. He eyed up girls and laughed and played with everyone. He smoked cigarettes, went to the beach, kissed girls on their cheek. Islamists don't do those kind of things,' a cousin told Bowcott. 'You would never think he would be capable of this terrible act, this crime. Those bombs were acts of terrorism, not Islam. It's a sick ideology.'

News of the arrests broke late on the day after the bombings. By the next morning, Saturday, all Spain knew that three Moroccans had been arrested and that at least one had fundamentalist connections. Political parties had suspended campaigning straight after the bombings. Saturday was, in any case, the official 'day of reflection'. Voters were meant to ponder their choice. Politicians were banned from campaigning.

During the day, however, the murmur of discontent grew to a roar. Opposition politicians had already let it be known they thought the government was lying, deliberately sticking to the ETA line to win votes. A new political phenomenon was born that day – the instant text message demonstration. Anonymous text messages began to fly from mobile phone to mobile phone. They became known as the *pásalo* messages, because each ended with an exhortation to 'Pass it on'. It was like chain mail, but instant. The first *pásalo* had landed on my mobile the evening of the attack. It simply said: 'A candle in the window for the dead. *Pásalo*.'

On the day of reflection the messages became frantic, political and angry. By mid-afternoon, my partner's phone had received this one: 'Aznar smelling of roses? They call this the day of reflection and Urdaci (head of news at state broadcaster RTVE) is working? Today, the 13th, at 6 p.m. PP HQ 13 Génova St. without parties. Silence for the truth. pásalo!'

Demonstrations are illegal the day before an election. But this was a call for one. In the space of a few hours, the messages flew from phone to phone. The internet picked them up. E-mails and message boards amplified the call. New protests were hurriedly called outside PP offices across the country.

At ten minutes to six I took up position outside the PP's Génova Street headquarters. There were a dozen or more journalists and photographers there and a handful of people, no more than twenty, hanging about. At six on the dot, a protest demonstration materialised out of thin air. Suddenly there were fifty, then 100, then 200 people gathered. The police ordered them to move on. They refused. The police demanded their ID cards. The demonstrators held them out to the TV cameras. 'We want the truth!' they shouted. '*¿Quién ha sido? ¿Quién ha sido?*', 'Who was it? Who was it?', began the chant. As the minutes ticked by hundreds more people arrived. Soon there were a thousand, then two thousand, then the street was blocked and the riot squad vans were arriving – always too late for the protesters as their numbers grew.

A small, determined woman was standing in the middle of the road, ignoring police orders to stay on one side and shouting at passing cars, many of which honked in support. I went up to ask her some questions. 'We are just people who want the truth. Our pain has been caused by Aznar's support for Bush,' she said.

Within half an hour, 5,000 people were sitting on the road chanting: 'We want the truth, before we vote!' Another chant was '*¡Vuestras guerras, nuestros muertos!*', 'Your war, our dead!' Madrid's notoriously baton-happy riot police looked on, unable to do more than prepare to stop a full-scale assault on the PP building, where only a few lights burned. The blue vans kept tearing up and disgorging their cargo of helmet-and-visored police officers. If the demonstrators had wanted to riot, they could have done. I expected violence and half wished I had one of those helmets disguised as baseball hats that news agency journalists seem to get these days. But nothing happened. The police did not charge. Nor did the demonstrators. One part of the text message was roundly ignored, however. There was no silence. The crowd howled.

A man walking a large, well-groomed dog started arguing furiously with the demonstrators. He was a university professor who, he told me, had been jailed by Franco. He was livid. 'They [the left] are doing this because they know that tomorrow they will lose the elections,' he fumed. The professor's prediction was one of the worst made that day. He was one of the few people who dared to predict anything at all. Most people thought the Socialists were going to win extra votes, but nobody was prepared to say how many – or whether they might oust the People's Party. Only at Aznar's Moncloa Palace residence and at the headquarters of the two main parties – where a select few had access to private polling – did people know that the professor's prediction was totally wrong.

The demonstrators kept going all night. It was remarkable, given the tension and the anger, that there was no violence. Spaniards, anyway, do not go in for riots. The only exception has been the Basque Country's angry, organised, and systematically riotous, separatist radical youths. Later the protesters would move to the Puerta del Sol – Madrid's answer to Piccadilly Circus or Times Square – and would wander loudly around the streets until the small hours of the morning.

It seemed nothing could add more tension to the situation. But, as protesters wandered the streets, the drama reached new heights. Telemadrid, the capital's television station, received an anonymous call. The caller said that a videotape had been left in a waste-paper bin outside what Madrileños called the '*mezquita de la M-30*', the shiny, Saudi-built mosque perched above the city's ten-lane M-30 inner ring road. Police picked up the tape. When they put it into a video machine, they were greeted by the sight of three machine-gun-toting, masked men. They looked like they had come from a Hamas suicide bomber's farewell tape in Palestine.

> We declare our responsibility for what happened in Madrid, just two and a half years after the attack on New York and Washington. It is our answer to your collaboration with that criminal Bush and his allies. It is like an answer to the crimes you have committed in the world, concretely in Afghanistan and Iraq, and, if God wills it, there will be more. You want life and we want death, which provides an example of what the Prophet Mohammed said. If you do not stop your injustices, blood will flow more and more. These attacks are just a little of what might happen in the future with what you call terrorism. This is a warning from the military commander of al-Qaida Europe: Abu Dujan the Afghan.

'You want life and we want death,' they had said. It was the mantra of angry, violent Islamists – an almost exact replica of what the imam Fizazi had reportedly said in Morocco.

The delivery of the tape was extraordinary timing. It drove the nation's political blood pressure to coronary-attack levels, and it did so just hours before Spaniards went to vote. Nobody who stepped into a polling booth the following day could have had any doubt about who had attacked Madrid.

Or could they? As Spaniards voted the following morning, Foreign Minister Ana Palacio was interviewed by Sir David Frost on BBC television's *Breakfast with Frost*. 'The idea that ETA might be behind [it] is still strong in the investigation,' she claimed.

There are many versions of why Spaniards voted the way they did, none of them provable. Zapatero likes to say he was going to win anyway – despite opinion polls which gave the People's Party a five to seven point lead days before the bombings. Spanish polls are notoriously bad, but that is clearly absurd. The People's Party blames the illegal demonstrations and rumour-mongering in the left-wing press. Others on the right see the old dark forces of Felipe González's corrupt Socialists and their friends in the police at work in the shadows. Right-wing commentators in the US and Great Britain saw straight-forward cowardice. They claimed Spaniards had voted out of fear, especially after Zapatero stuck to his long-term pledge to pull Spanish troops out of Iraq. 'Neville Chamberlain, en Español,' said one *Wall Street Journal* opinion piece, commissioned from an angry Spanish right-winger, on Zapatero. A few days earlier his nickname had been 'Bambi', because of his look of doe-eyed innocence. Most reasonable commentators, however, point to only four definite conclusions: the bombs produced a larger than expected turn-out at the polls; Zapatero would probably not have won without them; the People's Party would not have lost had it not supported war in Iraq and sent troops there; its huge error in insisting that ETA had planted the bombs drove the final nail into its coffin.

Spaniards have a history of rebelling against leaders who take them into wars they do not like. If they feel viscerally suspicious of war, one should not be surprised. Many countries have experienced its horrors. Few, however, are so convinced of its futility. As a child in 1960s and 1970s Britain, I grew up with the moral certainty that a previous generation of Britons – that of my schoolteachers – had fought a just war against Adolf Hitler. If the Auschwitz gas chambers proved they were right to fight, General Franco was proof to my Spanish friends that their grandfathers had butchered one another senselessly. The colourless decades of his rule hung heavily over the past, like a punishment for the bloodbath.

Spain's experience of war has been better painted than it has been written. The few hundred metres of central Madrid that embrace both the Prado Museum and the Reina Sofía modern arts centre, contain, within them, some of the most telling pictorial denunciations of war ever painted or etched. In his painting *The Third of May, 1808*, or *The Executions on Príncipe Pío Hill* and his *Disasters of War* series of etchings Goya tells of the Spanish uprising against Napoleonic rule in 1808. '*Yo lo ví*' – 'I saw it,' Goya scratched onto one of his copperplates of killing, rape and pillage. In the Reina Sofía, Picasso's huge, grey-blue *Guernica* is populated with terrified mothers, dead children, maddened animals and dismembered bodies. It evokes a world numbed by terror.

The horror of Guernica, blitzed by the German Luftwaffe on Franco's behalf in 1937, was real, and more so because it was innovative. An ancient human fear was turned into reality. Death rained from the sky. A local artist once showed me around the rebuilt town, telling me his memories of the fateful day. He had run for the hills as a boy and watched Guernica burn. What he saw was the invention of blanket incendiary bombing of civilian targets. What was shocking in 1937 became, sadly, commonplace within a decade. Guernica, and nearby Durango, were the experimental laboratories for the carpet bombing of Coventry or Dresden and, ultimately, for the nuclear wastelands of Nagasaki and Hiroshima.

War played its part, but the most likely reason for the 2004 vote was the People's Party's obstinacy in insisting on the one version of events that would help them politically – that ETA was to blame. A post-voting poll showed one in five Spaniards had that uppermost in their minds when they voted. It was enough to swing it for Rodríguez Zapatero.

In the end, it was not Al-Qaida that brought Aznar's People's Party down. It was ETA. Or, rather, it was Aznar's personal obsession with the separatist group. Under his guidance, the People's Party had been drawn into defining itself in terms of ETA or, rather, in terms of its anti-ETA-ness. If ETA was absolute evil, the People's Party saw itself as its only true opponent. It was, by extension, its noble, shining opposite.

The People's Party, and Aznar in particular, was so blinded by that idea of itself that, when the bombs went off, it was as if a prophecy had come true. ETA had shown its full vileness, further justifying Aznar's firm stance and shaming those he saw as appeasers. The People's Party had no need to lie to Spaniards. It was already fully programmed to fool itself. As its thesis weakened, it instinctively dug its grave deeper. Little wonder Spaniards voted it out.

Ten days later, Aznar, who was still caretaker prime minister, appeared on television for a rare live interview. It had, presumably, been at his own request. For the first time ever, he began to talk about himself as a victim, though a surviving one, of terrorism. A roadside bomb in Madrid had, on 19 April 1995, blown his armour-plated car halfway across the road and caused a nearby building to collapse. Aznar, then the opposition leader, insisted on walking to a nearby clinic and remained icy-cool in the aftermath. 'I recall the terrible smell of explosive powder, my face was scorching, my hair was singed and, as the whole place was thick with smoke, my first reaction was to feel my own body with my hands, to see if I was injured. On finding that nothing was missing, I asked the driver and bodyguard if they were all right,' he said later. Aznar, that day, showed both courage and cool. His advisers gloated. ETA, they said, had just blasted him into the Moncloa.

I had always been impressed, however, by his refusal to make political capital out of his status as the survivor of an ETA attack. It was a card he could have played many times, but did not – until it made no difference. Suddenly, stripped of power and personally responsible for his party's defeat, he seemed to be seeking sympathy. Not that he was admitting he had done anything wrong. He, and his party, still refuse to admit that.

Long before terrorism became one of the dominant preoccupations of global politics, it was the personal bugbear of José María Aznar. It overlapped, at least in his mind, with his other main dislike, Basque and Catalan separatism. Aznar always had a black-and-white view of terrorism. The only thing negotiable with ETA, his party liked to say, was 'the colour of the bars on their cells'. Terrorism was not a political problem, but a moral one. Terrorists were evil – and that was all there was to it. They had to be defeated. Little wonder that, even before 9/11, he saw eye-to-eye with George W. Bush. On a first, and somewhat fraught, visit to Europe, the US president made Madrid his first stop. Aznar blushed with pleasure when Bush rewarded him by pledging 'our government is committed to stand side by side with the Spanish government as it battles terrorism here in Spain.' He even dared to become Spain's first-ever out-and-out Atlanticist premier. General Franco had signed deals to give the US bases in Spain. He had done so, however, more out of geopolitical, Cold War expediency than out of admiration for the country that humiliated Spain in 1898. 'It causes me some anxiety to see the world in the hands of the North Americans,' Franco once said. 'They are very childish.'

Fighting ETA's terrorism was an obviously noble cause. It did not occur to me that there might be something personal about Aznar's determination until, during his term in office, I went to the Moncloa Palace to interview him. I did this twice, spending an hour with the man on each occasion in a room decorated with tapestries made at Madrid's Real Fábrica de Tapices from tapestry cartoons drawn by Goya. The first time I met him, he walked into the room in a jolly, back-slapping sort of a way – a man determined to make a friendly impression. He pretty soon returned to the dour, serious individual he really was. On one of these visits I asked him about the ETA attack against him. '*Son gafes del oficio*,' he said. 'It is a downside of the job.' It was a good reply. Then I told him I had met a lot of ETA victims – those wounded in attacks or those who had lost loved ones. All had told me that each fresh attack felt to them like a reliving of the first, definitive attack. Did he feel like that?

Aznar's reaction has stuck in my mind ever since. It is not what he said, trotting out a line about how it was important to maintain a calm, clear head, but the strange look he shot in my direction. When I said I had met lots of victims – which I had, as part of a book project – it was as though I had intruded on a private domain. Aznar, dubbed *el Sequerón* because of his dry, dour personality, is not the sort of person to let emotion show. It was the first time, in fact, that I had seen him at all ruffled. It was as though I could not possibly understand. I felt I was being told, in fact, that it was none of my business. It was impossible to guess what psychological cogs were turning behind the Aznar facade. This was, however, clearly not a run-of-the-mill political topic for him.

I had approved of Aznar when he was first in power. He got rid of a Socialist government that, because of its multiple corruption scandals, had long forfeited the right to govern. He was also the first professed right-winger to be democratically elected to power since 1934. He showed Spain that the political right was not just Franco, but that it could exist perfectly well in a democracy – that, in fact, it was a necessary part of one.

With no absolute majority in his first term in parliament, Aznar had also had to broker deals with Catalan and Basque nationalists of Convergència i Unió and the Basque Nationalist Party, respectively. They supported him in parliament, thus showing not only that they are conservatives at heart but also that the 'nationalist' centre and the 'nationalist' periphery could get along and make the country work. It was, again, something many had thought impossible. His rowdy supporters, believing opinion poll predictions of an absolute majority, had gathered outside the party headquarters on election night and shouted: '*¡Pujol, enano, habla castellano!*', 'Pujol [the Catalan nationalist regional premier], you midget, speak Spanish!'

Aznar kept his hands out of the till, and, with a few exceptions, made sure his party did too. He was rewarded, at the 2000 elections, with an absolute majority. Aznar, the *Sequerón*, shed tears as he waved at the crowd of supporters in the street. It was a strange sight. This man had always been accused of lacking charisma, of being unloved even by those who voted for him. There was more emotion behind the Aznar facade than met the eye.

Years before the September 11 attacks in the United States, Aznar had been ploughing an unfashionably hard line on terrorism. It was, he said, his first priority. He would be tough. Although he played host to Tony Blair and his family on a holiday in Doñana National Park in the days after the Good Friday peace agreement in Northern Ireland was signed, there could be no such deal with him. Each People's Party councillor killed by ETA was another twist on the screw that tightened his resolve.

The funerals he attended cannot have been easy. I once sat in an apartment in San Sebastián, talking to a young, attractive woman while a three-year-old boy called Javier rushed about in his dressing gown playing boyish games. Ana Iríbar's story was yet another tale of tragedy in the Basque Country. She was the widow of Gregorio Ordóñez. He was a city councillor shot at point blank range, in front of three lunch companions, as he ate lunch in La Cepa. This restaurant sits on the short Calle 31 de Agosto in the old part of San Sebastián, where ETA has now killed three times.

One of the assassins had walked down the street from his own parents' restaurant. The killers walked straight up to him and put a bullet in his head. When I met his wife, Ana, she had been widowed for barely a year. But, recently a father myself, what stuck in my mind was the little boy. Those sort of thoughts must have been a constant in Aznar's political life.

There was one ETA death, however, that intrigued me especially. The victim's name was Margarita González Mansilla. She had been born seventy-three years earlier in Badajoz but had migrated to Madrid and raised a family in a modest little house. When she died there were no mass marches. Nobody took to the streets. Her death, three months after she went into coma, occupied only a few paragraphs in the newspaper. Even that much space was due to the fact that the bomb had been the one that, on 19 April 1995, had been aimed at Aznar. I always wondered how much her death – which had, after all, meant to be that of Aznar himself – might have affected him. It could, of course, have left him cold, but somehow I doubted that.

Aznar's obsession with ETA grew. The police worked harder, the US pledged some kind of help – though numerous government officials I spoke to were unable to say how. The French police, above all, cracked down on them. By the time he left office, ETA had, for the first time, gone almost a whole year without managing to kill. It was not defeated, but it was close to it.

Aznar's friendship with non-violent Basque nationalists soured as soon as he gained an absolute majority. The old pacts fell apart, or at least became inoperative. The nationalists moved in the opposite direction. They ate up some of ETA's territory by loudly defending the right to self-determination and threatening to hold a referendum of their own. This was an attempt to split the difference, and push ETA and its Batasuna ally off the political map. It was also scrupulously democratic. For Aznar, it was close to treason. He even legislated so that he could lock up the Basque regional premier if he did call a referendum.

Spanish literature has provided us with the greatest honourable fool of all times. Don Quixote de La Mancha, that 'light and mirror of all knight-errantry' who is now 400 years old, was a man obsessed by 'the grievances he proposed to redress, the wrongs he intended to rectify, the exorbitance to correct, the abuses to reform, and the debts to discharge'.

Aznar, with his willingness to get into a fight and refusal to budge on matters he perceived to be of honour, had more than a few Quixotic characteristics himself. The temptation to draw parallels between Don Quixote turning windmills into giants and Aznar, after the Madrid bombings, turning Al-Qaida into ETA are almost irresistible, though there is nothing humorous about the latter. Don Quixote was deaf to Sancho Panza's warnings before he charged the windmills. 'One may easily see that you are not versed in the business of adventures: they are giants; and, if you are afraid, get aside and pray, whilst I engage them in a fierce and unequal combat,' he said before charging at them and being knocked cold by a windmill sail.

Aznar's faithful steed was not a horse called Rocinante, but a government apparatus run on presidential lines. It gave him the results he wanted. Where he was going to see ETA, it too had trained itself to see ETA. That particular trick was not new. British and American intelligence has done the same thing in Iraq, 'seeing' weapons of mass destruction that politicians insisted must be there – when they were not.

Aznar had already outdone both Bush and Blair in his assurances that the weapons existed. His stance then could also have been mouthed by the knight-errant of La Mancha. 'What I say is true, and you will see it presently,' Don Quixote said when convinced that a group of monks were really wicked enchanters. That was also the Aznar approach to the 11-M bombings.

The train bombing story did not end on 14 March. For the bombers had not gone away. Its final chapter was written four weeks later. By that stage the bombers had shown signs of being active once more. An attempt had been made to blow up a high-speed train on its way to Seville. A second failed attempt targeted the high-speed line to Zaragoza.

But police were getting closer. Eventually the bombers were

discovered in the dormitory town of Leganés. Police surrounded their apartment. A gun battle started. Then a special-operations squad was called in to storm the place. It was greeted by a huge explosion that blew out the walls of the apartment building, killing a police officer. The seven men inside had stood in a circle and exploded their remaining dynamite. Their bodies – or body bits – were scattered amongst the ruins. One had to be fished out of the building's communal swimming pool. Seven corpses were eventually identified.

One belonged to an Allekama Lamari, a violent Islamist who had been mistakenly released from jail because of a bureaucratic mix-up between Spain's two senior courts, the National Court and the Supreme Court. Communications between the two courts had, apparently, broken down – though they are barely 100 metres apart. The other bombers were a mixture of petty crooks, drug dealers and pious university graduates.

The profile of the Madrid bombers was depressingly low-life. They were freelance radicals, only loosely linked to Al-Qaida, but determined to follow the exhortations of Osama bin Laden.

The gang had a rural hideaway. It was a one-storey house in the countryside outside the town of Chinchón, just twenty-five miles from the capital. The bombers had held a barbecue party at their little retreat a couple of weeks after the Madrid bombings. They had stored their dynamite here and activated the mobile phones that would set them off. Neighbours remembered one of them, a hashish trafficker called Jamal Ahmidan, because he rode motorbikes and would appear with a couple of Spanish girls who had tattoos and piercings.

Spain, despite Aznar's obsession with ETA terrorism, turned out to have a lively black market in Goma 2 and other explosives used in the mining industry of the northern Asturias region. Here, it seems, police missed warnings about the traffickers. The dynamite was reportedly paid for with just 6,000 euros and a quantity of Moroccan hashish.

'It turns out that all this was done by a handful of petty crooks who were also police informers, but that police did not have the faintest idea of what was going on,' commentator Victoria Prego wrote in *El Mundo* newspaper. 'The judges must now reveal . . . the full degree of ham-fistedness and carelessness that we are discovering.'

Aznar's government, obsessed by ETA but rattling the Islamist cage with its vocal support for war in Iraq, had been looking the wrong way.

A parliamentary inquiry was set up. The politicians, however, were more interested in rowing about whether the government had lied or whether the Socialists had brought protesters out onto the street than what had gone wrong. Newspaper editors, even foreign correspondents, were, initially, placed on the list of witnesses to be quizzed. One morning I opened *El País* to find that I myself had been called as a witness – though the commission members later cancelled all the journalists.

The inquiry became a laughing stock. Political witnesses competed with one another to see how long they could go without stopping, even to eat. Acebes and Aznar both did more than ten hours. Zapatero lasted almost fifteen.

The inquiry was evidence of the divided Spain inherited from the Aznar years. The People's Party sat in one corner uselessly clinging to the idea that ETA must have had something to do with it. The rest – the left and the regional nationalists or separatists – tried to prove that Aznar had deliberately and knowingly lied. Aznar, in the commission, gave wind to the conspiracy theories. He talked about connections between ETA and Islamists. The 'intellectual authors', he added mysteriously, were 'not in remote deserts or far-off mountains'.

Zapatero, in turn, claimed Aznar had orchestrated 'a massive deceit'. Both theories are now engraved in stone on each side's version of events. 'The political wounds from March 11 are so deep that we may have to wait a generation for them to heal,' *El Mundo* columnist Lucía Méndez concluded. The commission of inquiry itself split along the now depressingly familiar lines of the Two Spains when drawing up conclusions. It blamed Aznar for 'manipulating' and 'twisting' the truth. The People's Party representatives voted against. The contrast with the US Joint Inquiry report into the September 11 attacks made the whole affair seem even more shameful.

The victims and their families, meanwhile, looked on in absolute alarm and disgust. Pilar Manjón, who lost her nineteen-year-old student son on one of the trains, accused the inquiry members of behaving like kids in a school playground. The victims, she told them, had become a political football for them to kick around. 'What have you been laughing at? Who are you trying to cheer on? What victories are you celebrating?' she asked.

It took a while for the technicians to repair a videotape found amongst the rubble where the seven bombers had blown themselves up in Leganés. When the tape was finally ready, investigators heard a name some may have recalled from school history lessons.

'The brigades that are in Al Andalus . . . will continue our jihad until martyrdom in the land of Tarik Bin Ziyad,' the three heavily armed, white-robed figures threatened in one of the undamaged segments. This was none other than the Berber who had sailed his troops across the Straits of Gibraltar in 711. 'Remember the Spanish crusade against the Muslims, the expulsion from Al Andalus and the tribunals of the Inquisition,' the bombers added, claiming Spain was Muslim by right and Christian only by force. They, like bin Laden and Aznar, saw an age-old conflict simply entering its newest phase.

Spain now has several hundred thousand Muslim immigrants. Many work in the intensive, plastic-tented vegetable plantations of Almería, in the south-east. There, the joint head of Spain's Islamic Commission, Spanish convert Mansur Escudero, told me that ordinary Muslims thought of Al Andalus as history.

'To argue that this country is impious and in need of a Muslim *Reconquista* is barbarous,' he said. The half-dozen Moroccans who stepped out from midday prayer at the Al Tawba mosque, a one-room outfit at Vícar, near Almería, pointed out that Al Andalus had a reputation for religious and ethnic tolerance. 'Al Andalus was a common project between Christians, Muslims and Jews,' they said.

Bin Laden would not agree. Nor would Aznar.

The arrival of Islamist terrorism, however, seemed to bring an unexpected bonus. For the Islamists may have sealed the fate of Spain's home-grown terrorists, the Basque separatists of ETA. Even the most radical separatists had claimed to be sickened by the 11 March train bombings. How could they now justify meting out more of the same? As this book goes to print an already weakened ETA is thought to be involved in a secret peace process. Even if it does stop killing, however, the scars ETA leaves behind will take generations to heal. In the meantime the Basque Country remains the supreme example of Spain's longest-running and most intractable problem. Is it really a nation? Or is it several nations squeezed into one?

10

In the Shadow of the Serpent and the Axe

It has the feel of a secret, slightly dangerous assignment – as if I was meeting someone from an underground, illegal movement. I have arranged to see Gotzone at the university, but I do not yet know where. Gotzone, when she is there, often has to hide. She is a lecturer, and has been in this faculty for almost thirty years, but that is no protection. I am to call her mobile phone before I set off. Her instructions, when we speak, are to get to the university and then call again. These are routine safety procedures, she explains. She does not want me to feel offended.

The campus is a compact, ugly jumble of glass walls and concrete pillars on a hilltop outside Bilbao, the Basque Country's biggest city. I sit on a raised circular dais in the atrium of the university library and call again. Gotzone tells me to wait. Someone will come and find me. A young man in black casual clothes hisses to me – that Spanish '*tsss, tsss*' that means 'look over here' – from the top of the staircase. He crooks a finger. He is too smartly dressed, and is just a bit too old, to be a student. There is a bulge in his jacket, too, where a pistol sits. This is one of her bodyguards. I walk up the stairs and he signals me to follow. He looks carefully around as we walk off.

I experience a sadly familiar, depressing feeling. I am back in the Basque Country. Once more I must talk to people about violence and fear. Why is it, three decades after democracy arrived, that this prosperous, northern patch of Spain is still stained by bloody hatreds? Domestic terrorism has, after all, almost disappeared from the rest of western Europe. It is early in 2005. I have been coming here as a journalist, on and off, for a dozen years. I am still, however, writing the same story. The axe and the serpent, symbols of the violent Euskadi Ta Askatasuna (ETA) – Basque

Homeland and Freedom – separatist group cast a shadow almost wherever I go. Rumour has it that a peace process might be starting. I hope it does. But, for the moment, ETA would still like to kill Gotzone. And, even if peace does arrive, the damage done over three decades of violence is too large for it to be overcome instantly by a few signatures on a piece of paper. ETA, or the violent emotions that drive it, will be present for a long time to come. If it is not here in person, its spectre will be.

We greet another bodyguard, who is standing in a corridor. He ushers me into one of the hundreds of nondescript offices dotted around the campus. Gotzone is in there with her cardboard boxes. 'As I change offices, they come with me,' she explains. Changing offices is part of her life.

She currently has three offices. One is official, but her bodyguards do not let her go there too often. So there are two other secret ones as well, like this, in different departments. When she gives a lecture, however, everyone knows where she is – even with two bodyguards at the door.

Gotzone Mora is small, with that neat, short haircut favoured by Basque women above a certain age. She wears frameless glasses over hazel eyes and has two solid gold earrings clamped to her lobes. Basques have more than double the normal incidence of the rhesus negative blood type. This is almost certainly a left-over – along with their remarkable language *euskara* – from their centuries as one of the most isolated groups in Europe. To me, however, the main physical aspect that differentiates some Basques from other Spaniards – apart from the women's practical, sensibly short haircuts – are their noses. Gotzone has a fine version of what might be considered the typical Basque nose – large, proud and strong.

Gotzone is hiding from western Europe's last significant armed separatist group. As well as lecturing on sociology here at the University of the Basque Country, she is a local Socialist politician and an outspoken ETA critic. Documents found in one ETA member's home revealed an elaborate plan to shoot her at the university. They contained the following commentary: 'Gotzone

Mora is so far-sighted that she would not see someone put a gun to her head.' A bomb planted in the faculty lift a couple of years ago failed to go off. Police believe it was waiting for Gotzone or one of two other professors here who have been vocal in their denunciation of separatist violence. 'They could have brought the whole place down,' she says. Now she takes the stairs.

An election campaign for the regional Basque assembly, which elects what is already one of the most autonomous regional governments in Europe, is on. ETA, it is said, has ordered its people to 'put corpses on the negotiating table', as it prepares for talks. Gotzone is a prime target. 'I have been told the more time I spend outside the Basque Country, or even outside Spain, the better,' she says. 'The trick is to make sure that, if ETA finally stops, you are not the last one to be killed.'

The locks to the door on her main office have had to be changed six times because the master-key keeps disappearing from the porters' room. She suspects colleagues, or university employees, who support ETA and are either prepared to help them kill her or just want her to be frightened. When we visit it, she shows me a bookshelf that had been mysteriously moved from the wall a few days ago, before the latest lock-change. 'We think they wanted to plant a bomb behind it,' she said. She now has the only key.

The high-pitched sound of a *txistu* (a Basque flute) and of drums floats up towards her temporary office. Somewhere on campus, she explains, there is a demonstration in favour of letting ETA members back to study – from their prison cells – on the university's courses. It was a right they lost after Gotzone discovered that lecturers were being threatened by their jailed students. A colleague had received a letter from Idoia López Riaño, alias *La Tigresa*, The Tigress. *La Tigresa*, accused of twenty-three killings, has been in jail for a decade. 'You know what to do if you do not want problems,' the letter said, according to Gotzone. She meant, Gotzone explained, that he was expected to pass her at exam time. That would improve her job prospects when she got out.

Gotzone tries to avoid walking past the regular demonstrations calling on the ETA prisoners – who can now study at Spain's distance-learning university – to be let back. '*¡Puta socialista, vete a España!*' 'Socialist whore, go to Spain!' they shout at her if she goes near them. One day she went to the bathroom and found '*Gotzone Mora; ETA, mátala*' – 'ETA, kill Gotzone Mora' – graffitied on the wall.

'The radicals are a minority, but they manage to spoil everything. Campus life is dead,' she says. Later on I see the two musicians. They are grey-haired, red-cheeked men wearing large, black, floppy Basque berets. They are wandering around the campus, still playing. Music should be pleasure. Hearing it now, with Gotzone's explanation, it sounds like menace. It reminds me of the Protestant Apprentice Boys on their marches through Catholic territory in Northern Ireland. Or am I just being infected by paranoia?

As I walk beside Gotzone, I find I have to make an effort to stick close by her side. The natural thing to do is drift away. The chances of anything happening to her, here, with two bodyguards and ETA on what may – or may not – be its last legs, is minimal. But she carries the mark of the hunted. Instinctively, and ashamedly, I am uncomfortable beside her. I notice that other people on campus either blank her out or avoid her. 'My neighbours at home complain. They worry that if my car is bombed, it might affect them,' she says. The impact on her social life is also devastating: 'People do not want to be seen out with me.' Then there is her family. Her husband, a law lecturer, has been sidelined at the university, she claims. Friends say his health has been affected.

I ask why she puts up with it. She explains that there have been political and trades union militants on both sides of her family. Spanish socialism had its first flowering right here, in and around Bilbao, in the 1890s. Dolores Ibarruri, the Basque communist firebrand known as *La Pasionaria*, once hid out in her family's house. *La Pasionaria's* most famous phrase was: '*¡No pasarán!*', 'They shall not pass!' It was uttered during the Spanish Civil War and directed at Franco's troops.

'When I can't stand it any more then I'll just leave,' Gotzone says. She would not be the first to go. There are no reliable figures but lecturers, politicians, journalists and businessmen – those on ETA's list of targets – are amongst those who have fled. It amounts to a kind of intellectual cleansing, she says.

Gotzone's biggest complaints, however, are reserved for the Partido Nacionalista Vasco (PNV), the Basque Nationalist Party. If Basque society is neatly sliced into two halves – one that favours unity with Spain and one that tries continually to either weaken or break the tie – then the *nacionalistas* are the leading force against the latter. They have, through a variety of coalitions, controlled the Basque Country's regional government for the quarter century since it was established. Since then, critics like Gotzone claim, the nationalists have set about moulding the Basque Country to their own desires.

Nationalism in the Basque Country, as in Catalonia, is as much an emotion – or an identity – as a set of political arguments. Its voters are people who put their Basque-ness before any other political desire. Because, like religion, it is based on belief and feeling, other politicians find nationalism hard to battle against. Its most fervent critics tend to be repentant former members of the clan. One of them, the writer and former ETA member Jon Juaristi, has described the dominant emotion of nationalism as 'patriotic melancholy . . . though they do not cry for the loss of something real. The nation did not exist before nationalism came into existence.' This contradiction, he claims, is resolved by inventing a past out of *historias* rather than *historia* – stories, not history. Those stories, he says, are inevitably about loss. There is always a victim, too. The victim must be Basque, if it is not the Basque Country itself.

Gotzone has a deep dislike and distrust of Basque nationalists. She complains that, amongst other things, Basque schoolchildren are now taught that their natural *patria* extends into the Basque region of France and into neighbouring Navarre. She obviously thinks that, consciously or unconsciously, the nationalists egg ETA on. The pro-nationalist media, she says, paint her as a dangerous madwoman. 'They are making me a target . . . If ETA kills me, it will be clear to everybody that I was already an *impresentable*, a disgrace.' Few are prepared to raise their voices against

ETA – or even Basque nationalism – as loudly as this. 'I know I scream, but some screaming has to be done,' she says.

I do not share all of Gotzone's ideas about the Basque Country or nationalists, but I cannot help admiring her determination to scream. For it is a dangerous, potentially lethal, thing for a Basque to do. Those who dare raise their voices are, however, privately thanked for doing so. 'I have cried for you and I have felt terribly frustrated for remaining silent, for not banding together with my classmates and coming to your aid . . . but we, too, are afraid,' one student wrote to Gotzone. 'Thank you for telling us that murder makes no sense; thank you for fighting for my freedom; thank you for being on the side of those who suffer; thank you for being there, day after day.'

Gotzone is a councillor in her home town of Getxo, which is governed by the Nationalists. She has spent years watching enviously as Nationalist councillors walk calmly out of the door onto the street after meetings while she squeezes into her armour-plated car. Her fellow Socialists and members of the Conservative People's Party all also have had bodyguards. These have been kept, as this book goes to the printers, although ETA – in a first sign that it is ready to talk – has said they are no longer targets.

I walk with Gotzone as she prepares to leave. The bodyguards, one behind and one in front, lead her through the campus. They call ahead to their colleagues in the cars. Two Peugeots await in the car park – a blue one with armour-plating for Gotzone to ride in and a silver one to follow her. Gotzone opens one of the doors. 'These doors are so heavy that they give me cramp,' she complains. The cars speed off. As I watch them go, I find myself hoping, once again, that this is my last encounter with Basque violence and the fear that goes with it. It may be. ETA has never been so weak. A new government is willing to talk. It may, still, be able to bow out without humiliation. But there have been talks and ceasefires before that were followed by more violence.

Long ago, when I first came here, I was captivated by the romance of the Basques. There is something deeply attractive, dashing even, about a small group of people proudly defending their culture in a globalising world. That unique language, those strange sports, the food, the steep, green valleys and the wide-open Cantabrian Sea are all captivating. They start to pall, however, if you only ever come here to talk about shootings, bombings and kidnappings. At my regular hotel in San Sebastián, a small, charming, secret place, the owners once told me that they thought I was jinxed. 'Something always seems to happen when you are here,' one of the family explained.

My view is, of course, skewed by the experiences of a journalist. Only a small minority of Basques have shared Gotzone's daily contact with violence. Even when I have tried to avoid it, however, the violence has had a way of throwing itself into my line of sight. Not even the gleaming Guggenheim Museum in Bilbao – its shiny, sculpted titanium roof picking up the clouds that scud over one of Spain's rainiest cities – has managed to quite avoid the curse of ETA. The dazzling museum designed by architect Frank Gehry is the glittering new image of a city, and a region, that, like the rest of Spain, has undergone profound change over the last three decades. Its opening, however, was marred by the shooting to death of a member of the Basque regional government's own police force by ETA gunmen. They had been trying to sneak a bomb into the forty-three-foot-high, flower-clad 'Puppy' sculpture (of a West Highland White Terrier) by Jeff Koons that stands outside the museum entrance. So it is that a place which boasts a unique language, *euskara*, and that has fine traditions in everything from sculpture to sport, to writing and cuisine is reduced to a tale of fear and loathing.

The Basques have always had their foreign admirers. Hemingway was one. 'These Basques are swell people,' says a character in *The Sun Also Rises*. George Steer, the twenty-seven-year-old *Times* journalist who told the world that the Germans had carpet-bombed Guernica during the Civil War, warned future visitors to mind their tongues. 'There are few things the patient Basque won't tolerate, and one is the suggestion that he is Spanish,' he wrote in *The Tree of Gernika* in 1938. Modern Bascophiles soon capture the anti-nationalist mood music arriving from the rest of Spain. This reached a crescendo under Aznar, when nationalism and terrorism were often – and unjustly – treated as one and the same thing. It is easy, however, to swing too far in the opposite direction. Mark Kurlansky's *The Basque History of the World* is, in most ways, a brilliant and informed journey through the delights of Basque cuisine, history, navigation, whale-hunting, fishing, music, customs and politics. The failure of a temporary and unilateral ETA ceasefire in 1998 is, however, laid firmly on Madrid. Kurlansky produces the most absurd of reasons. 'How would Spain justify its huge armed forces, Guardia Civil and police if it no longer had enemies?' he asks.

Gotzone Mora is right about one thing. Silence makes the Basque Country different. Spain is, in many ways, a journalist's paradise. Everybody has an opinion and everybody is prepared to share it with you. It makes the basic task of reporting a simple and enjoyable matter. Approaching strangers in the street in Bilbao or San Sebastián, however, I often find them politely declining to answer my questions. Polls have shown that a quarter of Basques believe they are not free to talk about politics.

It is not just politics that are dangerous ground. Start discussing anything from Basque history to folklore and you stand a chance of offending someone almost immediately. It is often wise, in fact, to find out which side of the nationalist fence the person you are talking to sits on before opening your mouth about anything other than the weather, food or relative merits of Athletico de Bilbao and Real Sociedad football clubs. Just by starting this chapter off with an avowed anti-nationalist like Gotzone Mora, for example, is to risk alienating a significant number of Basques.

History is one of the worst areas to venture into. Basques outdo even other Spaniards when stretching their political rows back in time. 'In conversations with Basques, it is not unusual to hear expressions such as "that only happened 5,000 years ago",' Basque anthropologist Joseba Zulaika observes. Another academic expert, Roger Collins, points out that the 'politicisation of normally abstruse and *recherché* anthropological arguments about the Stone Age' underpins nationalist ideology. 'Few statements relating to people, their history and their language can be treated as politically neutral,' he warns. 'Few statements? None at all,' adds *Dirty War, Clean Hands* author Paddy Woodworth.

There is another characteristic at work, however, when Basques stay silent, for they are famously timid. 'Short on words but long on deeds,' was the description of Basques given by a character in Tirso de Molina's seventeenth-century play *Prudence in a Woman.* 'A Basque, however courageous he is in the wild, is timid and shy when confronted by man,' agreed the Basque writer and philosopher Miguel de Unamuno more than two centuries later.

Basques have a reputation as adventurers, sailors and outdoorsmen. Kurlansky claims they made it to North America before Cabot 'discovered' it in 1497, but kept quiet about it because of the rich fisheries they found off Newfoundland. The first person to circumnavigate the globe was the Basque Juan Sebastián Elcano – who took over command of Magellan's ships when he was killed by Filipino tribesmen in 1520. Basque sports are rugged, outdoors stuff, too. They have axe-wielding, log-chopping a*izkolariak,* stone-lifting *harrijasotzaileak* and teams for *soka-tira*, tug-of-war. Broad-shouldered oxen, meanwhile, compete dragging heavy weights in *Idi-probak* trials. These are as much trials of endurance as they are of strength. Basques bet, too. Sometimes the bets are laid between competitors. In *Vacas*, Julio Medem's film of Basque wars, cows and rivalries, the source of one hero's wealth is his skill with the axe.

If a Basque is shy when confronted by man, he (or she) is reputed to be even more timid when confronted by the opposite sex. 'It's a straightforward choice,' the Basque comic Oscar Terol explains. 'Either you can be Basque, or you can have sex.' This has something to do with what Unamuno once called a 'puritanical' Basque approach to religion. 'Priests have told me that they know, from the confessional, that the exceedingly rare cases of adultery that occur in our mountains are owed, in great part, to the woman's anxiety to have children, when the husband does not give them,' he said. Traditionally Basques have often sought the company of their own sex. The *cuadrilla* – the same-sex group of friends who meet almost daily for a drink or two – can still be seen doing the rounds of bars in the evenings.

Nationalisms are, by definition, exclusive – despite the loud denials here in the Basque Country and in Catalonia. That makes them unintelligible to most outsiders, a red rag to other Spaniards and a cross to bear for fellow Basques who do not share their creed.

Many people blame one man for the fear, violence and hatred that runs through the Basque Country. Sabino Arana, the father of Basque nationalism, died a century ago. He had a short but eventful and controversial political life, creating the Basque Nationalist Party along the way. Today, his words and ideas continue to fire both nationalism and ETA. A hundred years after his death he has become one of the most argued over figures in Spanish history. I decided to visit the foundation that honours his name in Artea, a village on the old road inland from Bilbao up towards the regional capital Vitoria and the plains of Alava.

On the way there, I first looped around Bilbao to look at Neguri, Getxo and Las Arenas – the wealthy outer suburbs of greater Bilbao. Large stone mansions stand on the shores of the Nervión estuary where it opens out to the Bay of Biscay. The mansions look across the water at a south shore populated with dockside cranes, piles of scrap metal and smokestack industries. This is Bilbao's wealth staring across the water at its own source. In Las Arenas I drove my car onto the wobbly platform that hangs from the vast iron structure of the Vizcaya Bridge. This is the world's first 'transporter bridge', erected in 1893. Only thirteen of them were ever built, with seven of them in Britain. It is a monument to the Basque Country's – and Bilbao's – place at the heart of Spain's (late nineteenth-century) industrial revolution. A platform for half a dozen cars and a hundred or so foot passengers hangs from the 150-ft-high iron structure that spans the murky Nervión. It runs, swaying gently, along rails atop the structure. A dozen cables kept us suspended above the river for the two minutes it took to deliver me into the industrial left bank neighbourhood of Portugalete.

Locally mined iron ore and timber from Basque forests provided the raw materials of this industrial revolution. Hungry Spaniards from further south provided much of the manpower – for a miserable life of twelve hour days and twenty-five-year lifespans.

For Spaniards from elsewhere, one of the things that most hurts about separatism and nationalism in the Basque Country is that these are now amongst the richest people in the land. Per capita disposable household income in the Basque Country is the highest in Spain. It is not the poor who seek emancipation, but the rich.

As I drove on to Artea, I recalled the people I had met several years earlier, when I embarked on a project to make an oral record of Basque violence. Inspired by Tony Parker's *May The Lord in His Mercy be Kind to Belfast*, I wanted to give voice to those who lived the violence directly – both victims and perpetrators – letting each speak for themselves in their own words. The project did not prosper, but the research immersed me for a few months in the suffering caused by Basque violence.

'The trouble with the Spaniards is that they have never stopped being *conquistadores*,' said the barman in one village near Vitoria as he invited me to a *chato*, a small glass, of red wine and some slices of *chorizo*. 'They think they are better than us.' The *conquistadores* he was talking about were just two dozen miles away across the plain in the Castilian province of Burgos. The bar belonged to Blanca, a small, strong-willed and bitter woman in her mid-seventies. The youngest two of her seven children were ETA men. One was in jail. The other was in a niche at the cemetery after a police shoot-out. For Blanca, her sons were wronged angels. 'Nobody can say my boys are bad,' she swore. 'They never tried to harm anybody. Quite the opposite, in fact. When something needed doing here in the village, they always there to do it.' They were, she insisted, '*bellas personas*'.

José, an *etarra* (Eta member) who had been let out of jail with medical problems, told me he was pleased to see a new generation of activists appearing. He had been jailed after being caught taking part in the kidnapping, for ransom, of a businessman. He refused to see this as a form of torture. As proof that a kidnapping was no suffering for the victim, he told me anecdotes about how they had managed to play the card game *mus* with their captive. *Mus* requires a certain amount of secret nodding and winking between partners, something that, he admitted, had been complicated by the fact that he and the other *etarras* were wearing masks. More sinisterly, however, he was against a unilateral end to the violence. Basques, he claimed, had been fighting for independence for five hundred years. 'We should not give way out of tiredness. We have to pass the baton on to the next generation. There are youngsters now who are ready,' he said.

If the stories of those on ETA's side were hard, those of the victims were simply heartbreaking. In Seville I met María Dolores, the widow of a police officer who had been machine-gunned to death with three other colleagues. A distraught police sergeant, a friend of her husband, had grabbed a pistol from a colleague and blown his own brains out in front of the four coffins. 'I think it was a coherent thing to do, given the circumstances,' she told me. 'It is hard to see something like that, the shot in the head and the pool of blood . . . Those who practise violence make you live situations that are beyond belief. It is something you don't even see in the films.' María Dolores spent the next seven months dressed in black, without talking, almost without eating and with a permanent fever. 'The doctors did lots of tests, but they could not say why I had that fever. The body is a mystery. I guess it was the *fiebre de tristeza*, the fever of sadness,' she said.

A decade after losing his wife and two daughters, aged thirteen and fifteen, in a bomb attack on Barcelona's Hipercor supermarket that killed twenty-one people, Álvaro wept as he told me the story of his search for them. He eventually found them, charred black by smoke, in a morgue. 'I told them it couldn't be them, that my daughter was white, and my wife too. But eventually I had to admit it. It was my wife and daughter,' he said. A few hours later he was shown a third body. It was his other daughter. 'I don't trust anybody any more. I have made a world for myself, which is me, on my own,' he told me.

Some victims fantasised about ways of exacting revenge. A wheelchair-bound former Civil Guard officer – whose lack of bodily control meant he wore diapers that needed constant changing – still recalled the hatred in the face of his attackers. He suggested to me that *etarras* should be hung live on television. He also showed me a photograph of his uniformed daughter – one of the first women to have joined the Civil Guard.

Rosa, the widow of a murdered *ertzaina* – a police officer in the Basque government's own force – had had to cope with the fact that he had been shot while sitting at some traffic lights in his car, with her fourteen-year-old son sitting beside him. Her husband came from a *euskaldun* – a *euskara*-speaking – family. His grandmother, Rosa told me, had her hair shaved off as punishment for talking *euskara*. But even 'good' Basques – ethnic, nationalist, *euskara*-speaking – can be in ETA's sights. It is not just the *españolistas* who are targets. Graffiti that appeared on some walls in the Basque Country soon after her husband's killing read: '*Cabezón, devuelvenos la bala*', 'Hard-head, give us the bullet back.' 'My only worry is that something might happen to my children ... That they might go the wrong way because of what happened, and start fighting from the other side,' she said. Fortunately, if we except GAL and the dirty war, no one here seems tempted by that last option.

Taking the valley road up towards Artea, I was reminded that it was not just Bilbao that took to industry. Up and down the narrow, steep valleys of Vizcaya and Guipúzcoa, workshops and small factories, many making machine parts, thrive. A tradition of working iron in small, water-powered *ferrerías* extended back at least to the fourteenth century – with some three hundred of them in place by the sixteenth century. The Basques had, however, mainly been farming people. Their system of inheritance by primogeniture ensured that property – normally the family farmhouse, the *caserío* or *baserri* – remained undivided. The road to Artea followed one of these valleys. Factories, warehouses, workshops and sawmills were dotted along the valley floor. Lone cyclists, wearing the lurid Lycra colours of some local team, pedalled uphill through the truck fumes. Basques are as obsessed by bicycles as they are by balls. The five times Tour de France winner Miguel Induráin emerged from these pedal-obsessed valleys. His imitators continue to risk life and limb amongst the traffic every day.

Caseríos – large and squat with broad, gently sloping roofs – dot the hills. The best examples have three wide storeys – one each for livestock, the family and stores of grain or straw. They also have a generous inset porch that offers protection from the rain. Basque life revolved around these *caseríos*, sometimes grouped into small villages and hamlets, for centuries.

Caseríos had a life of their own almost above that of their occupants. In the Basque Country it is the people who belong to the *etxe* or *etxea*, the house, not the house that belongs to the people. Many Basque surnames begin, in fact, with *etxe*, or versions of it – Echanove, Etxeberria etc. These are families described by their houses. Some see the emotional roots of nationalism in this concept. '*Nire aitaren etxea defendituko dut, Oesoen kontra, sikatearen kontra, lukurreriaren kontra, justiziaren kontra*', 'I shall defend my father's house, against wolves, against drought, against usury, against the law,' starts a poem in *euskara* by Gabriel Aresti, who died in 1975 at the age of forty-two. In Aresti's poem, the narrator is prepared to lose all he has, crops, livestock, income, hands, arms and, finally, his life until: 'I shall die, my soul will be lost, my descendants will be lost, but my father's house will endure on its feet.'

There is graffiti here, too, in *euskara*. '*Presoak etxera orain*', 'Bring the prisoners home', it reads. The *etxe* is here, too, in '*etxera*'. The graffiti refers to the fact that, unlike other Spanish prisoners, unrepentant *etarras* are punished for their obstinacy by being kept in jails as far from home as possible. This can turn family visits into 1,000-mile hikes every other weekend. The only Spanish flag I see is hanging over the wall of a Civil Guard barracks. But there are no signs of the 'military occupation' that more radical separatists insist exists here. There are no roadblocks or army patrols. This is not Northern Ireland during the Troubles.

It is early March and, as I approach Artea, I see that the Gorbeia – one of the many mountains Basques have endowed with magical, mystical powers – is wearing a cap of solid snow. At the foot of the Gorbeia, I turn into the village and look for the large honey-stone building where Sabino Arana's legacy is carefully preserved.

Arana runs a close second place to Franco as the most controversial historical figure in Spain. Rabid racist and fervent Roman Catholic, he began by claiming that his *patria* – his homeland – was Vizcaya, the province based on Bilbao. He penned ferocious articles against the *maketos* – the Spanish immigrants of the industrial slums. He went on to proclaim that his *patria* was something wider than Vizcaya, that it belonged to a nation which he named *Euzkadi*. This was the nation of the Basques. Despite his ideological contortionism, Arana lit several fuses over ten intense years of political activity that ended when he died, aged just thirty-eight, in 1903. He himself would be elected as a deputy to the provincial assembly. Within four years of his death, the Basque Nationalist Party had a mayor in Bilbao's city hall.

For Arana, the people of Vizcaya were 'intelligent and noble' or 'vigorous and agile' while Spaniards were 'inexpressive and harsh' or 'weak and clumsy'. 'The Vizcayan cannot serve, he was born to be a *señor ('etxejaun')*; the Spaniard is born to be a vassal or a servant,' he declared. The *etxe* is here once more. '*Etxejaun*' is the head of the house. Shortly before his death, however, Arana did a political U-turn. He urged his party members to become *españolistas*, pro-Spaniards. 'Good Basques will continue working for their people, but not in isolation, rather within the Spanish state.' Some see, in this, a call for the kind of autonomy the Basque Country now enjoys. Others say that, after spending time in prison, he simply realised that Spain would never let the Basques go. 'The survival of his [Basque] country was at stake,' said the archivist. 'It was a sign of his grandeur.'

Arana and other Basque Romantics fiddled liberally with history as they sought to find a 'lost' Basque nation. This, some said, extended back to one of Noah's sons. The one thing they could definitely point to as something Basques had been slowly losing, however, was their language.

Euskara is truly remarkable. It has thirteen noun cases, has had to import most of its swear words, does not use the letters c, q, v, w and y and piles on suffixes to make impressively complex-looking words. It is generous with k, z and x, with the latter often combining with t to produce a 'ch' sound.

The language's most expert practitioners are the *bersolari* – poets who compete by composing ad lib on stage in front of a crowd. A scarcity of irregular verbs and irregular nouns eases the task of learning – though, as two-thirds of the population of the region's biggest city, Bilbao, will tell you, that does not mean people necessarily want to. About half of the Basques said they could understand or speak *euskara* in 2001, though fewer than one in six used it as much as, or more than, Castilian.

Try, as they do, linguists cannot find any other living language even vaguely connected to it (though there have been claims for everything from Pictish and Minoan to Sino-Tibetan and North America's Na-Dene languages). *Euskara*'s only known relative is ancient Aquitanian. This existed mainly on the northern, French side of the Pyrenees and in the mountains themselves as far as Catalonia. It died out in some areas and evolved into *euskara* in others, sometime after the appearance of the Romans. *Euskara* may be the sole surviving version of a family of languages that was, with all other previous western European tongues, wiped out by the Indo-European languages we now speak. Its forebears were being spoken in Europe thousands, if not tens of thousands, of years ago. Along with genetic and other evidence, it is persuasive evidence that Basques remained remarkably homogeneous – and secluded – until immigrants started arriving late in the nineteenth century.

Here is a small example of euskara: *Ezkutatu zuen Aitor'ek orduan altxor bat/leize baten sakonagonean,/iñoiz ez, iñork ez ebastu zezan/Eta an irauntzen da,/mendietan ezkututa,/aitalenaren isilekoa. / Bere emaitza./Orrela jaio zan enda bat,/orrela jaio zan erri bat,/euskotarrarena./Aitor'en semeak.*

It is taken from the *Legend of Aitor* poem. This describes how the 'seven tribes' of the Basque Country (the Spanish provinces of Guipúzcoa, Vizcaya, Alava and Navarre plus the areas of Soule, Labourd and Basse Navarre in France) were formed by the seven sons of Aitor. It was written by the nineteenth-century French Basque Romantic Augustin Chaho. He mistakenly thought that when Basques called themselves *aitorren semeak*, they were calling themselves the sons of Aitor. In fact, it seems, they were calling themselves 'sons of good fathers'. A rough translation reads: 'And so Aitor hid a treasure/ in the depths of a cave/in such a way that nobody could ever steal it/ And there it stays/ hidden in the mountains,/the patriarch's secret,/his legacy./ So was born a race/so was born a people/that of the euskaros/the sons of Aitor.'

Many clues to Gotzone Mora's difficult life are to be found right here, in the language. *Euskal Herria*, the language's own way of saying 'Basque Country', actually means 'the country of *euskara*'. By that definition, *Euskal Herria* had been shrinking – probably for centuries – before Arana. Numbers are, once more, growing. Most Basques, however, still do not know how to speak the language.

Euskara's system of building words with suffixes allows it to generate new vocabulary easily. Arana, having learned it himself as an adult, soon thought himself fit to invent new words. Many have since disappeared. Others, however, are now highly familiar not just to Basques, but to all Spaniards. What is most revealing about them, however, are the words *euskara* was missing when nationalism was born.

Arana's inventions included: *Euskadi*, the Basque nation; *ikurrin*, flag; *abertzale*, patriot; *gudari*, soldier; *aberri*, fatherland; and *lehendakari*, roughly 'person whose job is to lead'. The fact that he had to invent these words suggests that the Basque desire for statehood was either non-existent or, to be generous, unarticulated at the time.

Basques, however, now live in a region officially called Euskadi. Their president's official title is 'Lehendakari'. Their red, green and white flag (also invented by Arana and based on the Union

Jack) is known as the *ikurriña* and their national day (yet another Arana invention) is the Aberri Eguna. Bombs are planted by *gudaris*, as ETA members consider themselves, while the *ezker abertzalea*, the 'patriotic left' of radical separatists either applauds or tries to explain that this is all a result of centuries of continued Spanish oppression.

Language is another Basque minefield. Just choosing to call a place by its Spanish or Basque name, for example, is a political act. Do I say San Sebastián, for example, or Donostia? Should it be Bilbao, or the *euskara* version, Bilbo? A good nationalist will usually try to reach for the name in *euskara*.

In the small museum at Artea there are 1930s badges decorated with swastikas – an ancient Basque symbol for the sun – belonging to the *mendigoizales*, a mountaineering-cum-nationalist propaganda club of the 1930s. The *mendigoizales* were a peculiarly Basque phenomenon – a political rambling club. They organised groups to walk up mountains and reflect on the importance and meaning of being Basque. The swastika disappeared from Basque symbolism after the Nazis decided to use it too. It was replaced by its alternative form, the ubiquitous *lauburu* – with the four arms ending in oval shapes that make it look like a four-leaf clover. The *mendigoizales* were a reminder that mountains were more than just things to be admired – and climbed – to Basques. Two of Spain's most important mountain ranges, the Pyrenees and the Cordillera Cantábrica, meet here. Mountain spirits form a central part of pre-Christian Basque mythology. The mother-god *Mari* is said to use several Basque mountain caves as her home. Other cave-dwelling spirits are capable of transforming themselves into bulls or vultures. Hurl stones at certain mountains, the legends go, and you will incur their wrath.

Basques were amongst the last Europeans to have towns or become Christians. They have made up for it since then. Ignatius de Loyola, the Jesuit founder, was a Basque. His aristocratic family's *torre* – a large, square four-storey fortified house – has been conserved beside a huge baroque basilica and shrine devoted to him at Loiola. Some critics of nationalism say the Church, which kept *euskara* alive from the pulpits and by publishing magazines and books whenever it was persecuted elsewhere, is to blame for everything from Arana to ETA itself. Religion has certainly formed part of nationalism's historical essence.

Through Arana, nationalists trace themselves back to the Carlists. These were the reactionary, Catholic traditionalists who backed an absolutist pretender to the Spanish crown in the nineteenth century. Arana's father was a Carlist – opposing liberal reforms that attempted both to create legal equality across Spain and loosen the Church's power. The Carlists, colourfully attired with large red berets, fought two bloody civil wars in Spain in the nineteenth century. The leader during the first of them (1833–9) was the extravagantly mutton-chopped General Tomás de Zumalacárregui. The Carlists' great hero died while unsuccessfully besieging Bilbao in 1835. Though nationalists see these as wars against Spain, they also pitched Basque against Basque. Zumalacárregui's brother Miguel, as the Basque Country's leading Liberal, helped raise troops to fight him. He went on to be a Spanish justice minister as well as mayor of San Sebastián. Few Basque schoolchildren today, nurtured on stories about Tomás, could name his ultimately more successful brother. The Carlists, always underdogs, provoked the romantic admiration of some commentators. Karl Marx saw them as having 'a genuinely mass national base of peasants, minor aristocracy and clergy'.

A second Carlist war followed, and failed, in the 1870s. The level of atrocities carried out by both sides appalled observers. They were said to set the pattern for the Spanish Civil War less than a century later. The *Carlistas* reappeared in that war, on Franco's side. Basques and Navarrese were prominent amongst them. Some historians say more Basques and Navarrese fought for Franco than against him. His thank you included allowing Navarre to keep some of its autonomous powers – and the maintenance of a special funding regime for Alava province. It also included violent repression of anything that hinted at Basque nationalism. Franco certainly was not going to resurrect the semi-autonomous Basque government that, briefly, had appeared at the outbreak of Civil War. 'The horrible and sinister nightmare that is Euskadi has fallen defeated forever,' the first Francoist mayor of Bilbao declared. The Carlists' red beret, meanwhile, became part of the uniform of the Caudillo's Movimiento Nacional. '[The year] 1936 was, in fact, the first Carlist success. And they imposed on the rest of the Basques their social morals, their symbols and their monuments . . . My father well remembers the anti-*euskara* paranoia in 1938 of his mayor, who was a Basque Carlist,' says Juaristi.

The *Carlistas* were strongest in the Basque Country, though they also did well in Catalonia and had support elsewhere. They had said they would conserve the *fueros*, the ancient bills of rights of each Basque province and for neighbouring Navarre that were eventually, after a long period of decline, annulled in 1876. It was a good way of ensuring support. The *fueros*, each different from the others, dated back to the late Middle Ages. At their strongest, they amounted to a kind of shared sovereignty, partly in the hands of the monarch and partly in the hands of each province. Royal laws and decrees had to meet the conditions of the *fuero*, which acted like a provincial constitution, before they could be applied. Each province had its own parliament with representatives elected in myriad ways but usually representing a particular constituency of a town, village or district. Spanish customs were only payable at the border with Castile, meaning no export duties were paid to Madrid. Spanish monarchs, in turn, pledged to observe the terms of the *fuero*. In the case of Vizcaya, the parliaments were eventually held by the famous oak tree at Guernica. Ferdinand and Isabella swore an oath here in 1476, as did Emperor Charles V in 1526.

This Romantic picture of the Basques was captured by William Wordsworth in his ode to Guernica's oak, written as Spaniards – with help, in what became known as the Peninsular War, from Wellington – were trying to expel Napoleon's troops in 1810.

> Oak of Guernica! Tree of holier power . . .
> What hope, what joy can sunshine bring to thee,
> . . . If never more within their shady round

Those lofty-minded Lawgivers shall meet,
Peasant and lord, in their appointed seat,
Guardians of Biscay's ancient liberty.

The Basque *fueros* and their parliaments, however, were provincial affairs. Those of Vizcaya, Guipúzcoa, Alava and neighbouring Navarre acted autonomously of one another, swearing loyalty to whichever king ruled them. Rights varied, but could include not having to do military service outside their own frontier. What the *fueros* did not amount to, however, was independence – either as individual provinces or as a state called Euskal Herria, the Basque Country. The last Basque-centred kingdom was that of Navarre – which was conquered, and absorbed into the rest of Spain, in 1512. Both Vizcaya and Guipúzcoa had, in any case, gone into the orbit of Castile by 1200. The last time, in fact, that all the Basque lands – including those in France – were jointly ruled by a Basque was in 1035. This was when Sancho the Great held the kingdom of Navarre. He, however, titled himself King of the Spains, and ruled a far larger area. Collins says Sancho's rule had no impact on Basque 'self-awareness or aspirations'. They were too busy squabbling amongst themselves. Their social structure was based, instead, around the family. That does not stop ETA bloodily pursuing the impossible dream of a state that would, a thousand years later, again unite all Basques – be they French or Spanish – under a government of fellow Basque.

If Spanish history is today a political battlefield, Basque history is its bloodiest corner. The *fueros*, Arana, the tree of Guernica, the kingdom of Navarre and the Carlists are fought over tooth and claw. Even the Battle of Roncesvalles – when Basques fell on Charlemagne's retreating rearguard in 778 – is the subject of heartfelt, emotional commemorations by separatists. It is still possible, for example, to buy books that state 'the Basque *pueblo* was already formed in neolithic times.'

For my archivist in the Sabino Arana Foundation, the *fueros* obviously represented a golden era. Nationalists mourn what they see as a lost Basque Arcadia, where grass-roots democracy protected the rights of man and there was harmony between man and nature. It is a world of clover-filled pastures, isolated valleys, peacefully ruminating cows, deciduous forests, mountain spirits, sturdy farmhouses, noble souls and fiercely proud farmers, blacksmiths and lumberjacks prepared to defend their idyll against all comers.

I left the Sabino Arana Foundation unenlightened as to the true course of Basque history. One thing, however, was clear. The founder of the Basque Nationalist Party had planted his political seed in fertile ground. The robust nationalist tree, despite the efforts of dictatorial force and democratic persuasion, has grown and gathered strength ever since.

I drove around behind Artea's church and its *frontón* – a sort of large, open squash court with just two walls in the shape of a long L, where *pelota vasca*, literally 'Basque ball', is played. The *frontón* is a feature of almost any Basque village. Larger towns – in both the French and the Spanish regions – boast covered, all-seater *frontones* with a third wall at the back. Here the great players of the sport knock a hard ball against the walls using their hands, small wooden rackets or the long-curved baskets of the spectacularly fast and exciting *cesta punta* or *Jai-Alai* version.

I stopped at a large building on the other side of the village. Measured in historical time, this was a journey of more than six decades from the time when Sabino Arana died. I was moving on to the 1960s, to the time ETA first emerged as a fighting force. It was a time when younger nationalists became frustrated with the Basque Nationalist Party's peaceful opposition in exile and reached for their guns. I had come to see Xabier Zumalde, alias *El Cabra* (The Goat), who was one of the first to pick up a weapon in anger. *El Cabra* is in his late sixties now, though still lean, fit and keen. Years ago he was one of the first military leaders of what was still an embryonic, amateurish armed outfit. Today he is a maverick. 'I am a military man,' he said, as we tried to stave off the cold by an open fire. 'I don't understand politics. Give me fifteen or twenty men and I can do anything. Give me any more than that and I am lost.'

El Cabra considered himself a freedom-fighting revolutionary. He handed me a photograph of his younger self wearing a black beret and sporting a revolutionary beard. Che Guevara had been his hero. He spent the final years of the Franco dictatorship running a small group of Basque guerrillas from exile in south-west France, carrying out mostly sabotage and propaganda attacks. In fact, another ex-ETA leader told me, *El Cabra*'s group rarely, if ever, exchanged shots with the Civil Guard. He buried his arms in *zulos*, underground hideaways, after Franco died and an amnesty was announced in 1977.

Up until Franco's death, ETA had fought a classic war of provocation against the Caudillo and his Civil Guard. It had killed forty-four people – including a dozen civilians caught in a bomb attack on a Madrid cafeteria, the Rolando. Two dozen ETA members had also died – in shoot-outs, blowing themselves up, executed or summarily shot. ETA's original fame stemmed as much from Franco's violent reaction to it as from the handful of prominent assassinations carried out in those years. Franco declared eleven states of exception during his time in power. Four were nation-wide and six of the seven others covered the Basque provinces of Guipúzcoa, Vizcaya or both. At one stage, a quarter of his Civil Guard was said to be posted to the Basque Country. 'If Sabino Arana considered Euskadi to be an occupied country, Francoism made that occupation real and effective,' explains the Basque author of a history of ETA, José María Garmendia. ETA is, in fact, one of Franco's legacies to modern Spain.

Some of those released or allowed home under the 1977 amnesty law would rejoin ETA and participate in the orgy of killing that swept through the Basque Country in the first years of the *Transición*. Between 1977 and 1980, more than 250 people would be killed as not just ETA but a swathe of separatist, left-wing revolutionary or reactionary right-wing groups reached for their weapons. 'It was chaos,' *El Cabra* recalled. He, however, stayed away from the fight. 'I cannot impose my doctrine on others by force,' he explained. Plenty of others felt they could. Some still do.

Eventually, he set up a museum to the *caserío* in Artea. He still runs it, though it is clearly in decay as, having fallen out with all the politicians, he no longer receives a grant. It has, amongst other things, displays on farming, on whale-hunting – for centuries a traditional occupation for those living along the coast of the Bay of Biscay, where the first person to land a harpoon on a whale's back could claim the valuable tongue as a prize – or for hunting wild boar. He has even built a working copy of a medieval *ferrería* and of a water-driven flour-mill. It is an innocent retirement. *El Cabra* should be history.

That is what he would have been, had he not decided to mount an exhibition on ETA's early days and its fight against Franco three decades after the latter's death. The display included weapons – which had been disabled long ago when he lived in France – as well as mock-ups of *zulos* and dummies dressed-up as ETA men.

The interesting thing about this exhibition, though, was not what it contained but the uproar it provoked. The ethical narrative of Spanish history has changed. ETA long ago lost its heroic halo as the only armed group capable of inflicting real damage against Francoism. In 1973 it quite possibly changed the course of Spanish history by killing Admiral Luis Carrero Blanco, the man who had been expected to continue the Generalísimo's work when the latter died. 'Spain's transition to democracy started that day,' says Victoria Prego, author of various books on the period.

History, however, is being revised. ETA is now being painted uniformly black. Even its early fight is deemed to be no longer heroic or just. Even those like Gotzone Mora, who as a student leader in the 1970s led campaigns to prevent ETA members being executed by Franco's firing squads, now think they were wrong to support ETA then. 'We thought they were fighting Franco. In fact they were fighting for separatism,' she explains.

Under Aznar, the revising of history went even further. All ETA's victims – including, for example, the infamous San Sebastián police chief Melitón Manzanas – became official heroes. Aznar's government awarded them all a medal, the Great

Cross of the Royal Order of Civil Recognition to the Victims of Terrorism. If all the victims were now heroes, those who attacked or killed them had to be villains. *El Cabra* was accused of praising – even encouraging – terrorism. No court, however, found a reason for banning his exhibition. Eventually, given the political scandal, Artea's Basque nationalist mayor ordered him to close it as the museum was housed in town hall property. 'The mayor was in the town hall under Franco. When the *Transición* came he changed jackets and, as he was a banker, the nationalists took him in,' says *El Cabra*. 'It is the nationalists who have shut me down. They did not fight against Franco, they just sat around *tocándose los cojones* – playing with their balls.' Police were sent in to enforce the mayor's order. He tore off the tape which they placed across the exhibition's entrance in a wooden shed into which he had carved a saying in *euskara* '*edozen txoriri eder bere kabia*', 'every bird thinks its own nest is the best'. 'Now they are going to try me. Not even Franco managed to send me to prison.'

'In each family there is someone who receives from the Basque Nationalist Party,' he says. 'It has the vote of the grateful stomach.' This is a common complaint. The Nationalists have run the regional government for more than a quarter of a century. Their critics claim that they have bought the Basque Country up. 'Where else in the world do parties stay in power for twenty-five years?' one non-nationalist Basque historian asked me desperately.

If those who *El Cabra* calls 'grateful stomachs' have a modern patron it is not the man who now runs the regional government – the lehendakari Juan José Ibarretxe. It is Xabier Arzalluz, the man who commanded the Basque Nationalist Party for more than two decades.

It would be hard to find a greater hate-figure in Madrid (excepting ETA and its political allies such as the spokesman of the banned Batasuna party, Arnaldo Otegi) than this tough former Jesuit priest whose father had backed Franco during the Civil War. To many critics Arzalluz is the modern incarnation of Arana.

He has occasionally reached for genetic definitions of Basqueness. 'If there is a single nation that exists in Europe then that has to be Euskadi . . . there are objective figures such as cranial studies and blood (type) studies. Is there anyone who, after all the studies carried out by the world's best universities, dares to say that we don't have rhesus negative?' he once said.

Arzalluz retired as party boss in 2004. I went to see him in his new office perched a few doors up from the stone Arenal bridge over the Nervión River that connects Bilbao's old quarter with the modern city. He was beginning to look his seventy-three years. He had, however, lost none of his verbal vigour. Basque Socialists, he said, 'hate *euskara* or any form of difference' and 'most are not from here and they do not love this country.' ETA itself, he added, was 'consumed by hatred' and was a block to any progress towards independence. Its violence had been a main factor in bringing Aznar to power. During the key *Transición* years Arzalluz was the Nationalists' man in Madrid. His party called on Basque voters to boycott the 1978 constitutional referendum (which won the votes of only 31 per cent of Basques, or three-quarters of those who turned up). He helped negotiate, however, a Statute of Autonomy that gave a generous dose of self-government while making no mention of self-determination or Basques not being Spanish. Basques backed that referendum. I wanted to know whether the nationalists' long-term goal was really independence. Arzalluz, thankfully, does not dress his answers up. 'The Basque Nationalist Party was born to create a Basque state,' he replied. Its aim was to make the Basque Country one more star on the European Union's flag, like Holland or Spain. What mattered above all was that Basques should be able to express their own will.

The PNV was not in a hurry, he said, but that should be the ultimate goal. Given that between them, Nationalists and the *ezker abertzale* separatists consistently gain just over half of Basque votes in regional elections, that might be taken as a majority for independence. In fact many Nationalist politicians – and many of their voters – are more moderate than Arzalluz. Opinion polls show only a third of Basques want a separate state. A similar number – which has to include some Socialist voters – would like Spain to be a federation. The rest are broadly happy with it as it is.

Self-determination lies at the heart of the Basque problem. It is a right that does not, legally, exist – though the Basque parliament wants it. Ibarretxe claims Basques have a right to 'decide freely and democratically, their own framework of organisation and political relations.' He put forward a plan which would see them 'freely associate' with Spain, but also, in effect, push them a long way down the path towards self-determination and, potentially, independence. Aznar reacted by rushing through a law that would allow him to lock Ibarretxe up if he called a referendum. It was typical Aznar – a measure certain to drive more Basques into the nationalist embrace. Zapatero revoked that law. Ibarretxe's plan, meanwhile, was approved by a wafer-thin majority in the Basque parliament but rejected by a huge majority of Las Cortes, the parliament in Madrid. The final vote was 313 votes against, and just twenty-nine in favour.

So why not have a referendum on independence? It seems, at least superficially, a fine idea. One vote and, if opinion polls are anything to go by, the Basques would proclaim their desire to remain Spaniards. That should be the end of it – at least for a decent period of time. It would also, surely, be the end of ETA – which would lose even its small amount of support, if it did not hang up its arms anyway.

Self-determination for the Basque Country, however, does not win votes elsewhere in Spain (except, perhaps, in Catalonia). The two big Spanish parties – which jointly represent the other half of Basque society – dismiss it with the same arguments. Self-determination belonged to another age, they say, to the era of 'decolonisation'. The Basque Country is not a colony, the argument goes, therefore self-determination does not apply. There are deeper worries, too. The first is that Basque Nationalist governments, if allowed to, would call referendums ad infinitum until a vote went through – which would be irreversible. What, then, would happen to a million people born, and wanting to stay, Spaniards? What would happen to Alava province, where a pro-independence majority would be impossible to achieve? And if Basques were allowed to vote on independence, who else might want to?

The Catalans could be next. Perhaps the Galicians would follow? And where do you draw the self-determination line? In 1873, during the first Spanish Republic, the south-eastern seaport of Cartagena declared itself an independent canton and tried to persuade others to follow suit.

Another reason Spanish politicians give for dismissing self-determination is that this is part of what ETA demands. Any move in that direction could be interpreted as a triumph for terrorism. 'Our dead do not deserve it,' said Aznar's successor at the head of the People's Party, Mariano Rajoy. The obvious problem with that argument is that it makes anything ETA wants impossible – even if others, who oppose violence, want it too. It is, in fact, a way of turning ETA's violence to one's own advantage. It also, however, highlights ETA's status as a hindrance, rather than a help, on the path to self-determination or independence.

ETA's decline has been gradual, but steady. In 1980 it killed more than ninety people. An average of thirty-three victims a year died between then and 1992. In the late 1990s it could manage barely a dozen a year. At the start of this century, and despite its efforts to the contrary, it has shown itself incapable of killing for two whole years.

As the years went by, and it found it harder to kill, ETA widened its choice of targets. First it was the police, members of the armed services, *chivatos* – police informers – and senior politicians. (Also, though, it was many others who simply got in the way when the bomb exploded or the trigger was pulled. There are at least twenty children on ETA's list of victims.) Then it was judges and public prosecutors. After that, it was civilians working for any of the above. Finally, it became anybody who dared openly oppose the gang, be they intellectuals, journalists or business leaders. It was termed, in a display of warped logic, '*la socialización del dolor*', 'the socialization of pain'. The perceived suffering of a minority of pro-violence separatists, in other words, must be shared by everybody else – who should, thus, be forced to feel the terror. It is, unfortunately, a remarkably effective way of shutting people up – as the almost total absence of anti-ETA activity on the university campus shows.

One key moment in ETA's decline came when a young People's Party councillor, Miguel Ángel Blanco, from the Basque town of Ermua, was kidnapped in 1997. ETA demanded that, in return for his life, its prisoners be sent from jails around Spain to those in the Basque Country within forty-eight hours. It knew, however, that with Aznar in power, that was never going to happen. As the hours went by towards the deadline a sense of doom spread across Spain. Blanco's fate held the nation on tenterhooks. The Saturday of the deadline, I recall, there was a general air of anxious nervousness. I was in a village near Segovia, on what was meant to be a convivial day out – bathing in a river – with a party of friends. But everyone was thinking of Blanco, knowing the minutes were ticking by. Then the news came. Gunshots had been heard in woods near the town of Lasarte. A huntsman out shooting had gone to investigate. He had found a seriously wounded man with two gunshots in the head and his hands tied. Television pictures showed an ambulance delivering the man to hospital. ETA's attempt at cold-blooded execution of a defenceless prisoner had been ham-fisted and messy. But there was little that could be done. Within twelve hours, Blanco was dead. The screw of violence had been given another cruel twist. It was one of those moments when Spaniards showed their almost unique ability for protesting en masse. Up to 3 million Spaniards took to the streets two days later to show their disgust – with the streets of Basque cities such as Bilbao and San Sebastián also filling up. ETA's leaders were stunned by the reaction. Here, for the first time, was mass public opposition from Basques to their terrorism. 'When they saw those pictures they were amazed – they could not understand,' explained Iulen de Madariaga, an ETA founder who has left the group.

Two days after Miguel Angel Blanco was killed, my telephone rang. At the other end of the phone a voice began to speak in a heavily accented, inaccurate, but fluid and bizarrely idiomatic English. It was a voice I did not know.

'I am a friend of the people in Eeee, Teeee, Ayyy,' the voice said. 'I used to speak to journalists a lot, but I have not done so for a long time.' My caller sounded like one of those madmen who pester journalists everywhere with bizarre and improbable tales. I decided, however, to hear him out. I did not take an exact note of the conversation, but the important parts of it went something like this: 'I have seen the people who were responsible for shooting Blanco. You must know that this is not the end of it. There will be much more,' he said. The phrase that stuck in my mind was the one used to describe what, he claimed, would be a future campaign of similar killings. The mad professor reached deep into his bag of English idioms. 'This is the new *cottage industry* in the Basque Country,' he said.

Looking back, I see my caller was not so mad. Blanco's killing, which had been preceded by that of San Sebastián People's Party councillor Gregorio Ordóñez, was, indeed, the start of a rash of murders of small town councillors belonging to parties deemed to be *españolistas*. People who, until then, had spent their time arguing over such mundane matters as waste collection, building licences and children's playgrounds were now worried for their lives. Eleven would be killed over the next three years. Those not killed could find themselves, in radical heartland towns of industrial Guipúzcoa, burnt out of their businesses, their homes petrol-bombed or simply attacked by thugs on the street. One Socialist councillor found a note slipped into her two-year-old's pocket in the playground. 'We know where you are and we are going to give it you. Bang! Bang! Bang!'

Masked men would walk into bars where councillors were known to have breakfast and shoot them in the head. In some places even the mask was not necessary. Witnesses could be guaranteed to keep silent. When one of the killers of Gregorio Ordoñez was finally caught, the word was put out that he had been recognised, and reported to police, by a man from whom he bought a bicycle. Letters arrived at local newspapers warning the 'coward and traitor' who told police that Lasarte was in a shopping centre to 'hide well'. 'Euskadi is the size of a handkerchief and whoever betrays a *gudari* usually has health problems,' the letter said. The bicycle salesman soon joined the list of ETA's victims.

Perhaps the most senseless but revealing killing of all was by a drunken young radical, Mikel Otegi. He convinced himself that two Basque *ertzaina* police officers driving past his front gate had come to arrest him. He went for his shotgun and killed them in cold blood. A jury made up of ETA supporters and people too scared to oppose them declared him not guilty despite the fact that Otegi's own brother had called the police. It was a sign of how deep ETA had sunk its teeth into Basque society. The killer fled the country before a new trial could be called. He joined ETA in France and was recaptured several years later.

In the late 1990s things were still much better than a decade earlier, but the corpses of councillors were piling up. The state replied by providing them all with armed bodyguards. ETA responded by widening its list of targets further. Journalists, opinion-makers and intellectuals were next. *El Mundo* columnist José Luis López De Lacalle, a sixty-three-year-old former anti-Francoist militant who had suffered jail, was gunned down as he bought the Sunday newspapers. A bomb left in a flower pot failed to go off as Juan Francisco Palomo and Aurora Intxausti, journalists for *Antena 3* and *El País*, wheeled their eighteen-month-old son out of their house in San Sebastián in his buggy. Gorka Landaburu, of *Cambio 16* magazine, had his fingers blown off by a parcel bomb. More bodyguards arrived to protect the university professors, journalists and intellectuals now under threat.

Watching three city councillors in Bilbao leaving a bar after a coffee, I realised just how saturated with bodyguards the place had become. As they moved, six other people began moving too, getting ahead of them to scour the street, walking beside, behind or just in front of them for the fifty metres it took for them to get back to their offices. Town hall meetings in some places required the presence of dozens of bodyguards. The Basque Country must have had more of them per square mile than anywhere else in Europe.

An already weak ETA called a unilateral ceasefire in 1998. It was dismissed out of hand by Aznar's government as a trap. Fourteen months later ETA unilaterally brought the ceasefire to an end. For Basques it was a tantalising taste of peace. For *abertzale* radicals, it was a political boon. Their share of votes increased to between 18 and 20 per cent in municipal and regional elections held that year. For ETA, however, it was a time to rearm and reorganise. It came back fast and furious for a couple of years, but police slowly strangled its capacity for action. By 2002 it was already killing only in single figures. French police became especially active. In 2004, despite its attempts, it failed, for the first year in three decades, to kill anyone at all. The *abertzales*, now gathered in Batasuna, lost one-third of their voters. Then Batasuna was banned altogether.

Numerous ETA members were picked up at what were described as 'routine police checkpoints' in France. Rumours began to appear that the same French police officers were at every checkpoint where the terrorists were caught. France had been slowly increasing the pressure on ETA since GAL had carried out attacks on French soil in the 1980s. Now it was arresting dozens of ETA suspects every year. The group's leadership was broken up time and time again. ETA itself was said to be infiltrated all the way through. Some ETA members even broke the group's long-standing policy of not shooting back when in France – with *gendarmes* being wounded. That policy had been meant to ease police pressure on the hideouts in France where its leadership, training and logistics are based and from where it organises its attacks.

Spain can claim to have carried out one of the world's most effective anti-terrorist policies. ETA could keep going for years, if it wanted. It has enough support. Militancy often goes through more than one generation of a family. Even a fresh ceasefire would be no guarantee that it might not reappear at a later date. It looks, however, unlikely ever to become as dangerous as it was in the 1980s – unless, in a radical change, it turns to totally unrestrained attacks against arbitrary targets. That tactic would see its support all but evaporate. A definitive renunciation of violence, meanwhile, would probably see the *abertzale* left launched into the centre of Basque politics. If the 1998 temporary cease-fire gave it 18 to

20 per cent of votes – how much more could it get for a full-time one? Just a little more, and it would become the second power in the region. As its violence decreases at the time of writing this book, hopes grow that it may be tempted to follow that path. Parliament has given the Zapatero government permission to negotiate if ETA renouces violence permanently. Some analysts say that ETA must first recognise that, militarily, it has been defeated. ETA, however, is nothing if not unpredictable.

The one thing police have not been able to crack has been the group's financing. Much of this used to be provided by the rewards of kidnappings – usually of members of prominent Basque business empires. Several years have gone by, though, since the last kidnapping. ETA's other main source of income has traditionally been an extortion racket it calls the *impuesto revolucionario* – the revolutionary tax. Directors of large companies, small businessmen, lawyers and accountants are amongst those invited to pay up – or pay the consequences.

Those consequences can run from murder to the firebombing of your shop or business. José María Korta, a business leader from San Sebastián who refused to pay and called on others to follow his example, died when a bomb was placed under his car in August 2000. How many Basques share Korta's courage? How many pay up? And how many large companies are secretly topping up the group's funds in order to be left alone? One example serves to suggest that the extortion racket goes much further than most suspect. In 2004, a stock-market-listed vending-machine company called Azkoyen replaced several board members after Judge Garzón accused an executive of handing over £150,000 in extortion money. The company, which operates across forty-two countries and has an annual turnover of £85 million, admitted the cash may have gone missing from its accounts a few years earlier. Azkoyen executive Jesús Marcos Calahorra allegedly drove to Vert in November 2001 where, 'near to the church, he met two unidentified members of ETA to whom he handed over the money', according to Garzón.

'Calahorra, obeying an obviously illegal order from the board of directors of Azkoyen – using accounting practices to hide the real destination – handed over the 37 million pesetas in the full knowledge of its real destiny,' the judge said. Newspapers reported that Mr Calahorra was paid £4,000 for the task. Azkoyen sacked him when the payments became public. He was reinstated by a labour tribunal that said he had just followed the board's instructions.

The Basque attitude towards paying a tax that buys bullets can be strikingly ambivalent. Again, a single example serves to illustrate. Juan Mari Arzak is the most famous of a group of very famous Basque chefs. *The New York Times* has placed Spain ahead of France in culinary innovation thanks, in great measure, to Basque chefs. Arzak started a revolution from the kitchen of what used to be his mother's restaurant – and, before that, his grandparents' *taberna* – on a busy road out of San Sebastián. He has, deservedly, been rewarded with three Michelin stars. Other Basque chefs, people like Pedro Subijana and Martín Berasategui, also boast Michelin stars for their restaurants. San Sebastián has always produced chefs, both professional and amateur. Its *sociedades gastronómicas*, where the (traditionally) male members meet – and compete – to cook and eat Basque dishes, have a history stretching back to at least the mid-nineteenth century.

I have been to Arzak's restaurant once, to celebrate a birthday. We were lucky. Real Madrid were in town that night, playing San Sebastián's Real Sociedad. Ringing just a few days before, I was still able to get a table on a Saturday night. A hushed and reverential atmosphere was more than compensated for by the dishes placed before us. Norway lobsters, large *carabinero* prawns, hake and young *pichón* pigeon were brought to our table by serious waitresses in grey uniforms. A jolly Arzak appeared at one stage – his happiness undoubtedly increased by Real Sociedad's victory over Real Madrid – to enquire whether the food had been to our taste. The, not inconsiderable, bill paid, we left, happy, replete and excited by our immersion in Arzak's brave new Basque cuisine.

Newspaper headlines that appeared some time later, however, suggested that a fraction of our bill may have ended up in ETA's coffers. Arzak was, reportedly, called to court to explain why his name – along with three other famous chefs, who boasted a further five Michelin stars amongst them – had been cited by an alleged ETA accountant as a revolutionary-taxpayer. It has not been proved that Arzak, or any of the other chefs, paid ETA. Nor have there been any charges, so we must assume that no crime was committed or money paid. But the idea that they might have paid out was not considered shocking by other Basques. 'The only ones to blame are ETA . . . judgement should be cast on those who extort and not on those who are victims of extortion,' Basque government minister Miren Azkarate said. The chefs, she said, were good men. They were ambassadors for the Basque Country. 'With their daily effort, they have placed this country in first place when it comes to gastronomy . . . all we can do is offer them our support.'

In 1998 the nationalists broke their alliances with Madrid-based parties and began negotiations with ETA. The nationalists said they were merely trying to wean ETA away from violence. They claim no deal was ever agreed on, or signed. It marked, however, a sea change. From now on the nationalists would increase their demands for greater autonomy and self-determination. It has made them the whipping post of newspaper columnists and radio debate show guests, ever since.

The nationalists presented the attacks on them as further proof of the Basque Country's victim status. Much of the most passionate vitriol came, however, from the mouths of fellow Basques who write in *El Mundo*, *El País* or *ABC*. The barrage continues today – to such an extent that the nationalists' radio station, Radio Euskadi, now broadcasts a regular weekly résumé of outrageous comments on Basques and Basque nationalism by *tertulianos*. The barrage reached its most unpalatable extreme, however, when the film-maker Julio Medem made a documentary in which he aimed to present the differing opinions of Basques to a wide audience. Medem, born in San Sebastián, had dug deep into the Basque *arcadia* and into themes of violence and cowardice in feature films such as *Vacas* and *La Ardilla Roja* (*The Red Squirrel*).

La Pelota Vasca: la Piel Contra la Piedra (*Basque Ball: the Skin Against the Stone*) – designed to 'see hatred without hating it' – was the most controversial thing to hit Spanish cinemas for years. With Aznar's party and several prominent anti-ETA intellectuals, including the philosopher Fernando Savater, declining to take part, the result was inevitably skewed in favour of the nationalists. It did not deserve, however, the bile with which it was received by Aznar's government and others opposed to nationalism (including Gotzone Mora). Culture minister Pilar del Castillo backed calls for it to be banned from San Sebastián's film festival. The Spanish embassy in London mysteriously withdrew funding for the Spanish strand of the London Film Festival – where it was shown to packed houses – claiming it no longer had sufficient funds. Medem was compared to Hitler's film-maker, Leni Riefenstahl. One politician demanded he return money that state television TVE had paid to show a previous film.

The reaction was a sign of just how tough the Aznar government was prepared to play with anything that smelt, however faintly, of support for ETA. 'The majority of us Basques do not confuse nationalism with terrorism,' Medem complained. 'But when one travels around Spain one realises an increasing number of Spaniards do.'

With the People's Party in power, the crack-down on ETA also began to throw up concerns about civil liberties. There was no repeat of the GAL outrages committed under the Socialists. The results, however, still sound shocking: the Basque Country's fourth-largest political party has been banned; two daily newspapers and a magazine have been closed by the courts, with the editor of one claiming he was tortured by police; a court administrator was appointed to run a series of Basque adult education schools; and various groups supposedly devoted to promoting youth, culture or other pastimes have also been closed or had their organisers charged with collaborating with ETA.

With most of these cases still going through the courts, it is impossible to say just how far, if at all, the anti-terrorist overreach has gone. There is no doubt that, somewhere, parts of some of these groups morph into ETA itself. Others are, probably, just front organisations. Proving exactly where they overlap is difficult. It may be impossible. ETA itself is aware of this. Police claim that it tries to bury itself inside anything from ecology groups to trade unions.

When newspapers, such as the Basque-language *Euskaldunon Egunkaria*, are closed down on the orders of an investigating magistrate, however, but a trial is not due to be held for several years, it is obviously essential that the case be cast-iron. In 1998 Judge Garzón decreed the temporary closure of the radical paper *Egin* – which sold 50,000 copies a day – while its connections with ETA were being investigated. By the time he ordered it to be reopened more than a year later, the company that published it was considered bankrupt. When *Euskaldunon Egunkaria*'s editor, Martxelo Otamendi, accused police of torture, the Aznar government announced it would lobby for him to be charged with 'collaborating with an armed group'. By making the allegations, it said, he had simply followed ETA's instructions to its members. 'To sue alleged torture victims, or to describe allegations as false even before there has been a chance to carry out a thorough investigation, will only help foster and nourish a climate of impunity, in which fear of reprisals prevents the reporting of possible acts of torture,' Amnesty International said. It is difficult to know what to make of torture allegations in the Basque Country. Amnesty says there is no evidence of systematic torture against ETA suspects. It has demanded, however, that cameras be placed in interrogation cells during the five days in which terrorism suspects can be held incommunicado. In the meantime, police officers found guilty of torture are, Amnesty complains, regularly handed pardons.

The *abertzale* left knows how to capitalise on any opportunities it is handed to reinforce its image as a victim of Spanish persecution. In 1997 the twenty-three leaders of one of Batasuna's predecessors, Herri Batasuna, were jailed for showing a video made by ETA during an election campaign. The decision was overturned later by the Constitutional Court but not until after one leader, Eugenio Aramburu, had hung himself in his brother's *caserío* rather than go to jail. I went to film the funeral in the village of Mallabia. Folklore, death and hard-edged politics overtook a village where local businesses closed down for the day. There were pipes and drums and dancing girls in long red skirts and white blouses carrying long hoops decorated with ribbons. A male dancer performed a neat, austere and highly acrobatic dance – the *aurresku* – full of on-the-spot turns and impressively high kicks in front of the coffin. There were also angry speeches and denunciations of Madrid. It all ended with the surprising, high-pitched sound of women ululating and the turning-over by angry radicals of a radio reporter's car. I do not recall any masked men this time. But at another funeral in Soraluze – this time for an ETA gunwoman shot by the army sergeant she had tried to kill when he stopped his car at a traffic light – masked characters appeared with a huge banner bearing the axe and serpent of ETA.

ETA constantly invites crackdowns. The revolutionary's maxim of action-repression-reaction (which worked for ETA with Franco) predicts an increase in support if police can be provoked into overstepping the mark. The more 'martyrs' or 'victims' that are created, the more support holds up. It is a trap for the unwary.

The most controversial of the banned groups was the radical Jarrai youth group. This was considered to be behind a campaign of street violence, the *kale borroka*, that swept through the Basque Country for several years. Jarrai was, in an expression first attributed to Arzalluz, a meeting place for 'the pups of ETA'. Before it was closed down I went to see Jarrai in action at a three-day 'festival' in the Guipúzcoa village of Zaldibia. The mix of radical politics, Basque folklore and underground culture produced bizarre contrasts as three thousand teenagers and students camped out in a bucolic landscape of green pastures overlooked by steep, verdant hills. Perhaps the strangest thing of all was to see a group of tough, street-wise, medallion-wearing, black Los Angeles heavy-metal rappers called Body Count walking down a Basque Country lane. Their most famous song was 'Cop Killers' which, according to the radical daily *Egin*, had to be interpreted as the product of 'an oppressed people'. In the opposite direction came a group of traditional *ioaldunak* dancers dressed up in sheepskins, conical hats decorated with colourful ribbons and wearing huge cowbells attached to their waists. The *ioaldunak*, their bells ringing as they jogged rhythmically along, were there to make the youths feel Basque. The rappers were there to make them feel hard.

A large marquee housed political meetings, where stony-faced Jarrai leaders sat in silence while the audience struggled to think up suitable questions – all asked in *euskara*. The same marquee was transformed at night, as bands took to the stage. The words were unintelligible, but the music was good. A mixture of thrash guitar, rock and punk, it had the raw energy that only four angry youths with electric guitars and a drum kit can produce. Trying to leave that night, however, I was reminded that this was about more than music and folklore. I, and several others, wanted to take the short route out of Zaldibia. The road was blocked by Jarrai marshals – teenagers dressed in the grunge apparel of the times but determinedly and spookily disciplined when it came to maintaining the rules. They insisted we had to go the long way around. Nobody dared break ranks. I was glad to leave. Jarrai went on to provide many ETA recruits.

With the ban on Batasuna – which was Aznar's personal initiative – a significant shift took place in Spain's democratic arrangements. A law was introduced which required a special tribunal of Supreme Court judges to decide whether the party was, in effect, part of ETA. The judges said it was. This was the equivalent of Britain banning Sinn Fein. It also left some 140,000 Basque voters (more than 10 per cent) without their traditional party.

Most Spaniards, however, welcomed the ban. Amongst other things, the aim of the law was to cut off Batasuna's access to public funds. These go to officials and political groups represented in parliaments, provincial assemblies and town halls. Some of those receiving funds doubled, undoubtedly, as ETA members. Perhaps the best-known was Josu Ternera, a deputy in the Basque parliament who has since gone back into hiding. 'Since then we have no longer had to experience the shame of seeing terrorists occupying seats in parliament,' Aznar explains in his memoirs.

In Bera, a town on the River Bidasoa just a few miles from the French border, I went to see the ousted Batasuna mayor, Josu Goya. Goya, a friendly, bearded man in his fifties, ran a shop selling everything from umbrellas and underwear to tourist knick-knacks and ironmongery. Bera was a nationalist and separatist stronghold. It was also, Goya joked, a place where 'everyone should be considered a *contrabandista*, a smuggler, unless they can prove otherwise.'

Arriving early, I had driven up the steep winding road – avoiding sheep and cyclists – to the Ibardin Pass half a dozen miles out of town, where the French frontier lay. The French Pays Basque – Iparralde to Basque speakers – stretched out below me to Biarritz and Bayonne. The other side of the frontier was a place where, a Spanish Basque taxi driver in the frontier town of Irún had warned me darkly 'people get up early, eat lunch at 12 a.m. and nobody goes out after 8 p.m. – even though they are Basques.' It was an eloquent, if unintended, destruction of the idea of a single, culturally unified 'Basque nation'.

Goya had been mayor for four years, after Batasuna won five out of eleven council seats in an election held during the 1998 ceasefire. Socialists and the People's Party did not even bother presenting candidates in Bera, which lies in the *euskaldun*, or Basque-speaking, part of Navarre. The ceasefire had made life easier for everyone, he said. 'The end of the ceasefire was a blow to all of us,' he said.

The idea that Batasuna had been an ETA front was 'a lie', Goya insisted. Some people in it supported ETA, others did not. By stamping on the few, he suggested, they were squashing the majority. He admitted, however, that two of his fellow Batasuna councillors had been arrested for terrorism-related offences. He himself refused to be drawn into criticising ETA. 'Who am I to judge?' he said.

The irony of Basque political violence is that it occurs against a background of cultural renaissance almost unprecedented in

Europe. Nineteenth-century linguists predicted *euskara* would not survive the twentieth century. 'You are a people that are disappearing . . . This language that you speak, Basque people, this *euzkera* disappears with you; it does not matter because, like you, it must disappear; hurry to kill it off and bury it with honour, and speak in Spanish,' Unamuno had warned in 1901. Yet, today, that language has not only been rescued but is experiencing a true literary blossoming. If Darwinian rules of selection apply to the survival of languages, Basque is not only fit but has found, in Spanish democracy, its healthiest habitat for centuries. The number of grown-up Basques who claimed they could speak or understand *euskara* rose from 33 per cent to 41 per cent over the decade up to 2001. Those who said they used it more or as much as Castilian rose from 14.5 per cent to 16.1 percent. Those may seem modest figures. It is certainly true that a majority of Basques do not speak the language which, according to nationalists, is a cornerstone of Basque identity. The nationalist ideal of a nation of *euskaldunes* – Basque speakers – still seems a dream. Turning a disappearing language around, however, is a huge task.

The secret of this has been a school system that offers children education either mainly in *euskara*, mainly in Castilian or jointly in both languages. Gradually Basque parents have been opting for an education in *euskara* – even those who do not speak it themselves. Reasons vary. Some do this out of a genuine desire for their children to learn a language that they could not. Others know that future public sector jobs in – for example – teaching, will require their children to speak it. Most Basque parents speak only *castellano*. Eighty per cent of state schools, however, now teach almost entirely in *euskara*. *Castellano* is given as a separate subject. Amongst those responsible for setting up this system was Fernando Buesa, a Socialist who ran the education department when Nationalists and Socialists ran the regional government in coalition. ETA paid for his services with a bomb that killed him and his bodyguard.

Teachers are given up to two years' paid leave – and free classes every day – to learn *euskara*. Some of those who fail to learn have begun to find themselves without work. The result is, in some ways, artificial. Some classes are given in imperfect *euskara* by teachers who have learnt it relatively late in life and rarely practise it outside the school. Even those who do learn, say it can be difficult to keep the language up. 'I don't speak it at home, or watch it on the television or read it,' one Basque teacher told me. 'In some classes there are students who speak *euskara* at home and so speak it far better than the teacher who does not.' Even Ibarretxe only learnt his *euskara* as a grown-up. Critics claim the Basque nationalists use language as a weapon. 'The current political incorrectness of the concept of race . . . has caused nationalists to replace race with language,' says one of the most vocal critics, the Basque professor Edurne Uriarte.

Novelist Bernardo Atxaga has produced what have become the first widely translated novels in *euskara*. ETA's shadow falls over literature, too, however. One of the best Basque writers of Atxaga's generation is Joseba Sarrionandia, an ETA member who was sprung from jail in 1985 by a man who would go on to lead the group – Mikel Albisu, alias Mikel Antza. Albisu hid Sarrionandia in the speakers of a musical group that visited the jail. Sarrionandia still writes, sending texts from a hideout by e-mail – and even wins literary awards. Atxaga himself has taken ETA as subject matter on several occasions. His *El Hombre Solo* deals with a man who leaves ETA but makes the mistake of hiding two of its members who are on the run. In *Esos Cielos* he tells of a woman ETA prisoner's first days out of jail and her bus ride back to the Basque Country. Atxaga's former ETA members are disillusioned with violence, but eternally marked by it. His heroine in *Esos Cielos*, on leaving jail, has no trouble in getting herself out of trouble when she picks a low-life lover who turns nasty. She fashions a sharp edge out of a melted cigarette filter and attacks him with it – violence still part of her life.

Tired of all the arguing about nationalism and history – and looking for a place where thoughts of violence would disappear, I drove to the sculpture garden of Eduardo Chillida, just outside Hernani. Chillida, a former goalkeeper for Real Sociedad, crafted hefty great sculptures out of granite and iron – two quintessentially Basque materials. They look surprisingly light and delicate here, amongst the oak trees set beside a converted *caserío* that serves as an indoor museum. I walk the paths and drink in the peacefulness of it all. Chillida, it seems, found harmony and contentment in his Basqueness. But then a voice comes to me from the past. It is Chillida's rich, measured tones as they used to sound when repeated several times a day on the radio a message to ETA as it held businessman José María Aldaya for several months. 'I am Eduardo Chillida. A request to ETA. Free Aldaya,' it says. Even here, then, there is no escaping the shadow of violence.

In Medem's documentary, Atxaga suggests that, should Basques solve their differences and find a place where they were all comfortable, a form of mass levitation would take place. 'I think that, rather than walking on the ground, people will walk about twenty centimetres off it, that they will levitate. It will be only a slight levitation, in order not to provoke a scandal, but it will be the result of the weight we have taken off our shoulders.' It is a poetic idea. It would be nice to see Basques discreetly floating off the ground.

Before they do that, however, they might have to learn some lessons from Catalonia. For most of the same gripes – about language, nationality and, above all, about history – can be heard there too. In many ways, the nationalist issue in Catalonia is more clear cut. It is also more important. There are three times as many Catalans as Basques. They account, in fact, for one in six Spaniards. No blood is spilt, however, in pursuing separatism there. There is no Catalan ETA. This may be precisely because Catalans have their feet on the ground. That characteristic, some claim, forms part of the proof that they are different from other Spaniards. But are they really so different? To find out, I decided to go back to my favourite city – and former home – Barcelona. That is always a pleasure. For if any place in the world could make me levitate, it would be the Catalan capital.

11

The Madness of Verdaguer

I am Catalan. Catalonia had the first democratic parliament, well before England did. And the first United Nations were in my country. At that time – the Eleventh Century – there was a meeting in Toluges – now France – to talk about peace, because in that epoch Catalans were already against, *against* war.

Pau (Pablo) Casals, cellist and conductor, at the United Nations, 1971

Barcelona's bustling, tree-lined Ramblas boulevard is a boisterous fusion of noise, colour and activity. Herds of pedestrians push their way past the squawking menageries at the exotic birds stalls and the bright, sweet-smelling flower stalls. Circles of spectators form around dancing, juggling and fire-eating street entertainers. Human statues stand silent watch as teenage Moroccan bag-snatchers weave through the crowds and, at the port end, a handful of dumpy, cheap prostitutes pitch for business.

I know of no other city where a single street is so important. From sex shops and souvenir stalls to the opera house and, in La Boqueria, the best fresh food market in Spain, Las Ramblas caters – in one way or another – for the most elemental desires of life. This is where Barcelona celebrates, protests and riots. Built over the course of a stinking stream once known as the Cagalell – the Stream of Shit – it is, more importantly, where Barcelona meets itself. For it is almost impossible, in one of the densest cities in the Mediterranean, for one *Barcelonés* to walk down Las Ramblas without seeing another he or she knows.

I have lived in this city before. There was a time when I, too, would meet people I knew as I walked down the Ramblas. Coming back, I find the people have changed. There is more variety. I can hear Arabic and Urdu, most of the languages of Europe and others from Africa and Asia. Some of the *castellano* is being spoken with Latin American accents. Barcelona, I realise, has become a city of immigrants. The Ramblas does not care. It is as noisy and busy as ever.

Looking at all these new people pumping fresh life into the Ramblas, I question why I have come here. I am looking for just one language and one identity, Catalan. Are Catalans, whose capital city this is, really as different from other Spaniards as they claim? Are they, as a growing minority argue, not really Spaniards at all? Already the Ramblas is making my questions feel too parochial, too inward-looking.

At carnival time Las Ramblas ramps up its innate capacity for spectacle. The already colourful boulevard is swallowed up by a long procession of clowns, horse-drawn carts, floats, musicians, mounted police, acrobats, dancers, giants, strange creatures with monstrously large heads – the *cabezudos*, or 'big-heads' – and thousands of costumed revellers. These are accompanied by excited groups of children – and quite a few excited adults – scampering after the boiled sweets that rain down like confetti from carriages and floats. The first time I watched it, I found myself shamelessly fighting with four-year-olds for my share.

The best place to see the carnival procession when it comes down the Ramblas is from the windows of the Palau Moja. A solid, imposing eighteenth-century city palace, it is now home to the culture department of the Generalitat of Catalonia, the regional government. One year I watched from its wrought-iron balconies as, below my feet, the carnival procession dissolved under a sudden downpour of rain. The heavens rumbled. The skies opened. Sodden devils, tottering giants and wobbling big-heads ran for cover. It was a wash-out.

With the procession suddenly over, a friendly cultural bureaucrat showed me around the Palau Moja. When we reached the sumptuous, double-height, frescoed ballroom, he let me into a secret. 'Do you know our national Catalan poet, Jacint Verdaguer?' he asked. 'This is where they say he went mad.' The great late-nineteenth-century poet-priest Verdaguer, Catalonia's own 'national' poet, had lived in this palace, on the pay-roll of a wealthy marquis. Towards the end of his life, my host told me, he had taken to performing bizarre exorcism rituals. Demons, Verdaguer had been convinced, were stalking their way through Barcelona's huddled masses. His behaviour had become increasingly bizarre. The bishops, Barcelona's upper-middle-class *burguesía* and upright Catalans turned their backs on a man whose lengthy, Catalan-language epics to his homeland – especially the *Canigó* – had made him a sort of Catalan Tennyson. He was the towering figure of a prolonged renaissance – the *Renaixença* – of poetry and writing in the Catalan language. His genius had been recognised outside Catalonia. Unamuno considered him Spain's finest living poet. Yet some of Verdaguer's final writings – on exorcism – were rumoured to be kept firmly under lock and key, my host confided.

It was meant to be a piece of *cotilleo*, a titillating jewel of cultural gossip, to be shared in private. Innocently, I got the message wrong. This, I declared, was a great subject for a newspaper article, or even a book. My host's face fell. I had misunderstood. It would, he said, be wrong to broadcast this story. When I asked why, he struggled for a bit and then declared: 'That would be like saying William Shakespeare was mad!' I wanted to point out that, worse than that, Shakespeare stood accused of not even writing his own plays. I held my tongue, however. Verdaguer, I realised, was one of those untouchable 'national' symbols of Catalonia – a place which, depending on who you spoke to, was either just one more Spanish region, a nation within a state, or a country whose state had been stolen from it.

Verdaguer is part of a whole pantheon of Catalan holy cows. He is accompanied by such varied 'national' symbols as the Catalan language itself, the black-skinned image of the Virgin of Montserrat, a ninth-century count called Wilfred the Hairy, the Generalitat itself and, even, the *blaugrana* – claret and blue – shirt of Barcelona football club.

Catalans are, on the whole, convinced they are different from other Spaniards. They have a name for that difference. It is the '*hecho diferencial*' – the differentiating fact. This not only makes them different in the way that, for example, an Andalusian southerner is from an Asturian northerner. It is a qualitative leap. Catalans, it means, are more different than others (except, most would agree, the Basques).

I have come back to Barcelona having set myself the task of finding out exactly what this *hecho diferencial* is. The trouble is that there is no single, defining *hecho* to point to. Is it in there amongst all these carefully cosseted symbols? Is it something to do with Catalonia's history as a fifteenth-century Mediterranean power that never quite made it into the modern era? Is it their different character? The Generalitat – in one of those outbursts of unabashed Catalan self-obsession that so annoy other Spaniards – has defined the latter itself. Catalans, its publicity material tells me, are seen as 'well-mannered, hard-working, thrifty, enterprising, and generally prudent – with a bit of '*seny i rauxa*' (literally 'common sense and madness')'.

Catalans speak a different language to other Spaniards, but then so, too, do Valencians, Majorcans and Galicians. Catalonia has had counts and kings of its own, but then so, too, have Navarre and León. It has its own medieval architecture, but so does Andalucía. Perhaps the *hecho diferencial* is the sum of all these things?

Whatever it is, the idea has often provoked ire elsewhere in Spain. 'I notify those of the *hecho diferencial* that they have been defeated by force of arms and that, if they want to be brothers with other Spaniards, we will impose on them the law of the victor because . . . we consider the *hechos diferenciales* are also finished,' one of Franco's generals, Alonso Vega, warned at the end of the Civil War in 1939.

When I first came to live in Barcelona twenty years ago, I was blissfully ignorant of these things. A love story gone wrong had brought me here. Recently finished at university, I had planned to move to Madrid with a girlfriend as I attempted to add some languages to my qualifications. But, a few weeks before we were due to leave, we split up. I chose Barcelona for a reason that, I would discover, was one of its defining characteristics. It was not Madrid.

Barcelona was, of course, different then, in the mid-1980s. It still had a rough, port air to it. *Quinquis*, small-time crooks and pickpockets, were a threat on Las Ramblas and in the old city. Transvestite prostitutes did nightly sentry duty on the street corners of the Rambla de Catalunya, the extension of the Ramblas away from the sea. Gypsies would set up fold-out tables on street corners and rip you off with the *timo de los trileros*, enticing you to bet on which of three upturned cups or walnut shells hid a pea or a small plastic ball. You walked carefully, or not at all, through the *Barrio Chino* – the densely populated red light district on one side of the Ramblas. I spent my first couple of weeks in a run-down *hostal* in a charming but dilapidated square off the Ramblas. The *Plaza Real* had palm trees, peeling paintwork, a leaky fountain, a dozen drug-dealers and a weekly market in what looked distinctly like stolen goods.

I was looking for a job. I wore my hair short, my shirts almost ironed and a suit. The *plaza* low-life left me alone. In retrospect, I realised, this was because I looked like one of those clean-cut young American evangelists who, even today, pound the streets of Spanish cities seeking converts. I saw my first knife-fight in the *plaza*. Two drug-peddlers wove circles around one another, blades in hand. I did not stop to see the result, but I recall being impressed by the way they wound their denim jackets around one arm as protection. I saw a second knife fight – two men tumbling around the wasteland behind La Boqueria market. Somehow, it never seemed as though these people were going to kill one another or even do significant damage. When an American warship visited, the sailors disappeared into the Barrio Chino and went home without their wallets. I read in the newspaper that these, empty of money, were found piled up at the foot of the gangway the next morning. A good pickpocket, I was told, made sure you got your ID card and family photos back. Barcelona was like that. It felt dangerous, but not deadly. It was sophisticated, decaying and sinful. It had an edge. It was perfect.

I bumped into my first 'differentiating fact' when I found a flat-share. The tiny apartment was just off the main square of Gràcia, a barrio of low – two, three and four storey – buildings. I shared with Sònia, a student from Andorra, and her Catalan boyfriend, Xavier. They, to my initial annoyance, spoke Catalan to one another – though they always addressed me in *castellano*. In fact, I soon found, half of my new friends spoke Catalan. All were, again, scrupulously careful to speak *castellano* if there was someone present, like me, who did not understand them.

On one side of Gràcia's square was the barrio's 'town' hall. Big-bellied, armed city policemen (they are all armed in Spain) stood guard outside. A large, brick clock tower stood in the middle of the small plaza. On the other side stood three or four small-time drug-dealers. Spain was living through the anything-goes days of early socialism. The cops left the drug-dealers alone. People smoked their small blocks of Moroccan hashish at the cafe tables set out in the square. In those days, as Spain experimented with its new-found, post-Franco freedoms, people rolled-up and smoked almost anywhere – in bars, on street benches, in the metro. Waiters had to navigate the traffic of Vespa mopeds, the yellow and black, bumble-bee-coloured taxis and the groaning *butano*, gas bottle, lorries to get to our tables in the square. I learned to drink *cremat* – blazing dark rum with coffee beans and lemon peel roasting in its alcoholic fumes.

I walked up the narrow staircase of our three-storey building to the flat, red-tiled roof. I lay in the sun and read Manuel Vázquez Montalbán's *Los Mares del Sur*. Vázquez Montalbán's detective, Pepe Carvalho, showed me around the city without my having to move. From the posh heights of Pedralbes, at the top of the one-sided cauldron that is Barcelona, to the stewing mass of the Barrio Chino, he gave me a feeling for my new home. Carvalho, an avid gastronome, even took me on exotic fictional shopping trips to La Boqueria – with its displays of octopus, bulging-eyed sea bream, sheep's brains and fat, white Catalan sausages. It was late summer when I moved in. There seemed no need for central heating. In January, however, snow settled on the city's palm trees. We took the gas ring and the *butano* bottle out of the kitchen and put it in our tiny sitting room. We sat round it with our coats on, warming our hands.

I found work teaching English. I studied at the city's university and at the Brazilian Institute on the top floor of the Casa Amatller – a beautiful modernist building on the Paseo de Gràcia. Looking out of the window I could gaze upon what some Catalans would describe as further evidence of their 'difference'. Paseo de Gràcia is home to some of the best work of Barcelona's emblematic architect, the turn-of-the-century modernist Antoni Gaudí. I could see the strange organic forms and Darth Vader-shaped chimneys above the sculpted, soot-encrusted stone facade of Gaudí's Casa Milà – long ago dubbed *La Pedrera*, the Stone Quarry. Gaudí's Casa Batlló was next door. Its scaly, undulating, ceramic-tiled roof represents the dragon slain by Catalonia's patron saint, Sant Jordi. It was, and is, breathtaking stuff – a lesson in how adventurous and imaginative the Catalan mind could be.

I walked everywhere. Stepping on Gaudí's jellyfish, conch-shell and starfish-decorated hexagonal tiles on the Paseo de Gràcia, gravity pulled me down to the Ramblas. It was a short hop from there to the narrow, dark, medieval, washing-adorned streets, tiny squares and austere, voluminous stone churches of the Gothic Quarter.

Barcelona recognised that it could not match the wild *movida* that Madrid was enjoying at that stage of the 1980s, but it was still intent on having a good time. On weekend evenings I wandered out to the squares of Gràcia. I knew I would always bump into someone, be invited to sit down and have a night out. Even then, though, the city was changing. Barcelona was ambitious to recover its lost glories. Gràcia's squares, some little more than strips of baked mud, were being dug up. New ones, all smooth concrete paving blocks, chrome railings and futuristic street lamps, would appear in their place. Something similar was happening to bars and night-clubs. Most were still seedy or sleazy. Some were full of men with big moustaches picking up part-time prostitutes to the sound of 1970s disco. One had a mini-golf course in its garden. Another had tables made of coffins and flashed a slide-show of human organs – hearts, kidneys, livers – onto a bare wall. It was a Barcelona version of counter-culture. New clubs, however, were big, open and slickly designed. The *clientele* was silently cool, busy looking and being seen. Catalans, I learnt, cared deeply about how things looked – starting with themselves.

I ate lots of *botifarra*, a Catalan sausage, with *mongetes*, white haricot beans. On Sundays I went down to the rabbit-warren of ramshackle restaurants on the beach to eat *arròs negre*, rice cooked in squid ink. I wrote my first magazine article on the British vedettes who danced topless at the theatres on the Paralelo – El Molino, the Arnau – or, with more glitter, at the Scala on passeig de Sant Joan. I never dared enter the Sala Bagdad, which had live sex acts that, legend had it, had once included a donkey.

I found my next Catalan national symbol at, of all places, a football match. I was not the only new Englishman in town. Gary Lineker had signed for F.C. Barcelona. I went to the biggest football stadium I had ever seen, the Camp Nou, to watch him play his first match against Racing de Santander. I expected thunderous noise from the 115,000 fans in Europe's biggest soccer stadium. But the Camp Nou was remarkably quiet. Instead of the bellowing and singing I had encountered in British stadiums, the fans standing around me formed little *tertulias* discussing the technical merits of the players and the failings of the coach. Barça fans, I discovered, always knew better than the coach. Lineker scored twice. The fans approved. They seemed to like the season's other British signing, Mark Hughes, just as much – pronouncing him to be *una tanqueta*, a little tank. I had found a club to support. But Barça, as people told me repeatedly, was 'more than a club'. I had bought into what was, in effect, the Catalan national team. It did not seem to matter that most players were not – and, increasingly, are not – Catalan. Under Franco, supporting Barça had been one of the only ways to show outward hostility towards him – and 'his' team, Real Madrid – and support for Catalonia. It was still the main popular emblem of war against the old enemy – Madrid.

I was having a good time, but mainly I was here to learn a language, Spanish. To my surprise, my new friends were also studying a language. It was their own, Catalan. For the first few weeks it was difficult to tell the difference between this and what I learned to call not *español*, Spanish, but *castellano*, Castilian. Catalan sounded drier, more clipped. It was both less exuberant and less coarse. Sometimes it sounded a bit like French. Half of my new friends spoke it at home. Few, however, knew how to write it properly. They had done their schooling in Spanish. Franco had banned Catalan from schools, universities and a vast array of official forums. Franco wanted national unity 'with a single language, Castilian, and a single personality, that of Spain'. My new friends had left school a few years after his death. That was before responsibility for education was handed over to the Generalitat and radical changes – too radical for some – were introduced. I was impressed by their diligence. They went to night classes. They were shocked at their own ignorance. They could not spell. They did not know the rules of Catalan grammar. Shame drove them to study harder. Other friends, born and bred in Barcelona to families who had migrated here from other parts of Spain, did not speak a word of Catalan. Nor did they want to.

A gradual linguistic change was taking place on the street, too. Street names were slowly being changed from Castilian to Catalan. In practical terms it was often a question of changing a few letters. *Calle* became *carrer*, *avenida* became *avinguda* and *paseo* appeared as *passeig*. The street called *Paralelo* changed, intriguingly, to *Paral.lel*. Written down, Catalan looked more like Spanish than it sounded when spoken. The big state enterprises – railways, post office and the phone company – refused, however, to follow suit. People would graffiti Catalan words over signs in railway stations, and on post or phone boxes. The protests were mostly good-humoured. Pink paint was a favourite weapon. Separatist protesters sometimes stopped outside the McDonald's on Las Ramblas. '*¡Botifarra si! ¡Hamburguesa no!*' they cried. If all they were worried about was Catalan sausages, the chances of *catalanismo* turning violent seemed slim.

Catalans did not seem cut out for violence. Terra Lliure, a Catalan attempt to emulate ETA, failed so badly that all it managed to do was kneecap a journalist, blow up three of its own members by mistake and kill an innocent woman in the town of Les Borges Blanques by blowing a wall down on her. It dissolved itself in 1995 after fifteen fruitless years and covered in anything but glory.

One day I walked up a scruffy wooden staircase and knocked on a door bearing a sign that read: '*Crida a la Solidaritat*', 'Call to Solidarity'. There was a complicated telephone entry system. *Crida* was a Catalan-language pressure group. Their main weapon was the aerosol can. The people at their offices, however, were jumpy. A few months earlier a man had walked through the same door with a false nose, a pistol and a bomb. He had forced everybody out and then exploded the small bomb. I walked away with a map of Europe that looked like none I had ever seen before. It was a map of stateless peoples and minority languages. The normal frontiers of Europe disappeared. Replacing the countries were languages and regions which, in some cases, I had never heard of. A large slice of southern France, for example, was now called Occitania. Spain itself was divided up into more than half a dozen bits, including Asturias, Aragón and Andalucía. The Catalans occupied a long wedge of Mediterranean coast, more than twice the size of what I knew as the Spanish region of Catalonia. The new Catalonia started somewhere near the French city of Perpignan. It stretched west into Aragón and tapered south, via Valencia, to a stiletto point somewhere after Alicante. There were island outposts, too. All the Balearics were coloured Catalan. There was even an outpost on the Italian island of Sardinia at a town Catalans called L'Alguer.

The northern part of this region on the map coincided roughly with what, at the beginning of the ninth century under Charlemagne, was called the Spanish March. The rest was a reminder of how the Aragonese kings who – despite their title – were based in Barcelona and spoke Catalan had built a fourteenth- and fifteenth-century Mediterranean empire that stretched to Sicily. Amongst their most infamous exports to Italy was a family of Catalan Popes – the despotic and debauched Borgias.

The dialects spoken in other places are not known as Catalan.

They are *valencià, mallorquí, menorquí,* etc. In one of the more pointless rows in modern Spain, the Valencian regional government has fought for its version of Catalan to be recognised as a separate language. This is considered absurd by linguists. In an attempt to placate them, however, the Spanish government came up with two identical translations of the European Constitution – one marked 'Catalan', the other marked 'Valencian'. Language, like history, is political stuff in Spain.

I did not learn to speak it, but I began to feel a creeping sympathy for this language. Catalan had been repressed or persecuted, on and off, for almost three centuries. Successive Spanish kings had tried to encourage it to disappear from the early eighteenth century onwards. Two dictators, Primo de Rivera and Franco, had done their best to squash it in the twentieth century. There were, however, still meant to be more than seven million Catalan speakers – more than either Danish or Norwegian. But how could it compete with *castellano*, a language with 330 million speakers world-wide?

I did not realise just how hard some Catalans were prepared to fight. A new Catalan semi-autonomous regional government had been set up in 1979. This was revival of a Generalitat that, barring a brief reappearance between 1931 and 1939 – had not existed since 1714. One of the first lines of the new Generalitat's statute said, in Catalan, '*La llengua pròpia de Catalunya és el català*', 'Catalan is the language of Catalonia.' At the time, this was more a wish than a reality. Some serious social engineering was required to make it true. Half of all Catalans spoke Spanish as their first, or only, language. All spoke Spanish but, in 1975, only 60 per cent could speak Catalan (compared to 75 per cent in 1930). A language crusade was launched, which continues to this day.

For the first quarter century of its life the Generalitat was run by a Catalan nationalist called Jordi Pujol. He stated that the predominance of *castellano* was the result of 'an ancient act of violence'. Pujol set out on a process that was given the unfortunately Orwellian-sounding name of *normalització*, normalisation. The main idea was to replace Castilian with Catalan as the language of education. Linguists say that, if you speak Spanish, you are already 80 per cent of the way to speaking Catalan, and vice versa – so it did not raise many practical problems. With *castellano* as the language of the schoolyard, television, pop music and the street, it was hardly going to be lost. Some people, however, did not like the idea of their children being 'normalised'. It was, they said, not just a reversal of the policies of Franco. It was the mirror image of them.

I left Barcelona, and Spain, after two years. The city, however, stayed – and, along with its football team, stays – in my heart. Five years later I came back to live here again. Barcelona was preparing to host the 1992 Olympic Games. It was bursting with energy, pride and self-importance. The first two, at least, were infectious. There were other differences too. It was less seedy. Some of the world's biggest architectural names – Frank Gehry, Norman Foster and Arata Isozaki – were at work. Glittering new modern buildings were going up.

Barcelona had become smarter and cooler, if more boring. The edge had gone. The sexiest things to be now were either a designer, an architect or a town planner. There can be no other city in the world where the latter has achieved such status. Advertising is another of Barcelona's specialities. '*Barcelona, posa't guapa*', 'Doll yourself up!' the city hall urged, appealing to the natural vanity of Spain's trendiest, best-turned-out people. It scrubbed up well – renewing much of its *modernista* facade – for the games. Olympic Barcelona also, however, saw the start of a long, and continuing, Barcelona obsession with transient design trends. At one club the urinals had stroboscopic lights triggered by the jets of urine aimed at them. Your piss blinked back at you.

I found a tiny flat on top of a nineteenth-century apartment block near the all-night flower market in a part of town known as the Eixample. An idealistic nineteenth-century city planner, Ildefons Cerdà had traced out a neat grid of streets here with each square filled by a block known as a *manzana*, an apple. Where the core of the apple was meant to be, Cerdà had proposed gardens, parks and schools. Property speculators had eaten the cores up years before. My flat was on the roof – where the doorman of our block had lived before he was replaced by an electric buzzer. I furnished it with old chairs, cupboards and tables that people left out once a month for the municipal rubbish collectors. I had to get onto the street before the gypsies came past, throwing the best stuff into their vans. It was heavy, old-fashioned furniture. Getting it upstairs was backbreaking work. There were seven floors of steps up to my rooftop flat but no lift. (A heavily pregnant woman came for lunch, climbed the stairs and gave birth soon after getting back down to street level.) My terrace was the building's roof – about four times the size of my flat. When the city lit bonfires and shot tons of fireworks into the sky to celebrate the eve of Sant Joan and the summer solstice, I sat out drinking *cava* – Catalan champagne – as fizzled-out rockets rained down onto the rooftop around me. Barcelona was still magical.

There were linguistic changes, too. The railway company and utilities were now using Catalan. Some friends now spoke Catalan to one another in the office – though they wrote up their meetings in Castilian. By now some two-thirds of Catalans said they could speak the language. More people answered my phone calls with the abrupt Catalan command '*¡Digui!*' which means 'Speak!' but sounds like 'Diggy!'

Generalitat-run Catalan television, which had been finding its feet when I first came, now had two channels and good viewing figures. Many people were listening to, or watching, their news exclusively in Catalan – on television or radio. Catalans were getting a different view of the world to other Spaniards.

Something special happened in Barcelona over a fortnight in the summer of 1992. Barcelona had won the right to host the Olympic Games partly because one of the city's own sons, Juan Antonio Samaranch, was president of the International Olympic Committee. The city knew how to design the kind of games Samaranch wanted. Both the man and the city got it right. Barcelona's games were a success. Barcelonans felt, and acted, like hosts to the world. More than 30,000 people became Olympic volunteers. They were proud of what they had, and they wanted to show it off. They put the Olympics, in the doldrums after decades of financial disasters and Cold War bickering, back on track.

A former senior Catalan Francoist, Samaranch was ideally suited to his job. The pseudo-democratic Olympic decision-making processes, conducted by minor princes, faded sports stars and sporting bureaucrats, must have been highly familiar. He is a difficult figure for Catalans. He is that most desirable thing – an internationally important Catalan. He is also, however, something that is not meant to have existed – a Catalan Francoist. There are old photos of him in the uniform of the Movimiento, shaking hands with the Caudillo or giving stiff-armed fascist salutes.

Catalonia, Catalans are mostly convinced, was always anti-Francoist. The Francoists and Falangists were '*ocupantes*', occupiers from elsewhere. Dictatorship was a Castilian invention. A true Catalan would never have supported the Caudillo. It was an idea that Catalans took to almost as soon as the dictator was in his grave. 'On the one hand, the Francoists wanted to disappear from the map so nobody would make them pay and so they could reappear, protected by *olvido* (forgetting), years later. On the other hand, the emerging *catalanismo* needed to present the image of a homogenous country,' the Catalan writer Arcadi Espada explains. 'It was a country determined to prove to itself that it had been good, beautiful and sacred – without fissures, without Francoists. A blanket of silence covered the nation.'

Even when gunning for Franco, Catalans are remarkably shy about naming their own. I found further evidence of this in a book written to prove how badly the Catalan language had been treated – *Catalan, a language under siege*. It informed me that Antonio Tovar, the Madrid academic who masterminded Franco's 1940s crackdown on Catalan, 'had a number of intellectuals in Catalonia who were his allies'. Rather than tell me who they were, however, the authors coyly declared that these were 'names we will not mention because some are still alive'. It was okay, in other words, to name Madrid Francoists, but not one's own.

Reading Anna Funder's study of East Germany under communism, *Stasiland*, I found that East Germans had a similar attitude to Hitler and Nazism. 'History was so quickly remade, and so successfully, that it can truly be said that easterners did not feel then, and do not feel now, that they were the same Germans as those responsible for Hitler's regime,' Funder says. She calls it the 'innocence manoeuvre'. Just how innocent, I wondered, had Catalans really been? The answer, one prominent Catalan publisher explained, has yet to be written.

Catalans have always shown an ability to adapt themselves to circumstance. In the eighteenth century their aristocrats upped sticks and moved to Madrid. Their chameleon nature was noted by George Orwell when he arrived in 1936 to fight in the Civil War. 'Down the Ramblas . . . the loud-speakers were bellowing revolutionary songs all day and far into the night. And it was the aspect of the crowds that was the queerest thing of all. In outward appearance it was a town in which the wealthy classes had practically ceased to exist . . . Practically everyone wore rough working-class clothes, or blue overalls or some variant of militia uniform . . . I did not realise that great numbers of well-to-do bourgeois were simply lying low and disguising themselves as proletarians for the time being,' he wrote in his *Homage to Catalonia*.

Catalans were indignant when the head of Spain's Constitutional Court, Manuel Jiménez de Parga, recently claimed they had welcomed Franco with open arms when he visited in 1972. 'Few places welcomed Franco with the enthusiasm shown by the Catalans,' he said. It was a blatant piece of Catalan-baiting which, predictably, worked. As for history, Jiménez de Parga would later claim that, in the year 1000, his native Andalucía (then Muslim) boasted fountains of coloured or perfumed water while other self-proclaimed 'historic communities' in Spain 'did not even know what washing themselves at the weekend was'. Pujol tried to take him to court.

After the Olympics, I left Barcelona for Madrid. Of all the great rivalries between all the great cities of Europe, few can summon up the bile that Spain's biggest cities – which are almost equal in size – reserve for one another. Up to now I had only ever experienced the rivalry from one end. Barcelona, according to this story, was always the victim. Madrid was always the villain. I had noticed, however, that Sergio, a Barcelona friend whose company car had a Madrid licence plate, always made sure it was in a car park in the days before a Real Madrid–Barcelona match. 'I don't want it scratched,' he explained.

In Madrid, I found, people often threw up their hands at the mention of Catalans. 'If they want to go, let them!' said one. 'To think we used to sing their songs,' said another, referring to the protest songs that a generation of Madrileños had learned to sing, in Catalan, in the final years of Franco.

A few months later the so-called '*Guerra de la Llengua*', the 'Language War', broke out. This was a rebellion against linguistic normalisation. A group of mothers in the resort town of Salou set up an association to lobby for less Catalan at school. They demanded the right to choose, as Basque parents could, between schools that taught mainly in Catalan and schools that taught mainly in Castilian. One night, one of their leaders, Asunción García, claimed to have been kidnapped and beaten. Her car was torched. A group of intellectuals, from both the left and the right, set up something called the Foro of Babel. They called the Generalitat's linguistic policies 'xenophobic and reactionary'. They, in turn, were accused, in semantic overkill, of being 'the intellectual heirs of those who sought to commit genocide against Catalan during the Franco regime'. The other allegation, which revealed that the strains between Catalonia and its migrant working classes were by no means new, was of a phenomenon that strikes fear into good bourgeois Catalan hearts, *lerrouxismo*.

The left-wing populist Alejandro Lerroux had been the 'Emperor of the Paralelo' at the start of the twentieth century when that area of Barcelona housed the city's immigrant slums. Barcelona already had a reputation as the capital of European anarchism. Anarchists and paid pistol-wielding assassins employed by factory owners fought a dirty war against one another. Regional nationalism in Catalonia has traditionally been a strongly bourgeois thing, so this was, to a certain degree, the nationalist class protecting itself against the immigrant masses who laboured in mills and factories.

Italian Giuseppe Fanelli – a friend of the great anarchist theorist Mikhail Bakunin – had introduced anarchism to Spain in 1869. It spread like wildfire through Barcelona's shanty towns and the countryside of Andalucía. Spain was the only country where anarchism truly took off. In the 1890s Barcelona's anarchists became Spain's first bomb-throwers. The most spectacular attack came in 1893 when a young man called Santiago Salvador tossed two bombs down from the cheap seats at the Liceu opera house in the Ramblas during a performance of Rossini's *William Tell.* They landed in the stalls, amongst the rich of a city whose upper classes had grown fat on the almost slave labour of their factories. Twenty-two were killed. Salvador and five other anarchists were garrotted. He shouted 'Long live anarchy!' before the iron collar of the garrotte – a very Spanish invention – tightened slowly around his neck.

Lerroux arrived on the scene a few years after the Liceu attack. He was a great, angry hater. He hated the Church, the monarchy and Barcelona's upper classes of industrialists and bankers. Most of all, however, he hated *Catalanistas.* His followers were known as the 'the young Barbarians'. When the city rebelled against a general call-up to send troops to Morocco in 1909, they led a week of violent rampaging. The Tragic Week, as it was called, remains seared into Catalonia's political memory. Some eighty churches, monasteries, convents and church schools were sacked or burnt. Mummified corpses of nuns were pulled out of crypts and put on display. *Lerrouxismo* has terrified Catalonia ever since.

My search for Catalonia's 'different' soul took me onto the outdoor escalators than run up the side of a Barcelona hill called Montjuïc to the National Museum of Catalan Art. This, in the words of one of its first directors, was established in order to 'construct a history of its own for Catalan art . . . that will allow us to show the differences that exist between Catalan art and hispanic or foreign art'. As museums around the world looked for connections between all kinds of art, Catalonia had decided to use its greatest gallery to look inward. The choice of building – a neo-classical monster known as the Palau Nacional – was apt for the stated aim of the project. It had been built, in the years of dictator Primo de Rivera, for the 1929 International Expo – a patriotic attempt to impress Spain's brilliance on the world. It took fourteen years to turn into the shining new symbol of a different nation, Catalonia. The museum finally opened all its spaces in 2004.

The result, I find, is both tasteful and spectacular. Whatever the original intentions, it does not seem to be about seeking 'differences between Catalan art' and 'foreign art'. Perhaps the curators, when it came down to it, realised that it was ridiculous to apply absolute frontiers to art. If anything, those who finally put it together after the ex-director was moved on have been careful to show how local art fits in with the rest of Europe. The museum's jewels are a series of Romanesque wall paintings dating back to the eleventh century. They are taken from churches high in the folds of the Pyrenees – especially the valley of the River Boí. Experts ripped them out in the 1920s, fearing they would fade and disappear. They were brought to Barcelona, to be installed in what has now become the MNAC. Art critic Robert Hughes has pronounced this place to be 'to wall painting what Venice and Ravenna are to the art of mosaic'. He adds, however, that: 'It seems unlikely these murals were painted by locals.'

Art is one of those things Barcelona and Madrid like to squabble over. In the first half of the twentieth century Barcelona produced some of the most remarkable artists of the time. The *modernismo* of Gaudí and his fellow architects was accompanied by that of artists like Santiago Rusiñol and Ramón Casas. They looked to Europe and loved all things modern. Like Gaudí, however, they also looked back at the Romanesque, at the twelfth-century Cistercian monasteries of the Catalan countryside and at Barcelona's own, unique, Gothic architecture. Their headquarters, in true Spanish style, was a bar – *Els Quatre Gats*, The Four Cats. A teenage Pablo Picasso who, although born in Málaga, spent his formative years in Barcelona – was welcomed here. One of his first exhibitions sat on the café's walls.

Picasso had been studying – and his father teaching – at the fine-art school lodged in the top floor of the fourteenth-century Llotja, the old stock exchange. Another pupil there was Joan Miró, who started off painting the countryside and farms of his father's native Tarragona before moving on to Paris and surrealism.

The mad, moustachioed, paranoid surrealist Salvador Dalí was a notary's son from that most conservative of Catalan places, Figueres. When Dalí died it was found that he had recently changed his will. Instead of giving his work to the Generalitat, he donated it to the Spanish state. Catalans cried foul, claiming Dali had been manipulated into changing the will at the last moment. The inventor of the so-called paranoid critical method left behind him a museum installed alongside his old Torre Galatea house. He had topped it with giant eggs and encrusted, on the outside, plaster imitations of Catalan bread rolls. It is now one the most visited museums in Spain. Dalí is perhaps the last person to have willingly sported a *barretina*, the sock-length, floppy red beret of the Catalan peasant. Some *catalanistas* prefer to forget his enthusiasm for Spain. This included highly formative years in the company of the poet Lorca and film-maker Buñuel as a Madrid student. It also included a fawning reverence for Franco.

A comic tug-of-war between Madrid and Catalonia involved that unlikely-sounding symbol of national pride – Dalí's *The Great Masturbator*. Catalan separatists insisted in the Madrid parliament that the picture, currently hanging in Madrid's Reina Sofía museum, should be returned to Figueres.

I was not convinced that art – however brilliant the things produced here were – was proof of a defining national characteristic for the Catalans, so I decided to look elsewhere. Nationalism and religion always seem to go together. This is especially so in Spain – National Catholicism was, after all, the name given to Franco's political ideas. It is as if each 'nation' needs, apart from its symbols, some sort of spiritual home. In Catalonia that home is to be found on the extraordinary-looking, towering outcrop of rocks known as Montserrat, the Serrated Mountain.

Montserrat must have provoked wonder in those who set eyes on it long before the temple that is considered the religious soul of Catalonia was established here in the eleventh century. The jumble of upright, rounded peaks here are unlike any rock formations nearby. From far off it looks like a dumping ground for giant menhirs, stacked as tight as space allows. Closer up, they look like the weathered backs of the carved stone gods of Easter Island. Catalans call it 'the Sacred Mountain'. Legend has it that a statue of the Virgin Mary was found in a cave here at the end of the ninth century. True, or not, there were, by the year 900, four separate chapels tucked into the hillside. The main Benedictine monastery was founded in 1025. A Montserrat monk, Bernat Boïl, travelled with Columbus to the Americas, giving this mountain's name to a Caribbean island along the way.

The original buildings were ravaged by man. Most of the monastery was destroyed by Napoleon's troops in 1811. It later suffered temporary disestablishment. During the Spanish Civil War, it was saved from being looted and razed by anarchists thanks to the Catalan regional government – though twenty-three monks were killed. Its current facade, made of polished rock from the mountain, was not finished until 1968. The symbols of Catalonia, especially the red and gold striped flag, are to be found discreetly draped around the monastery. The most important feature here, however, is another Catalan symbol. It is a statue of the Virgin Mary. Almost uniquely, the Virgin of Montserrat is black – probably the result of too much exposure to candle-smoke rather than design. Her nickname is '*la moreneta*', or 'the little dark girl'. On the folds of her golden robe sits a crowned child Jesus, also with a darkened face. A queue of visitors wishing to meet her stretches out of the monastery doors. They are waiting to kiss her right hand, which holds a sphere representing the universe. Anyone doubting her significance should come here on the weekend after Barcelona football team, that other symbol of Catalan pride, wins a major trophy. The trophy is brought here, to receive her blessing.

Montserrat has a reputation for producing rebellious monks. Under Franco, the monks continued to talk, read, write and preach in Catalan. In 1962 the then Abbot, Escarré, became one of the first church rebels by giving an interview to *Le Monde* in which he accused Franco of being a bad Catholic. A famous protest saw three hundred Catalan intellectuals lock themselves inside the chapel in 1970 while Franco's police sat helplessly outside. Even then, though, many of this self-styled *gauche divine*, divine left, were champagne radicals. Barcelona's Bocaccio nightclub delivered salmon sandwiches to keep them going. Franco knew he dare not touch the place. Jordi Pujol's Convergència Democràtica de Catalunya party was founded here and, as its propaganda eagerly points out, this was where he married.

Today the monastery's ninety monks include respected experts on the Catalan language, with their publishing house producing seminal works. They remain, however, an argumentative bunch. Recent reports suggest there has been a bout of infighting. Older, more strident *catalanistas* have, it is said, been moved on. One newspaper claimed they had lost out in a factional power struggle that involved a clique of gay monks.

I find Montserrat dull and uninspiring. The singing of a wonderful boy's choir – the oldest in Europe – fails to cheer me up. It is too new, too much a place for coach parties and day-trippers with foil-wrapped *bocadillos*. It has a cable car and a funicular railway. There are restaurants, gift shops and a post office. It feels like a religious-nationalist theme park. Catholicism and nationalism are, together, a spooky phenomenon, especially in a Spain that can recall Franco's version of it. I think of another Benedictine monastery with a choir school and a nationalist aura that I have visited recently – at Franco's Valley of the Fallen. My soul, Montserrat reminds me, is neither Catholic nor Catalan.

I drive on to another Catalan monastery. I have no trouble, however, feeling the pull of Santa María de Poblet. As I arrive the sun is going down and an icy wind is blowing through the neighbouring vineyards. The tourists have gone. The walls of the vast monastery complex, sitting under the wooded slopes of the

Prades hills, emit a warm, pinkish-ochre glow as they catch the reflections of the day's final rays. This is one of three Cistercian monasteries – the others are at Santes Creus and Vallbona de les Monges – built in the Catalan countryside in the twelfth century as the Moors were rolled south towards Valencia.

I find myself alone in the huge courtyard. Dogs are barking at the wind. A fountain provides the only other sound. I go into a huge, triple-nave chapel. It is dark, so I wait outside. A sign hangs in the entrance. 'The services are in Catalan. Please be punctual.' Bells ring out – a warm, booming noise that announces vespers. I go back into the cavernous chapel, where lights are slowly being turned on. A woman is confessing in one gloomy corner. Two dozen white-robed monks file in to the stalls that occupy part of the central nave. Poblet, I am surprised to see, is as multiracial as Las Ramblas. The younger monks mostly look as if they come from south America or north Africa.

There are only three of us in the congregation: the woman who had been confessing, a young man in a puffa jacket and myself. A monk offers me a copy of the *Antifonari* so I can follow proceedings. 'Where are you from?' he asks. 'Britain,' I reply. 'Better not then,' he says, retiring the book. 'It is in Catalan.' I persuade him that I can follow it anyway – both the music and the words. In fact, the words turn out to be easier. The musical score is dense and mysterious. It loses me quickly. The singing is soft and harmonious. It feels as though it is issuing from the stones and the walls. The monks somehow manage to fill the three broad, high naves of the chapel with their music. Incense wafts slowly down from the far end of the chapel, which seems a very long way off. The chapel is not just cold, but damp. A deep chill creeps into my bones as I sit on my wooden pew. My hands go numb. I wrap them in a scarf. The monks keep singing, standing, sitting and bowing as they go through their rituals.

Towards the back of the chapel, beyond the monks, I can see an elaborate stone tomb. I wonder who it belongs to. This is the last resting place of many medieval Catalan rulers, counts and kings. Most have nicknames. The Chaste, the Conqueror, the Lover of

Elegance, the Benign and the Humanist are all here.

When I leave, it is night time. I am alone again in the courtyard and the spotlights send huge shadows against the walls. For a moment I am a silhouette giant, as big as one of the hexagonal towers at the Royal Gate. I walk out thinking that, were I Catalan, I might feel the pull of history, some essence of my identity, in a place like this.

As I leave, I think about Catalan history and identity. So what makes a nation a nation, or a country a country? Does it have to be an independent state? Obviously not, if you think about Scotland. When can a country be said to have disappeared, or come into existence? And what does it mean to be a country – or, if you want, a nation – inside another country? Catalans account for nearly one in six Spaniards. They are an essential part of the mix. It is a very Spanish conundrum.

It is not a new one. 'They are neither French nor Spanish but *sui generis* in language, costume and habits,' the great British chronicler of early-nineteenth-century Spain, Richard Ford, reported. 'No province of the unamalgamating bundle which forms the conventional monarchy of Spain hangs more loosely to the crown than Catalonia, this classical country of revolt, which is ever ready to fly off.'

History sometimes helps. Sometimes it does not. In Spain it is, to a great degree, something to argue over – another political weapon in the battle of identities. Catalan history is no exception. 'History is a trap,' the separatist writer Víctor Alexandre warned me. 'What matters is now, and the future.'

The facts of Catalan history are fairly straightforward. Northern Catalonia had been recovered from the Moors relatively quickly, in the early eighth century. Charlemagne's son helped take Barcelona in 801. This was the Spanish March – a series of counties that acted as a buffer zone between the Franks and the Muslims. Barcelona was ruled by counts. Wilfred the Hairy, considered by some to be the founder of Catalonia, brought Barcelona and other counties together. He was, however, still a vassal to, of all people, Charles the Bald.

Catalans liked giving their counts – as those buried at Poblet showed – nicknames. If Wilfred was Hairy – and he certainly is in later sculptures of him – his successors over the coming centuries were one of the following: Crooked, Old, Towheaded, Great, Fratricidal, Saintly, Chaste, Catholic, Liberal, Humanist, Benign, Just, Generous, Ceremonious or just plain Careless.

In 988 one of these counts, Borrell II of Barcelona, broke his vassalage to the French king Hugh Capet. It was not exactly 'Freedom for Catalonia', but it could be called 'Freedom for Barcelona'. A thousand years later, in 1988, the Generalitat would decree the millennium of the political birth of Catalonia. The Counts of Barcelona expanded their territory southwards and became, through a marriage in 1137, the Kings of Aragón – a title they used from then on. The southward roll would continue until they passed Alicante in 1266. The Aragónese kings then looked east. They gained control of the Balearics (after slaughtering or selling into slavery most of the male population of Menorca), Sicily, Corsica, Sardinia and, by the fifteenth century, Naples and the southern half of modern Italy. But the lines with Castile were already getting blurred. The original dynasty ran out of heirs on the death of Martí, the Humanist, in 1410. Martí turned out to be the last Catalan to rule. A Castilian, Ferdinand of Antequera, was brought in as king. Six centuries later some Catalans would rather that had never happened.

In 1479 the new rulers would, again by marriage, help unify Spain under the joint leadership of Isabella of Castile and Ferdinand of Aragón. Thirteen years later they conquered the last Spanish Muslim kingdom at Granada. Castile plus Aragón minus Moors meant, basically, that Spain had been founded (though there was still work to be done in Navarre). The rest, as they say, is history. But it is not. This is Spain. History, once more, is the stuff of debate, disagreement and politics.

The origins of Catalan discontent with the results of Isabella's and Ferdinand's marriage can be found, some say, in an oath. It was one sworn by subjects of the Aragonese kings and it went: 'We, who are as good as you, swear to you, who are no better than us, to accept you as our king and sovereign lord, provided you observe all our liberties and laws – but if not, not.'

With the court now displaced from Barcelona to Castile, Catalans began to lose out. Trade to the Americas was given to Andalucía. Plague, famine and an overstretched Mediterranean empire were, anyway, taking their toll.

The Catalan national anthem, adapted from a folk song in the late nineteenth century, recalls what the Generalitat refers to as 'the War of the Catalans against King Philip IV' in 1640. For a while I could find no other reference to this war. Then I discovered it was usually given another name. It is the Revolt of the Reapers, or the Reapers' War. Whatever its proper name – and the motivation – the peasant rebels were Catalans down to their canvas *espardenyes*, espadrilles. They invented, as a password, a tongue-twister full of sounds that only a Catalan could hope to say: '*Setze jutges d'un jutjat menjen fetge d'un penjat*', 'Sixteen judges from a court eat the liver of a hanged man'. It was, for your average lisping Spaniard, as confusing and impossible a phrase as the words 'Manchester United' are to today's football commentators (who, for some reason, never quite make it to that final 'd' sound). The Catalan aristocracy joined the peasants, Catalonia saw off the king's army and momentarily declared independence under French protection. France did not like the idea of an independent Catalonia. A week later, Catalonia swore allegiance to the king of France 'as in the time of Charlemagne, with a contract to observe our constitutions'. Catalans stayed French subjects for twelve years. They spent much of that time falling out amongst themselves. Eventually, with the Aragónese and Valencians refusing to help them, they were reabsorbed into Spain.

The anthem is called 'Els Segadors', 'The Reapers'. 'We must not be the prey/ Of those proud and arrogant invaders!/Let us swing the sickle!/Let us swing the sickle, defenders of our land!' it urges. The proud and arrogant (*gent tan ufana i tan superba* in Catalan) they rail against every time they sing their anthem are, of course, Castilians. Again, the Generalitat cannot resist offering a po-faced explanation for the anthem. 'It is solemn and firm, and unites the will of the people in favour of the survival of a nation which proclaims its full national character.' It is, in fact, a celebration of the last time Catalonia actually managed to break from the rest of Spain.

Then, in 1705, the Catalans made a mistake. In a tussle over who was to get the crown, they backed a loser, Archduke Charles of Austria. A ferocious siege of Barcelona ensued, ending in defeat on Catalonia's own version of 9/11 – 11 September 1714. Modern Catalonia has taken the Dunkirk approach to remembering that event: 11 September is now the day Catalonia celebrates the Diada, its national day – a celebration of defeat. Like the anthem, it also reminds Catalans that their natural enemy is in Madrid.

The winner in 1714, Philip V, took his revenge by passing the Nueva Planta decree. Catalan was barred from schools – a measure that left the illiterate and uneducated peasantry indifferent. Castilian became the language of government and the courts. Catalonia also had some ancient institutions of its own which would now disappear. A century before England got its Magna Carta, Catalonia had already developed, in the early twelfth century, what is claimed to be Europe's first written bill of rights – the Usatges. While this did not help the serfs, it provided a legal framework for free men to argue peacefully over their affairs.

A parliament, les Corts, had been set up with limited powers in 1283. It represented the clergy, the nobles and the wealthier merchants. Its affairs were run by a standing committee of twelve men, the Generalitat. By the late thirteenth century Barcelona, too, had a sort of parliament – known as the *Consell de Cent*, the council of one hundred men. The Generalitat and the city's *consell* eventually conducted their business from fourteenth- and fifteenth-century Gothic palaces facing one another across the cobbled Plaça de Sant Jaume. They still do. Catalonia's modern-day politicians and administrators have no way of avoiding history. They work in the middle of it.

Corts, *Consell de Cent* and Generalitat were, however, all abolished by Philip V. Les Corts, anyway, had met only once since 1632.

The 1714 defeat led, in Jordi Pujol's own words, to 'Catalans returning to their homes and staying there, without aspiring to anything more than to survive without ambition or any collective project, for 200 years'. None of this prevented them, however, from prospering economically over the next few centuries. They exported wool and paper. In the nineteenth century the cotton trade was smaller only than that of England, France and the United States. Barcelona embraced the industrial revolution long before most of the rest of Spain.

Growing wealth allowed Barcelona to expand, giving Ildefons Cerdà a chance to design the Eixample, where I would later live through the 1992 Olympics. Cerdà was, however, more than aware of where the money was coming from. He was one of the few to warn about the vile living conditions into which factory hands were forced. Catalan peasants had held occasional revolts. Soon the urban working classes would be at it too. Church-burning was a particularly Catalan sport. In 1835 a bullfight was held in Barcelona. It was not a success. The crowd became angry. A popular rhyme in Catalan explains what happened next. '*Hi haver una gran broma/ dintre del Torín./ Van sortir tres braus,/ tots van ser dolents:/ això fou la causa/ de cremar convents.*' 'There was a big set-to/ inside the bull-ring./Three fighting bulls appeared/but all were weak: and that was the cause/ of the burning of the convents.' Not for the first time, or the last, Barcelona's skyline was streaked by plumes of smoke coming from church buildings. The Church, rich, powerful, arrogant and unpopular, had already seen its buildings burnt in Barcelona fifteen years earlier. Even Poblet, miles away in the fields of upper Tarragona, was torched. Lerroux's young barbarians, or their anticlerical heirs, would be back with their matches the following century. Modern Catalans often proudly proclaim that bullfighting has nothing to do with them – but it has obviously been around for almost two centuries.

Catalans were, of course, not all church-burners. Antoni Gaudí, the architect of the Sagrada Familia cathedral which is still rising – its colourful, ceramic-encrusted spires already a symbol of the city – eighty years after he was run over by a tram, was a deeply conservative, religious man. One of his first projects was the restoration of Poblet, which had become a crumbling, vandalised wreck. In later life Gaudí became a pious, ascetic eccentric. He lived on the Sagrada Familia building site, sleeping on a small four-poster bed in the middle of a workshop piled high with plaster models of his ongoing designs. He became a strict vegetarian and turned into a seedy-looking, emaciated, white-bearded old man. 'We must beg God to punish and then console us,' he once said. 'Everyone has to suffer.' When he wandered in front of the number 30 tram on Barcelona's Gran Vía, it took a while for someone to recognise him. He died a few days later. Legend has it he died in poverty. His will, however, turned up recently – showing that he still had a pretty pile in the bank.

Modernisme had emerged from the mid-nineteenth-century *Renaixença*, the Romantic Catalan renaissance that found its local hero in the exorcist poet Verdaguer. Literature in Catalan has had an irregular history. In the Middle Ages it produced three great writers – though none were, by today's definition – Catalans. The Majorcan priest Ramon Llull wrote more than 250 texts of philosophy, poetry and theology – in Catalan, Latin and Arabic. He was eventually lynched to death while trying to convert Tunisia's Muslims in the thirteenth century. A Valencian called Ausías March, wrote, amongst other things, impassioned verses to a mysterious mid-fifteenth-century married woman, his '*llir entre cards*', or 'lily amongst thistles'. Another Valencian, Joanot Martorell, produced a raunchy fifteenth-century novel about knights in shining armour which tossed old values of unconsummated courtly love into the literary dustbin. In his *Tirant lo Blanc*, considered a precursor to Cervantes's *Don Quixote*, the eponymous hero's manservant rejects a would-be lover's offer of a few strands of hair: 'No, my lady, no. That time is past. I know quite well what Tirant desires: to see you in bed, either naked or in your nightdress.' It seems that Catalans, still more French than Spanish in their amorous arrangements, always were more sophisticated in sexual matters.

Catalan literature slackened until Verdaguer's time in the mid-nineteenth century. Today's Catalan writers can choose between two languages. One offers them a larger market. The other offers, via the Generalitat, to buy the first 300 copies of their book.

The *Renaixença* broke the emotional ground for the emergence of political Catalanism. Gaudí, when presented to King Alfonso XIII, addressed him in Catalan. His example could be an inspiration to the Generalitat's latest language campaign which encourages people to start their conversations with strangers in Catalan. '*Parla sense vergonya*', 'Speak [Catalan] without shame', it urges them.

Gaudí's most fervent admirers believe, however, he is more than just a model of virtuous Catalanism. He is, they say, also a model of saintliness. The Vatican's Congregation for Saints' Causes seems to agree. It is studying a petition for his beatification, which looks set to go ahead. He is already known as 'God's architect'. God and Catalonia – the cornerstones of traditional nationalism – meet in Gaudí.

Catalans, generally, are good at celebrating their own culture. They eagerly sign up to belong to groups and do things together. They form clubs to go rambling, to dance their peculiar *sardana* or to form those scary (seven- or eight-storey) human towers, the *castells*, that balance small children precariously on their top.

Catalan politicians, however, have sponsored some quite absurd attempts to create a distinctive Catalan culture. Pujol made this – along with language and history – one of the main battlegrounds of Catalan nationalism. The rules set for his functionaries in the Palau Moja were simple. There was money for things in Catalan. There was relatively little, or no, money for things that were not. Half the population, which naturally did things in Castilian, was out of the loop. Catalonia has some interesting theatre, but quality, critics complained, was not always a criterion when handing out funding. The policy reached its most absurd when El Tricicle, a group of comic mime artists, presented a short film for the National Film Awards of the Generalitat. They were told, however, that their wordless film did not qualify. The reason was simple. The silent movie's title, *Quien mal anda, mal acaba*, was in *castellano*.

As culture in Catalan frequently depended on financing from the Catalan state, those on the receiving end were careful not to bite the hand that fed them. Catalan nationalism, as a subject, was, therefore, taboo. In the theatre world, there was one shining exception – Albert Boadella's *Els Joglars*. Boadella was quick to turn his attention to the new holy cows of Catalonia. Nationalism had built him a whole new set. They were waiting to be knocked down like fairground coconuts. The chief holy cow was Pujol himself.

Pujol embodies the view many Catalans had fashioned of themselves after Franco's death. He was a proven anti-Francoist – having been jailed for two years for his involvement with a group of people who stood up and sang *Els Segadors* at Barcelona's magnificent modernist concert hall, El Palau de la Música Catalana. He was a Catholic conservative. He was also a banker. A man who understands money is admired in Catalonia. '*La pela és la pela*', 'Money is money', is one common local saying. A Catalan-language poet, the Majorcan Anselm Turmeda, wrote an eloquent ode to cash in his fifteenth-century 'Elogi de Diners' ('In Praise of Money') which ends: '*Diners, doncs, vulles aplegar./Si els pots haver no els lleixs anar:/si molts n'hauràs poràs tornar/ papa de Rom*', 'So you must get money!/If you get it, don't let it go!/If you have lots, you can become/the Pope in Rome.' The Borgias had almost certainly read that one.

Pujol was a formidable politician. He was, in fact, too good. Over his quarter-century in charge he became Catalonia, and Catalonia became him. He was referred to simply as '*el President*'. He added a few Napoleonic touches of his own. He insisted, for example, that journalists stood for him when he arrived – usually late – for his press conferences. He sent self-interviews to Barcelona newspapers – questions and answers by Jordi Pujol. Worse still, these would be printed.

There was a rationale behind this self-grandeur. Pujol was building, or rebuilding, a nation. The nation needed national symbols. One of those symbols was *el President*. By this logic, Pujol turned himself into a symbol of Catalonia. 'When seeing him in action it is impossible not to recall De Gaulle's '*La France, c'est moi*', the Irish–Spanish writer Ian Gibson said.

An Els Joglars show inspired by Alfred Jarry's *Ubú Roi*, called *President Ubú*, saw Pujol and his wife pilloried mercilessly. The Pujol offered up by Boadella was, according to one critic, not just maniacally ambitious and money-grabbing but also showed 'homicidal tendencies, a double personality and delusions of grandeur'. Boadella did not bite his tongue when explaining his vision: 'Ubú Excels [Pujol's alter ego] invades our privacy daily, recriminating, advising, threatening, moralising and laying down the law . . . explaining even how we Catalans have to urinate,' he said. His punishment included a long-running, if undeclared, veto on Els Joglars by Catalonia's television and its national theatre house. Culture, once more, was wielded as a political weapon. It still is, even without Pujol in power. When Catalonia was invited to exhibit at the Frankfurt Book Fair in 2005, the Generalitat said it would concentrate on those who wrote in Catalan – though many of Catalonia's best writers do not. The new regional government that made that decision is headed by a Socialist, Pasqual Maragall, who has also shown some strong *catalanista* tendencies – and is allied with a separatist party, Esquerra Republicana de Catalunya.

There is a terrible ambiguity to Pujol and his nationalists. They proclaim Catalonia to be a nation. They want to '*desenvolupar la plena sobirania nacional*', 'develop full national sovereignty'. They deny, however, having separatist ambitions. But, they add, who knows what the future will bring? In practice, Pujol's nationalists have turned to an age-old Catalan tradition – *pactisme*, deal-making. Catalonia's *burgesía* has been striking deals for centuries. Barcelona, after all, was a major Mediterranean trading city when Madrid was little more than a large village.

Catalan nationalism is still the strongest political force, even though a coalition of other parties currently keeps it out of power. It has always been determined to maintain its *seny*, to be moderate and sensible. On several occasions Pujol's party has held the balance of power in the Madrid parliament, Las Cortes.

It has never used it to destabilise or drive extravagant bargains. It has propped up both left and right. It has, however, always made sure it walked away with a bit more power. The result, as he himself admits, is that 'not once over the past three hundred years have we, continuously, enjoyed such a degree of political power'.

Pujol's wife, Marta Ferrusola, represents the more visceral, unpleasant side of Catalan nationalism. The former first lady of Catalonia stirred up a major controversy when she declared that immigration might lead to Catalonia's Romanesque churches being empty within a decade. Catalonia would, instead, be full of mosques. Her husband, she insisted, was fed up with giving council housing to 'Moroccans and people like that'. Family aid was going to people 'who do not even know what Catalonia is'. These were people who only knew how to say '*¡Hola!*' and 'Give me something to eat!' she said. 'Whoever stays in Catalonia should speak Catalan,' she added. Her comments coincided with the public support offered to Austria's chief xenophobe, Jörg Haider, by Heribert Barrera. Barrera was a head of the separatist, and supposedly left-wing, Esquerra Republicana de Catalunya. He had also been a president, or speaker, of the Catalan parliament. 'If the current flow of immigrants continues, Catalonia will disappear,' he claimed. 'When Haider says there are too many foreigners in Austria he is not being racist.'

These outbursts were worrying. As a young man Pujol had been damning about *xarnegos*, describing the typical immigrant from Andalucía or Murcia as 'a destroyed and anarchic man' who 'if their numbers come to dominate, will destroy Catalonia'. He long ago repented of that attitude, however, saying Catalonia should be 'just, respectful, non-discriminatory and in favour of all that can help the immigrants'. That was his public stance anyway. He must have told his wife something different. In any case, the feeling persists amongst non-Catalan speakers that they are looked down upon. The message they perceive is this: Good Catalans speak Catalan. Bad ones do not.

Catalanism is a car with no reverse gear. It may go slow, it may go fast, but it only goes in one direction. At what stage, I wondered, would nationalists say: 'That's enough. We have achieved our aims. We don't want any more power here. You can keep what is left in Madrid'? The answer to that question is almost certainly 'never'. A nationalist needs, by definition, to keep demanding more – and to claim always that they are the victim of injustice.

I can understand separatism. It is a straightforward and honest credo. The ambiguity of Catalan nationalists, however, makes it impossible to guess where they want to go. It also ensures that the tension between Madrid and Catalonia can never be resolved. It might vary in degree, but it will be eternal. The nationalist definition of Catalonia seems to require it.

Jordi Pujol finally retired as president in 2003, though he still looms large, presiding over the *Convergència Democràtica de Catalunya* party. His successor, Artur Mas, won most seats in the elections that year. But he did not win an absolute majority. Mas was outflanked by Pasqual Maragall, the same Socialist who, as mayor, had seen Barcelona so brilliantly through the Olympics. He stitched together what, on the surface, was an unlikely coalition of left-wing parties. It included Esquerra Republicana de Catalunya – the separatist party which had doubled its support to take one in six Catalan votes.

The best explanation of the growth in separatism has been provided by Ricardo, a cartoonist at *El Mundo* newspaper. He drew a cartoon of Aznar, the belligerently centralist Conservative prime minister at the time, rubbing a lamp. A genie came out and offered him a wish. 'I want you to make all those who radicalise the nationalists disappear,' he said. The genie responded by turning Aznar to dust.

Maragall, however, not only needs the support of separatists to run the Generalitat but also has some nationalist tendencies of his own. His grandfather, Joan Maragall, was a major Catalan poet and admirer of Verdaguer. He penned a famous ode to Spain, which chided it for ignoring Catalonia after the disastrous losses of Cuba and the Philippines in 1898.

On ets, Espanya? – No et veig enlloc./ No sents la meva veu atronadora?/ No entens aquesta llengua – que te parla entre perills?/ Has desaprès d'entendre an els teus fills?/ Adéu, Espanya!

Where are you, Spain? – Nowhere to be seen./ Do you not hear my resounding voice?/ Don't you understand this language, speaking to you amongst dangers?/Have you stopped listening to your children? /Farewell, Spain!

Joan Maragall's poem reflected, amongst other things, Catalonia's pain at losing its valuable markets in Cuba. The relationship with Cuba had been strong. Catalans still sing *havaneres* – Cuban songs brought back by its sailors. Bacardi – the world's most famous rum – owes its name to its Catalan founders. The disaster of 1898 marked a moment when Catalonia's upper middle class lost faith in Spain and turned towards regional nationalism as an alternative. If Madrid could not run their affairs properly – or guarantee their markets – they would run them themselves.

Under the poet's grandson there will be no turning the clock back on education and language reforms. A Pujol law imposing fines on shopkeepers who fail to translate their signs into Catalan is still there, as are the offices where people can denounce those who do not comply. Maragall, meanwhile, is demanding a reform of Catalonia's statute that will see it accrue further powers. He wants it formally recognized as 'a nation' – a concept that drives Spain's traditional right apoplectic.

A Catalan journalist explained the progress of *catalanismo* like this: 'The train is going down the track. All the major parties in Catalonia except the People's Party [which gets only one in eight votes] want it to keep moving. The only argument is where it should stop. The Catalan socialists will get off at federalism. Separatists want it to reach the end of the track. Nobody knows where the nationalists will stop.' He might have added that the latter were, however, determined to make sure the train never ran out of coal.

Maragall's reforms are set to happen despite the opposition of leading Socialists in other parts of Spain. Such views can coexist in the Spanish Socialist Party because it is federal. What is strange about the Socialist Party, which currently governs Spain under Zapatero, is that it does not formally propose the same solution for Spain itself. 'Federal' is a word it has begun to toy with. It is not ready, however, to go the whole way. Some argue that, with so much devolution of central power, Spain is already a long way down the federal track. A formally federal Spain remains the ideal, only, of the far left and the Socialists in Catalonia – even though it seems an obvious solution to what Spaniards call '*el problema territorial*'.

The political father of Catalan nationalism, Enric Prat de la Riba, reached a similar conclusion in 1906. 'Catalonia is a nation . . . a collective spirit, a Catalan soul, which was able to create a Catalan language, Catalan law and Catalan art.' How to square the principles of 'to each nation, a state' and 'the political unity of Spain'? Prat de la Riba's solution was '*l'Estat compost*' – basically a federation. In 1914 Catalonia got something much less than that – an administrative body called the Mancomunitat. It was short-lived. In 1925 the dictator General Miguel Primo de Rivera dissolved it. Primo de Rivera would, amongst other absurdities, ban the *Sardana* – the painfully earnest and unexciting Catalan group folk dance. The striking down of cultural symbols, however minor, was part of yet another determined re-engineering of the Catalans.

As would happen with Franco and, to a lesser but demonstrable degree, with Aznar, a militant centralist in Madrid only served to popularise Catalan nationalism. After Primo de Rivera had gone it came back with a vengeance. This time, however, it was driven by the left. In 1931, a leader of Esquerra Republicana de Catalunya, Lluís Companys, proclaimed the Catalan Republic to a crowd in Barcelona. The then head of the ERC, Fransesc Macià, claimed this new republic was part of 'the Federation of Iberian Republics.' Federal Spain poked its nose above the parapet. It was, as in 1640, a short-lived idea. Three days later Macià backtracked and agreed to the idea of a semi-autonomous government to be called, once more, the Generalitat. It would last until the Spanish

Civil War, with Companys as its last president. Companys was forced into exile. Extradited from occupied France by Hitler while Franco's brother-in-law, the *Cuñadísimo* Serrano Suñer was foreign minister, he would be shot on a hill above Barcelona in 1940. Companys' party would later be led, for a while, by that future Haider-lover Heribert Barrera. The current generation of leaders have distanced themselves, and their party, from his racist discourse.

Thinking of Barrera, I travelled to the town of Vic. This is the heartland of traditional Catalonia. Hairy Wilfred had begun its ninth-century rebuilding after it was recovered from the Moors. Verdaguer was born nearby. Here I found a group of 'language volunteers' giving free lessons to immigrants. They were making a heartfelt effort to help these people integrate in Catalonia. I wondered, however, what really motivated them. Were they zealous missionaries of Catalan, converting natives? Or were they genuinely welcoming, just trying to help them out? When I heard one enthusiastically explain to a classroom of Africans what the idiom '*treballar com un negre*' – 'to work like a black man' – meant, I wondered even harder. She did not notice the sharp intake of breath from some of those – hard-working, lowly-paid and black – in the room.

Moving back to the Ramblas, I found another group of immigrants studying Catalan. They were here for money, not love. 'I went for a job and they said come back when you can speak Catalan,' explained one Ecuadorian. She complained that, in the city's hospitals, nurses and doctors often addressed her in Catalan. In fact, with Catalan required for many public-sector and some private-sector jobs, speakers are now up to 5 per cent more likely to find employment. People from abroad, or elsewhere in Spain, shout 'Discrimination'. My Catalan friends – some of whom now work and live almost exclusively in Catalan – find that hard to accept.

I would like to move back to Barcelona one day. This has always been where I have felt most at ease in Spain. My conscience, however, tells me that, if I do so, I should learn Catalan. I am, after all, no longer the innocent foreigner who stepped off a plane at Barcelona airport in the mid-1980s with a rucksack, little idea of Spain and – like those immigrants Mrs Pujol complains about – none at all of Catalonia.

But I can think of many other, more useful, languages I would rather learn first – Arabic, Chinese, perhaps Italian. It makes a move to Barcelona about as attractive – and likely – as going to, say, Helsinki or Athens. Does that mean I am being excluded? Or am I excluding myself? Perhaps I just take it all too seriously. Pujol recently complained that Catalonia felt 'uncomfortable' in Spain. Maybe I should go to Barcelona and allow myself to feel 'uncomfortable' too.

As my quest for Catalonia's 'differentiating fact' drew to a close, I set off to visit the least popular museum in Barcelona. It is dedicated to none other than that great and beloved poet Verdaguer. I drove up a twisting road past the funfair at Tibidabo – the highest point in the hills that rear up above the city. This peak's name comes from the words of the Devil's offer when he tempted Christ. Would he have had the will-power, I wondered, to reply 'get thee behind me Satan' had he been offered Barcelona?

I drove through dense woodland. Here, a stone's throw from the city, a shepherd was tending his sheep. A sign pointed me towards a converted *masía*, an eighteenth-century Catalan farm house, called Villa Joana. This is where Verdaguer, disgraced and distraught, died in 1902. 'I am in a sea of troubles that do not let me think or write, let alone sing,' he complained. A few years earlier he had been banned from saying Mass. Although he was reinstated, the elite of Barcelona – his former patrons – had mostly turned their backs on him.

It was a Saturday morning. I was the only visitor at the museum, silently trailed by a uniformed security guard. There was obviously no taboo, or at least not any more, on mentioning his supposed madness. His exorcism writings, I found, had now been published. The museum explains how Verdaguer became the leading light in the *Renaixença* and the star turn at its annual poetry competition, the *Jocs Florals*. The *Renaixença* had included, in

1841, the publication, in the preface of a poetry anthology, of a call for cultural independence by Joaquim Rubió i Ors which claimed that Spain was no longer 'the fatherland' of Catalans.

The clarion call came from a man who, like many of the *Renaixença* figures, were from Catalonia's prosperous upper middle class of merchants and financiers. Bonaventura Carles Aribau eventually spent much of his time in Madrid, running Spain's treasury, mint and state holdings. That did not stop him waxing lyrical in *La Pàtria* (*The Fatherland*) about his roots and his language, which he referred to by the medieval term of *llemosí*. '*En llemosí soná lo meu primer vagit,/ Quant del mugró matern la dolça llet bebia/ En llemosí al Senyor pregaba cada dia,/ E cántichs llemosins somiaba cada nit.*' ('My first infant wail was in Catalan/ when I sucked sweet milk from my mother's nipple./ I prayed to God in Catalan each day/and dreamed Catalan songs every night.')

The *Renaixença* gave birth to political *catalanismo*. In Catalonia, the poets came first, then the politicians. That explains why language and culture – and not the bullet or the bomb – are the chosen weapons of *catalanismo*. It also explains why some Catalans can be so touchy about Verdaguer.

My search for the *hecho diferencial* ends here. Catalans are obviously different. But I do not see that this conflicts with being Spanish. In any case, it strikes me as something an outsider cannot judge. The *hecho diferencial* can only be felt from within. If a Catalan feels that he or she is Catalan above all else, and that this makes them different to other Spaniards – or, even, not a Spaniard – it is a wholly subjective sensation. Perhaps, like Aribau, one must first dream and suck a maternal nipple in Catalan. The outsider cannot share it. Nor, I am sure, can the immigrants on Las Ramblas.

Catalans are not, however, the only Spaniards whose first dreams normally come in a language other than Catalan. The Basques, as we have seen, cannot compete. *Euskara* is still far from being their first language. The people of Galicia, however, do mostly speak their own language, *galego*. They, too, have their own poets. So how do they fit into the jigsaw puzzle that is Spain? To find that out, I would have to leave the warm and placid Mediterranean behind me. I would need to head for the wild, wet Atlantic, to a place that is home to The End of the World.

12

Coffins, Celts and Clothes

I met Manuel standing beside his coffin. The long, wooden box, lined with quilted, padded white viscose, was standing upright, leaning against the wall of the church at Santa Marta de Ribarteme. Manuel and four friends were standing beside it, quietly waiting for the moment when he would step in.

Santa Marta is a small village, more a loose collection of farmhouses, in the hills that rise up from the River Miño in Galicia, Spain's misty and mysterious north-west corner. Manuel, a forty-nine-year-old, one-eyed former quarryman, had a love-heart and the letters L-O-V-E, in English, tattooed on one forearm. He had come up from the nearby cathedral town of Tui, which sits on the border with Portugal, to join the procession that is the highlight of Santa Marta's annual fiestas.

'I have stomach cancer. I have been very, very ill,' he explained. While others walked, or even crawled, Manuel would be riding in his coffin. 'I have prayed all I can and I have survived. It is a small miracle, so I have come to give thanks.'

The coffin parade at Santa Marta de Ribarteme was, I had been assured, one of the supreme examples of those twin Galician characteristics of religiosity and superstition. I had come here as I tried to work out a problem that was just as mystifying, if not more so, than that posed by the Catalans or Basques. Why was it that Galicia, the most far-flung and historically abandoned corner of Spain, did not feel the same intense mistrust of Madrid as them. Why, in short, were Galicians happy being Spaniards? This, after all, was also a place with its own language. Four out of five people spoke *galego* – a far higher percentage than native *euskara* speakers. Galicia, too, could boast its own literature and culture. Geographically, it was more distant and isolated from Madrid than either the Basque Country or Catalonia. It had certainly suffered more. For centuries, and until very recently, Galicia was a byword for poverty, hunger and emigration. It was recognised, alongside the other two, as 'a historic nationality' – marking it from Spain's other autonomous regions. Fewer than a quarter of Galicians defined themselves as nationalists, however. Only one in thirty wanted a separate state. There was no real argument that, in Galicia, one was amongst Spaniards.

In Santa Marta de Ribarteme it was lives and souls, not mundane politics, that were at stake. 'He prays to Santa Marta,' explained one of Manuel's friends, here to act as pall-bearers for a still-living man. 'The cancer hasn't killed him, not yet.'

I asked whether they had weighed Manuel before volunteering their services. 'He weighs sixty-eight kilos,' said the friend. 'We'll try not to drop him.'

Inside the tiny, stone church, a queue of men and women was barging its way noisily forward towards a polychrome statue of Santa Marta – Lazarus's sister, who once served Jesus his supper. A man with a microphone and a weary expression was berating them. 'If you could hear yourselves,' he said. 'You would realise that this sounds like anything other than the house of God.' But still they pushed anxiously forward. They were sweating in the summer heat – a hot crush of frail bodies, frayed nerves and raised voices.

Some of the people here – children, women, old men – wore strange, short, transparent white tunics, made of gauze or mosquito netting, over their clothes. It made them look like baggily clad sugar-plum fairies, though none seemed particularly aware of their outer aspect. Most clutched long, thin, yellowed wax candles, as tall as a man, their flames protected by small, white cardboard cones. Some carried *exvotos* – rough wax sculptures of parts of the body – bought from vendors who had set up trestle tables outside. As they reached the saint, the pilgrims added their *exvoto* to a growing mountain of yellowy arms, legs, ankles, heads, chests, breasts and tummies that was piling up under her pedestal. I heard a steady 'clink! clink! clink!' of coins hitting the bottom of a money-box.

The sickly and the well reached out to wipe the statue, or its pedestal, with their handkerchiefs. Once the saint had been touched, the handkerchiefs were immediately passed over the owners' brow, neck or face. Santa Marta's ability to intercede with God to bring about cures gives her great weight amongst these devout, superstitious, Galician villagers. Most were here asking for her to bring an end to their ailments – though many, like Manuel, were also giving thanks for help, and cures, already given.

Most people were talking what sounds to the untrained ear like a straight mixture of Portuguese and Spanish – the harder, rawer edges of Castilian rounded off by the smooth, musical tones of Portuguese. This is *galego*, the language of the Galicians – a direct descendant of the language used by many thirteenth- and fourteenth-century Iberian *trovadores* to sing their *cántigas*, or lyric poems, of love, desire and death.

I had driven up to the village on a road that wound its way through eucalyptus woods. Small plumes of smoke still rose from the charred, smouldering soil where a forest fire had swept through the previous day. Road signs along the way had been blackened by the blaze. Forest fires are an ever-present part of the Galician summer. This one looked like a modest gust of wind might make it suddenly sputter back into life. Large, menacing clouds of black smoke spread in the distant sky from blazes still burning elsewhere. Fire-fighting helicopters were dipping their buckets into the broad River Miño and dropping the contents on flames that could be seen leaping through woodlands on the Portuguese side of the river.

The farms may be small, but the farmhouses here are large – at least by the standards of most Spanish housing. Many still conserve the *hórreo*, the separate store for maize and grains, standing up on stone stilts and shaped like a small chapel, sometimes crowned with a tiny cross.

Galicia's countryside is a land of smallholders. Here, along the Miño valley, they grow the long-trunked vines of the *albariño* and *treixadura* grapes across head-high, horizontal trellises. These go towards making the young, crisp Rías Baixas white wines. There are also vegetable gardens and modest plots of maize. The odd conical haystack, shaped like a giant straw breast, rises voluptuously from the ground around a tall pole. Much higher up, on top of the hills, stand two dozen of the modern wind-farm windmills that have appeared like mushrooms wherever, in the country of Don Quixote, a decent breeze blows.

The tiny church – all beautiful, weathered granite on the outside – had been unfortunately restored on the inside. The walls were fresh with new plaster and shiny stonework. The interior resembled that of an *asador*, one of those cavernous, meat-roasting restaurants that do their best, with fake stone walls, heavy furniture and wrought-iron lampshades, to look like they have been around since the Middle Ages.

It was late July, and the sun beat down on the small crowd leaning on the railings above the church. Itinerant vendors had set up stalls selling everything from T-shirts and hats to power drills and electric fans. Some, intriguingly, were manned by immigrant Ecuadorians dressed in the frilly, white shirts with colourful embroidery and the black felt hats of the Otovalo Indians. A couple of makeshift bars and restaurants were doing brisk business under canvas marquees. The smell of *pulpo a la gallega* wafted across the village from huge copper vats where octopus was stewing away in boiling water, olive oil and paprika. The priest's voice rattled out from a tinny loudspeaker attached to the bell-tower as he entoned prayers in that inexpressive, droning voice favoured by Spanish priests. We had come here, he reminded us, in the belief that 'by the intervention of Santa Marta, you may be cured of your ailments'.

By this stage there were three coffins arranged against the wall. It was not clear who owned the second one. A chubby boy of about thirteen leaned his back nonchalantly against it, chatting to his mother. An orange baseball cap sat backwards on his head. He wore a sugar-plum-fairy outfit over his brightly coloured shorts and sleeveless basketball-shirt. A sickly looking woman in her late thirties, equipped with a prayer book, a blue bum-bag and a small, battery-driven white plastic fan, had reserved her place in the third coffin. A young, heavily made-up woman who had squeezed her ample upper half into a tight T-shirt had, by this stage, donned knee pads and a pair of blue slippers. She was preparing to crawl behind the procession that was due to set off soon. In a gesture that even the priest was unable to explain later, two women also appeared, each with a brand-new, red clay tile sitting on their heads. The tiles were held in place by pieces of bailing twine tied under their chins. They looked like they were trying to stop the sky falling on their heads.

A uniformed wind band struck up some doleful marching music as two statues, a smaller San Antonio leading out Santa Marta herself, lurched out of the church door, borne on the villagers' shoulders. Manuel and the others stepped into their coffins and were raised aloft by their pall-bearers. Manuel lay there calmly, his hands held together, looking suspiciously as though he was taking the opportunity for a siesta. The coffins were open and the sun shone directly into Manuel's eyes. Someone handed him a fan, which he unfurled and held across his face. And so, with the band playing, the priest with an amused look on his face, Manuel in his coffin, the blue-bum-bag woman in another one, the third one being carried empty, one woman crawling and two others with tiles on their heads, the procession of some three hundred people set off.

Less than an hour later, after wandering up through some woods, the procession arrived back at the church. Manuel entered in his coffin. He said his prayers, stepped out of his box, and, having paid the priest 180 euros to borrow the coffin, handed it back. It was carried over to a stone shed where it joined a dozen others. Manuel, and his exhausted friends, headed back to Tuy.

The following day, I visited some Madrid friends at their summer house in Asturias, the next 'autonomous community' east along the Cantabrian coast from Galicia. They listened to the story of the Santa Marta procession, incredulous. 'You have found "*la España profunda*",' one said. She was referring to that mysterious 'deep Spain' which, like the American Deep South, Spaniards associate with strange goings-on and the dark, secret lives of country folk. Whenever some backward tradition or grim, rural tragedy involving land boundaries, water rights and shotguns hits the headlines, city folk sigh and remind one another that *la España profunda* still exists.

In fact, you can find *exvotos*, normally wax casts or plastic moulds of body bits but also, as I once saw, a motorcycle crash helmet, in other Galician churches. I do not find anything inexplicable about them. Miracles are part of Roman Catholic belief. Hiring a coffin may be an extreme way of giving thanks, but then there are no more traditional Roman Catholics in Spain than the Galicians. There are also no people as traditionally superstitious as the Galicians.

Gallegos are proud of their supposedly Celtic origins. They have legends of *meigas* and *brujas*, good and bad witches. There are mysterious beings called *mouros*, who hoard treasure under the abandoned *castros* (iron age settlements) that sit on hilltops and promontories. Death, the afterlife and Purgatory are particular obsessions. A band of tortured souls from Purgatory known as the Santa Compaña, for example, wanders remote country roads at night, awaiting a chance for redemption. 'You have to remember that, although Galicians go to church a lot, we are more superstitious than religious,' a schoolteacher in a country town near Lugo explained to me. The bestiary of Galician folklore is large and scary. It includes *lobishomes* (werewolves), deceptively beautiful *nereidas* (fishwomen) and *mouchas*, melodic owl-like spirits whose calls announce the coming of Death. Even without them, the countryside was always scary enough. Wolves roamed much of Galicia well into the twentieth century. A stone cross on a rock near the village of Berdoias marks the spot where, locals insist, a pilgrim monk was eaten by a pack of them on his way to Santiago de Compostela. The wolves are still present. Thanks, partly, to a new sense of ecological protection in Spain, some estimates now put their numbers at more than 500. A further 2,000 are believed to inhabit the neighbouring regions of Asturias and Castilla y León.

The Galicians have, in the Bloque Nacionalista Galego, a growing, left-leaning nationalist party. But they are traditionally conservative folk. Franco was born here. His home town of el Ferrol was temporarily renamed El Ferrol del Caudillo in his honour. The Conservative People's Party ran the regional government for sixteen years – until 2005 – under the leadership of Manuel Fraga. This octogenarian former Franco minister's opponents have jokingly given him the nickname of an invented dinosaur, '*El Fragasaurio*', the Fragasaurius. Fraga, one of the authors of Spain's 1978 democratic constitution, combines one of the largest brains in Spanish politics with the reflexes of those not used to being argued with. Like many of those who succeeded under both Francoism and democracy, his curriculum has been retouched to present him as having been a tireless worker for progress towards the latter. It is worth noting, however, that his most famous description of Franco, coined in the 1960s, was: 'the hero turned father, who stands vigil, night and day, over the peace of his people'. Fraga's most enthusiastic following is in the poorer, rural areas of Galicia. In 2005 he was still the most popular politician in the region. He lost power, however, when the Bloque and Socialists jointly obtained one more seat in the regional parliament.

Fish and farms – mostly vineyards, arable and dairy cows – have been the lifeblood of Galicia. The scattered farmsteads, often clustered in tiny *aldeas*, or hamlets, are a huge change from the piled up, cheek-by-jowl housing of the towns and villages of central, eastern and southern Spain.

I saw my first Galician cow within seconds of leaving Santiago de Compostela airport on my first-ever visit here a decade ago. The cow was on the end of a piece of rope. An elderly peasant held the other end. It looked as though he was taking the cow for a walk and, indeed, the intention of this peculiar *paseo* was clearly that the animal should graze on the grassy, banked verge beside the airport fence. That was about all I got to see. Within minutes I was plunged into thick fog. I struggled to find my way along the road. Eucalyptus trees closed menacingly in on me. I began to wonder whether what I had heard was true: that Galicia was all cows, Celts, eucalyptus, fog and fishing boats. All I needed was for a few Christian pilgrims looking for Santiago de Compostela and a trawler-full of cocaine – this is, after all, the main entry point for the drug in Europe – to appear through the mist and I would, in happy ignorance, have reckoned to have had a fairly complete Galician initiation.

Manuel Rivas, a poet and novelist who writes in *galego* but has been translated into several languages, once calculated that there were a million Galician cows – one for every three inhabitants. EU milk quotas and mad-cow disease have reduced the numbers since but, as the early twentieth-century Galician nationalist politician Alfonso Daniel Castelao once said, the cow, the fish and the tree are Galicia's holy trinity.

Progress came later to Galicia than the rest of Spain. Until a few years ago, driving here from Madrid was a nine-hour affair as you slogged over the 4,000-ft-high ridge of Cordillera Cantábrica. This mountain range dips south along Galicia's border with neighbouring Asturias and Léon. It forms a formidable natural barrier that sets Galicia, and the Galicians, apart from the dry, austere monotony of Castile and the Castilians – and from the rest of Spain. In the late eighteenth century the journey to Madrid took a week. Even with new, EU-subsidised motorways sweeping over bridge after spectacular bridge and through dramatic cuttings in hills and mountains, there are still six hours of hard driving from Madrid to the region's biggest city, La Coruña. Along with the ever-present, Wellington-booted women in nylon housecoats carrying hoes, rakes or spades over their shoulders, I still sometimes bump into someone with a cow, or two, on a rope when I come here.

Galicians are probably not real Celts. But they would like to be. Many, thanks to some self-interested tinkering with history by nineteenth-cntury Galician Romantics, are fully convinced they are. 'Most of the Celtism found by local historians in Galicia is utter claptrap. It is decoration to cover the gaping holes in that particular story,' the philosopher Miguel de Unamuno wrote in 1911. The independent tribes that inhabited this area in pre-Roman times certainly had, from the sea, contacts with Brittany,

Ireland and other Celtic areas. Modern genetics has shown, also, that there is a shared gene pool around the European Atlantic in which the people of northern Spain, including the Basques, share. There is even an ancient Gaelic text, the pre-eleventh-century *Leabhar Gabhala* (*The Book of The Invasions*), which claims that Ireland was once successfully invaded and overrun by Galicians. These were known as the 'sons of Mil' and, improbably, took Ireland in a single day.

Whatever the truth of the Celtic origins – and they do not shout out at you in the physical aspects of Galicians or in their language – people like them. Vigo's football club is, for example, called Celta de Vigo. In front of the Tower of Hercules, the ancient lighthouse overlooking the ocean at La Coruña, a huge, round, modern, mosaic *rosa de los vientos,* a wind compass, bears the symbols of the world's Celts – including the Irish, Cornish and Bretons. Bagpipe players are here as common as in Scotland. Some even make it as local pop stars.

One bright, cold December day I climbed the steep, sinuous, stone path up the Monte do Facho. This is one of the most exposed spots in the *rías,* the western sea lochs of Galicia. The *monte* rises abruptly up from the Atlantic at the end of the Morrazo peninsula between the two wide-mouthed *rías* of Vigo and Pontevedra.

Slippery, lime-green moss lined the rocks and boulders of the pathway as it snaked up the hill through the inevitable Galician eucalyptus wood. I was alone. A few sharp sounds, of dogs barking or doors slamming, ricocheted up from the village below. The only other noise came from the sea, the wind and the birds. It was easy to conjure up images of the ancient Galicians who had walked this path from Iron Age times onwards. The view from the top of the *monte* was breathtaking. The Cíes islands seemed close enough to touch and, to the north, the islands of Ons and Sálvora lay placidly in a deceptively calm ocean. I could see the mouth of the Ría de Arousa to the north. The view stretched beyond that reaching, at least in my imagination, to mainland Europe's most westerly point – Cape Finisterre, the End of The World. The

Atlantic, almost bare of ships, stretched out towards America. Inland, meanwhile, chimney-smoke drifted across the lowlands and onto the glassy waters of the *ría*.

How could one not be awe-struck by the mysteries of nature, or be given to thoughts of deities and spirits, in such a spot? Wide, flat slabs of granite, very slightly hollowed out, are scattered on the peak here. There is also a tiny, round, weather-beaten eighteenth-century look-out post of grey, lichen-clad blocks. The little mountain gains its name from the fires that used to be lit here to guide boats home. The flat stones, or *aras*, of which 130 have been found, were used as sacrificial altars in Roman times. The God worshipped then was called Berobreo. Like Santa Marta, he could cure. Archaeologists believe this, too, was a place of pilgrimage. Some *aras* still bear inscriptions asking for the gift of good health.

Galicians had been here for centuries before the Romans. Galicia was rich in primitive iron and, even, gold mines. It also had, and has, a wealth of natural resources in the sea. Molluscs and other seafood are still basics of both diet and economy. On the inland side of Monte do Facho's peak, the remains of a typical Galician Iron Age settlement – a *castro* – are being dug up by archaeologists. Living in round, stone, thatched buildings and protected by defensive walls, people lived in this *castro* until the time of Christ.

The *castros*, some five thousand of them, are dotted on hill tops and promontories across Galicia. Their inhabitants – who also had little workshops and stores – sought safety, from enemies, bears and wolves, in height. An information board on Monte do Facho explains that, some time in the years after the birth of Christ, 'the inhabitants went downstairs to get land near the sea' (*sic*). Monte do Facho, with its six-foot-long, granite *aras* lying here as if cast onto the mountain top by the Gods, must have remained, however, a fine place for a sacrifice.

Like almost any Atlantic coastline, the weather here is unpredictable and unforgiving in equal proportions. To drive around the tips of the peninsulas between the *rías* when the storms are coming in, buffeting you with near-horizontal rain and wind, is to wish for a thick set of walls to hide behind and a warm fire for comfort. To come here on a bright, sunlit day, or glimpse it when the clouds suddenly roll away, is to gaze with awe on dramatic landscapes conjured up by sea, rock, wind and rain.

At Finisterre, the relative protection of the sea lochs runs out and the exposed coast starts turning east, gaining the spine-chilling name of the Costa da Morte, the Coast of Death. This is the point where Romans thought the world ran out and where, it is said, they would come to watch the sun being swallowed up by the sea at night.

The *rías*, with their calm waters, are homes to neat rows of *bateas*, the large rafts from which chains of mussels grow on cords hanging below them. Gangs of gumbooted-women, bent double at the waist and dragging buckets behind them, dig up winkles, clams, cockles, scallops, razor clams and oysters when the tide runs out on the long, shallow beaches. The exposed cliffs of the Costa da Morte, however, are the territory of the *percebeiros*, who risk life and limb to scrape off the *percebes*, the prized goose barnacles, which cling like bunches of purple claws where the Atlantic waves crash in.

For years this remotest of Spain's remote corners was a place of shipwrecks, pirates and sea legends. A local historian, José Baña, has logged some 200 shipwrecks here between 1870 and 1987, with more than 3,000 dead. Hefty granite crosses dotted along the cliffs recall some of those who drowned within sight of land. Gallegos are still fishing folk, their mighty trawler fleets now criss-crossing the globe in search of food for a fish-hungry nation. From Argentina to Angola, passing via the Irish Box, the Galician fleet tenaciously battles on where those of other European countries gave up long ago. As a result, some twenty Galician sailors and fishermen still die at sea every year. There are also stories of wreckers, *raqueros*, who tied lanterns to the horns of cattle in order to draw boats onto the rocks. The Royal Navy training ship *Serpent* was smashed against the rocks near Boi Point when it ran into a violent storm on its way from Plymouth to Freetown, Sierra Leone, in 1890. Of 175 boy sailors on board only three survived.

A small, lonely, walled cemetery, *el Cementerio de Los Ingleses*, sits near this remote point – the only reminder of the tragedy.

Finisterre is still a key point on mariners' charts. More than 40,000 merchant vessels round this cape each year, including some 1,500 oil tankers. Inevitably, they, too, sometimes go down. Every decade or so, Galicia's coastline is painted black by their foul cargoes. Three of the world's twenty worst tanker disasters have happened here, making this the most regularly oil-polluted coast on the planet. The names of the sunken tankers run easily off Galician tongues, each one a black mark on recent history. *The Urquiola*, in 1976, spilt 100,000 tons of oil on the beaches around La Coruña. *The Aegean Sea* crashed into the rocks under La Coruña's ancient Torre de Hercules lighthouse, in 1992. The world's only remaining Roman lighthouse, first built in the second century and reformed to its current state in the eighteenth century, was obviously no use to the ship's captain. *The Aegean Sea* tipped a further 74,000 tons of oil onto the coast.

Then, in 2002, came *The Prestige*. News that it was adrift, and bearing 77,000 tons of heavy fuel oil, reached the Costa da Morte on the night of 13 November 2002. *The Prestige*'s hull was splitting as it lay some twenty-eight miles off the coast. When the people of Muxía, one of the most exposed towns on this coast, woke up the following morning, *The Prestige* was on their doorstep. It floated, dangerously out of control and clearly visible, several miles beyond the solidly built sanctuary of A Barca, where large, pancake-shaped rocks run down into the sea. Well before the sanctuary was built, this was a magical place. The wind and sea-smoothed *pedras*, the rocks, have both names and magical powers. The Pedra de Abalar can be rocked by a crowd of people standing on it and has, in the past and depending on how it rocked, provided yes–no answers to important questions. The Pedra dos Cadrís has a low, wide archway eroded through it. People suffering kidney and back pains or rheumatism scramble through it, hoping it will provide a cure. Stones and rocks have a central role in the superstitions of Galicia. Eighteenth-century priests launched campaigns to prevent couples seeking children from copulating on rocks deemed to have special fertility powers.

There was little the magic stones of Muxía, themselves supposedly petrified remains of a sailing boat belonging to the Virgin Mary, could do about *The Prestige*. Over the next few days the ailing, leaking vessel was pulled this way and that by rescue tugs as European nations lobbied to keep it away from their coasts. Eventually, the salvage tugs were ordered to tow it far out to sea and drag it towards Africa. The cynical logic was that it would not matter if it spilt its noxious load off the coasts of the Third World. When it finally went down some 130 nautical miles off Finisterre, on 19 November, the fuel oil refused to solidify in its tanks, as the government had predicted it would. Instead, it sent much of it onto the beaches of the Costa da Morte. The oil destroyed the *percebes* clusters, ruined coastal fishing grounds and threatened the rich seafood beds and the *bateas* of the rías. Parts of Muxía itself were painted black by oil-thickened waves. The television pictures provoked instinctive horror in a country where cleanliness is, if not next to godliness, at least the obsession of every self-respecting, bleach-bottle-wielding *ama de casa*. While the government sent in the army but took a while to turn up in person, cleaning up Galicia became a popular obsession. Coachloads of volunteers appeared from across Spain. Provided with masks and white boiler suits, they shovelled up the dirty sand and scrubbed the rocks by hand. Galicia rebelled. Demonstrators and fly-posters demanded '*Nunca Máis*', 'Never again'. Their fury forced the government to introduce rules keeping tankers away from the coast. It was an unusual rebellion. 'The Galician does not protest, he emigrates,' Castelao once said. This time it was not true.

More than fish, cows, rocks, *castros* and *meigas*, what defines the Gallegos is their language, *galego*. I had my first encounter with *galego* by accident. Looking for books to study Spanish with when I first arrived in Spain, I decided that – apart from detective novels – poetry would be my best study material. It could be taken in short chunks and studied intensively with a dictionary. My first book-buying spree provided, more by luck than judgement, rich pickings. I chose the Chilean Pablo Neruda, who I had just about heard of. I cannot recall why, but I also chose the Galician poetess Rosalía de Castro, who I had not heard of.

Opening the Rosalía de Castro book, I discovered, to my delight, that it was in two languages. On the left-hand page was a Castilian version of the poetry, on the right was the original Galician. Without knowing it, I had bumped into the mother of modern Galician literature. Rosalía was a Galician Romantic who, in the nineteenth century, did more than anybody else to reinvent *galego* as a literary, written language. In proper Romantic style, she was brilliant but sickly and, allegedly, the illegitimate daughter of a priest. She died aged forty-eight, having had six children.

Galego had, centuries before, been pushed aside as the language of writing by Castilian Spanish. The language of the *trovadores* and their *cántigas* lost out to Castilian, (just as Galicia would, after brief rule by the Moors until 740 and despite a couple of short experiments with 'independent' monarchs in the tenth and eleventh centuries, always be ruled by kings from Asturias, León or Castile). One of the most famous composers of *cántigas* was King Alfonso X, who once penned a filthy ditty about the sexual prowess of the Dean of Cádiz – perhaps a precursor to the cheeky, popular *chirigotas* that are now sung at Cádiz's carnivals. The *trovadores*, however, also helped spread the ideal of romantic love. It was, perhaps, apt that a new generation of Romantics should return to the language they used. Rosalía was, nevertheless, swimming against the current. The melodic, soft sound of *galego* was an obvious aid, however, to her sometimes dark, sometimes saccharine, descriptions of her homeland. In *Cantares galegos*, her most famous work in *galego*, she explained herself like this:

> *Cantarte hei, Galicia, teus dulces cantares, que así mo pediron*
> *na beira do mar.*
> *Cantarte hei, Galicia, na lengua gallega, consolo dos males,*
> *alivio das penas.*

> I must sing to you, Galicia, your sweet songs, because that is what they begged me at the edge of the sea.
> I must sing to you, Galicia, in the Galician tongue, consoler of troubles, lightener of grief.

It was enough to help set off a modest literary and cultural revolution, O *Rexurdimento,* the Galician 'resurgence'. Successive generations have picked up the baton, though there is still much to do. Two-thirds of Galicians have grown up with it as either the main or shared language of their household. Some 83 per cent speak it fluently. That compares to just 16 per cent of Basques who speak *euskara* as much as, or more than, *castellano*. 'She lived in a country without its own voice, and she was the first, with class, to find the name of things, the unwritten name of our things,' wrote one recent publisher of her work. Her 'Cantares', published in May 1863, marked a new beginning for a language which, for five long centuries, had been written off as *inculta*, uncultured.

Despite general recognition of Rosalía's literary qualities, not everyone was convinced that *galego* and literature went together. '*Galego*, which is a sweet, harmonious language abundant in vowels, is of no real use for life or for literature. In *galego* you can write a few poems – Rosalía did marvellous ones – buy a few fish and talk to the chickens, the birds and young village girls. But who would ever consider writing, in *galego*, a political article or a piece of journalism, yet alone a work of philosophy?' the Galician writer and journalist Julio Camba wrote more than half a century later.

Rosalía was enamoured of the nobility and gentility of the rural poor and the fishing folk dotted along the rugged Atlantic coast. Her enthusiasm for *costumbrismo* – for the detailing and describing of local tradition – went too far for most people, however, when she spelled out one, more unusual, custom. In 1881 she told the readers of Madrid's *Imparcial* newspaper that: 'Amongst some people it is accepted, as a charitable and meritorious act, that should a sailor who has not touched land for a long time arrive at a place where the women are decent and honourable, the wife, daughter or sister of the family which has given the stranger a roof to stay under, allows him, for the space of a single night, to occupy her bed.'

Aware that she was sailing into a storm, Rosalía justified her mention of this practice as further proof of the Galician peasant's warm heart. 'This must seem as strange a practice to our readers as it does to us, but for that very same reason we have not doubted about making it known, considering this strange idea of such extreme generosity is redeemed by the good intentions that it harbours.' Galicians were outraged. She paid back their anger by refusing to write again in *galego*. Her final poems were in Castilian Spanish.

Galego is now the official language for local road signs. Galicia's winding, unmarked country roads are hard enough work already. They take you through the confusing systems of *concellos* (councils), *villas* (towns), *parroquias* (parishes), *aldeas* (hamlets) and, ambiguously, *lugares* (places, which usually seem to be *aldeas*). On a larger scale, there are four Galician *provincias*. Each, in turn, is divided into a dozen or so *comarcas*. Sometimes a single name is shared by three of the above, which fit inside one another like Russian dolls. Galicians have had a thing about drawing concentric circles since prehistory, with the motif appearing repeatedly in the abundant local rock engravings. The concept seems to have been transferred to modern administrative planning. As a visitor, however, all you see is the same name repeated, confusingly, over and over again. At moments of tension between driver and navigator, I have secretly entertained the idea that Galicians do this deliberately.

One of the great Galician characteristics is meant to be *retranca*, a devious refusal to let others know what you are doing or thinking. Meeting a Galician on a staircase, other Spaniards like to say, it is impossible to know whether they are going up or down. Ask a Galician their opinion, they add, and the answer will be deliberately fudged. '*Depende . . .*', 'That depends . . .', the Galician will say. Like all stereotypes, *retranca* annoys Galicians when used to describe them by outsiders. They themselves, of course, feel free to use it. But then they see it differently. *Retranca*, to them, is also humour. They are not being shifty, they are being ironic.

This is one of the great, absurd misunderstandings in Spain. Even Spanish and Galician dictionaries give their own, different meanings. Other Spaniards, who do not always have a sense of irony, suspect they are being lied to. In fact, they are having the mickey taken out of them – which some would actually consider worse. Could it be, I have sometimes wondered, that they have organised their place names, and road signs, for just that purpose?

Manuel Rivas went some way to explaining my wider confusion about Galicia to me in a witty introduction to his home region, *Galicia Contada a un Extraterrestre* (*Galicia Explained to a Visitor from Outer Space*). With farms and communities so widely scattered, he says, Galicia accounts for half the place names in Spain – some 250,000 of them. 'We have . . . valleys that bear the names Sea, Love, Gold and Silence. And there is also a Sacred Peak and a Mouth of Hell. One of my favourites is a forest bordering with Portugal: *A Fraga de Escuro Vermello*, The Deep Red Forest.'

The *galego* names now on the road signs tend to bamboozle the non-Galician visitor further, especially if their road map remains obstinately in Castilian. The result, however, is that, as you meander, lost, through pastures and eucalyptus groves, you can find yourself passing through such delightfully sounding places as Goo, Zoo, Pin or Bra.

This has always been a land of smugglers. Sea routes to continental Europe, Britain, Ireland and beyond, as well as the land border to Portugal, have offered ample opportunities for those prepared to cheat the laws of the day. Until the 1980s, this was relatively harmless, even romantic, stuff. Tobacco, alcohol, even white goods like television sets, would arrive on trawlers, yachts or motor boats. The Civil Guard often looked deliberately in the opposite direction. But what was once an almost quaint local industry changed when Galicians, through their extended network of emigrant cousins in south America, started working with the Colombian cocaine cartels. In just two decades they have made it the main gateway into Europe for the drug.

In the 1980s pairs of Colombian men, one acting as bodyguard to the other, would appear in port towns like Vilagarcía. 'They would stay together in hotel rooms, and everybody knew that was not because they were gay,' a Vilagarcía schoolteacher said. The Colombians brought wealth. They also brought the brutal methods of the cartels, with their paid *sicarios* and loaded pistols. Large houses, fast cars and strange business ventures, there to launder money, popped up in coastal towns and villages. Corpses also began to appear. Strange deaths of young men remained unexplained. The outboard motors on the *planeadoras*, the fast speedboats that seem to glide over the *rías*, got larger. Some nights they would nip out to collect bundles of cocaine from vessels that had sailed from south America.

The names of the big drugs barons soon became legend. There were, for example, the Charlines, the Oubiñas, Prado Bugallo and Sito Miñanco. Police caught many of them, but the clans divided up into smaller, tighter groups. Now they provide a simple courier service for the Colombians. Trawlers pick the drugs up from merchant vessels or yachts off the African coast at Cape Verde. When they reach Galicia, small fleets of *planeadoras* and Zodiac-style boats speed out of the *rías* to rendezvous with them. The speedboats then head for hidden beaches where the drugs are picked up and taken to secret hideaways. There they stay until the Colombians send someone else for them, and they are distributed around Europe. The Galician cut is said to be a quarter of the cocaine's value.

In the first decade of the twenty-first century, Spain – mainly Galicia – vies with Mexico for third place on the global ranking for the amount of cocaine it captures each year. Only the United States and Colombia constantly outdo it. With more than 44,000 kilos of the drug being found in a single year, Spain accounts for 60 per cent of European cocaine busts. At a wholesale price of around 40 euros a gram, that makes for 1.76 billion euros worth. Assuming, as Spanish police do, that more than half as much more gets through than they capture – and with the Galicians getting a 25 per cent cut – that makes up to 660 million euros of cocaine cash for the region. Picking up the newspaper one morning, I found a succinct explanation of Spain's status in the cocaine world. It came from a senior customs official. 'We are not the tip of the iceberg, as we once thought. We are the iceberg,' he said. Spaniards are now also Europe's biggest cocaine consumers, along with the British, with one in fifty admitting that they have taken it 'recently'. Cocaine, meanwhile, causes more than half of drugs-related deaths in the country.

A doctor who, as a young man, had been a general practitioner in Galicia, told me how the influence of the local *narcos* spread beyond the criminal world. He had always wondered why a large furniture retail warehouse outside the town was open only occasionally. 'The warehouse was owned by the local *narco*. He used it for money-laundering, but also for buying friends. On those weekends when it was opened, people would go in and explain that they wanted a kitchen suite or furniture for a bedroom, but could not pay the full price. He would ask them their names, tell them he knew their parents well and offer them a large discount or tell them they could pay 'at some later date', he explained. It was a way of buying silence and allegiance.

When the *narco* men went to jail, their women took over. The most infamous of these women capos was Josefa Charlín, daughter of the biggest capo of them all, Manuel Charlín. For years she moved with ease backwards and forwards across the Portuguese border with police often one, perhaps well-remunerated, step behind.

Josefa liked the Colombian way of doing business. That, at least, was what Colombian hitman Hernando Gómez claimed after shooting, allegedly on her behalf, Carmen Carballo and her husband Manuel Baúlo. Baúlo – who was threatening to give evidence against Josefa's father – died. Carmen, although wheelchair-bound, is still very much alive. Kidnappings and killings, by one side and the other, were reported to have followed. Josefa went on the run and remained loose for another five years, despite appearing, for example, at her son's graduation ceremony. She eventually went to jail for seventeen years for cocaine trafficking.

Two of the Baúlo children were arrested in 2005, accused of helping organise one of the biggest-ever cocaine smuggling operations into Britain.

Galicia's peasant women have long taken pride in their role as strong-willed matriarchs with considerable power over house, farm and family. With husbands often away at sea, they are used to coping single-handed. Rosaliá de Castro divided them into 'the widows of the dead and the living'. Running the family drug operation was, for Josefa Charlín, just an extension of that tradition.

There are few more telling monuments to the female capo than the Pazo de Baión. The *pazo* is an imposing country palace surrounded by 35 acres of trellised vines of *albariño* grapes. The main building is an imposing turn-of-the century invention replete with coats of arms, square turrets and battlements. It is famous in Spain, but not for wine. For this was the chosen home of another celebrated female drug smuggler, Esther Lago, and her husband Laureano Oubiña.

Both were eventually caught and locked up. At their trial, they tried to make out that they were simple farming folk. 'He only knows about farm work,' she insisted. Oubiña, meanwhile, said she was in charge of everything. 'If I want a thousand pesetas (four pounds) to drink a bottle of *albariño* with my friends, I ask her for them, and if she does not give them to me, I stay at home.'

None of this fitted with their palatial new property. When I rang on the video-phone at the *pazo's* elegant, wrought-iron entrance gate, a modern gate next to it slid silently open. A voice invited me to drive up the long, gently curved gravel path. The *pazo* was, temporarily, in the hands of the Spanish courts. A deal had been struck with a well-known wine company to tend the vines and produce the Pazo de Baión *albariño* wine until the place was auctioned off.

'The *narcos* are not exactly famous for their good taste,' warned an estate worker as he tugged at the *pazo*'s heavy front doors and prepared to show me around.

This was deliberate understatement. The *pazo* was built at the turn of the century by a Galician emigrant who made his fortune in Argentina and wanted to impress the neighbours when he returned with his ex-prostitute wife and thirteen children. The man had time to build a remarkable house before his wife gambled the fortune away. They never moved in, being forced to live in a smaller, older building on the estate. Styled after a French chateau, the *pazo*'s spacious rooms had beautiful, carved wooden ceilings and intricately laid parquet floors.

These, however, proved not to be to Esther's taste. The first thing she did after buying the house was have the floors pulled up. She replaced them with the sort of bleach-resistant, heavy, shiny brown tiles that one sees in Spanish motorway service areas. Outside, a large concrete plinth was erected on the flight of steps sweeping grandly up to the front door. The plinth had been, my guide insisted, due to hold a life-size statue of Esther herself. Four other plinths were also set up in the garden: there was one for her husband and partner in crime, Laureano Oubiña; there were two for her daughters; and the last one, conveniently tucked around a corner, was said to be for her mother-in-law.

Fortunately, she did not have time to indulge in much redecoration. First a judge arrested her, seizing the *pazo* and its contents. Then, when let out, she drove her SUV off an empty straight road into a wall. That was the end of Esther Lago. Was it an accident? Or was it another professional hit? Many believe it was the latter.

A wall of silence, however, surrounds the *narcos*. Their wealth has helped pump new cash into what, until recently, was one of western Europe's poorest, most backward regions. Fear and admiration prevent locals tipping police off, even though everybody knows, or claims to know, who they are. The wives of three traffickers who disappeared together one night, and are widely believed to have been murdered, are said to be swimming in cash. Their silence, it is said, was bought with money backed by threats. One local *narco*, the Vilagarcía schoolteacher told me, was famous for the glass-bottomed swimming pool he had on the second floor of his house. Naked prostitutes were said to frolic in it when he and his friends partied downstairs.

Some of the *narco* stories sounded too good to be true. Where did reality end and story-making start? In a region fond of myths and stories, I decided, the *narcos* were becoming the stuff of modern legends.

It was, perhaps, inevitable that the first public opposition to the *narcos* should come from another group of Galician women. In the port city of Vigo a group of mainly middle-class mothers who watched their children succumb to cocaine and other addictions decided to make the *narcos*' lives as difficult as possible. Their most famous action was to try to tear down the iron gates of the Pazo de Baión. They once chased Carmen Carballo down the street in her wheelchair after she had appeared in court. And they were there at Esther Lago's funeral, shouting '*asesino*', 'murderer', at her husband.

I met a roomful of these fierce mothers, some attired in fur coats, twin-sets and angora sweaters, in Vigo. Cocaine, not surprisingly, is both cheap and plentiful in Galicia. The mothers' aim was to break the silence surrounding the clans. 'Galicia is a closed society,' explained Carmen Avendaño, the group's leader. 'But Galician women are not naturally submissive. The *narcos* do not scare us.'

The *narcos* are one of the least attractive modern phenomena to have appeared in a country where the juxtaposition of old and new, accentuated by the speed of progress, is a constant source of surprise and wonder. Nowhere, however, is the contrast so great as in Galicia. Leave one of the fast new roads or motorways that, suddenly, seem to criss-cross it and you soon find yourself back in the lost world of country farmsteads, confusing road signs, eucalyptus and cows. 'Down a winding road, a turbo-charged diesel car overtakes a tractor, which is overtaking a cart,' is how Rivas explains it.

On a summer's afternoon I found myself, lost again, in the mountainous country – wolf territory – around Mondoñedo, near the border with Asturias. I was looking for somewhere called Santo Tomé. As usual, in a region where a single place name may be shared by up to two dozen locations, there was more than one choice. Also, as usual, I chose the wrong Santo Tomé first. I was looking for a *rapa das bestas*, a rounding-up of wild Galician ponies from the mountainside. By the time we got to the mountain top, however, the ponies had already been corralled and the foals branded to match that of their mother. They were handsome chestnut beasts, with dark manes, small, slim and famously sure-footed. Some of the Galician cowboy horse-herders rode them with just one rein. The horses were normally left to roam for their first three or four years of life. 'That way they learn to keep their footing on the uneven land up here,' one rider said.

At the *rapa das bestas* we bought T-shirts off a local environmental group and were given, as a present, a small, thin book with dark green, cardboard covers. The title was '*El Valle de Oro. Sociedad de instrucción, protección y recreo. Memoria Social 1928*'. It was a reprint of the report on the work of an association of emigrants from this valley who had fled its poverty for Cuba, made money and decided to form a charity to fund school-building and other activities back home. The book was a reminder of just how neglected Galicia had been. 'There probably wasn't a single family in the Valle de Oro that did not have a relative on that island. Cuba was, for us, something more than a distant country and Havana was more familiar than many a Spanish city,' commented Antonio Orol Pernas in an introduction to the book.

An estimated 900,000 Gallegos left the region in the nineteenth century, mainly for Latin America where, in some countries, those of Spanish origin are still routinely called *gallegos*. Boys, most unable to read or write, were shipped off at ages as young as twelve. Well over a million more followed in the twentieth century. 'The biggest Galician city is still Buenos Aires,' says Rivas. 'And the biggest Galician graveyard is the Cristóbal Colón cemetery in Havana.'

The Valle de Oro report contained pictures of smart, bow-tied and besuited Cuban–Galicians with carefully combed and oiled hair. Their sophistication contrasted with the pictures of the openings of their *Casa-escuelas* back in the valley, attended by peasants clad in their Sunday best of thick, woollen trousers and jackets, and collarless shirts with their top buttons done up.

'*Escuela que se abre, celda de cárcel que se cierra*' ('For every school that opens, a prison cell closes') the Cubans reminded their poverty-stricken brothers back home.

The emigrants even tried to intervene in the valley's courts. They had raised 160 dollars for the defence of a young man, Manuel Acebo Rey, who had murdered his sister's lover. In a letter to the governor of Lugo, they spelt out why Acebo should be treated leniently. 'The deceased (may God pardon him) cheated on and dishonoured the sister of the accused, who was working in his house. After leaving her in a sorry state, he then declined to have her in his service: she, naturally, returned to the parental home, where he would go to see her with one does not know what intentions . . . On one of these occasions he was required to explain himself by the master of the house, whose soul was greatly pained by his daughter's disgrace and the trampling of his honour: but, unable as he was to control his arrogance, the [deceased] man attacked the old man, which caused the son to intervene. There was a scuffle and, finding a kitchen knife to hand, young Manuel grabbed it and, without premeditation and in order to defend himself, killed the aggressor who had tricked his sister.'

Perhaps only the Irish can fully understand the Galician experience of emigration. For here, as there, famine drove the desperate away. Rosalía de Castro was, as a child, appalled by the sight of the hungry masses begging in her home town of Santiago de Compostela in 1853. 'I don't know how our country can resist such supreme pain,' she wrote, at a time when she herself contracted typhus on a trip to Muxía. Her husband, the *rexurdimento* writer Manuel Murgía, said those scenes were repeated in 1880 at a time when 'the inhabitants of the province of Lugo ate grass'.

Only the cows eat grass in Galicia now, but centuries of emigration mean there is an easy two-way flow between this corner of Spain and other parts of the world. Standing one day with the women dropping off their clams and cockles at the Vilagarcía *lonja* (the dockside shed where wholesalers buy the fresh shellfish) I found myself chatting to two with New Jersey accents. On other occasions I have bumped into Gallegos from Hammersmith, Notting Hill, Luton or Sydney, Australia. And those are just the ones with *anglosajón* connections. In the 1960s and 1970s Gallegos headed for the car factories of France and Germany and the restaurants of Switzerland. They have also been huge migrants within Spain. There is, for example, a Gallego restaurant on the corner of my block in Madrid. A second one lies fifty metres away. And, the same distance further on, there is a third. The result is that, at sometimes exorbitant prices, yesterday's catch from Vilagarcía's *lonja* is available for lunch around the corner today.

Poor, desperate and easily exploited, other Spaniards looked down on Galicians for centuries. They were the country's cheap labourers. A strong back and an obedient attitude were their only virtues. 'The Galician is a very similar animal to a man, invented to relieve the ass,' the nineteenth-century Madrid commentator Mariano José de Larra wrote.

Many *emigrantes*, and their children, can still vote in Spain. In fact, every ninth Galician voter lives abroad – usually thousands of miles away. Voters far outweigh actual residents in some towns. In the *concello* of Val do Dubra, for example, the vote is decided in Argentina, where some 40 per cent of its 7,318 voters live. In Avión, almost half the 4,370 voters live abroad, many in Mexico. Emigrants can, therefore, choose mayors in towns and villages some have not visited for decades or, indeed, may never have seen. It is some consolation for the *morriña* (nostalgia) Galicians are meant to feel for their homeland.

Manuel Fraga, while regional premier, did regular tours of Argentina and other Latin American countries. He is great friends with, of all people, that other long-lived populist of Galician origins, Cuba's Fidel Castro. On one visit to Buenos Aires, however, he was greeted by shouts of '*asesino*' as the children of exiled former Republicans reminded him of his own Francoist past and called out names of those killed by Franco's governments.

Here, as in the rest of Spain, emigrants often come home to retire. A large, modern house – just that much bigger than the neighbour's – is the traditional sign of their relative wealth. In the nineteenth century, for those who had made money in Cuba, the house would included a palm tree in the garden. These houses, the *casas de indianos*, can still be found, the palm trees bigger than ever, dotted around Galicia and Asturias.

Emigration was proof of the Galician's hard-done-by status. *Morriña*, felt for Galicia rather than Spain, was proof of their love for their own land. Neither explained the Galicians' continued attachment to a Spain that is, relatively, so unloved in the Basque Country and Catalonia. The reason for that, I felt, must lie in Galicia's place in the founding legends and myths of Spain. To understand them, I would have to follow a road already trodden by millions of pilgrims, to the Galician capital of Santiago de Compostela.

As miracles go, the one that brought the remains of Santiago El Mayor, St James The Apostle, to the site where a city named after him, Santiago de Compostela, would grow, requires a larger than normal suspension of rational thought. Legend has it that Santiago, brother of St John, was the first to bring Christianity to Spain. He later returned to Judaea, only to be put to the sword by King Herod Agrippa in AD 44. His disciples, Atanasio (Athanasius) and Teodoro (Theodore), placed his corpse on a boat with neither oars nor sails and, guided by an angel, travelled the length of the Mediterranean. They passed through the Strait of Gibraltar into the Atlantic. Then they headed north, eventually reaching the Galician Ría of Arousa. The trip took just a week. The boat came to a stop against a rock at the neck of the *ría* at a place known as Pedrón, Big Rock, and now known as Padrón. A devious heathen queen tried to trick Santiago's disciples by offering them a cart and two wild bulls to pull it. These fierce, dangerous beasts, however, turned into docile oxen as soon as they discovered the importance of the job in hand. They wandered inland, dragging the saint's body behind them, and came to a halt in the middle of a forest known as Libredón. This, it seems, was a sign that Santiago should be buried there. And so, they claim, he was.

Mysteriously, it took locals another eight centuries to discover this fact. Apparently the forest grew denser and greener, hiding its secret occupant. Then, sometime after 813, locals began to notice that, at night, they 'could see shining lights in the same place where it was said that angels had frequently appeared'. Closer investigation revealed the hidden tomb. Santiago de Compostela – said to derive from Campus stellae, the field of stars – was born. That, at least, is the official, Church version. The appearance of the tomb happened at a time when Christianity in Spain was, quite literally, cornered. The Moors had come, and then gone, from Galicia in the first half of the eighth century. The Christian *Reconquista* was still taking its first, unsteady steps out from Asturias and the north west.

News spread fast. Within a few decades, pilgrims were making their way here from across Europe. Santiago de Compostela would eventually be hailed as Christianity's third most important place of pilgrimage, after Rome and Jerusalem. By the twelfth century, the flow of pilgrims had become an avalanche. The expansion of the shrine followed that Galician habit of doing things in concentric circles. Around the tomb a church was built, then a cathedral and, around this, another, larger cathedral. Beyond the cathedral a wealthy city – the largest in Galicia until the end of the nineteenth century – of stonemasons, religious bureaucrats and, then as now, pilgrim-fleecers began to grow.

The great Muslim general Almanzor sacked the city in 997, destroying much of Santiago. He took the cathedral's bells to Córdoba but left the tomb intact. According to legend, he ordered his troops to mount guard beside it after finding an elderly monk praying there.

This act of Muslim generosity was all the more remarkable given that Santiago had, according to legend, miraculously appeared on a white horse at the Battle of Clavijo in 859. There he tipped the balance in favour of the Christian armies against the Moors. He gained the nickname '*Matamoros*', 'The Moorslayer', as a result. His appearances in battle, always on the side of Spain, allegedly number more than forty since then. Perhaps that is why, in a remarkable example of insensitivity, Spanish troops sent to support the occupation of Iraq in 2004 wore the Moorslayer's red cross as their symbol. More importantly, however, it made this city – and this saint – part of the story of Spain. That, in turn, helps Galicians feel that Spain is theirs.

Franco, another Galician, was an avid fan. The old battle cry of '¡Santiago y Cierra España!' 'St James and close up Spain [safely from its enemies]!' was one of his regime's slogans. When he entered the cathedral here to get his indulgence in the *Año Santo* of 1938, Archbishop Muñiz de Pablos prayed for 'eternal light and success for the undefeated Caudillo'. He later stood beside Franco and gave a stiff-armed fascist salute to the crowds.

Unsurprisingly, given that St James died 2,500 miles away, other theories about who is buried here have also emerged. One favours Prisciliano, a charismatic renegade bishop reputedly of Roman–Galician origins with an abundant and enthusiastic female following. He was beheaded in 385 by the Emperor Magnus Maximus. His alleged crimes included sorcery, diffusing obscene doctrines, conducting strange midnight meetings with groups of women and praying in the nude. His modern-day supporters argue that Compostela actually owes its name to a late Latin expression, derived from *componere*, for 'little burial place'. Certainly, archaeologists have found early Christian graves here dating back to before the ninth century 'discovery' of the tomb. 'This was never "The Field of Stars", which was something invented by those favouring his usurper,' maintains one recent history of the charismatic heretic. Some Spaniards, it seems, would rather there was a real Galego buried here, instead of a Palestinian fisherman from Galilee.

An eleventh-century pope declared any year when Santiago Day fell on a Sunday to be a special Holy Year. That meant plenary indulgence for those who made it here, confessed, attended Mass and gave to charity. It was a ticket out of that very Galician obsession, Purgatory.

Santiago de Compostela's name became famous across Europe. Dante declared the definition of a pilgrim to be 'that they go to the House of Galicia'. Goethe claimed that the idea of Europe itself was made on the path to Compostela.

The *camino* was the first great European tourist route. Its first travel book, the twelfth-century Codex Calixtinus, described it as a sort of walking Tower of Babel. 'They come from all climates and nations of the world and even further away [*sic*], French, Normans, Scots, Irish, Welsh, Teutons, Gascons, those from Navarre, Basques, Provincials, Anglo-Saxons, Britons, those from Cornwall, Poitiers, Danes, Norwegians, Russians, Sicilians, Asians, Indians, Cretans, Jerusalemers, Antiochans, Arabs, Moors, Libyans, and many others of all tongues, who came in companies or phalanxes and they all sing in unison to the Apostle,' its French author, said to be a friar called Aimeric Picaud, wrote.

Picaud promised pilgrims 'absence of vice, mortification of the body, increase of virtue, forgiveness of sins, penitence . . . distancing from Hell and the protection of the Heavens'.

He also warned however, that you needed a strong stomach to make it to Santiago de Compostela. 'Whether it be the fish which are so vulgarly called barbel or that which the Poitvins call the Alose (shad) . . . in no part of Spain nor in Galicia should you eat them, for without any doubt you will die soon afterwards or fall ill.'

A sixteenth-century British traveller, Andrew Boorde, agreed that mortification of the body was fully guaranteed. 'I assure all the world that I had rather go five times to Rome out of England, than one to Compostella; by water it is no pain, but by land it is the greatest journey that one Englishman can go on,' he wrote.

When George Borrow came here in 1833, with the Carlist wars raging, his descriptions of living conditions could have come from the era of the *castros*. 'Roofs were thatched, dark and moist, and not infrequently covered with rank vegetation. There were dunghills before the doors, and no lack of pools and puddles. Immense swine were stalking about, intermingled with naked children. The interior of the cabins corresponded with their external appearance: they were filled with filth and misery.'

By that stage, the *camino* was in serious decline. St James's miraculous bones had been lost some two hundred and fifty years earlier, apparently after being hidden out of fear that

English pirates would get them. The Black Death, Protestantism and local warfare nearly killed the *camino* off. In 1867 only forty pilgrims could be found in the city on St James's Day. The bones were found again in 1878 and a papal bull was issued to state that they were genuine. They now sit in a silver urn under the high altar.

As the number of pilgrims dwindled, the first cultural tourists arrived. The Victorians fell so in love with the Pórtico de la Gloria, the twelfth-century facade sculpted by Master Mateo, that a cast was made for what was then the South Kensington Museum, now the Victoria and Albert. John Charles Robinson, sent to write a report on it, compared it to Michelangelo's work in the Sistine Chapel. 'I have no hesitation in stating that I consider it incomparably the most important monument of sculpture and ornamental detail of its epoch,' he said.

The Pórtico had become part of the inside of the cathedral when a new, baroque and infinitely inferior facade was built in the eighteenth century. Richard Ford, visiting in the mid-nineteenth century, complained that Master Mateo's work had been disfigured. 'The vulgar hand of some local house painter has bedaubed the central figure of Christ, and painted the countenances of several apostles, so as to give them the appearance of purblind wooden dolls,' he wrote. Master Mateo, who immodestly placed a statue of himself at the base of one column, is now revered almost as much as Santiago. Pilgrims queue up to rub foreheads with him, hoping his genius will be passed on.

Tourist board planning, cheap pilgrims' hostels and New Age esoteric superstition have, once more, made the pilgrimage a phenomenon of the masses. The routes to Santiago now fill every summer with backpackers who have replaced the traditional pilgrim's conch shell and drinking gourd with the modern fetish objects of eco-tourism: Goretex, Timberland, mountain bikes, mobile phones and GPS navigation devices. In Holy Years the city is inundated with the curious and the pious. The cathedral fills, cash tills ring, coins drop into the hats put out by bagpiping buskers and everyone, it seems, is happy. Numbers have increased twenty-fold over the past fifteen years. More than 70,000 people a year now pick up the sheet of paper in Latin, the 'Compostela', from the cathedral's Pilgrim's Office to show they have slogged along the obligatory 100 km of *camino*. In the Middle Ages they would have gone on to Finisterre to marvel at the end of the world. Now they head for the souvenir shops and Santiago airport.

Over the past decade a new sort of people have been arriving in Galicia, this time to stay. A trickle of younger *emigrantes*, or their children, are coming home. The reason for their return sits on an ugly industrial estate at Arteixo, near La Coruña. Here, under the roofs of a network of uninviting, cavernous modern buildings, clothes for more than 2,500 fashion shops in fifty-six countries move along 120 miles of rails. This, some say, is where the future of Galicia is being built.

It is known by the unexciting name of Inditex. It is the personal empire of one man, a reclusive Galician billionaire called Amancio Ortega. For years Ortega was remarkable for two things: he was Spain's richest man; and nobody had ever seen a photograph of him. His employees knew him well. He would wander the ever-expanding shop floor in his shirtsleeves and eat in the company canteen. But no photographer ever got close to him.

Media paranoia and, some claimed, fear of kidnap, kept him a faceless mystery. Spaniards, meanwhile, found that they were all wearing his clothes, bought from store chains with names like Zara, Massimo Dutti, Stradivarius and Bershka. His photographic coming out did not happen until, as he prepared to float shares on the Madrid stock exchange, a passport-sized picture appeared in the 1999 Inditex accounts.

For such a historic photograph, it was unremarkable. Amancio Ortega refused to don a tie. With his jowly face, stout build and receding grey hair, he looked like an average, small-town Galician businessman. Only his unseasonal tan spoke of a man worth, at the time, 4 billion pounds – more, according to *Forbes* magazine, than anybody in Britain. He remains one of the half-dozen richest people in western Europe and one of the forty richest in the world. That is good going for a man who started out, at thirteen, as a shirt-maker's delivery boy in La Coruña. He learnt to cut and design clothes in his sister's dining room. His first sales hits, when he branched out on his own, were housecoats and dressing gowns.

Ortega's favourite spot is said to be the womenswear design section of Zara. His eye is obviously good. Even most French *Vogue* readers admit to shopping regularly in Zara – paying a fraction of the price they might pay for clothes elsewhere.

Ortega employs some 45,000 people. Much of his sewing is still done by seamstress co-operatives spread throughout rural Galicia and northern Portugal. One of the secrets of his success, indeed, is that so many Galician women can sew.

Rivals use words like 'innovative' and 'devastating' to describe Ortega's impact on global fashion retailing. His secret, developed over the past thirty years, is simple. Zara, the flagship that turns in the bulk of sales, has some two hundred designers. New models can get from the drawing board to the shop in two weeks. It allows a lightning response to fickle fashion tastes the world over. They call it 'live fashion', and churn out 10,000 new Zara models a year. Customers are treated like political focus groups, their tastes minutely monitored and instantly responded to.

There is no brash self-promotion and no fashion posturing. Ortega does not give interviews. He does not even advertise. Instead he bombards shops with new styles, dropping ones that do not sell and mass-producing ones that do. Advertising, he believes, is a pointless distraction. When a famous Spanish actress asked to do a photo shoot in one of his shops, Ortega said no. 'You haven't got the idea yet have you?' he told the newly appointed executive who suggested it would be good for the Zara name. It seems somehow appropriate that a Galician, and one so suspicious of showing off, should have so thoroughly punctured the mystique of fashion.

Ortega, in his faceless way, is the symbol of new Galicia. Somehow, he still fits alongside the old superstitious Galicia of the coffin-occupiers at Santa Marta de Ribarteme. Perhaps it is because Ortega, in his secrecy, seems just as superstitious and mistrustful as a Galician peasant queuing up with his *exvoto.* Or, maybe, Ortega's silence is just *retranca*, a good-humoured attempt to confuse those who try to read the Galician soul.

Ortega's clothes are becoming the new face not just of Galicia, but of Spain itself. In the new world of globalisation, he is Spain's first global conquistador. His self-effacing, hard-working, innovative manner, however, does not fit the image we foreigners have built for Spaniards.

Mention Spain, indeed, and most people prefer to think of the loud, the extravagant and the colourful. Another modern Spaniard who has triumphed around the globe fits that image much better. Oscar-winning director Pedro Almodóvar has filled cinema screens around the world with kitsch colours, outlandish characters and – though often in a subversive form – the traditional icons of Spain. It is a story that is best started, as the opening line of Don Quixote says, 'In a village of La Mancha . . .'

13

Moderns and Ruins

At the Kodak Theatre in Los Angeles, California, it was 5 o'clock in the afternoon but in Calzada de Calatrava, a large farming village on the parched, red-soiled plain of La Mancha, it was already 2 o'clock in the morning. The only living beasts visible in the streets were the cats, busy shredding bin bags and scattering the contents across the pavements. Candles burnt at the shrine in the hermitage of Saint Isidore, lit by elderly women seeking divine support for the village's favourite son – film director Pedro Almodóvar.

Apart from that, the only sign of life – as the director competed for two Oscars with his film *Talk to Her* – was in the Círculo Agrícola, the village's faded, if spacious, Farmers' Club. The hat racks and polished table legs suggested this had once been the smart place to be seen in Calzada de Calatrava. Here in the public saloon where, as a boy, Almodóvar saw his first films, some forty of us had gathered to watch the ceremony. On one wall, under a vast black-and-white picture of the nearby castle where an order of medieval knights was founded, a screen had been set up. The television picture from Los Angeles was projected onto the screen, but the words being said were lost in the disastrous acoustics of the room.

We were a mixture of the young, the elderly, the curious and the drunk. Sleepily, we awaited the moment, three hours later, when the Oscar winner would be announced. A victory for Almodóvar in either of the mainstream categories for which he had been nominated (as best director or for the best original screenplay) would be the first ever of its kind for a Spanish film – and a rare tribute to a foreign-language director. His double candidacy was further proof that Almodóvar had become Spain's new face to the world. From Hollywood to the art-house cinemas of Europe, his sometimes kitsch, often camp and almost always subversive take on Spanish life and mores was the colour-drenched new facade of the country.

His message is taken seriously. In 2005, *Time* magazine declared *Talk to Her* to be the film of the decade (so far). 'At its simplest level, this transgressively witty film is about how a hospital orderly's sexual obsession achieves the unlikely awakening of a comatose woman. But there's actually nothing simple about this lovely, lightly dancing film's reflections on all the big topics: life, death, dreams – and ballet,' *Time*'s critics declared.

As the night wore on, the drunks got drunker and the rest of us got sleepier. Spaniards are generally good at holding their alcohol – they are not given to the binge-drinking, falling-over nights out of northern Europeans. Tonight, however, one or two were well over the top. One of these – another medical orderly – had decided I should be his new friend. He drew up a plastic chair and leaned over at me, his head almost resting on my shoulder. 'We should go to the hills of the Sierra Morena to watch the sun go up,' he suggested. 'We can take some pork sausage with us.'

Spaniards, wherever they are, know how to stay up late. Village fiestas always last until the small hours of the morning. On fiesta nights children scamper around the streets until they drop. As the night goes on they can be seen asleep on public benches or in their parents' arms. Spaniards have a special verb for seeing the night through until the sun rises: *trasnochar*, literally to cross the night. It has been a point of pride amongst my friends to occasionally link night with day and arrive at the office without having slept. An even greater point of pride is that nobody at the office should notice. In playful Andalucía, meanwhile, a decent *juerga* can sometimes be measured in days. Siestas, sadly, are largely a thing of the past (except where it is too hot to work in the early afternoon). It is still a mystery to me how so many Spaniards can function on so little sleep.

In Calzada de Calatrava a brave few were trying to uphold the tradition of Spanish nocturnal staying-power. The local florist, a small, formal man, recalled how Almodóvar used to come and play at his house as a boy. He was always 'a bit special', he said. 'As a boy he stood out, all right. He would do things that other people didn't do. If he thought people were ignoring him he would do some mischief to get our attention,' he remembered. He was about to tell me a tale of some prank involving his chickens when his wife clamped a hand on his knee to shut him up. Discretion was being called for. The village's most famous son should not be spoken of badly. Apart from that, however, few people could remember anything very much about him. He had moved away as a child and now made only occasional family visits to the old family house. His parents' graves, however, were here. Calzada de Calatrava, as Almodóvar's brother once put it, 'is the sort of place where people spend their whole life saving for a decent headstone in the cemetery'.

Sitting in a moulded plastic chair for three hours, there was plenty of time to reflect on a simple conundrum. How is it that the arch-proponent of modernity in Spanish culture – a man who has triumphed around the globe – should come from such a sleepy, backward, dry and barren cultural void? The answer became apparent well before Almodóvar lifted his 'best original screenplay' statuette above his head shortly after 5 a.m. It was that one would do anything to escape a place like this. If ever there was a case for throwing out the old and bringing in the new, this was it.

The party folded soon after Almodóvar had lifted his statuette. I went out into the street in front of the Círculo Agrícola. Anastasio, one of the one-man-band cultural animators who are the saving grace of places like this, was rummaging around in his car boot. He pulled out three fireworks – large rockets. He lit them one by one, there in the street. They exploded above the sleeping *pueblo*. There were three loud bangs. I expected half of the 5,000 inhabitants to appear shouting – in anger or joy – on their balconies. Nothing, however, stirred. One newspaper reported 'great festivities' in Calzada de Calatrava. It obviously had not been there.

Almodóvar's first films – with their kitsch 'new wave' costumes, electric colours, complex sexual relationships and relentless drug-taking – were all a reaction to this drab, hard environment. 'It was the kind of harsh place where nobody understood sensuality, the joy of life or even the idea of colour,' Almodóvar once explained. His mother, who plays small roles in some of his films, wore black – the once obligatory colour of mourning – for twenty years as a young woman. 'Perhaps that is why there is so much colour in my films,' he said. Trips to the cinema were liable to be cut short by paternal disapproval. Almodóvar's father, who traded goods off the back of a mule, would order them out if anything too risqué appeared on screen. A family outing to see *War and Peace* ended after the second kiss.

'I was not born in the right family, in the right town, in the right language or in the right moment to make movies . . . It's like dreaming of being a bullfighter when you're born in Japan or England,' he once explained.

His *pueblo* upbringing, however, shaped Almodóvar's future. 'It allowed me to discover what I didn't want to be, the mentality I didn't want to live with.'

When Spaniards want to refer to something, or someone, as backward, they often say they are '*de pueblo*', 'from the village'. Village life means old-fashioned values, hardship and lack of education. It also means the suffocating atmosphere and intense rivalries of a place where everybody watches everybody else. The *pueblo* is one of those things that not just Almodóvar, but Spain as a whole, in its headlong rush into modernity, has been desperate to leave behind. His early films, the writer Maruja Torres said, represented exactly that. 'It is a synthesis of what we want to leave behind, and what we want to have,' she said.

Flight from the countryside has been the biggest revolution in Spanish life over the past century. Hundreds of villages have, in fact, been abandoned altogether. Many more have just one or two families left in them. The killer blow has often been provided by electricity at a neighbouring village. That has been enough to force out the last few residents of those places it had not got to –

who have gone and plugged themselves into the grid at the other village.

The process of decline is all too familiar. First the young families go, then the primary school closes. This is followed soon after by the shop and – the death blow – the bar. Mayors in some remote rural communities have started importing Latin American immigrants in an attempt to stop themselves disappearing off the map. They have paid for whole families to fly from, say, Argentina to underpopulated Teruel. Some one hundred villages most under threat – mainly in rural Galicia, the highlands of Valencia, the bleak, harsh Maestrazgo hills of Teruel, or the slopes of the Pyrenees mountains in Huesca – have even formed a club to seek new occupants from abroad. It has meant reversing the time-worn flow of Spaniards towards Latin America that started in the sixteenth century.

The *pueblo* is the old world. The city is the new. And, for most Spaniards, new is infinitely better than old. This is something that is obvious in a hundred small things – a virtual absence of second-hand shops, for instance, or the rarity of old cars. Nowhere is it more patent, however, than in architecture. Here great new things are being built – and great old things are left to crumble.

Ask famous international architects like Norman Foster, Richard Rogers, Richard Meier, Frank Gehry or Arata Isozaki where the best place in Europe to build exciting new buildings is, and the answer will most likely be: 'Spain'. A vast amount of, mainly public, money has been poured into giving the international gods of architecture spectacular new contracts for spectacular new buildings across the land.

This craving for new buildings is partly due to Spain's status as a 'new' country with plenty of space, new wealth and fresh needs. Even where the great architects are not at work, cities expand visibly. New motorways and high-speed-train tracks, meanwhile, roll out across the country. This is often thanks to European Union funds. There is something about the relationship between spare space and development which makes me think not of other places in Europe but, once again, of the US or Australia. For Spain has plenty of room to grow. Greater Madrid, for example, can keep expanding for dozens of miles in most directions before running into significant geographical, urban or other barriers.

The desire for great new architecture is insatiable. The bigger the name, the better: Foster has the Bilbao metro system (whose glass-clad station entrances are affectionately known as *fosteritos*) and Barcelona's telecommunications tower; Rogers has Madrid's new airport and a transformed bull-ring in Barcelona; Richard Meier has his MACBA modern art centre in Barcelona; Frank Gehry has his Bilbao Guggenheim and a giant monumental fish on Barcelona's water front; Arata Isozaki has Barcelona's Olympic indoor sports stadium and a museum in La Coruña; and that list does not even include the prodigious home-grown talent, and output, of Rafael Moneo, Santiago Calatrava or Enric Miralles. Calatrava, a polymath – sculptor, artist, architect and master engineer – has designed a dove-shaped airport for Bilbao, daring bridges like Seville's Alamillo Bridge, and Valencia's soaring complex known as the City of Arts and Sciences.

Spain is currently in a league with Japan and Holland as the new experimental laboratory of world architecture. Rogers, who does almost a quarter of his work in Spain, has called it 'Europe's architectural hothouse'. The can-do, even must-do, attitude in Spain amazes him. '[Madrid airport] is the biggest infrastructure project in Europe. It's three times the size of [Heathrow's] Terminal Five which is our biggest airport in Britain. We won T5 as a competition fourteen years ago and work hasn't started yet; we won Madrid four years ago and it's halfway up,' he explained in one newspaper interview.

There is an essential optimism to modern Spaniards, a belief that life is always going to get better – and that it will do so at the same velocity it has acquired over the past three decades. Progress is not only unstoppable, it happens at a dizzying speed.

A recent Rogers conversation with the head of Madrid's subway system reportedly went like this. 'Subway man: "How many kilometres do you need?" Rogers: "Ten kilometres." Subway man: "Ten kilometres? We guarantee one kilometre per month

– ten months." Rogers: "We need two new stations." Subway man: "One month each – twelve months. If you want to be kind, give me fourteen months."' That deal eventually ran into financing problems. The subway man's reply, however, was a sign of how used Spaniards are to building the new. Tunnelling machines are constantly at work under Barcelona and Madrid, driving through new metro and rail lines.

Cities have now started to compete to have great buildings. When Bilbao got its Guggenheim, San Sebastián, the next city along the coast, had to get its Rafael Moneo Kursaal conference centre. When La Coruña got its Arata Isozaki Museum of Mankind, neighbouring Vigo got an Aldo Rossi maritime museum. Santiago de Compostela, the other major Galician city, now awaits a Peter Eisenmann arts complex.

This love of modernity hides what Spaniards sometimes call an *huida hacia delante*, or 'running away forwards', this time in its cultural form. The facades of these 'brave new world' buildings hide a certain disrespect, even contempt, for the old. For these new shrines to modern architecture divert attention away from the numerous ancient churches, hermitages, monasteries, fortresses or castles that are falling down – buckling under the weight of time and the force of nature.

It is probably unfair to criticise Spain for its treatment of its historic buildings. They are so many, and so widely spread, that it is difficult to know what to do with them. Prehistoric, Greek, Roman, Muslim, Romanesque, Mudéjar, Mozárabe and Gothic buildings, or the remains of them, dot the landscape. This is a land of eight thousand castles and other fortifications and hundreds of monasteries and convents. Much of the best has been saved, if not always in the finest taste. Such a widely scattered, and rich, national heritage is a headache, however, for those whose job it is to decide what should be kept and what left to rot. Some of those buildings are in the same villages that were abandoned by their residents decades ago. Should a Romanesque church tower be saved in a village where no one lives and which only a handful of adventurous types with four-wheel-drive vehicles, trail bikes, mountain bikes or sturdy walking boots will ever visit? Does it matter if, as happened recently to the Torreón de Santis – an eleventh-century fortress in Aragón – the last remaining section of its battlements comes tumbling down? And should Spaniards care if the Romanesque paintings that were still visible on the walls of the hermitage at Alcozar, in Soria, in the 1970s have now faded out of sight, or that the building itself looks set to collapse?

This state of affairs is a delight for visitors who like discovering ruins on their own. In Soria, one of southern Europe's most sparsely populated regions, it means one can stride through the largely unspoilt hilltop ruins of the vast tenth-century Moorish fortress of Gormaz – once reckoned to be the biggest citadel in Europe. The fortress is not on any of the main tourist routes of Spain. Nor, in fairness, has it been left to fall down completely. It is unspoilt, however, by the visitors centres, gift shops, cafeterias or any of the other paraphernalia of overgroomed ruins. Visitors may find they have the whole one-kilometre perimeter to themselves. It is an opportunity to imagine the times of Rodrigo Diaz de Vivar, El Cid Campeador, the legendary eleventh-century freebooting knight and mercenary. He once held this castle as it stood on the front line, changing hands continuously, between Moor and Christian. The scale of the task of conserving ancient Spain is exemplified by Gormaz. A village of just nineteen people, it also boasts the remains of a Celtic *castro*, a fourth-century-BC necropolis with some 1200 (Iberian) graves, a hermitage – possibly dating back to the seventh century – with medieval wall paintings and an eighteen-span Roman-origin bridge which was rebuilt in the nineteenth century. That works out at one major monument per family.

In the early twentieth century one could come here and snap up entire ruins. American and other buyers did exactly that, shipping them home stone by stone. One hermitage from nearby San Esteban de Gormaz was dismantled and shipped to Catalonia in the 1920s – though it had originally been destined for the US.

There are many examples of how, in architecture, the new gets priority over the old. So it was that Barcelona – generally one of the best conservators of its own past – managed to put up its Isozaki and Foster buildings in time for the 1992 Olympics, while the museum that was to house the world's finest collection of Romanesque wall-paintings – as well as a wealth of Gothic and Baroque art – was not fully opened for another dozen years.

The Prado Museum in Madrid, meanwhile, is now overcoming years of chaos, neglect, leaking roofs and botched repair work. An ambitious new expansion is to see it absorb a number of neighbouring buildings. Unfortunately, this includes ensuring the virtual disappearance from public view of the cloisters of the nearby Jerónimos Church. These, though rebuilt in the nineteenth century, date back to the sixteenth century. They have now been swallowed up by a brick cube by Moneo. A campaign to leave the cloisters alone was greeted with indifference by politicians and *Madrileños* as a whole – in a city which can hardly claim to be bursting with sixteenth-century buildings.

When ruins are restored, Spain sometimes falls into the temptation of 'improving' and sanitising them. The arch-example is the Roman theatre at Sagunto, near Valencia, where the Supreme Court had to order that the 'renovation' – which included large amounts of spanking-new, shiny marble – be completely undone.

'Every day we awake with another piece of architecture . . . left to die so that speculators can carry out, under the name of restoration, changes that are both unnecessary and irreversible,' one specialist architect, Antonio-José Mas-Guindal, says.

Even the 'old new' can be swept away. One of Madrid's landmark modern buildings, the Christmas tree-like *la Pagoda* of Miguel Fisac, has already been pulled down to make way for an anonymous glass office block – thus stymieing moves to make it a 'protected' building.

All this, perhaps, should not be surprising in a country where new houses and apartments are worth more than old ones or where *moderno* is always a positive adjective. New apartments in Madrid fetch 20 per cent more, per square metre, than old ones. Older apartments and houses are, anyway, almost inevitably deemed to need *reforma total*, complete renovation. The reason given for this is often one of 'hygiene'. It as if there was actually something sick or infectious about the old. It is heartbreaking to see the skips of Madrid fill up with patterned 1920s *cerámica hidráulica* floor tiles, made from pressed concrete, old wrought-iron radiators and wooden window frames. The latter are often replaced by PVC.

The situation is even more alarming outside the major cities, in those much maligned *pueblos* where, thanks to the internal migration of the Franco years, most city-dwellers' parents or grandparents came from. In Las Navas del Marqués, a relatively prosperous town in Ávila province that lives off weekend tourism from Madrid, I have watched as brick summer villas from the early half of the twentieth century are torn down to be replaced by crude, ugly apartment blocks. Town planning has failed across the country – even in Catalonia, that supposed haven of architectural and urban dignity. A Catalan friend once asked me doubtfully what I thought Catalans had, if anything, in common with other Spaniards. She obviously thought there was very little. We were walking along the seafront at Badalona, a town just north of Barcelona, so I pointed to the one- and two-storey beach-front houses that were being knocked down and replaced by gleaming new blocks of flats. Even she had to nod her head.

The eagerness with which the new is embraced has something to do with the memory, real or inherited, of poverty. Again, there is an element of *huida*, of flight. Old, in many minds, still equals poor.

The countryside fares little better. Many of Spain's frequent summer fires are put down to speculators seeking building permission. With the land already burnt, the logic goes, the local town hall will be unable to find 'environmental' reasons for banning building. That will make the building of an *urbanización* of weekend *chalets* or the creation of an industrial estate, that much easier.

One of the greatest abuses of all was to rid Europe of what is said to be the only river on the continent that reaches the sea in a waterfall. The spectacle of the River Xallas, in Galicia, pouring from a height of 100 metres into the Atlantic, disappeared in 1986. This Galician Niagara was sacrificed to a local factory which built two dams along the course of the river. Public protest finally saw water redirected to the waterfall – but only on occasional Sundays and then only for a few hours.

Part of this love of the new is a desire to catch up. Spaniards spent the best part of two centuries looking enviously over the Pyrenees at what was happening in the rest of Europe. When a Spaniard wants to be down on his own country – or complain, in a rare burst of irony, of an old French attitude to it – he still sometimes reproduces a tired, overused phrase: 'Africa, you know, starts at the Pyrenees.'

Suspicious Spaniards, or those whose pride is hurt by the way foreigners have written about their country, are not completely without reason. For European and *anglosajón* writers Spain has, until quite recently, always been 'the other' – a shining example of what they, themselves, are not.

Anglosajones, especially, are accused of having spent the past four hundred years putting about a version of Spain known as the '*leyenda negra*', 'the black legend'. From the times of Philip II – who sent the Invincible Armada to a stormy grave in 1588 – onwards, they claim, we have had it in for them. Amongst other stories to have been exaggerated beyond belief by *anglosajones* and *protestantes* generally, they say, are Philip's imprisonment of his son Carlos (and his subsequent death, turned into an opera by Verdi and a play by Schiller), the extent of the Inquisition and the treatment of the Jews, Moors or *moriscos*. Foreign criticism of the country's Roman Catholic hierarchy is still, for some diehard conservatives, just an extension by *anti-españoles* of the centuries-old plot to do them down.

Until the twentieth century, Spain caught the attention of only the braver or more rugged of Europe's great writers. Those of a more delicate frame of mind gave it a wide berth. It was too primitive, too mountainous and too dangerous. There were gangs of bandits. There were sudden, violent upheavals. It lacked acceptable restaurants or decent food of any kind. Travellers came back with tales of ragged hordes of filthy, naked children and of people living in caves. Protestants saw sinister flocks of raven-like priests still stained by the sadistic cruelty of the Inquisition. If you wanted museums, Greek or Roman ruins, art, opera, classical music or poetry – better Italy, France or central Europe. The Prado Museum, the baroque finery of Seville and a few remnants of Al Andalus were deemed its few saving graces. 'To travel in Andalucía you need three francs a day – and a gun,' said one Frenchman who accompanied the writer Alexandre Dumas on a mid-nineteenthth-century trip.

Spain was not, generally, part of the Grand Tour. It did not have the sophisticated allure of Italy or, even, the ancient charm of Greece. A young Alfred Tennyson was briefly attracted to the cause of Spanish liberalism against the absolutist Fernando VII. His friend William Boyd was executed on the beach at Málaga after trying to start a revolt in 1831. Tennyson later extracted vengeance against the Spaniard in his elegy to Sir Richard Grenville's foolish and suicidal attempt, two centuries earlier, to fight his way through a fleet of fifty-three Spanish vessels in the appropriately named *Revenge*. Tennyson's Spaniards are 'Inquisition dogs', 'the children of the devil' and 'a swarthier alien crew'.

Still, historical chauvinism is a two-edged sword. My children will learn at school that Sir Francis Drake was a *pirata*, rather than the valiant hero I was taught about. They will be getting a more accurate picture of the man who robbed the Spanish blind in the New World and 'singed the king of Spain's beard' by sinking his ships in Cádiz harbour, than I did.

Byron spent a few weeks visiting south-west Spain, skirting around the ongoing Peninsular War, in 1809. He saw a bullfight, refused the amorous advances of his Seville landlady, Josefa Beltram and heard the following ditty '*La Reyna es una puta/ El Rey es un cabrón/Viva el rey Fernando/ Y muera Napoleon*' 'The Queen's a whore, the king is a cuckold, Long live King Fernando, And death to Napoleon'. It was enough, however, to help inspire him to write his *Don Juan*. Perhaps it was Josefa's very matter-of-fact forwardness that helped make Byron's version of the great Latin lover, unlike most of the numerous other Don Juans or Don Giovannis conjured up by European literature and opera, someone pursued by – rather than a cruel pursuer of – women.

Those writers who made it here in the nineteenth century were often wild adventurers. Their lurid tales of bandits, public executions, castanet-clicking dancing girls and bullfights often sold well. France gained a sudden interest in popular Spanish culture thanks, in part, to the wilful, capricious and man-devouring Carmen of Prosper Mérimée and, in turn, Bizet's opera.

Right up until the middle of the twentieth century, Spain was deemed the preserve of the courageous. 'Neither in France nor in Italy can one be so frankly frightened,' wrote V. S. Pritchett in 1954, after thirty years travelling to Spain, including a two-year spell as correspondent for the *Christian Science Monitor* in the 1920s. Visitors often felt, in fact, that it was not Europe at all. It was, if not Africa, at least part of the east. The border itself was a place where Pritchett could 'feel the break'.

'Spain is the old and necessary enemy of the West. There we learn our history upside down and see life exposed to the skin,' said Pritchett who, for precisely that reason, could not get enough of it. On his way back there in the 1950s, he found himself 'impatient for the drama of the frontier and for the violent contrasts, the discontent and indifference of Spain'. The continent's Wild West awaited.

For European writers, Spain was often like this. It was so opposite as to provide proof of the values – or, alternatively, the deficiencies – of their own cultures. For the Romans, the men of what they called Hispania were people who enjoyed war, cleaned their teeth in stale urine, ate bear steaks, drank bull's blood and read the future in the entrails of their executed enemies. For the handful of Romantics prepared to rough it through Spain, they were noble savages, blessedly untouched by the polluting atmosphere of industrial civilisation. For the Wellington-loving Richard Ford – writing in the early nineteenth century – they were at once charming, but also proof of the natural superiority of the British race. George Borrow, meanwhile, wallowed, more entertainingly and possibly more fictionally, in Spain's nineteenth-century low-life. Frenchman Théophile Gautier came, amongst other things, to ogle at the cigarette-rolling girls of Seville's tobacco factories in 1840. He was as enraptured by what he considered their animal sexuality, as he was by the 'violent emotions' and colour of the bullfight. He wrote:

> We were taken to the work-rooms where the leaves are rolled into cigars. From five to six hundred women are employed in preparing them. As soon as we set foot in the room, we were assailed by a hurricane of noise: they were all talking, singing and quarrelling at the same time. I have never heard such an uproar. They were for the most part young, and some of them were very pretty. The extreme negligence of their dress enabled one to appreciate their charms in full liberty. Some of them had a cigar-end stuck resolutely in the corner of their mouths, with the assurance of a cavalry officer.

Mérimée's Carmen, who was one of the cigarette girls, became the prototype of the wild and sensuous Andalusian woman. 'She wore a red skirt, very short, which displayed her white silk stockings, with more than one hole in them, and tiny shoes of red morocco, tied with flame-coloured ribbon . . . She had a cassia flower in the corner of her mouth . . . and walked along swaying her hips like a filly from the Córdoba stud farm. In my country, a woman in such a costume would have made everyone cross himself. At Seville, everyone paid her some gallant compliment,' one of her victims, the Basque Navarrese Don José, recounts in Mérimée's novel. 'Finally, taking the cassia flower, she threw it with a twist of her thumb and struck me right between the eyes. It seemed to me, *señor*, that a bullet had hit me.'

Bullfighting was, for some visitors, the ultimate expression of the Spanish attitude to life and death. No one was as obsessed by the bullfight as Ernest Hemingway. He found Spaniards both noble and violent in the manly kind of fashion that he admired. The honour, pride and cruelty of the confrontation between the legendary 1950s bullfighters Luis Miguel Dominguín and Antonio

Ordóñez epitomised a rugged masculinity that he sought wherever he went. The wine-fuelled bonhomie and man-against-beast adrenalin rush of the running of the bulls during Pamplona's San Fermín fiestas fitted happily into this virile world. Men could prove themselves in front of half a dozen charging, horned, half-ton animals. With so much overexcited testosterone about, women, or at least visiting ones, did not really fit in, Hemingway thought. 'Pamplona is no place to bring your wife,' he says in *The Dangerous Summer*. 'It's a man's fiesta and women at it make trouble.'

When the Civil War broke out it got even better. Hemingway liked war. Spain, he declared, was 'good country'. It had given him a large dose of his subject matter. His image of Spain still enraptures American college students, who often arrive with copies of *Death in the Afternoon* or *The Sun Also Rises* in their backpacks. Perhaps that is why they always seem to be the first ones gored in Pamplona's streets every July. Death, or the proximity of it, is the key ingredient of that fiesta. At the time of writing, the last fatal victim was drawn from those US collegiate ranks.

Even in the early 1960s, Jan Morris found Spain still not just markedly, but deliberately, set apart from Europe. This was a country proudly and obstinately turned in on herself. 'Spain is almost an island,' she wrote. 'Whichever way you enter her . . . instantly you feel a sense of separateness – a geographical fact exaggerated by historical circumstance.' Morris's entrance to Spain, via the Roncesvalles pass in the Pyrenees to the River Ebro, shows just how the country seemed petrified in time – and just how much travellers loved it that way. 'In the middle distance a group of gypsies hastens with caravans, donkeys, and skinny dogs along the road, and beyond them all of Spain seems to be expecting you – Spain of the shrines, Spain of the knights-errant, Spain of the guitars, the bull-rings, and the troglodytes.'

Spain, it often seemed, remained frozen in one of Goya's eighteenth and nineteenth-century etchings or the earlier portraits of Velázquez. It was a place of haughty, aristocratic Grandees, of poor but noble peasants and of picturesque fiestas.

It was also, however, a playground for the Grim Reaper. The dark, primitive forces of war, hunger and violent death constantly threatened to overwhelm it.

'What about the bloodlust that, as the Civil War and the Carlist War and the Napoleonic War all show, comes over them on particular occasions – that morose, half-sexual, half-religious passion in which they associate themselves with Death and do his work for him?' Gerald Brenan asks in *The Face of Spain*, after his post-Civil War return to the country.

'The daylight Spaniard is the man one sees – sociable, positive, capable of great bursts of energy and animation . . . and not very imaginative. In his ordinary conduct he is rather a simple person, as one can tell from a glance at Spanish literature,' Brenan says. But there was another side to Spaniards, which he called 'the night side'. 'It is associated with thoughts of death and contempt for life . . . *Menosprecio de la vida*, disdain for life! That phrase is like a bell that tolls its way through Spanish history. The Spaniards are great destroyers.'

This was something Protestants felt especially keenly. 'For nearly two centuries she was the she-butcher, *la Verduga*, of malignant Rome; the chosen instrument for carrying into effect the atrocious projects of power,' said the Protestant bible-seller George Borrow. But Spain's problem was not uncontrolled violence. It was something far more sinful: 'Fanaticism was not the spring which impelled her to her work of butchery; another feeling, in her the predominant one, was worked upon – her fatal pride.'

The upside of Spanish pride, however, was the nobility that makes savages so admirable. 'The suspicion common in industrial society, the rudeness of prosperous people, have not touched the Spaniards; one is treated like an equal amongst equals. There is never any avarice. One sits before the hearth, the brushwood blazes up, the iron pan splutters on the fire, and conversation goes on as it has always gone on,' says Pritchett.

It made Brenan, returning to London, feel floods of nostalgia. 'As we pass through the packed and sordid streets, I see all about us a throng of plain, rounded faces that lack the distinction of real ugliness. Faces like puddings that seem never to have desired or suffered, smooth vegetable faces, placid cow-like faces, lightly creased and rippled by small worries,' he complained.

Add in the sensuality of the women, the joyfulness of fiesta, the deadliness of the bullfight and a widely assumed but largely undefined dose of Latin 'passion' and the picture of the Spaniards as close to nature was complete. That, often, is how we want them still. A major BBC series on Spain – broadcast in the early 1990s – was called *Fire in the Blood*. The wacky excess of Almodóvar's early work fits in too.

Some Spaniards, however, do not take much persuading that the foreign view is more accurate than their own. That is why, for example, Brenan is far better known in Spain than in Britain.

There is more than a touch of masochism in this, because Spaniards are often their own most bitter critics. Fraga's 1960s advertising slogan still jangles at the back of their minds. '*España es diferente*', 'Spain is different' it tells them – but not proudly so.

'They tell me the English are a people who travel all over the world to laugh at other countries,' one Andalusian told Brenan. 'That's fine. I thoroughly approve of it. I hope you are having a good laugh at us . . . I find things to laugh at all day long.'

Brenan's Andalusian was not the only one who thought like that. Spaniards have a long history of being gloomy about themselves. Often they have ended up crying, rather than laughing. With their last colonies lost in 1898 and an average of a coup, a revolution or a counter-revolution every three years – they spent much of the nineteenth century and most of the first half of the twentieth century in a state of maudlin self-contemplation. Franco's appearance only encouraged more of it. This was despite of or, perhaps, because of, his promise that he would guide them to '*la plenitud histórica y espiritual de España*', 'Spain's historical and spiritual fulfilment'. The problem, many agreed, was Spaniards themselves.

Mariano José de Larra's epitaph for his country was: 'Here lies half of Spain. The other half killed it.' The poet Antonio Machado added his cheerless welcome to newly born Spaniards with his:

'May God protect you. One of the two Spains will freeze your heart.'

This national self-flagellation carried on well into the twentieth century, with Ortega y Gasset leading the way. 'Spain is falling to pieces, falling to pieces,' he wrote in 1921. 'Today, more than a People, it is the dust that remains.' Salvador de Madariaga went on to provide the most damning of all verdicts, diagnosing the national illness as *yoismo*, me-first-ness. 'Obedience and discipline are hateful things to a Spaniard . . . Spain is a mound of blocks of uncut granite that support one another with the minimum number of points of contact and the largest amount of mutual bothering per square centimetre as possible.'

Spain is no longer so hard on itself. But it is, once more, in the grip of a round of self-doubt and self-questioning. What is Spain? What is her history? Is it one nation, or several? What sort of a country is it? Is it pulling together, or falling apart? Torrents of ink are now being used up in an attempt to defeat the arguments of nationalists and separatists in the Basque Country or Catalonia. Foreigners may be quoted as support for one or other argument – the idea being that they may, somehow, be above the fray.

All this interest in what foreigners make of Spain means it is a remarkably gratifying place for a newspaper correspondent to work. Radio and television shows seek your opinion. Spanish newspapers reprint your articles. By belonging to the world of the written word, one is often considered to be part of the cultural elite. There is even social cachet. It makes a pleasant change from being punched on the nose on a London doorstep or finding that your profession rates you amongst the least trustworthy people in Britain.

One of the first surprises about reading Spanish history is that many of the great men and women of the discipline are not Spanish at all. Firmly installed amongst them are the *hispanistas* – foreign experts on Spain. Their names, like that of Brenan, are often better known here than in their own countries.

The *hispanistas* have been helped by the fact that, for many years, they could write in an atmosphere of intellectual freedom that their Spanish colleagues did not share.

One reason why *anglosajón* historians of Spain have done so well, however, is because of the way they write. A certain Spanish idea of culture as medicine – good for you, even when hard to swallow – is to blame. The *hispanista's* flowing, story-telling style contrasts with the often dense and learned, but ultimately turgid, prose of their Spanish rivals. A Spanish editor once explained to me that historians and biographers were either excessively dry and serious or excessively short on real investigation. This helps explain the success of historians like Paul Preston – (biographer of Franco and Juan Carlos) – Hugh Thomas (*The Spanish Civil War*), Stanley Payne, J. H. Elliott, Raymond Carr, Henry Kamen and the great expert on García Lorca and Dalí, Ian Gibson. These are names that trip easily off the tongues of cultured Spaniards (though not that easily, for only the British are worse linguists than the Spanish). Another reason for their success, however, remains the fact that Spaniards are not always sure whether to trust what their own writers have to say about them.

Spaniards reach for the Bible (Matthew) to explain this suspicion, often driven by envy, of their own great or successful children. '*Nadie es profeta en su tierra*' , 'No one is a prophet in their own land', they say. It is certainly true of Pedro Almodóvar. *Talk to Her* was Hollywood's choice for the best original screenplay of any film in English or any language. Spain's own film academy did not even choose it that year as the Spanish candidate for best foreign film at the Oscars.

A recent Spanish study that infuriated Almodóvar pointed out that his characters spent 14 per cent of their time getting off their heads on drugs or alcohol. A total of 170 characters, mainly women, were said to be hashish, heroin or cocaine users. The director said the study, by Spanish university psychologists, left him with 'a Kafkaesque sensation of fear, disgust, astonishment, fury and indignation'. An artist's job was not to judge his characters, he said. It was to explain them. 'Imagine that we analysed Scorsese's films and found 60 per cent of his characters were gangsters or delinquents who owned weapons and used them a lot. We would have to conclude that Scorsese was a member of an organised crime group.' *Moralistas*, he warned, were on their way back.

Moral strictness has always been a generator of the avant-garde. In this Almodóvar, with his childhood in Franco's rural Spain, is no exception. Both the voyeuristic painter Dalí and the provocative film-maker Buñuel emerged from similar – if more bourgeois – stiff moral backgrounds. *Bad Education*, the Almodóvar film that came after *Talk to Her*, featured a paedophile priest and his victims. Almodóvar has said that *Bad Education* has only a few autobiographical touches. Abuse scenes in the sacristy and river, he said, were based on stories told to him by friends at the school where he boarded. In a 1982 interview, however, he admitted he himself had suffered 'terrible things' at the hands of priests. 'It was a shame, because sex should be discovered naturally, and not brutally, suddenly. For two or three years, I could not be alone, out of pure fear.' If the priests at his school were only slightly as bullying and abusive as their fictional counterparts, they could be credited with helping imbue in him an abiding interest in what, for the Roman Catholic Church, is the perverse and sinful. To that extent he is a son of the *pueblo* and, especially, of the *pueblos* of Francoism. 'I think my life and all I have done goes against all that, but that is where I am from,' he says.

Almodóvar is also thoroughly Spanish, taking a special pleasure in using folkloric, religious and popular culture symbols – be they bullfighters, bolero singers or nuns – and subverting them to his own ends. In the 1980s and early 1990s his films were designed to provoke, shock and enthral. It was as if the new space of liberty had, somehow, to be filled up to the edges as quickly as possible – in case it disappeared. That may explain why, when asked by an interviewer for an unrealised erotic fantasy, he replied : 'My erotic fantasy is to go on a bus, pass by a school, and to see, for example, a father of about thirty-eight picking up his thirteen-year-old daughter. What I would really like to do is go to bed with the father and the daughter at the same time, because I like pubescents a lot, and their fathers, even those with respectable jobs that give them a bit of a paunch.'

To the deluge of kitsch colour was added a torrent of sexual experimentation. *Pepi, Luci and Bom*, Almodóvar's first feature-film, introduced Spaniards to the golden shower and featured a penis-measuring contest. His characters have included a truck driver turned transsexual prostitute, a drag-queen judge, several porn stars, an incestuous transsexual and a retired *torero* who is into post-coital murder. Mostly, however, these characters manage to have a heart of gold. So it is that in *Tie Me Up! Tie Me Down!* Antonio Banderas takes Victoria Abril captive and ties her up, declaring: 'I'm twenty-three years old and have 50,000 pesetas. I am alone in the world. I would like to be a good husband to you and a good father to your children.' Almodóvar's first heroes were weird but somehow good – at a time when weird finally could be good. They were also, however, transparently unreal. How many heroin-taking convent abbesses are there out there, after all?

Almodóvar was the muse and just about the only durable cultural product of Madrid's *movida*. Apart from him, and a few passable musicians, all it produced were a couple of photographers. The best of these is Alberto García-Alix. To view his *movida* work now, however, is to mourn the dead. Looking at his photos in his flat near Madrid's Plaza de Santa Ana, I was struck not so much by the undoubted quality of his black-and-white images, but by a photo of a handsome young man in a black bomber jacket, with a touch of the rockabilly to his hair. Young, healthy and happy – this was García-Alix's brother. He died, like many of the *movida*'s casualties, from an overdose. 'Heroin was just part of the scene,' someone who lived it explained.

The colour and wackiness of Almodóvar's films have reduced in intensity since the *movida* died. Almodóvar, like Spain, has matured and moved on. His films are deeper, more intense, more emotional and less noisy. His central characters, however, are still misfits, some to the point of criminal insanity. Almodóvar sets about trying to make us understand or, even, empathise with them. It is as if, having emerged from decades of intolerance, it is now important, if not to tolerate then, at least, to understand everyone. This is, at once, one of modern Spain's most enduring and potentially dangerous beliefs.

Almodóvar himself is aware of this. 'I love characters who are crazy in love and will give their life to passion, even if they burn in hell . . . But this is art. When my friends start behaving that way, I tell them to stop. They say "But look at your movies." I say: "That is art. Art has its own world."'

In *Bad Education*, his dark depiction of child abuse by 1960s priests, Almodóvar even makes a last-minute attempt to help us understand the chief pederast. 'I have a tendency to redeem my characters,' he admits. 'It is very Catholic.' The *pueblo* – a phenomenon that crops up increasingly in his films – reappears in the closing scenes of *Bad Education* in the voice of a brother who has murdered his transsexual sibling. 'You don't know what it is like to have a brother like Ignacio and live in a *pueblo*. You can't even imagine it!' he says.

Who else but Almodóvar could have persuaded Hollywood to give him an original screenplay Oscar for a film in which the hero rapes a comatose woman who is the object of his obsessive, self-invented love? That is what happens, off-screen, in *Talk to Her*. Almodóvar's invitation, again, is a very modern Spanish one – to understand, or empathise, rather than moralise. He must have felt a special satisfaction at getting that one past those 'moralistic' *anglosajones* – and, especially, censorious Hollywood – of whom many Spaniards so disapprove. Could a film-maker from a different country have made the same sort of films? Almost certainly not. Would Almodóvar still be testing the limits were it not for the era – and the *pueblo* – he grew up in? I doubt it.

There are signs, however, that Spain may be coming to terms with the *pueblo*. The Sunday evening traffic jams into Madrid or Barcelona are full of people coming back from weekend escapes to *pueblos*. Many have second homes in the places where their parents or grandparents were born. In August some villages find their populations multiply several times over as families come back to enjoy a holiday away from the noise and bustle of city life. The summer fiestas have generally survived – being the last thing any self-respecting *pueblo* will let go of. It is the slow pace and enforced intimacy of the pueblo, however, that begin to seem attractive again. The attraction grows further as Spaniards become increasingly hard-working and stressed.

The film cameras are back in the *pueblos* too. Almodóvar was one of the first. In *The Flower of My Secret* his heroine, after being abandoned by her husband, found a zeal for life again after returning to the *pueblo*. He chose Almagro, just twenty miles away across the scorched and red plain of La Mancha from Calzada de Calatrava. He was there again in 2005 working on a feature film, to be called *Coming Back*. Death and ghosts returning from the past were scripted to play a major part. 'The death culture is very strong,' Almodóvar has explained of his native La Mancha. 'My mother once told me that my grandfather reappeared after dying, and the whole village collaborated in sending him back to the sweet hereafter. I don't believe in that, but that's part of the culture where I was born, and it is part of me.'

Almodóvar was echoing something that García Lorca once said to explain why death was an essential part of *duende*, the fairy-like Spanish creative spirit. 'In all countries death is an ending. It arrives and the curtain falls. Not in Spain. In Spain the curtain is raised,' he said.

The *pueblo* is also the star of a documentary film – *The Sky Turns*, by director Mercedes Álvarez. It follows a year in the life of her family's former *pueblo* – Aldealseñor, in Soria. Álvarez was the last person born there, more than thirty years ago. The film, shown at Spanish cinemas in 2005, watches the old grow older as the last few inhabitants head towards the grave. Álvarez compares the village's plight with that of a painter friend who is going blind.

Aldealseñor's villagers are, naturally, heavily concerned with death. 'Right up to the end you think you are going to live forever,' says one. They also remember the Civil War, and tales of those executed by Franco's people. An elderly shepherd sits against a stone wall and recalls one man's final words in front of the firing squad. "*¡Viva la República!*" ("Long live the Republic!"), he shouted,' says the shepherd shaking his head and cursing to himself.

First-hand memories of those terrible, bloody years will soon be buried, along with the last remaining villagers, in the local cemetery. The passing away of the Civil War generation is part of the wider explanation of why Spain is now looking back to the past. A dark page of history is being definitively turned, and Spaniards finally feel liberated from it. That is both good and bad. They no longer feel constrained by the Pact of Forgetting. Digging up Civil War graves may not be easy, but at least it can now be done. The time lapse since Franco's death in 1975 is not so great if you compare it with other European countries. It was the generation of 1968 in Germany, two decades after Hitler's death, that asked how their parents had been involved with the Nazi dictatorship. The French took even longer to seriously assess Vichy and collaboration with Hitler.

If the *Transición* was a success, it was because Spaniards made a supreme effort to find consensus. That effort was driven, to a large degree, by the Civil War ghosts still haunting so many Spanish households. The divisions now visible in Spain have much to do with the release of those historic constraints. How Spaniards deal with them will be the ultimate test of that *Transición*.

Spaniards seem to be taking a breather – and taking stock. They have stepped back to contemplate, and to come to terms with, the achievements of the past three decades. These are both many and considerable. They include, largely, the communal Spanish aim of becoming more like other Europeans.

Spain still has its own particular set of historical ghosts. They, above all, are what makes this country, as the hated 1960s advertising slogan put it, 'different'. What many Spaniards have not yet learned to do, however, is love the idea of their own difference. And that is strange. Because it is precisely why so many outsiders, including this *anglosajón*, love them so.

Epilogue

Ernest Hemingway declared that books on Spain should be written 'as rapidly as possible after a first visit as several visits could only confuse the first impressions and make conclusions much less easy to draw.'

That is truer than ever today, for the dizzying speed at which Spain is changing has added to an already mercurial nature. In the year since the original manuscript of this book was handed in, there has been no slowing down. This epilogue to the paperback edition (which has been slightly revised to correct typographical and other errors from the first edition) takes a brief plunge into the latest events up to October 2006. Those wishing to keep up-to-date with changes after that can turn to the book's accompanying web-site at www.faber.co.uk/ghostsofspain. This will also contain a full bibliography, footnotes and further notes for those wanting to study any of the subjects raised here.

After months of procrastination, the Socialist government has come up with a draft *memoria histórica* law. It is a response to those exhuming Civil War graves and demanding some form of moral redress for Franco's numerous victims. The draft law is, however, tempered by an obvious fear of the past. It has also, perhaps inevitably, led to a fresh round of rowing. Once more, the fault-lines are familiar to students of the 'two Spains'. The suggestion at the moment is that victims, or their families, should apply to a special committee of experts who will investigate and issue some sort of certificate detailing the facts of their case. This system, in the words of deputy prime minister María Teresa Fernández de la Vega, is designed 'to heal wounds without reopening anything'. It is criticised by the Right as an attempt to awake old ghosts. For the hard Left, and those digging up mass graves, it is too tepid.

In the long term, the most important part of the proposed law is that it sets aside money to do something about Spain's abandoned Civil War and Franco-era archives. They will provide valuable extra material for historians and investigators, who continue to flood the market with work on the period.

The proposed new law also recognises that Spain's transition to democracy produced victims, especially those killed by the police in the first years after Franco's death. Political demonstrations at the Valley of the Fallen, meanwhile, will be banned. Whether that means the police will patrol the basilica when Franco's annual memorial mass is held, has yet to be seen.

The pact of forgetting, however, remains intact as far as the naming of perpetrators is concerned. The draft law says documents emitted by the committee of experts will 'omit any reference to the identity of anyone who took part in the events'. There will, in other words, be no individual guilt. The only bad guy will be Franco himself. No one else must be blamed or punished, whatever they did in his name. Francoism, in that respect, remains an abstract thing.

While some light is to be shone on the darker recesses of the Civil War, the Islamist train bombings of 2004 look set to become murkier. Conspiracy theories now abound – including, once more, the idea that ETA was somehow involved. The People's Party, aggrieved by the way it lost the elections that year, continues to give the theories a fair wind. Even the forthcoming trial of twenty-nine of those accused of taking part (who do not include any ETA members) will, I suspect, fail to heal the wounds. Spain looks set to stay forever divided over the events of that dark day.

Perhaps the brightest light of all, however, is being shone on corruption. In March 2006 police arrested the mayoress and numerous town councillors in Marbella. The town hall was deemed so rotten with corruption that a board of administrators was appointed to run it. No trial has yet been held. The accusations against them, however, appear to show that those in power routinely demanded bribes for council contracts and building permits. As Marbella's sun-tanned and wealthy councillors contemplated the inside of their prison cells over the following months, there was a sudden avalanche of corruption allegations in town halls across the country. These are, it seems, finally being taken seriously by police, the courts and central government.

The most hopeful change in Spain has been a cease-fire declaration by Basque terrorist group ETA. Talks with the government are widely believed to be under way. The results of those talks, however, remain unpredictable. A definitive peace is by no means assured.

A new autonomy statute for Catalonia, meanwhile, has been approved at referendum. It gives Catalans more powers of self-government and provides another nudge towards the federalisation of Spain. The statute's preamble, however, plants the seed of future arguments. 'The parliament of Catalonia has defined Catalonia as a nation', it states, while going on to recognise that the Spanish constitution has not. The Catalan statute is set to be followed by reforms giving greater powers to many of Spain's other sixteen regional governments.

Perhaps the biggest change happening in Spain, though, is that wrought by immigration. The figures are, by European standards, extraordinary. Spain has taken in 2.8 million people over six years, thus multiplying the immigration population by four. 'The reality of the situation overwhelms the provisions of desk-bound sociologists', El País commented as the total number hit 3.7 million, or 8.7 per cent of the population, by the end of 2005. Spain's booming economy may need a similar number of fresh immigrants over the next fifteen years.

A decade of continuous growth means there are jobs for all. The social security payments of immigrant workers have, in fact, provided an unexpected bonanza for the state. So far this sudden wave of immigration has had little social impact. Overt racism, although it occasionally raises its head in the abuse that football crowds hurl at African players, is largely absent.

There are two reasons for this. Spain has, in Latin America, a deep pool of potential immigrants who already have shared cultural, linguistic and religious values. The experience of migrating is also, however, still alive in the country's own communal memory. Only thirty years ago Spaniards were themselves still emigrating, looking for work in northern Europe and the Americas. They know, in other words, how it feels.

Immigration is, in fact, the most obvious sign of modern Spain's success. A country that people once fled from is now a beacon of hope for those looking to improve their lives. As long as everybody has jobs, the potential for friction remains low. Opinion polls, however, now show that Spaniards are beginning to rate immigration as a major problem. The big question is what will happen when Spain suffers, as it inevitably will, an economic downturn. This will be the ultimate test of how well Spain has adapted to its own success. Will the Spaniards' natural sense of hospitality and generosity break down when they find themselves competing with immigrants for the same, scarce jobs?

There is no reason, however, why this new Spain should not pass that test. In my own privileged and *anglosajón* fashion, I am also an immigrant. And, like those who have arrived in recent years, I intend to stay in this, my adopted home – come good times or bad.

Madrid, October 2006

Acknowledgements

Many of those who have helped me over the past three years are named in the pages of this book and my first thanks must go to them. I hope to have done justice to them all. On a handful of occasions, in order to protect privacy, I have changed names. I have made this clear in the text where I have considered it important.

Professor Justin Byrne, Isabel Yanguas and Christopher Skala generously gave their time to read through early versions of the text. Their encouragement has been key to keeping the writer writing. I am indebted to Paddy Woodworth for looking through the Basque chapter and for his expertise on the GAL affair. David Fernández de Castro Azúa and Stephen Burgen similarly read through, and put me right on, Catalan affairs. Alan Goodman, Elizabeth Nash and Paul House also helped scrutinise the text. Responsibility for any errors that escaped, and for all the opinions expressed, remain exclusively mine.

In the Tiétar Valley I am indebted to Federico Martín and to many of those, especially Federico's mother Clara, who shared painful memories of events from almost seventy years ago. In Barcelona my special thanks go to Silvia Català – not just for her help but also for two decades of friendship. Iñaki Gorostidi, Iñaki González, Nick Gardner, Iulen de Madariaga and Rosa Aliaga were invaluable in the Basque Country. The Elkarri peace movement has been a constant help there over the years. Prison officers at Spanish jails, who are targets for ETA, do not like their full names to appear in print. My thanks, therefore, go to Mercedes at Seville jail and Víctor in Granada. Alfonso de Miguel was a crucial flamenco contact as were many workers at the Esqueleto in Seville. Clea House and Monica Pérez diligently checked translations from Spain's varied languages – though, once again, I have had the final word on these.

Amongst the institutions and public bodies to have helped me are the Biblioteca Nacional, the Audiencia Nacional, Patrimonio Nacional, the Museu d'Història de Catalunya, the Dirección General de Instituciones Penitenciarias, the Secretaria de Política Lingüística of the Generalitat de Catalunya, Omnium Cultural, the Fundación Nacional Francisco Franco, the Fundación Sabino Arana and the Mancomunidad de Municipios de la Costa del Sol Occidental.

Santiago Macías, Jusèp Boya, Montse Armengou, Justin Webster, José Antonio Sanahuja, Pedro del Olmo, Gijs van Hensbergen, David Sugarman, Ángel Palomino, Carlos Velasco, Mercedes Munarriz, Isambard Wilkinson, David Sharrock, William Chislett and several descendants of Salvador Ripoll have all provided help, often without knowing it.

Commissioning editors in London allowed me to chase stories that have provided much of the background, and some of the backbone, of the book. Ed Pilkington at the *Guardian* encouraged me to devote more than the usual time to looking at Civil War graves, while Harriet Sherwood generously gave me the three months off that I needed to finish writing. My thanks to them and the rest of the *Guardian*'s foreign and features desks. Elsewhere, thanks are owed to Bronwen Maddox, Gill Morgan and Tony Turnbull at *The Times* and to David Meilton.

My agent Georgina Capel has been an invaluable and enthusiastic guide. At Faber and Faber special thanks go to Walter Donohue and Nick Lowndes for their patience and understanding when dealing with a writer schooled in the rhythm of journalism. Thanks also go to Graeme Leonard for his seamless editing.

My most heartfelt gratitude, however, goes to my in-house editor, advisor, expert on flamenco matters and so much more, Katharine Blanca Scott. Two young Tremletts, Samuel and Lucas, have helped the author more than they can possibly know.

Index

INDEX

LIBRARY, UNIVERSITY OF CHESTER